DAVID FELLMAN
Vilas Professor of Political Science
University of Wisconsin
ADVISORY EDITOR TO DODD, MEAD & COMPANY

Modern Government
Third Edition

DELL GILLETTE HITCHNER

University of Washington

WILLIAM HENRY HARBOLD

Whitman College

MODERN GOVERNMENT

Third Edition

DODD, MEAD & COMPANY

New York 1972 Toronto

To Kathleen
and Mary Jo

Veritas vos liberabit.

Preface

THE reception afforded this book has provided justification for a third edition. Although the political world has seen many changes since the first edition appeared, events generally have confirmed the validity of the basic lines of analysis undertaken herein. Thus, the thrust of this book remains that of previous editions: to introduce the broad and complex subject of contemporary government and politics, and to provide not only information about the governmental process but standards for its evaluation as well.

Changes in this edition, even so, are once more extensive. In response to the current preference for shorter texts, it has been reduced in length by nearly one-third. While it retains all the basic topics of previous editions, it introduces a number of new subjects of contemporary interest and significance. The revision is substantial throughout and all chapters are brought up-to-date. Finally, the Study Guide to reference materials at the end is entirely new and reflects the latest thinking and writing on its topics.

Debts owed for assistance in a work of this sort, and accumulated over the years, far outrun the possibility of their adequate acknowledgment. I must mention especially my appreciation to Professor William H. Harbold, friend, former colleague, and coauthor in previous editions, who made useful contributions to an early draft of the revision but did not participate in the preparation of this edition in its final form. I wish to acknowledge also the assistance of Professor John S. Reshetar, colleague and friend, who generously afforded me the benefit of his scholarship at a number of stages in the preparation of this volume. Finally, I am grateful once more for the kind and efficient aid of members of the Dodd, Mead editorial staff in bringing the manuscript to its present form. I should add that since I did not always accept advice tendered me, I alone am responsible for what appears in these pages.

DELL G. HITCHNER

Contents

1

The Study of Modern Government

THE world around us is clearly a political world. All mankind has been drawn into some political association through which men engage in cooperation and conflict. Indeed, that the world is becoming ever more political seems one of its most important aspects. Even today, most of us would support the sentiments of a thirteenth-century king: "Had I been present at the creation of the world I would have proposed some improvements." It has always been a human ambition to change and improve the world. The first practical step in setting out to make such changes, however, is to decide what is the political world really like. This volume is a response to that question.

How do we proceed with a sensible discussion of the nature of modern government? It would seem we should begin by reaching agreement on what we are talking about, but attempting to do this can raise disputes. "If you wish to converse with me," said Voltaire, "define your terms!" "Definitions are hazardous," warned Samuel Johnson. "I hate definitions!" said Disraeli. However we have it, it remains that to converse we must share some common meanings for the terms we use, and a common understanding of the nature and scope of the subject we are considering. Unfortunately, in this realm there are no accepted agreements and understandings. The political world we seek to examine, for example, is introduced through books with a variety of titles: "modern government," "government and politics," "politics and government," "introduction to politics," "the political order," "political systems," and so on—with each title having common or variable meanings according to its user. Since there is no way to reconcile the irreconcilable, one makes a start here somewhat arbitrarily.

I. The Nature of Politics

The term "political science" is commonly used to describe an established academic discipline. Since political science is a way of saying "the systematic study of politics," the meaning of the word "politics" is immediately crucial to our discussion. At first glance, "politics" is a simple and familiar term. Most of us encounter it every day, applied commonly to the affairs of politicians and political parties, to electioneering and maneuvering for partisan advantage, and to some behavior of government officials.

Such activities certainly are a part of politics, but political scientists generally believe that its scope is much broader than that. Yet when they extend their view to comprehend the whole subject, they fall into disagreement. Like politics itself, political science is rooted in controversy; the discipline is not unified, either in its scope or terms of analysis. One finds in it instead competing perspectives both in identifying politics and in studying it.

This is not a situation that political scientists like, since it casts a shadow over the validity and value of their work. Some of the greatest thinkers of western culture have attempted to define politics in terms that would permit scientific work and political life to proceed harmoniously. Amid a host of attempts, three perspectives on politics stand out. Since each seems to possess its own grain of truth we will consider them briefly.

What is Politics? The first perspective on politics comes to us from ancient Greece. Our word "politics" was derived from the Greek name for their "city-community," the *polis*. To the Greeks, political life was the distinctive way of life in the *polis*; as expressed by Aristotle, politics was all that concerned the "good life" in a well-organized, stable, and self-sufficient community. Political science in ancient Greece, therefore, had to study the nature of that good life, and discern the types of political order and laws that would promote it. Aristotle's conception of political science—the statesman's "master art"— a conception strongly infused with ethics and devoted to the whole range of community affairs, has had great influence. Yet no single and integrated science of society has resulted from the classical Greek beginning. As we have said, the Aristotelian approach was based upon the comparatively small community of the *polis*, seen as the self-sufficient and ultimate organization of human life, with the individual realizing himself most fully by citizenship therein. Since these conditions no longer exist, either as fact or ideal, Aristotle's idea of politics is too broad a base for political science.

In more recent times many writers have sought another, more limited, perspective that would be practical and realistic. They have defined political science as the study of the state. Institutions and activities are considered to be political, therefore, according to how they are related to the state. Unfortunately, though, it has proved most difficult to identify this entity, especially in those frequent periods of considerable social change when legal and philosophical notions are uncertain. The term thus becomes least useful just when it is most needed. Although the basic concept—that politics embraces only some and not all social relationships—is sound, it does not specify which relationships are embraced; thus, no one definition of the state satisfactorily meets our needs or obtains general acceptance. For convenience any political community, order, or system may be called a "state"—often with qualification, as in "city-state," "nation-state," or "modern-state"—but the name contributes little to our understanding of politics. For this, we need to look behind the legal concept to see why the state is a political phenomenon.

A third and more modern perspective has its roots in the reflection of the sixteenth-century Florentine writer and diplomat, Machiavelli, that politics is "power." To thinkers of this persuasion, political science is the study of the power relationships between men—the forms these take, the institutions they create, and the benefits to individuals that result. Those rigorously taking this position eliminate from political science any moral content. Politics is domination, they say, and we must simply be observers and analyzers of the fact. Power can equally serve good and evil, they insist; and the political facts, unlike moral judgments, are independent of which is served. Considerable force must be admitted to this claim, especially if power is broadly enough defined. Aristotle was aware that in every *polis* a ruling class defined the good life for others and enforced its definition. We know today that power considerations are at least as important as moral ones in any effective acts of government. Thus politics can be seen in part as the accumulation in various ways of sufficient power to achieve particular ends.

Two difficulties prevent this perspective from being adequate. One

Is that defining politics simply as the exercise of power, without qualifications which would beg the question, makes impossible any distinction between political and nonpolitical relationships. The phenomenon of power is discernible throughout the entire realm of social activities, and the network of power relations in a community, by and large, is coextensive with the community itself. Many governments obtain compliance with most of their policies without resort to force. And, because there are various kinds of power, coercion may be present in contexts that are not political. In the second place, we rarely think of politics in connection with the exercise of raw power. When the search for power, or its exercise, impresses us as being political, it is because it occurs within a context of institutions and laws. Politics does embrace power, but only by virtue of being something other than power.

Obviously, such a complex and age-old problem as determining what is politics is not to be resolved simply. Let us adopt a practical expedient, therefore, which will get our study under way—one which we can extend and clarify as we go. All of us in our normal experience have come into some kind of contact with tax collectors, license clerks, policemen, judges, and legislators. We are aware that the existence of these offices has a concrete impact on our lives, both limiting and supporting our activities. We are also aware that these offices do not exist in isolation, but are interrelated within a structure of authority and influence we call "government." These officials do not ordinarily act in an unpredictable way; as officials, their behavior is partly controlled by a system of rules we call "law" and is thus related systematically to the larger community in which they function.

It is this rather ordinary experience with officials and offices which, in all its dimensions, political scientists attempt to understand. However sophisticated political analysis becomes, this commonsense perspective is its base and starting point. We begin, then, with a consideration of government as the regulation of the people's activities in a community by an organized body of officials according to the community's legal rules. Often, however, we are less concerned with the fact of regulation, or that it is by officials, or that there are rules, than we are with the broader question: how are the activities of government—the ends sought and the means used—determined? We thus move into the realm of politics, which we may identify as the process through which such determinations are made. It is in politics, not just by government, that problems arising in social life are identified and clarified, possible solutions proposed, power to deal with them organized, and decisions made. The process is not conducted this neatly, of course, nor does it always appear explicitly in a problem-solving situation. It may appear rather in a situation in which rights and interests are defended or advanced, or more simply, in one in which order is maintained. Since rights, interests, and order are essential elements of any problem and of any solution, politics embraces all these phenomena.

While this process of government manifests broad patterns of order wherever it is found—it must if political science is to be possible— we can recognize also the great diversity and complexity of political orders, reflecting differences in human experience over time and place. Political behavior springs from diverse forms of thinking and feeling, which in turn affect the differing ways in which people envisage politics. Thus men attempt to understand their world and act in it according to several approaches—artistic, scientific, and philosophical.

Politics as Art. The art of government among men, of ruling and being ruled, must surely be as old as society itself. Since art is a skill which principally depends upon gift and practice, rather than upon conveyed knowledge, one of the greatest accumulations of human artistry lies in the governmental process. Political skill certainly was at first, and to a large extent remains, an eminently practical art—"the art of the possible." Thus some today still consider politics a form of human activity incapable of objective determination. Politics in this sense stresses the value of experience gained from common sense and insight, as well as the importance of creative imagination and vision, and of achieving the chosen end successfully; thus, it demands practical, rather than theoretical, wisdom. Such qualities are hardly gained through formal instruction and logic alone. They depend largely upon native talent and intuitive reasoning, and experience contributes to their development not so much information as understanding and appreciation. The successful statesman or politician of any age, the skilled craftsman of politics, is more often than not self-taught in his art; he may even be spoken of as a "born politician," with his political lore having little to do with books.

To some degree, therefore, a share of the political scientist's attention must be devoted to the art of governing as such, not only because this aspect of the subject does not—or will not yet—lend itself to scientific inquiry, but because it seems capable of revelation by a kind of impressionistic treatment akin to artistic perception. The political scientist is obliged, much as is the art or literary critic endeavoring to appreciate a painting or a novel, to concern himself with matters of aesthetics, balance, and harmony. Some of political science's most useful conclusions, moreover, have been provided by those with the shrewdest perception of human nature. Thus, the study of politics is not likely ever to become solely a process of collecting facts about government; at its most rewarding, it must always have regard for and be alert to wisdom and imagination.

Politics as Science. The ideal has long existed that man could be governed in accordance with scientific knowledge—that is, by means superior to chance and guesswork, and without reliance upon intuition and personal skills, which are largely incommunicable and difficult to control. Scientific knowledge is organized and verifiable knowledge, based upon observation and experience; it is obtained from inquiry guided by the subject matter as completely as possible, and not by the hopes, fears, and prejudices of the scientist. This is what is meant when it is said that scientific inquiry is "objective." The essential elements of the scientific method include the definition of the problem to be solved; the acquisition of relevant data; the construction of hypotheses, or tentative theories, to explain the data in terms of the problem; and finally, the attempt at verification of the hypotheses. These steps produce the most notable characteristic of science: the basing of conclusions upon the best available evidence.

Since man began to organize his information about human association over two thousand years ago, he has collected much knowledge about the process of government. Though methods and results diverge in important ways from those of the physical and mathematical sciences, clearly a political science exists. Furthermore, the knowledge of political science has been made available to those participating in the process of government, so that politics may be more rational and its results more dependable. Few political practices today reflect only the creative art of politicians; they embody also valid conclusions reached from the application of scientific processes to political phenomena. Science in politics is less advanced as yet than political art, but it plays an increasingly active role. In the long run, the science of politics will undoubtedly help us organize ourselves more effectively.

Politics as Philosophy. When Plato observed that men would never be well governed until "philosophers are kings, or the kings and princes of this world have the spirit and power of philosophy," he stated clearly that politics cannot be understood apart from its philosophical foundations. Philosophy and science both stress the rational element in our experiences. The philosophy of politics differs, however, from the science of politics in that the former seeks the foundations for some justifiable commitment to government. It insists that we ask such questions as: why must men be governed, how, and to what purpose? Neither empirical study nor artistic perception will finally answer these questions.

The philosophical element of the political mind provides the insight to evaluate the institutions and processes of the concrete political world. This is no esoteric matter, but one of practical importance. Democracy demands a great deal from its citizens; and, far more than a technical knowledge of government, they need an understanding of the objectives sought through it. Lacking this, they will be unable to fulfill the proper role of citizens: intelligent criticism of their leaders and their institutions. This is not to claim that every citizen must be a practiced philosopher, any more than a consummate artist or a methodical scientist. But there must be critical thinking in any political order if politics is not to degenerate. Thus, there is in every political order which has not become stagnant a philosophical dimension that seeks to interrelate in value and harmony all aspects of human experience.

Politics in Perspective. Our consideration of the roles of art, science, and philosophy in the governing of men has sought to suggest that politics is not to be found exclusively in only one of these approaches. The functions of the three approaches in politics are complementary; for neither art, science, nor philosophy can advance without the stimulation that each provides. If philosophy considers primarily the values in political life, distinguishing the courses of action we ought to pursue among the many possible ones, we must recognize that neither ends nor means are discovered simply by contemplation. Without reference to the controlled knowledge of the conditions of existence, which only science can render, philosophy would lose contact with the possible and the real.

The ideal, then, would seem to be a mutual relationship between these two: for philosophy to give science its direction, science to prevent philosophy from becoming unrealistic, and the result to be a harmonious and effective political life. Yet this is only an ideal, since neither the philosophy nor the science of politics has attained a level of development which enables either to perform its full role. There remains a need therefore, for the art of the gifted practitioner of politics, with his flair for the possible, which can bring together science and philosophy and fill the gaps that exist in our more systematic knowledge.

II. The Dimensions of Political Science

The study of political science, particularly as it is administered in the United States, may be divided broadly into four major academic fields. A brief description of these will indicate the broad dimensions of the discipline and how it touches the other social sciences. The four fields are distinguished both by the focus of their attention and by the varieties of approaches and materials they employ. There are not precise boundaries setting the fields apart, of course, for they necessarily overlap. Such classifications are simply conveniences to provide rough groupings of political data and to point out specialization and division of labor.

American Government and Politics. For Americans, reasons for concern with their own institutions and processes are fairly obvious. These are also entitled to, and do receive, considerable attention from abroad, given the current influence of the United States in the world, its contribution to the development and defense of representative and democratic government, and the extensive literature that has been produced on the subject. This field deals with American affairs from the perspective of public law, which is concerned with the relations of individuals and their government according to fixed rules; from the perspective of practical politics—dealing with parties, public opinion, interest groups, legislators, and voting—which treats the ways in which the contest for political power is conducted; and from the perspective of public administration, which centers on the application and enforcement of public policy. Political scientists in other countries naturally give major attention here instead to their own national system.

Comparative Government. The field of comparative government is directed toward the study of the political experience, institutions, behavior, and processes in the major systems of modern government.

The approach of this field is very broadly based; it emphasizes the universal character of government, seeking to determine which phenomena among political systems are variable and invariable, and which are unique or common. Its objective is not only to delineate the forms and patterns of the various political systems as they operate within their national settings, and to relate or distinguish them by comparative treatment, but to draw from them generalizations about the governmental process in practice. Thus, the field is a useful one in which to integrate many of the otherwise isolated findings of political science based upon the analysis of particular national systems. Although none of the diverse governmental systems appearing throughout the world has been entirely ignored by political scientists, they have tended to concentrate on those systems with the largest world influence, those representative of fundamental types, or those with unusual characteristics.

International Relations. The field of international relations is concerned with the affairs of the world political community. The range of political phenomena in world affairs is so great that this field is further subdivided into three major areas: international law, dealing with the legal rules and practices of international relations; international politics, the study of the contest for power and influence between the states of the world; and international organization, the examination of the institutional structure and agencies of the world community. Here the political scientist seeks to analyze the character of state interrelationships, and evaluate the forces of conflict and cooperation determining them. The range of global affairs is obviously great, extending over topics from foreign policy, diplomacy, international trade, and regional international organization to arms control, alliances, and war.

Political Theory. Finally, political theory is devoted to the philosophical and speculative consideration of politics. Its task is integrative; that is, through theoretical consideration of the area of politics as a whole and its relationship to the rest of social life, it seeks to give meaning and direction to more particular subjects of political investigation. For this reason it is the broadest of the political science fields, and provides the core of its discipline. Within this field, political scientists undertake two tasks essential to the study of politics. The first is the process of definition, generalization, and classification necessary to establish the basic terms and concepts with which and about which we do much of our political thinking. The second is to discover the underlying nature, functions, and purposes of the political community. In this field are gathered the body of ideas, doctrines, and ideologies that provide the frame for the whole pattern of politics. It is through the theoretical approach that we come to grips with some of the fundamental questions of political value: the source and basis of political authority; the scope of political activity; the determination of the individual's rights and duties; the nature of the obligation of obedience; the meaning of law; and the character of the ideal state, for example. Obviously, all aspects of politics may be subjected to theoretical analysis, and theory should be a major concern of every political scientist, not only those calling themselves "theorists."

Political Science and the Social Sciences. The social sciences—those disciplines dedicated to the principle that "the proper study of mankind is man"—are devoted to the study of man in society. The affairs of civilized man are complex and many-sided, and invite contemplation from numerous points of view. Man has a physical heredity bequeathed by previous generations; his birth and every day of his life give him further human relationships; he becomes a member of many kinds of groups; with other men he draws on those physical resources of the earth available to him and gains a livelihood; he thinks and feels, and through communication with other men acquires knowledge and beliefs; he regulates his affairs and promotes his interests by action within political communities.

The meaning of all these facets of human society, viewed simultaneously, can be bewildering. To get a clearer and more detailed view of how and why humankind behave both similarly and variously in these activities, scholars attempt to isolate certain kinds of behavior. This means that they have relinquished the construction of a single science within which to explain the whole of social interaction for a number of such sciences. This division permits a higher degree of expertness and efficiency within each of several formally distinguished categories of learning, and better assures that no phase of social action will be overlooked. And given the vastness of the information man has or seeks to have collected about himself, and the limited possibility of finding single minds that can comprehend all of it, some kind of academic division of labor in this regard becomes a practical necessity.

As one of the disciplines concerned with man's affairs, political science has close relationships with the several other social sciences. It has always been indebted to history as a source of some of its data, as well as for the depth of perspective history provides in considering the political past. Economics and political science were once studied together in a discipline known as "political economy." Though now separated, the factors of economic and political life still bear closely upon each other in the realm of public policy. Sociology, like political science, is generally concerned with man as a product of group life; however, the former tends to leave the subject of political association to political science, and instead deals broadly with social behavior and the social order. Recently, political scientists have been placing increased emphasis on the use of psychology in explaining the phenomena of political behavior. Some of geography's concern with the territorial aspect of the state is linked to political science through political geography. The study of government and politics also parallels in some fashion or draws upon such studies as anthropology, ethics, jurisprudence, and philosophy, among others.

III. The Methods of Political Inquiry

It is generally understood that differences in methods employed in any discipline reflect differences in questions and problems being investigated, that methods must be adapted to the subject being studied, and that the conclusions reached depend upon the methods used. Evidently, what may be appropriate methods for political science is an important question.

We shall treat the question only in broad terms here. The research methods of political science are generally those of the other social sciences, or are appropriate counterparts applying to particular bodies of political data. Obviously, political scientists develop their findings by specific techniques that are highly disparate and sometimes controversial. These techniques may best be examined and their utility weighed through study of the considerable and detailed literature on the subject, which is sampled and reviewed in the latter part of this volume. Any adequate methodology for political science must, of course, be pluralistic; that is to say, for a full understanding of politics we must employ simultaneously several different kinds of study and thought, harnessing them for a common task. Such an approach inevitably mirrors the complexity of our subject. In political inquiry as it is practiced, there are three basic techniques of study and thought.

Philosophical Speculation and Analysis. Philosophy is reflection on the nature of reality, with emphasis upon what has been referred to as "the nature and destiny of man," and his relationship to the universe. As it proposes ideas on these fundamental matters and develops their implications, philosophy serves as both stimulus and starting point to the study of politics.

Philosophy contributes in two ways to the consideration of politics. In the first place, that branch of philosophy called ethics undertakes a systematic examination of the values of a society—that is, the things, behavior, and achievements which are considered desirable. It attempts to examine them critically, to test their validity, and to determine if the fulfillment of some values renders impossible the realization of others. Many philosophers of the past, however, have gone beyond the simple indication of conflicts to propose new formulations of social values, hoping to eliminate the conflicts and thus make possible a better life. Such speculations are vital to political science because they define and clarify the problems needing investigation, and suggest solutions. The second way in which philosophy contributes to the study of politics is in its efforts to sharpen the tools of investigation. Techniques of investigation and communication must be properly adapted to the nature of the particular study involved, or the results of the study may be false. Furthermore, the limitations of any such tools must be kept in mind, to avoid misleading conclusions. We need a variety of techniques of inquiry, but they are valuable only when properly used.

Political theory is the mediating study between general philosophy and political science. One of its principal tasks is to translate into terms relevant for political life the concepts of more general philosophy, such as ethics and metaphysics. It thus treats of such items as rights, duties, and responsibilities, whether of public authorities or citizens; the proper scope of governmental action; and the best organization of political life to accomplish the multifarious ends assigned it. Most important, it attempts to form a coherent system of thought from its conclusions on these matters, so as to bring all aspects of political life into perspective. Political theory deals also with methods of political inquiry, attempting to reconcile practical needs and limitations at any given time with more universal requirements, as in logic and ethics.

We must remember, finally, that the study of politics inevitably involves considerations of speculative and analytic philosophy. Those who deny this are unaware of the bases of their activity; a major premise is not less a major premise for being inarticulate, but it is certainly the worse for being unexamined. The serious student of government, to some extent, must also be a philosopher.

Historical Inquiry. History is a record of past experience, and as concerns us here, of man's political experience. Research into the past experiences of men has been conducted with sound scholarship, giving us a fairly complete knowledge about the past and its relation to the present. We have already mentioned the value to political scientists of such information. As may be noted, too, one of the major problems of the social scientist is that he lacks the means of manipulating his data so that he can observe processes working themselves out under controlled conditions. Quite often he cannot find a sufficient number of current examples of the particular institution or event which he wants to study to enable him to generalize. But if his contemporary environment is thus limited, he can always turn to the past. Historical study, thus, by enlarging considerably the materials available to him, and giving him often more complete information than he can obtain concerning his own time, is a great asset to the student of political phenomena.

The value of history, however, goes beyond this—and more needs to be said, even though we enter into a realm which has always been controversial. The eighteenth-century tendency to deprecate history resulted from the belief that history was not important: man lives in the present, it was said, and in accord with reason, once he is freed from the trammels of superstition. However, what we assume to be "reason" is always, at least in part, received opinion, based upon past traditions and customs; a man who believes that he is thinking for himself is likely at best to be doing no more than extending or developing his intellectual heritage. If this is true even of exceptional individuals, it is the more so for the so-called masses. A similar idea has been raised recently: that we need only consider what is relevant to the present, the problems and issues of today. But without knowledge of the past, we cannot understand the present; for the present can appear only as chaotic and meaningless unless we see it as it is—a continuation of past trends and the culmination of earlier developments.

Under the stimulus of such a view, men in the nineteenth century undertook the study of history, trying to discover the origins and original forms of social institutions, and their lines of development. They felt that in this way—and often that *only* in this way—could the significance of contemporary events and institutions be portrayed, and guidance for the future be found. Of particular importance to political science was the work begun at this time on the background of law and legal institutions, of political philosophy and morals, of the functioning of various types of political and governmental forms; and, occasionally, on the relationship of political struggles to other social developments. Such historical research has continued to the present, and we have profited greatly from it; but in analysis of the results we have tended to become more and more critical. The past is not a collection of errors, nor is it sacrosanct, the repository of all wisdom; both of these positions of our recent ancestors are extreme. We must always go beyond the lessons of past experience, supplementing them with philosophy and with empirical observation.

Empirical Research. Empiricism is a point of view (in epistemology) which assumes that valid knowledge can be derived from direct experience. Empirical research, then, attempts to found our knowledge of social life upon such experience, approached through intelligent and controlled observation and experiment. This is the approach generally referred to as "science." However, as both history and philosophy can be quite scientific in their own ways, this usage is somewhat misleading. It should be kept in mind that the word "science" has both a narrow, popular meaning, and a broader, more comprehensive one, in which it signifies a method of study best adapted to its object and yielding the most fruitful results.

It is the ideal of empirical study to attain knowledge in the form of generalizations of high probability. When we observe the world about us, the immediate result is only knowledge of this or that particular event; and as particular events do not repeat themselves, such knowledge cannot take us very far. It is necessary to discover what may be common to many events, and to arrive at a statement which will apply to a large number of individual cases. To the extent that such generalizations prove to be true—that is, that things do actually happen (or at least that there is a high probability that they will happen) as indicated—the generalizations are frequently referred to as "laws" of behavior. Thus is reached the goal of scientific prediction: the ability to state what will happen in particular conditions. But even in the absence of such established generalizations, empirical study can test the correspondence of our opinions to what is actually the case, and can suggest alternative ideas more descriptive of political reality, thus promoting knowledge.

While few of the writers on politics since the days of Plato have ignored observed phenomena, or failed to attempt valid generalizations from the particular events or relationships observed, this approach to the study of politics has become increasingly important. More recently it has manifested itself especially in the prominence of behavioral analysis. Those of this orientation—while not necessarily denying the value of traditional philosophic, historical, or legalistic analysis—argue that political science most properly is concerned with observable patterns of political behavior and activity, whether within governmental institutions or not, and that the task is to identify as precisely as possible the structures of these patterns of behavior and their causes and effects. The result of this approach has been that the techniques of observation and of handling the data resulting from observation have steadily been improved. Especially has there been a growth and constant refinement of polls and surveys, of the use of psychological and sociological concepts to interpret political data, and of the use of mathematical devices to order that data. In addition to the use of measurement and quantification, and of devices such as game theory and simulation, the behavioral approach has sought to separate empirical explanation and ethical evaluation, and to integrate material broadly from the social sciences. The approach emphasizes the behavior of individuals in politics rather than institutional structures, and aims to reach value-free conclusions. In its beginnings, some behavioralists concentrated inordinately on method in their determination to be scientific; some so emphasized the functions of political systems as to neglect the role of important political institutions. But the behavioral approach to the study of politics has become well established, and has resulted in enhancing the sophistication with which political realities are observed.

The empirical study of contemporary events and relationships plays, and must play, an important role in political science. Dealing with the given materials of experience, the political scientist tries to select those relevant to his study—to describe them, classify them, indicate the relationships between them—and ultimately from these data tries to make valid explanations and predictions about the phenomena of politics. It seems likely that political science in the future increasingly will develop and depend upon knowledge obtained by empirical research.

In sum, we suggest that the knowledge which empirical research can give us should be joined with the results of philosophical and historical analysis. Facts are not necessarily science nor useful information, and they do not speak for themselves. The chapters that follow seek thus to integrate fact and theory with the perspective history affords us; no one approach will prosper effectively in isolation.

2
Society and the State

MAN is by nature a political being. Thus in the ancient world Aristotle stated the fundamental principle of his social science: that man achieves his highest excellence as a citizen. The simplicity of this view, however, did not long survive. Before the end of the middle ages, St. Thomas Aquinas had interpreted Aristotle to say that man is by nature a political and social being. To John Locke, early in the modern era of England, the observation required yet further alteration. Though recognizing fully the necessity of government, Locke found it sufficient to observe that man is by nature social. This bit of intellectual history is extremely important to us; it reflects the growth of a fundamental distinction and persisting tension in western culture between the social and political orders, between society and the state. While Aristotle could largely ignore these differences, we must grasp them if we are to understand politics today. No institutions of government, no public policies, no political values and ambitions can be comprehended if the distinction between society and the state is not kept in mind.

To say that the state is one thing and society another, however, is not to advance our understanding very far. We need criteria by which we can recognize the one order and the other. Since virtually the same men participate in both orders, we need to see how the orders are related, whether they support or oppose one another, and which is predominant. While the distinction between state and society may seem firmly engrained in our political culture—in our institutions no less than in our opinions—that distinction is a historical phenomenon, changing as the circumstances of the western world have altered. Despite some persistent characteristics, neither society nor the state are entirely today what they were yesterday or what they will be in some tomorrow. To avoid arbitrariness, consequently, we must consider the terms "social order" and "political order" according to the meanings they have acquired in our historical development. We can then suggest a more adequate definition of politics for today than that proposed in the previous chapter, treat the relationships between social and political phenomena, and examine how the western political regimes developed into the modern state, thus laying the foundation for all subsequent discussion.

I. The Social Order

We do not think of human beings—apart from a rare few—as isolated individuals living in only occasional and casual relationships with others. Mankind has always lived in intense and continuing association of groups small and large; the sort of men we are is largely shaped in such relationships. Yet man is not simply a gregarious animal, and man's social order—and man with it—have changed dramatically over time. While we know rather little about our remote ancestors, it appears that primitive men lived in self-contained kinship groups that imposed all obligation and regulation. These kinship groups were the exclusive source of benefits and duties, offering no sense either of a personal individuality or of a transcendent humanity. They also made few functional distinctions of responsibility, office, or role other than those necessitated by differences in age and sex. Obviously, this is not the world we know; such an undifferentiated primitive order has been replaced by our highly diversified and differentiated society, whose emergence we must briefly consider.

The Growth of Social Complexity

Many events and ideas have contributed to the growth of diversity in social life and to man's changed conception of the nature of social organization. Our discussion of this development must be limited by our particular interest: the clarification of the distinction between social and political orders. After dealing briefly with the initial breakdown of the primitive community, we shall proceed to later developments significant in western political history: the rise of Christianity, medieval pluralism and the rise of individualism, and the independent economy.

From Kinship to Citizenship. So commonplace has been the homogeneous and exclusive community based upon kinship that men have been able only gradually to emancipate themselves from it. The emergence of an alternative—a transition from kindred to civic relationships—was only imperfectly realized among the Greeks, since they tended to view their city as a new and enlarged family, no less exclusive than the kinship groups it replaced. The development is more clearly exemplified in ancient Rome, where the civic order began as an association—or a federation—of primordial families and never entirely lost this character. As a result of territorial expansion and conquest, peoples who were not original members of the city nonetheless had to be absorbed; that they were absorbed so effectively was due to the genius and flexibility of Roman political institutions. Even then, eight hundred years passed from the first grant of limited citizenship to the Roman plebs—commoners, not of the noble families—to the extension of citizenship to all free men throughout the then broad empire.

This development has a simple explanation. The Roman community early became too large and complex to be organized on the narrow basis of kinship alone. First the plebs and then others became too important, economically and militarily, to the life of the city. The ultimate extension of citizenship came from the need to broaden the tax base of an empire in serious financial straits—thus continuing the pragmatic Roman response to changing conditions and practical problems.

The nature of the community was now radically altered. What plebeians and patricians acquired in common was not the kindred and religious ties that were the foundation of early Rome, but rather a more limited and mundane social intercourse. Although the Roman community and law were never entirely divested of religious associations, these became increasingly secondary. Instead, the law emerged as a framework of rights and duties tending to secure the harmonization of diverse and distinct interests, and the community comprising all those living within that law. An association defined in such broad and pragmatic terms is not only capable of indefinite expansion but is also totally different from the primitive community from which it sprang. Although persisting civic religions and nationalistic sentiments show that the transformation is not complete, the first important breach in the homogeneous and undifferentiated social order had been made, and events of succeeding centuries were to extend it.

The Rise of Christianity. In primitive culture religion pervaded every aspect of life. Later, the increasing diversity of the population in pagan Rome compelled some measure of religious differentiation and tolerance. With the appearance of Christianity, however, the principle "Render unto Caesar the things which are Caesar's; and unto God the things that are God's" was introduced. Although there has always been difficulty in determining what in particular belongs to God, and what to Caesar, western culture has generally accepted two distinct, if interrelated, realms in human life. Diversity thus became a cultural norm, and this promoted respect for the individual person. The principle also implies that religious obligation is distinct from other social obligations.

Further, Christianity created an ecclesiastical institution parallel to that existing in the civic or imperial realm. It could not attempt to displace the latter—the realm of Caesar—which had its own special role in an imperfect world: the coercive maintenance of standards based in large part upon utility and expediency. But performing as spokesman and governor for the spiritual side of man's nature, and concerned with obedience to divine law, the Church was to remain independent and inviolate. For the first time in history a division of social authority within a community existed both in fact and in principle. And since religious attitudes had been a central expression of the homogeneity of primitive culture, that unself-conscious and simple unity had now definitely been broken.

Medieval Pluralism and the Rise of Individualism. During the thousand years between the fall of Rome and the rise of the modern world, western man became further accustomed to a community both unified and diversified. The decaying Roman empire could not be held together by the leaders of the Germanic tribes that overran it; and in time there emerged a new system of distributing power and responsibility, rights and duties, among many territorial and functional groups. The basic unit of medieval society was the manor, a relatively complete local community. It existed within a broader community, including the feudal nobility, the emperor, the Church, and a variety of corporate economic and cultural entities—all of them enjoying a partial independence from each other. As a result the associational life of the middle ages was enriched, compared with that of earlier periods, and the idea that human life is fundamentally pluralistic was established.

In medieval pluralism the individual was rarely seen as independent of his place within established associations. After the fifteenth century, however, primacy of the individual came to be emphasized. Increasingly the groups to which men belonged were no longer accepted as given, but accepted only as means to activity and development. Long since, men have been free to decide whether a group is appropriate to their particular ends or means. With the assumption accepted that their needs are diverse and changing, men are no longer obliged to stay within existing groups—even those into which they were born—but are free to shift from one group to another or to form new ones. Since the advent of pluralism, individuals have been able to use social organization for the realization of their purposes, rather than being dominated by it. Though such freedom has its limits, the organization of human life in western civilization has become as a result ever more complex and changeable.

The Independent Economy. One of the ways individuals exercised their new freedom of activity and association was in economic ventures. In the nineteenth century particularly, the theory and practice of laissez faire predominated, rejecting traditional, moral, religious, and political limitations on economic activity. This doctrine of "let alone" was firmly rooted in the scientific perspectives of the age. Adam Smith, in his renowned *The Wealth of Nations* (1776), applied the term "the invisible hand," which presumably guided individual endeavors to the general advantage without additional regulation being either necessary or desirable. Later economists constructed on Smith's insights an imposing system of economic thought, comprising a considerable number of "laws" seen as both necessary and beneficial. In short, the economic aspect of human life was taken to possess its own rules, derived not from politics or religion but inherent in its own nature. Economic activity should be left free, it was held, to follow those laws for the sake of efficiency and progress. Economics thus followed religion in asserting its autonomy.

The Modern Community. The modern western community, shaped by and extending the ideas and forces sketched above, has thus become intrinsically pluralistic. Compared to the primitive community, or to the Greek *polis* with its homogeneity, common purposes, and all-pervading authority, it hardly seems a community at all. More realistically it is a common space or realm, rather difficult to define or describe, in which individuals pursuing diverse ends act through innumerable autonomous organizations according to rules appropriate to each. Of course, this description exaggerates; perfectly self-conscious individual freedom, autonomous organizations, and specialized functional rules are rarely found in the world of ordinary experience. Yet, in describing the community as a whole, this conceptualization seems more adequate than any other. When we try to identify a common good for the modern community, we are generally reduced to such formal and external purposes as protection against foreign enemies, maintenance of order and security, and preservation of personal freedom. These are important, but far from the Aristotelian "good life." To a considerable degree, then, what the community provides has been reduced to the form of human life; the substance is provided in more particular and limited associations.

Modernity Challenged. The fact that men continue trying to give a richer and less formal meaning to such phrases as "our way of life," however, suggests that the modern community does not altogether meet men's needs. In the nineteenth century, various communitarian sects—such as the Amish, Mennonite, and Mormon—attempted to isolate themselves to preserve an integrated life for their members according to an older style. In the present century various totalitarian movements, fascist and communist, entirely disdaining religious objectives, have attempted to integrate men into one unified community to which they owe an exclusive and total allegiance. Recently some hippie and similar counter-culture groups have undertaken experiments with communal living. Whatever the ideology, these tendencies all suggest that the highly integrated and pervasive community of earlier times had certain attractions in providing a form of cooperative life, minimizing anxiety and maximizing certain limited benefits. Its contemporary advocates are thus able to attract persons to whom the values of freedom and diversity have little meaning.

That many people find no meaning in their lives is a worldwide problem today, but it is unlikely that the remedy is a restoration of some form of the primitive community. In the past, as human life became more complex, homogeneous and undifferentiated communities proved unable to meet emerging social needs and could not survive. In the even greater complexity of modern life, therefore, totalitarian and other efforts to restore the primitive community are a fundamentally irrational response to the undeniably serious problems and emergencies of the late twentieth century. They are, indeed, an atavistic and unrealistic attempt to escape the consequences of over two thousand years of history.

A Conception of Society

In any community, there are common standards of value and judgment which pervade the lives of its members; present also are ways in which those standards are established and maintained. In primitive life this distinction is not very sharply developed; standards are dictated by custom, so that one lives, labors, loves, and fights within essentially the same frame of reference. The primitive community is at the same time a family, a church, an economy, a military organization, a society, and even a political system. In modern western life, by contrast, distinctions between these diverse activities have become part of our social behavior and organization, and the activities have to a considerable extent their own standards, presupposed by our ideals of freedom and limited government.

To the modern mind some of these distinctions, such as that between family and economy, are easily made on self-evident grounds, if only because we now view the family as a consumer and not a producer. The more abstract entities, society and state, are often confused with one another, and with community. Yet it is the task of political science to distinguish them; and we are helped to do so if, in the historical development just sketched, we can see not only the collapse of the homogeneous community into diversified and interdependent activities, but also the emergence of two different processes through which persons are related and appropriate patterns of behavior determined. Thus, within any modern western community will be found what may be called the "social" and the "political" orders, distinguished primarily by how things are done rather than by what is done.

Society as the Voluntaristic Order. The modern western community has many activities and organizations in which people choose to participate, but are not obliged to do so. One may quit his job, abandon his business, even leave the economic order entirely for subsistence farming, if he chooses to accept the costs. In any event, no man is bound to any particular job, church, or social group. Though existing

informal class structures may raise particular problems, one fundamental aspect of life in the modern community, then, is the reality of
free individual choice, and of standards and relationships maintained
through voluntary acceptance. Some term is essential to identify this
aspect, which distinguishes modern western civilization from all other
civilizations, and enables us to identify the quite different and specific political realm which emerged alongside it. *This voluntaristic
realm we shall call "society," or the "social order," being a network of
associations created through relationships and obligations voluntarily
accepted.* Here the presence of voluntary agreement is superior to
any particular objectives. Most appropriately, therefore, it is the
sphere of small and intimate groups, shared purposes, and considerable informality in procedures.

Our definition of "society" is theoretical, of course, and is of little
value to those social sciences which make no distinction between
legal obligation and any other sort of necessity. It is intended less to
identify any particular associations as social than to identify a quality
which any association may possess—dominant and crucial in some, in
others subordinate. Economic and family life, for example, include elements not altogether voluntary, while in democratic political life
consent to government is highly important. Such ambivalences do
raise problems, and we shall deal with them in the following pages.
Nonetheless, that a social order of this sort exists has been assumed to
some degree in all western political and social thought since the seventeenth century. Thus John Locke's position was continued and extended a century later when Thomas Paine argued that society is always a blessing, but government is only a necessary evil; the former
springs from our wants, the latter from our wickedness. In keeping
with a bias in favor of individual spontaneity and freedom, and recognizing that the modern community was coming to give those attributes considerable scope, Paine and other liberals distinguished actions and groups in which those attributes are primary as "social."
Our definition is rooted in this historical experience and thought.

II. The Political Order

We now turn to our principal concern, the clarification of modern
politics, and note how the developments discussed above in relation
to society also contributed to the emergence of a distinct and limited
concept of politics.

The foundations of a distinctive political order were laid early in Greek and Roman times, when a division emerged between the city, or public realm, and the private sphere of life. The private realm was that of families in their internal affairs, and later of special religious sects, recognized as existing independently and having their rights—as we would put it today. The public realm was that of affairs common to all citizens, having its own special institutions, procedures, and purposes. For our immediate concern, the distinction is important because it suggests that the term "political" is applicable only to certain aspects of human experience. The contribution of Christian doctrine to determining the nature and role of political order has been neither entirely clear nor consistent, because of the belief that even what is Caesar's belongs ultimately to God. Nevertheless, a distinct realm for government was generally recognized by Christianity, too, its role being that of a remedy for man's sins, limited in its purpose and domain.

The political thought and practice that emerged granted universal and unqualified legitimacy to only one responsibility and function of government: the provision of order and security. Rarely in modern times—fascist regimes excepted—has government been seen as a creative force, or having any intrinsic moral value. It has rather been seen as an agent of people, who are not considered primarily as citizens but as private persons who need order and security for their private purposes. In this view, a political system performs two functions: it first enables people to identify their needs; it then protects their rights and provides appropriate services and opportunities so that they can effectively satisfy those needs. It should be obvious, however, that political systems differ significantly as to whose needs are taken into account and how they are satisfied. As a result, many recent political scientists have assumed that their major task is to discover "who gets what, when, and how," thus identifying politics simply as the struggle among interests. Though the reality of such a politics is undeniable, the perspective is not comprehensive enough to account for all political facts, and we must proceed further.

A Conception of Politics

A conception of politics appropriate to our needs—not only as political scientists but also as citizens—is implicit in the historical developments sketched above. Because these developments have shaped the thought and practice of western culture, and reflect its essential characteristics, such a conception of politics should help us identify and understand the realities of political life. It should also be sufficiently persuasive that we intuitively recognize it to be meaningful.

Politics as the Foundation of Modern Community. The effect of these historical developments on politics may be summed up in three propositions. First, the modern political order is only one aspect of community life; the realm which is not political may be referred to as that of conscience, voluntary association, or private affairs. Second, the political order exists to identify and safeguard the individual's rights and to aid him in satisfaction of his needs. Third, government can best achieve these purposes by maintaining a common framework of order through both legal rules and basic services and opportunities.

On the whole, these propositions define the liberal view of politics and government. Because this liberalism has been a powerful force in shaping the modern community, any great departure from it would make understanding modern government impossible. At the same time, however, it is not entirely adequate to our needs. Liberalism produced the view that political order is the protecting framework of society, within which other more primordial and important aspects of life may go on. This reduces the political order to being only a means to an end, about which it has little to say. Yet if we reflect on our history, we must realize that the modern community was forged through political revolutions, and that its social order was created and sustained through political action. The social order, with its private individual rights and associations, is therefore no more historically prior nor ultimately important than is government; both are equally natural phenomena in historical sequence, and interdependent one upon the other. Obviously, then, the role of politics is more than to accept and protect an established social order. It helps to shape it, and does so with particular power in the complex modern community.

This is not to deny the equally obvious fact that the social and political orders are mutually supportive. The unusual character of the modern community reflects a close interdependence among highly differentiated elements in it. Political order is one of the elements—one which political science studies. Political science must, therefore, have a definition of political order that reflects our liberal history and recognizes a political world rooted in the past but constantly changing.

Let us say that the "political order" is the foundation of the modern community, and "politics" is activity concerned with the creation of such an order and the maintenance of its essential values. Politics is not identical with the community, as in ancient Greece, but only with one aspect of its life. Its special character, and the distinctive responsibility of the political order—recognizing the coequal existence of the social order—are that it prescribes conditions within which social groups must operate and private activities be conducted, sometimes to the extent of affecting their values and objectives. Since politics is a control, however partial, of private activities, it must exercise this control according to values and procedures not necessarily those of private life. For this reason it is different in important ways from the control of religious, economic, and family life; standards of conduct derived from these activities are not necessarily relevant to the political realm. And politics does have an appropriate perspective of its own: in the historic values of western culture, wherein politics arose, the best political order supports freedom and diversity in social life.

Despite its importance, a political order is difficult to establish and maintain. In good part this is because modern social life has been dynamic, producing a society more complex and fragmented than others in history. But unless we can integrate the fragments through shared values and common standards, not only progress but even survival is unlikely. In a dynamic community the search for an effective integrating order never ends, so that different communities will have different political orders. Political processes and public policies, therefore, have no necessary stability or universality. We can discern when politics has failed, however; for the result is either chaos or totalitarianism, in neither of which can modern man live "the good life."

The Scope of Politics. There is a distinctive scope to politics which can be fully developed only in the course of our study, but which here can be briefly introduced. Our definition of politics, like that of society, is abstract and theoretical. It does not describe any particular behavior, but simply indicates the political dimension of behavior that is never solely political. The continuing disagreement over what is political and what political institutions and policies are appropriate suggests that no theory will adequately explain more than a few instances of politics and the political order. Among other reasons for the difficulty, people are involved in politics in different ways and for different motives—sometimes without being aware that they are; politics is a matter of circumstance, and is thus variable in its form and content; and political power, inseparable from government, is not always clearly definable either in the functions its serves or in its sources and effects.

In considering the scope of politics, it must be remembered, first, that few persons in any community are consciously and deliberately engaged in creating, maintaining, and perfecting political order. In fact, most appear to be engaged in their own private affairs, seeking to obtain from government some special advantage, to manipulate other persons through existing power systems, or to gain power and prestige through public office. However, we must see these motives and behavior in context. That businessmen pursue profit rather than an efficient system of production and distribution does not invalidate the laws of economics; it simply gives economists the task of relating profit-seeking to the larger pattern of economic life.

Political scientists must similarly attempt to understand, as facets of a larger political life, a politician's campaign for election, an interest group's attempt to obtain a subsidy, and even a revolutionary conspiracy, because they have no political meaning in isolation. An interest group may be seen as a political phenomenon because, in its quest for protection, assistance, or honors, it declares its importance to the community as a whole. Politics is not always rational—or, perhaps better, it has a peculiar rationality of its own—but, even so, such forms of behavior as we have just mentioned truly participate in the creation of the order government maintains. People may act politically by accident or design, out of self-interested or public-spirited purposes; no political system has ever depended solely upon conscientious and civic-minded citizens for its existence. Consequently, it is always difficult to identify accurately the range of political phenomena.

Second, in considering the scope of politics, it should be noted that the character of any political order depends largely upon circumstances. The institutions, procedures, and policies that serve to integrate the social order and promote equality or justice are not necessarily the same in different times and places. Political institutions and policies transplanted from a native to an alien soil yield rather surprising results, if they survive at all. It is the case, then, that we can identify politics only by examining what institutions enable a particular community to evolve policies sustaining a common life. In doing this, attention must be paid to the entire political environment within which the political system operates. Such a system maintained successfully for any length of time develops, indeed, its own political culture; we shall give some attention to this later in the chapter. In any case, the viability of political orders is tested, not in a priori speculation or in scientific laboratories, but in political experience. In sum, the most applicable conception of truth for politics may well be the pragmatic one—that something works!

Finally, power is necessary if any order is to exist, and there are always men who seek opportunity to exercise it. A political order necessarily supports a concentration of the more potent forms of power —especially physical coercion—in the hands of government officials, whose activities therefore constitute especially striking instances of politics, as do struggles to gain and control those offices. As every analysis must have some starting point, in political science governmental and immediately related phenomena are usually seen as the core of political life. Nevertheless, it is undesirable to give power-seeking an independent significance; this is especially so in the study of democracy, wherein it is difficult to relate government and its power clearly to its context. Political science must consider many things not immediately or inherently political if it is to discern the full scope of political life and the dimensions of the political order.

The Interrelationship of Society and State

We have distinguished two orders within the modern community: the social and political. We know from experience, however, that in our communities few matters are exclusively political or social; they contain elements of both. We must now endeavor to see how the social and political orders are related to understand either in practice.

Neither the social nor the political order exists for its own sake. Men cannot live without cooperative association. Especially in western culture, they have to this end created two important and different ways of cooperating: one of voluntary and often evanescent relationship, and another of more or less permanent, generalized, and authoritative organization. Paine was thus right in his assertion that society and state could be distinguished as to their sources, objectives, and methods. Yet he was wrong in his somewhat casual assumption that government can only be understood in terms of the needs and character of social life. The social order is as often shaped by the political, and distinctively political values do exist.

The Social and Political Orders Influence Each Other. Much private practice and opinion we now take for granted in social life—in which we assume government has no part—is really the product of past political activity. On the other hand, we can easily see the degree to which political standards and activities are affected by prevailing social practices and attitudes. The relationship between the two orders is clearly one of mutual influence. The role of politics has never been so negative as Paine suggested, and is certainly not likely to become so. Indeed, government seems destined to become ever more important and powerful. Communities are becoming more complex and their aspirations more demanding. In these circumstances realistic and compatible goals and appropriate techniques of cooperation in our communities are increasingly difficult to discover and maintain. It is therefore possible that politics as we have known it will vanish in an emerging totalitarianism—though this has not happened where politics was firmly established. Hence, the fear of those who oppose expanding government is comprehensible. But whether we like it or not, as the means for identifying and implementing a framework of order for society, government must continue to be the central and controlling force in modern life.

The Nature of Political Values. Certainly politics must express some central values in life. In the first place, the preservation of the political order itself is a political value of the highest rank, especially if taken to mean preventing degeneration into chaos or totalitarianism. Within this, then, we may distinguish two categories of political values. One comprises those values so essential to community life that they must be enforced, if necessary coercively. No one has suggested that uncontrolled killing of fellow citizens might be tolerated, and few that contractual obligations should go unfulfilled. The second category includes values whose realization requires widespread and highly organized cooperation beyond that available through any other association, and perhaps of a type not appropriate to any other. Foreign relations, military activities, and monetary systems are examples of long standing, to which have been added more recently programs of national economic development. Differences over these programs, as well as disputes concerning to what extent racial or sexual equality should be a value of the first category, indicate the dynamic nature of political life and its values.

Rather than a necessary evil that can and should be limited, government is realizably a potent force and a positive good—an instrument for organized achievement when other means fail. It is a misguided concern for private interests to hope to promote them through abolition of public authority; it is only upon such authority that the security of their rights and the possibility of broad and enduring cooperation depend. Still, governments are scarcely perfect instruments even to the best ends. Apart from the possibility of their corruption and of their great power being used imperfectly, they cannot serve all human purposes, and whatever they do inevitably runs counter at some point to such values as privacy and individual spontaneity. Even those values it does serve acquire their full meaning only in the context of other more intimate and personal values. We are no longer the Greeks of Aristotle's day; politics, however important and exciting, is not an end in itself. Ultimately and ideally, the political order is important because it promotes human freedom in an ever richer social life.

III. Historic Patterns of Political Organization

A political order must have some organizational form, and that of modern times is generally called the "state." Yet the modern state is not the only form of political order that has existed or is likely to appear. Furthermore, it has grown out of earlier and quite different regimes, and cannot be fully comprehended except when seen in an historical dimension. To broaden our perspective, we should briefly survey these earlier systems before considering modern times.

Governments in Antiquity

The cradle of western civilization was the eastern Mediterranean area and the Middle East. We know relatively little about the governmental institutions of these early civilizations. Successive kings and emperors—from the rulers of the first dynasty of Ur about 2550 B.C. to the Persian Cyrus, who captured Babylon in 539 B.C.—succeeded in building great regimes, including systems of law and organizations of officials. The Code of Hammurabi, from before 2000 B.C., was remarkably complete, dealing with property, commerce, and family relationships, yet it was a codification of law probably centuries old. Kings and emperors derived their power partly from military effectiveness and partly from priestly support. The range of governmental activities was already wide, extending from postal to irrigation systems.

Yet as far as their power reached, these regimes were totally despotic. They rested entirely upon the activity of a few ambitious, energetic, and relatively enlightened men, and the vast mass of the community was more acted upon than led. Such regimes could maintain a fairly high degree of internal order in a relatively static culture, but they were not effective organizations for more unified or progressive purposes. They fell before the attacks of less civilized but more aggressive nomadic groups, or by their own degeneration into internal rivalries, leaving little but ruins to later ages.

The Classical Age: Greece and Rome

The communities of Greece and Rome developed after 750 B.C. a more dynamic political life, undeniably influencing later western culture and politics. Each community had its own special characteristics, and consequently a different impact on later developments.

The Greek City-Community. Originally nomadic invaders of the eastern Mediterranean, the Greeks made a relatively rapid transition to life as city dwellers; what had probably taken several thousand years in Mesopotamia was compressed for them into a few hundred. Perhaps for this reason, and because they were a people of unusual and quick intelligence not much inhibited by superstition, the Greeks soon came to show a considerable diversity among their city-communities and a rather dynamic changeable character within. Their cities remained small, however; they did not create empires. The core of Greek life remained the city with its surrounding rural area. The largest of these, Athens, was at its greatest about one thousand square miles in extent and comprised less than 40,000 citizens, plus their families and a large number of resident foreigners and slaves. Most cities were much smaller; indeed, in their political commentaries Plato and Aristotle expressed a preference for cities of no more than six thousand citizens.

An explanation for this attitude is to be found in the nature of the Greek city. It was not just a place where Greeks resided, but the framework and substance of their lives. It was a way of life, clearly delineated and intensely shared. As such, it could not be divided into private associations and benefits, nor could it be submerged in a greater union. Each city had its own peculiar personality, expressed in its traditions, and in each the primary aim was that every citizen be raised to that city's standard of human excellence. For the Greeks this was political life, and it represented freedom. However different may be our experience, we can sense our Greek inheritance in attitudes we take toward government and its place in life, particularly when we maintain that government is the people's concern and that citizenship is morally significant.

Roman Law and Institutions. The glory of Rome was its empire and its law. Both emerged within a republican constitution, further developing within an imperial constitution, and enduring as a whole close to nine hundred years. Rome's influence, both then and since, has been enormous. The explanation of its success—although perhaps for its ultimate failure as well—lies in the eminently practical approach the Romans took to their political problems. The complex and often confusing pattern of institutions developed to meet immediate practical needs of the city, however, proved by the end of the second century B.C. no longer an effective government for Rome as an empire. After Julius Caesar, consequently, the office of emperor was superimposed on the institutions of the republic and generally dominated them.

The particular Roman genius was manifested in the techniques devised to govern the far-flung dominions. Roman demands were generally quite limited—that peace and order be maintained, trade kept free, and taxes paid. They could therefore permit local customs to stand and local leaders to continue in power. To protect imperial interests, they developed and maintained a colonial administration of great effectiveness. Provincial governors, or proconsuls, of unusual competence and integrity, were dispatched throughout the empire. The justly renowned Roman armies were used not only to conquer new areas, but to maintain order. One of the most cohesive forces of the empire, however, and one of its most enduring accomplishments, was the Roman law. This came into wide use, systematizing legal standards for the many peoples throughout the empire and providing a foundation for political order, after the empire's collapse. Rome could bequeath this heritage because of the practical and thus potentially universal nature of its law, but it fell because it could not invent federal and representative political structures to match its creativeness in law and administration.

The Medieval Political Order

The fall of the Roman empire was primarily the collapse of the great administrative system it had created. The idea of some sort of universal order did not vanish, however, nor was the legal order Rome had built totally destroyed. Both were important elements in the feudal system, an extremely complex social and political order, which in time arose on the ruins of the empire. Furthermore, the medieval political order included an important role for the Roman Catholic Church, now freed from an earlier dependence upon the emperor and able to exercise a leading and unifying influence throughout the western part of the former empire. In the East, on the other hand, both the Orthodox and Islamic religions promoted the unity of what western analysis distinguishes as religious and secular realms; while the peoples of the East had governments, they thus had no distinctively political orders.

The Feudal System and Limited Government. Despite the efforts of Charlemagne at the beginning of the ninth century, the leaders of the conquering tribes were able neither to preserve nor replace the unified governmental system of Rome. Thus, from roughly A.D. 500 to 1500 government in Europe was highly decentralized and divided. Community in the middle ages was for the most part, and for most people, extremely localized; and the manor—a village, in effect, dominated by its defensive walls and moat and by the living quarters of the lord of the manor, and surrounded by agricultural and hunting lands—was the realm in which all but a few passed their entire lives.

The feudal system, which comprised the relationships between diverse manorial lords in a hierarchical structure that came to include numerous kings, was capped by the "Roman" emperor. The relationships were of mutual service and protection, with the obligations consecrated in an oath of fealty. Between the customary laws of the manor and the equally customary laws of feudal relationships, the rights, duties, and authority of every person were identified. These were attached not to persons as such but to the positions they occupied in the hierarchy based on land ownership. Everyone had some position—even the serf, who had his customary rights within the manor and could not be expelled.

The feudal superstructure, in particular, was based upon the supremacy of law, since in the absence of any overriding and unified governmental power, only law could define in any settled way the relationships among the various barons, counts, and kings. From this arises the most striking characteristic of medieval government—the stress placed in both thought and practice upon limited government, with its authority based upon law, and its power flowing from consent. Ultimately, in feudalism's declining years, this relationship was applied to the king and all his free subjects. The idea that government flows from consent of the governed and is responsible under the law was passed on to the emerging modern community.

The Roman Church and Medieval Government. Besides the manor and the feudal system, Christianity as organized in the Roman Catholic Church played an essential part in the government and politics of medieval Europe. The Church, considerably unified in doctrine and organization before the fall of the empire, survived and was for many years the sole power transcending tribe and village. Its hierarchy—from parish priests through bishops to the Pope in Rome—was more tightly organized than that of the feudal system at its best. Furthermore, few apart from its clergy were literate; the feudal lords were often dependent upon the Church for more than religion. Since this was a devout age, it is easy to understand how the Church was able to maintain and even extend its authority throughout the period, claiming responsibility for faith and morals. Evidence of this authority is well preserved in documents, including many admonitory letters from bishops to kings, which were commonly heeded. Also, such matters as marriage and inheritance were regulated by the canon law of the Church, which maintained its own courts; the legal systems of central Europe still reflect this situation. In the medieval period, then, the Church was itself a central part of the governmental order from the manor to the Holy Roman Empire.

IV. The Modern State

The medieval political order—dividing public power and responsibilities among various persons, groups, and orders—was an interesting attempt to combine localism and universalism, and to coordinate public authority and private interests; since these are continuing problems the period is fruitful for political study. Nevertheless, its tensions eventually proved too great, with its government largely depending for stability and effectiveness upon everybody's agreeing to accept customary arrangements. But in the twelfth century some of the more powerful lords began to extend their dominions and to escape from the feudal restrictions on their authority. By the seventeenth century the collapse of the medieval order was complete in western Europe, where there emerged the typical political organization of modern life, the state. By consolidation in the places of its original establishment and extension to new places over the following centuries, the state dominates political life today.

The Nature of the State

Examples of the state are not hard to find; England and France have been thus organized for many hundreds of years, and the United States since 1789, at least. Nevertheless, the term is somewhat ambiguous. The reason for this is that the modern state is neither in theory nor in practice a logical concept, but a historical fact. The complexities of historical development have thus produced in the state a political phenomenon that is extremely difficult to comprehend as a whole.

One can without difficulty, of course, identify some elementary and reasonably constant characteristics of the state. Political scientists have traditionally held as distinctive marks of the state the existence of an independent and unified government, effectively controlling a determinate population and territory. Thus, the modern state is distinguished from the overlapping jurisdictions and diverse legal rules of the middle ages by the unity and distinctness of its order, and from provinces, colonies, and dependent territories by its independence. Yet these criteria do not enable us to distinguish the special ethos of the modern state from that of the ancient city-state or of other regimes reasonably independent, unified, and effective. They do not provide a definition adequately sensitive to the state as a political order. To obtain this we must consider its historical development.

Origins of the "State." Words describing types of governmental systems, such as "kingdom," "republic," and "democracy," have been in use since antiquity, but the political order of which they are aspects has been known as the "state," rather than "city," "commonwealth," or "empire," only for the last few centuries. The term appears in the writings of Machiavelli and his contemporaries around 1500, but even then the usage was not general. It is closely related to the words "status" and "estate," when used to mean some condition or thing enjoyed or possessed. Originally a state as a legal entity was either an estate—a bundle of privileges and responsibilities—or the status of someone who possessed such an estate. In the feudal system, many such estates distributed rights and duties among the population in a hierarchical order. Although the status of king or emperor was superior in dignity to others, it was not for that reason different in essence from that of baron or commoner; all were founded in customary law.

Gradually the modern order emerged out of the medieval, using its vocabulary and political relationships even while transforming them. Thus, in the late middle ages the more powerful lords succeeded in extending their dominions and increasing their power within them. In some areas the political order was better integrated and demanded greater unity and centralization of legal rights, responsibilities, and authority than the medieval order provided. Changes in law and political thinking now accompanied the changing power relationships. At first, quite naturally, the increasing power of the king gave to his status a significance all of its own, becoming a majestic and special estate upon which that of all others seemed to depend. In this integration of the diffuse medieval political order the modern state was born, often identified with the person and position of the king. In seventeenth-century France Louis XIV is said to have exclaimed "*L'état, c'est moi*"; the remark is fully characteristic of the early stage of the modern state's emergence.

Opposed to this appropriation of the state by the king, however, were those who insisted that the political order is founded not on mere power but on common law which is superior to any estate or office, even that of the king. These were traditionalists seeking to preserve their customary privileges; but in attacking royal absolutism, they did give rise to the idea that the state is the community as a whole, manifested in its common law and in the agreement of all its ranks and orders. This perspective was dominant in England after the thirteenth century. In other developing states, such as France and Spain, it was advanced with less success; the state continued to be identified with the king alone until the popular revolutions of the eighteenth century.

These popular revolutions heralded still another pattern of the state, one which rejected both the royalist conception and the traditionalist view of the state as law. This view—held by those who were commoners in class and, often, individualists in philosophical perspective—accepted the traditionalist idea of the political order as a community, but denied that a hereditary class structure is essential to it. Since individualism tends to deny any basic differences of interest or value among men in its assertion of freedom and equality, the community came to be seen not as a whole, or a blending of different parts, but as a unity of like parts. This view of the state was expressed most radically in the French revolution, when the Abbé Sieyès insisted that the commons (third estate) is all. The state, then, is the organization of the commons to promote their common interests.

Different Concepts of the State. From this historical discussion three quite different conceptions of the state emerge. Each presupposes a highly unified political order—although not necessarily or even generally the integration of the social order into it—but they differ as to who or what serves as the core of that unity. The state appears, in one view, as a legal order, within which the diverse parts of the community are politically related. In a second view, the state is seen as the supreme power and authority of the king, or the government; by simple extension we may also see the state as the political means through which a dominant class or other group rules the rest of the community. Third, it is seen as an association through which common purposes are promoted among a community of equals. All three conceptions are reflected in the reality of the modern state, yet we can well ask how both law and a supreme power could be the basis of the state, or how the state as a cooperative association of equals can be reconciled with the dominance of one man or class. The reply must be again that political associations are not logical but historical facts. Developed by men over long periods of time, such institutions reflect the various objectives sought through them and the varying conditions in which they have worked. Political experience suggests that power is usually supported by some legal and institutional base—but someone had to create that base. Cooperation even among equals requires some sort of authoritative leadership. Political systems thus tend to become complex, and in time more rather than less difficult to comprehend. Any definition of the state, then, can only highlight some of its aspects.

The State as a Sovereign Legal Order. Despite its complexity, however, the modern state does possess some distinctive characteristics. It arose in a revolutionary age, in which the complex and customary order of the middle ages was destroyed by the movements known as the Reformation, the Renaissance, the commercial revolution, and the "age of discovery" in science and territorial exploration. Western culture was radically transformed—the means of power no less than the ends toward which they were employed. The severe reduction of customary and religious sanctions in political life, together with a great expansion of the sorts of values that men sought to realize, made necessary a fundamental transformation of the political order and of the organization and powers of government. The new character of political power may be summed up in the term "sovereignty"—which means, basically, the ultimate authority of some person or group to make law, unlimited either by customary law and rights or by any foreign lawmaking authority.

Early modern times, when the idea of sovereignty emerged, have with good reason been known as the "age of absolutism." Emphasis was placed on the absolute authority of rulers, tempered by appeals to their benevolence or enlightenment, as the only way anachronistic survivals of the feudal regime could be eliminated. However, no state since, whether monarchical, oligarchic, or democratic, has been able completely to escape at least a tinge of the absolutism—the potentially irresponsible power—inherent in its foundation. The reason is that change and innovation in the modern community limit the possibility of stable and precise standards to which government can be held responsible. Not only in its foundation, therefore, but as a continuing function within it, the modern political order in some manner contains the power of sovereignty. Various political regimes are distinguished primarily by where and how this power is exercised.

One should not assume that sovereignty is inherently an absolute and despotic power, or a claim to it. The term "sovereignty" is a legal one, and refers to authority and right more than to power, although power there must be. Taken even as power, sovereignty is limited by its context and circumstances as well as its end, which is the effective regulation of social relationships to preserve the community. From this view, sovereignty is the counterpart on the political level of private rights and associations on the social level; expressing the effective will of the community toward a well-ordered life, it is also the counterpart of the individual's free will in his private social affairs. These various concepts stand or fall together; and taken together—as they must be—they reflect the normal tensions of modern western life.

The modern state, then, represents an attempt to maintain an effective integrating order in a relatively large, diversified, and dynamic community through the establishment of centralized control. Such an order cannot be created and maintained by sheer force alone. We can rightly be skeptical of the sovereignty of selfish and power-seeking dictatorships—whether individual or collective. The authority they wield is that of the primitive community, and their despotic power aims at the destruction, not the fulfillment, of politics. Constitutional law is needed to furnish a stable basis for the exercise of political power, identifying the sovereign authority which is the source, not the product, of legal order. Moreover, given the disparate forces and political objectives to be coordinated in the modern community, that authority must reflect the needs and opinions of many. The modern state tends to be democratic, or at least popular, as a result, and to rest upon the unifying sentiment of nationalism.

The State and the Nation

Nationalism in the last two centuries has been one of the most potent political forces ever known. It has been so closely associated with political developments that we speak of the modern state as the "nation-state," meaning that its citizens possess a common nationality, and see statehood as the nation's most appropriate and characteristic form. Although nations have existed independently of any political embodiment, and states have been formed with multinational populations, their relationship has now become almost inseparable. From England and France centuries ago to the peoples of Africa, Asia, and the Middle East today, nationalistic sentiments have led to the destruction of traditional orders, multinational states, and colonial empires; to the building of new states on their ruins; and to the great increase of political power in the process.

The Modern Nation and its Nationalism. If the power and effects of nationalism are evident, the precise nature of the nation is not.

Broadly speaking, the term "nation" is used to refer to a body of people of common origin, language, and historical experience. But these commonly shared attributes create nationalistic sentiments only if men consider them important, which is not always the case; and men have altered languages, customs, and interpretations of history to serve nationalistic needs. Nationalism reflects also a sense of common life and destiny for a people—or for those who nationalistic leaders think ought to share that destiny; it is as often a nation-creating force as it is recognition of a nation existing. Nationalism is ultimately a construction of human imagination, springing from the fact that men live in and are attached to particular communities, and feel separate from those communities that are alien.

As distinct from tribal or civic loyalties, nationalism had its beginnings in the loyalties of common people to kings against foreigners—including emperor and pope—in late medieval England and France. However, it was primarily in the American and French revolutions toward the end of the eighteenth century that nationalism as we know it emerged. Initially reflected in a moderate love of a traditional way of life and independence, it soon acquired a different force, as when Paine wrote in *Common Sense* that "a government of our own is our natural right." The French revolution, seeking "liberty, equality, fraternity" against a regime that denied these ideals, not only overthrew a government but transformed a society. In the ensuing struggles the French were driven to a deeper sense of national community, and similar sentiments spread over Europe. Nationalistic and independence movements in this century have stressed the increasing awareness of virtually all people about the world of their cultural differences, similarities, and potentialities.

We may see now that the state is a political and legal association, membership in which entails subjection to its law, enjoyment of the rights that its law provides, and sharing in its objectives. It creates bonds that may be completely independent of the physiological, sociological, or psychological characteristics of its population—characteristics which might define a nation. Yet the state alone could never arrogate the power men have freely granted to the nation-state. It is unlikely that the great political realms of the modern world could have come into existence, or be continued, without the communal loyalty called "nationalism." However one may evaluate its effects, nationalism has revolutionized political life by rooting it in a mass support it never before possessed and which shows no signs of waning. The nation-state is clearly the principal organization of political power and loyalty in the world today, but this is no guarantee of its future. Like any historical phenomena, political regimes appear, change, and disappear as they reflect prevailing needs. We can only be certain that whatever the political order of the future, it will have grown out of that prevailing today.

The State and the Political Environment

We have given attention to the common characteristics of the modern nation-state; we need to conclude our discussion with some examination of those qualities which produce the considerable differences in the varying political systems of the nation-states. Each such system is, after all, part of a larger environment; and much of what we can observe within particular states is the direct product of that environment.

The Political Background. The political environment is shaped by a state's history. As we have seen, the quality of its nationhood is important: some nations demonstrate a political continuity of centuries, as England, Spain, and Turkey; others may be mainly the arbitrary product of recent colonial administration, as is the case with many new African states. A long experience of political stability can encourage free institutions and orderly government; a tradition of political instability will likely produce repressive institutions and frequent changes of regime. Racial and nationalistic divisions in states are usually the residue of grave political episodes in the past, and frequently combine to produce discrimination, conflict, and violence.

Geography is one of the obvious influences on the social and political structure of the state; location, topography, climate, and other physical characteristics have always set some dimensions of national life. But today more emphasis is placed on how a nation shapes and utilizes its share of the physical world than on how it is influenced by it. A state's economy—in part the product of its geography, but far more of its inventiveness, skill, and enterprise—ordinarily exists in close interrelationship with the political system. Advanced technologies, like effective self-government, have been established in only a limited number of countries; elsewhere in the world political and economic underdevelopment tend to go together. Religion can provide a cohesive basis for national life; but the presence of conflicting religions may be an additional source of controversy in national affairs. The nature of a state's communications is also an important variable conditioning the political process. Here it is important to determine who are the influential communicators—and what is the structure of the communications media—in the relationships between government and governed. The educational system of a state also bears significantly upon its political process in such matters as literacy, access to modern technology, and opportunities for improving economic and social status. In sum, the ways in which these physical and institutional characteristics interact and relate produce important national differences; comparing any two nations will show that their differences are legion.

The Political Culture. Political systems are explained in terms of the political culture, as well as political background. The term "political culture" has come to be used broadly to refer to patterns of behavior in the political order; more specifically, to refer to the distinctive customs, habits, skills, and attitudes learned by individuals as a result of the shared experience of their political system. Even a quite limited observation suggests that the members of a nation tend to display certain common and predominant traits distinguishing them from others—and this, of course, without denying a common humanity. These regularities in behavior patterns, usually recognizable by members of the nation itself as well as by outsiders, range too widely to permit their cataloging here. Three of especial importance concern attitudes to political authority, political recruitment, and political style.

Political authority, for example, may rest on traditional, rational, or charismatic claims to legitimacy; it may receive either secular or religious support, or both together. Again, political leadership is recruited by various means: among others, by hereditary succession, monopoly by a social group, co-option by an elite, or popular election. Thirdly, popular attitudes to the political process and degrees of identification with it give a distinctive political style to the national culture. For instance, in particular societies men may normally seek their interests by the use of force, by bargaining and negotiating, or by appealing to their just due under the law. Some societies enjoy wide consensus and a strong civic spirit; others are highly fragmented, reflecting apathy and alienation, and so on. These are all matters that must be left for further elaboration.

It is important to note that the political culture, like the general culture of which it is a part, is learned; it is the product of history and not heredity. The political culture is transmitted through means that have come to be called "political socialization." The conveyance and maintenance of the behavior patterns, skills, attitudes, and values constituting socialization are performed by both generalized and specialized institutions: family, schools, church, formal and informal groups, media of communication, and government agencies. The political socialization process differs considerably, of course, from culture to culture—and differs notably between traditional, democratic, and authoritarian societies. Finally, we may note that the differences in political systems are in part a product of the ideologies dominating them or competing within them; this is the subject of our next chapter.

3

Modern Democracy
and Its Challenges

"GOVERNMENT of the people, by the people, for the people"—these words of Abraham Lincoln are the classic statement of the democratic principle. The phrase is unchallengeable as a symbol and as a powerful expression of the meaning and quality of democracy. Yet its virtues as a definition are limited; what it tells us depends on how we read it. In the political context, what does "government" include, who are "the people," and how is government "of," "by," and "for" them? These are not easy questions. Most political thinkers now recognize that democracy is neither so simple nor easily realized as many believed a few generations ago; it is instead complex, often difficult, and sometimes frustrating. The achievement and preservation of democracy depend upon its understanding and its determined defense. Since it also requires favorable circumstances, which sometimes are matters of historical accident, it is not always a practical possibility. To understand democracy, we must not be complacent, but must carefully consider its essence, its values, its feasibility, and the challenges offered to it.

I. The Meaning of Democracy

Through most of history, democracy as a form of government seemed to present an easy target. In ancient Greece Plato, an accomplished aristocrat, spoke of "democracy, which is a charming form of government, full of variety and disorder." Barely a half century ago, H. L. Mencken, a professional iconoclast, could insist that "democracy is the most expensive and nefarious kind of government ever heard of on earth." But World War I tied the term "democracy" to the aspirations of much of the world's population, and practically no political leader thereafter has dared to reject the label.

Adolf Hitler asserted that "real democracy" was possible only within a racially pure and dictatorial state. Mussolini argued that fascism was an "organized, centralized, authoritarian democracy." After World War II, communist dictatorships called themselves "people's democracies." Among popular autocrats, Sukarno established "guided democracy" in Indonesia, while General Ayub Khan installed "basic democracy" in Pakistan, though both regimes were short-lived. Even Mao Tse-tung boasted of creating "a people's democratic dictatorship" for China. This almost universal attempt to appropriate the term "democracy" is rooted in the fact that all modern governments are popular in some sense. Almost everywhere the spirit of nationalism is strong, and national goals cannot be realized without the cooperation of great numbers of people. No contemporary political leader, therefore, can forego employing some of the forms, symbols, and slogans of democracy, and the claim to be democratic. Yet distinctions among governments must be made, and there is no reason to assume that all are democratic. As the term "democracy" has acquired some distinctive meaning through its use in western political history, we shall seek to clarify what this is.

A Preliminary View of Democracy. Like many political terms, the word "democracy" came to us from ancient Greece, where it meant the power (*kratos*) or rule of the people (*dēmos*) or citizens. Yet this group did not then include women, children, aliens, or slaves; even in Athens, the model democracy, only about one-tenth of the population were citizens. "We are called a democracy," declared Pericles, the greatest of Athenian statesmen, "because the government is in the hands of the many, not the few." In the broadest sense, democracy still means popular self-government, but democracy today is very different from what it was for the Greeks. As we have seen, the Greek *polis* was a small community, intensely united in the common affairs of the citizens; and nothing was considered more important than the opportunities and responsibilities of public life. To the Greeks, the citizen's service by direct participation—in the army or navy, popular assembly, courts and councils—constituted a way of life superior to any other.

By contrast, the political activities of the modern democratic citizen are modest; nor would he generally desire such intensely personal and demanding citizenship. To modern man politics is not a way of life, much less the supreme way; politics is a specialized function in the community. Requiring the constant participation of all citizens in government, direct democracy, is impossible because of the size of modern states; only representative democracy is now appropriate. Nor is democracy best used as a term for all good things, as in the phrase a "democratic way of life." Viewing democracy as a way of life has led to psychological theories concerning the "democratic personality" as contrasted with the "authoritarian personality," and so on. Likewise current are terms such as "economic democracy," presumably meaning an economy favorable to the workers alone, and "participatory democracy," proposing that all individuals must share in any decisions affecting them.

These phrases introduce such variable factors into the discussion that it is impossible to attain any clear idea of what is being talked about. We do not know for certain how personality types, economic and other social processes, and the forms of political life are related in today's complex communities. At the same time, "democracy" is not simply another word for "equality," "freedom," or "brotherhood." These more general terms can stand by themselves; and they are unlikely to refer to the same things when variously applied in politics, factory, family, or university. Consequently, it is to government and its related values and institutions that the term "democracy" must apply. More immediately, we seek the meaning of "democracy" as applied to the institutions that enable a people subject to a government to control and influence it in a continuing and effective manner.

II. Patterns of Modern Democracy

Democracy is government controlled by its citizens. Democratic government thus rests upon the consent of the governed, and its threat or use of coercion is minimal. These characteristics are not necessarily limited to democracy, of course; moreover, democracies do occasionally use coercion with considerable effectiveness. The distinctive qualities of democracy lie then not only in techniques which maximize consent and minimize coercion, but in particular attitudes toward men and the community.

The Traditional View of Community. An early discussion of the issues dividing democrats from their opponents arose during the English civil war of the mid-seventeenth century. Cromwell's parliamentary army, debating what to do with power gained by defeat of the royalists, was strongly influenced by the democratic ideas of a group known as the Levellers, who were advocates of constitutional reform, religious toleration, and manhood suffrage. The Levellers protested against the tradition of reserving suffrage only to those with substantial landed estate, and rejected the idea that political privileges were themselves a form of property. As one of them, Colonel Thomas Rainborough, put it, "The poorest he that is in England hath a life to live as the greatest he," and ought to have a voice in choosing any government regulating that life.

Reasonable though the argument may seem today, to Cromwell and other landed gentry of that time the position of the Levellers was hardly comprehensible. To the conservatives, a man must be defined in terms of the community to which he belongs; for a community is a traditional set of customs, and the values and rights established in them. This traditionalist view, which has appeared in various guises in criticism of democracy throughout the years, stresses the order, structure, and hierarchy of interests that the community exhibits. It is not persons as such that count, but the role they play in social life and the rights inherent in that role. As rights flow only from social position, and persons occupy quite different positions and responsibilities, persons cannot possess the same rights.

The political order being part of the community, these ideas are naturally applied to government as well. According to the traditionalist view, only some responsibilities require participation in government; and only those trained in the exercise of such responsibilities can capably use political power. Well into the present century, as a result, the ownership of real property has been the principal evidence of political interest and capacity. As well, payment of taxes, nationality, sex, race, religion, education, social class, and family headship have been employed in various western countries to justify differences in men's share of political life. Such arrangements thus rested on the assumption that the social characteristics, interests, and capacities of men—distinguishing one from another—are alone relevant in government and are the proper basis of political rights.

The Democratic View of Community. In the democratic view, on the other hand, a community is primarily one of persons. Men are first of all men, and only secondarily are they rich men or poor men, nobles or commoners, philosophers or fools. Their political concerns transcend differences of wealth, education, family connections, and the like; and these concerns will be adequately met only if citizenship is independent of such distinctions, if political rights attach to persons in virtue of their humanity alone. Unlike interests or social position, humanity is something we all have equally in common. There is, at this level at least, no adequate reason for discriminating between persons. If people are different, how does one decide which is the more perfectly human? In the community, therefore, there are no "natural" superiors and inferiors—either of race, class, or profession. With no one having either greater or lesser claim to political rights, citizenship must be universal and equal. Each man to count for one, and no man for more than one, is the logical conclusion of this argument.

Differing Conceptions of Democracy. Unfortunately no universal pattern exists in the organization of democracy as the realization of political equality; since the concept of democracy extends over many ideas and practices, it is neither precise nor entirely determinate. Without avoiding all difficulties or contradictions, however, it may help our understanding to examine two different conceptions of it: "populistic democracy" and "liberal democracy." While neither is descriptive of specific democratic regimes, they may assist in showing what is democratic in any political system, and in distinguishing democratic from nondemocratic regimes.

Populistic Democracy

The populistic version of democracy has a principal characteristic: an unqualified insistence that the larger number of persons in a community should determine what government does. Its virtue is thus its simplicity—that majority rule is the basic political technique.

Equal Treatment for All. The idea of political equality has roots deep in the western tradition, which early asserted the equality of all men before God, before the law, and before reason. Men thus became accustomed to consider themselves equals within a political system that was godly, lawful, and rational. Emphasis was long laid on the rational and ethical aspects of social life rather than on man's immediate equality. But after the fourteenth century, with a breakup of the feudal system, customary and religious justification for the special privileges of rank became weakened—"when Adam delved and Eve span, who was then a gentleman?" Inequalities of status and privilege, no longer justified by common experience, were seen as rooted not in human nature but in illegitimate impositions to benefit a few. Belief in equality of treatment was also supported by the developing conviction that all men in many respects were much alike.

There thus emerged an idea of modern egalitarian society: its foundation one of equal rights, its values and needs those shared by the unprivileged, and its ultimate judge of the common good—for the reason that it was his good—the common man. The common man was not only unprivileged, of course, but shared with many others a simple and traditional way of life in contrast to that of the privileged orders. Thus came the further assumption that this popularly-shared life should be dominant in the community. Traditional monarchical and aristocratic institutions, being neither egalitarian nor reflective of this common life, could no longer serve the new aspirations of the common people. Hence, new political institutions were now required.

Political Equality and Majority Rule. Within the framework of populistic democratic thought, then, political equality is ideally expected to lead to government from which unequal influence is removed. Yet absolute equality is an ideal unlikely to be realized; only when decisions are unanimous would no one be discriminated against. But unanimity is possible only among small groups of the like-minded; it can hardly be employed as a normal method in politics, where controversy is inevitable. With unanimity impossible in practice, then, a majority must suffice. Therefore, the technique of translating political equality into actual influence on government is majority rule.

The legitimacy of rule by the larger number of persons in the community rests on several assumptions. In a community of equals, the larger number will reflect a wider consensus than the smaller; the larger number could coerce the smaller; it is more deserving and aware of common needs. To admit a minority right to rule, by contrast, leaves the problem of "which minority?" Minority groups are commonly seen as claimants for special privilege, and not as spokesmen for general rights in a common life. Thus, the majority is more likely to be correct in its views of the common good.

Democratic forces in the past were generally composed of the ordinary man—the family farmer, small businessman, artisan, and village worker. In those simpler days, the "common people" were distinctive as a class and homogeneous in their virtues and values; as the most numerous in the community, they could be regarded as the real foundation of it. This situation inevitably influenced the development of democratic thought. It seemed only appropriate to conclude further that such people should dominate political life, as with majority rule they could. In democratic thinking, consequently, government of, by, and for the people came to mean government of, by, and for the majority of them.

Difficulties in Populistic Democracy. The argument of populistic democracy must appeal to all who favor any form of democracy. Yet it raises immediate difficulties when considered either as a guide to action or as an aid to understanding actual democratic governments. It assumes fundamentally that there is in any community *a majority* which has distinctive interests, and that the majority knows what those interests are and can promote them as the only legitimate ones. If these assumptions are not true, however, then absolute majoritarianism is not an adequate vehicle for popular government.

Modern democratic thought has largely been concerned to protest against prevailing inequities. Against the hierarchical regimes of aristocracy, democrats urged equality; against special privilege, common rights; and against minority rule, majority rule. But whether a modern society could actually be organized on the basis of equality, common rights, and majority rule, they scarcely considered. As well, in those western communities where democratic movements first appeared, the political order was already organized and unified, and the character and needs of the majority were already well identified. Now that we have had considerable experience with actual democratic governments, we can doubt that democracy is defined by simply contradicting hierarchy, privilege, and minority rule. The conditions within which contemporary governments exist, the demands upon them, the ways they must operate, are very different from those which gave rise in the past to populist democratic thinking.

The established democracies of the present are built upon complex communities and eliminating rigid social divisions—particularly any which would set apart a mass of unprivileged common people. These communities are marked by a greater individualism—and a correspondingly greater pluralism in group life—than ever before. None of their social groups is constantly dominant, and none receives the continuous support of the majority of the population. In contemporary life, therefore, the term "majority" cannot have the significance attributed to it by early democratic thought. A majority may still be found, of course, as the larger number whenever the community is counted off; but it is not a sustained political force. Indeed, since majorities are no longer naturally present in contemporary democracies, it is the great task of national leaders at intervals to create them; in any country today, majorities are the product of effective leadership. Strictly speaking, then, the majority does not really rule, nor are the leaders merely agents of the majorities they create.

It might appear that the populistic version of democracy is more appropriate to newly independent nonwestern states, so unlike the complex modern communities of the west. The leaders of such states have commonly organized a majority of the "common people" into a mass movement based largely on anticolonialism. But in these movements the people are simply followers of the leader; this permits no control of the leadership by the majority, and there is no recognized place for opposition. One is either for "the people," which in practice means supporting "their" leaders, or one is held to be against them. Serious criticism or organized opposition is then easily equated with disloyalty and suppressed. Thus what may have begun as a proclaimed system of populistic democracy may well end as a tyrannical personal dictatorship. Clearly, the kind of popular acclaim accorded a Nkrumah, Sadat, or Castro is very unlike the modest, generalized, and uncoerced support given political leaders in Canada, Great Britain, or the United States.

The populistic version of democracy, we conclude, is no longer even a desirable aspiration. Most people today expect a continued improvement in their condition; but the progressive change to achieve that improvement requires diversified technological programs whose benefits, in any particular form, are unlikely to be widespread. Furthermore, disadvantaged peoples today are often minorities—in terms of income, education, race, or age; the rest of the population may be unable to understand their problems or solutions to them. The populistic image of democracy, as we have seen, would thus work to withhold majority support from those who need it most. Finally, as the nineteenth-century historian W. E. H. Lecky observed, "The tyranny of majorities is, of all forms of tyranny, that which in the conditions of modern life is most to be feared and against which it should be the chief object of wise statesmen to provide."

Populistic democracy is thus an inadequate perspective: it does not realistically explain government as it now exists; it does not promote political equality but can justify inordinate power for the politically popular; it ignores the modern need for forward-looking leadership; and, it affords neither promise nor protection to minorities. While its ideal of political equality is the foundation of any democratic order, it does not provide means of achieving it in the sort of world we know and want. To meet that challenge, we must take a more complex view of democracy.

Liberal Democracy

It should now be evident that we do not get democracy simply by substituting "the people" or some majority of them for a dominant ruler or oligarchy. The many cannot exercise political influence effectively through the same procedures as the one or the few; such procedures establish dictatorship or oligarchy, whether or not the name of the people is invoked. Radically different from any other kind of government, democracy must find procedures appropriate to it. The more complex conception of liberal democracy suggests what are those procedures and related attitudes.

The term "liberal democracy" is well established historically, for democracy arose in close association with the liberal demand for individual freedom. In the nineteenth century, the term "liberal" was primarily associated with the idea of limited government and, more recently, with government in the interest of social reform. But the word is appropriately retained in its broader connotation: "liberal" as connoting an open-minded, generous, and tolerant attitude. Its use also encourages us to adopt a more empirical view of democracy—one based on the range of its values and institutions in the more highly developed regimes.

Basic Aspects of Liberal Democracy. It is obvious that democracy cannot mean that the people become the government, nor are representatives simply agents of the majority. Populistic thinking, failing to recognize this, simply assumes an effectively governing majority, and pays little attention to the all-important matter of continuing popular control over those who actually rule. Consequently, the door is opened to a quite undemocratic tyranny. The problem of democracy is not how to enable the majority of the people to govern or direct government, but rather how to develop governments that can win and retain the support of popular majorities on specific issues, and the general loyalty of most of the population as well.

The liberal democratic mode, therefore, emphasizes the conditions within which political power is acquired and exercised, and the effect of such conditions upon those who exercise power and upon what they do with it. In liberal democratic thinking, majority rule remains crucial as a realistic means to maximize "consent of the governed." But its meaning and possibilities must be partially qualified, for there are other features of importance. Underlying all democratic values and techniques is the ideal of political equality. This is no simple idea. Men differ too considerably in their personal values, capacities, interests, and pleasures for all to have the same wants. Liberal democracy has been concerned, therefore, that all persons pursue happiness according to their ideals, develop their own personalities, and participate in government according to their capacities and interests. In liberal democracy, consequently, equality refers primarily to freedom and opportunity; all persons can and should be equal by this standard.

Public policies that grant and preserve special privileges are not compatible with equality, even if they are those of a majority. Only rights which all can at least potentially enjoy and benefit from, which do not create special advantages for their possessors or special disadvantages for others, are appropriate to a society of the free and equal.

Majority Rule in Liberal Democracy. Democracy implies political equality, and political equality implies majority rule. A majority is a matter of numbers, but complications arise once we move beyond abstractions to ask what majorities actually are and in what sense they are said to rule. When democratic movements first appeared historically, the majority was the commons, a distinct class or estate. In the established democracies today, majorities of this sort cannot be found. Indeed, in the modern community, interests and activities are so diverse that majorities are neither initially present nor do they arise spontaneously. Instead, there exist a variety of persons and groups with varying ideas of what government should do. Out of all these a majority must be organized.

The majorities of democracy, then, are like all political forces: they are created by leadership and inseparable from it. And if democracy is not adequately defined as simple majority rule, the exercise of governmental authority in it nevertheless depends on the continuous support of popular majorities. *Democracy in practice, thus, is a continuous interdependence of leaders and popular majorities supporting them, and at its core are those procedures and values which work to preserve that interdependence.*

Leadership in democracy must be strong enough to create popular support, but not so strong that it creates dependence on the leader, instead of interdependence between leader and led. There are no rules that tell us clearly what qualities support democratic, rather than autocratic, leadership. Yet a few observations are pertinent. Leadership based on coercion or its threat is not compatible with democracy, but neither is leadership based on hero worship; such leaders do not sufficiently depend upon the people. One-sided relationships of fear or worship are likely to produce dominance. In practice, leaders are those whom others will follow, and democratic leaders prevail as a rule through their ability to persuade people to grant them support on fairly specific issues.

At the same time, the existence of democracy depends upon the capacity of a people to respond to this sort of leadership. They must be able to give their support according to the issues raised, and not simply surrender themselves to a leader; they must criticize reasonably rather than idolize mindlessly. A modest distrust of politicians and campaign oratory is probably a healthy sign; yet politicians should not be denied a certain respect. They create the popular majorities at the heart of democratic life—it could not long survive without them.

Further essential to democracy, especially in its modern representative form, are certain conventional arrangements. Whether a majority has formed to support a leader or a program can be known only through a free election with universal suffrage. Elections must also be regularly recurrent to ensure that officials are sensitive to public opinion. If democracy is to be a continuing interdependence of leaders and people, there must be regular testings of popular support. Channels and media should be available through which issues can be raised and their alternative solutions proposed. Alternative leaders should be able to challenge previous or proposed decisions, and to attempt to win the support of new majorities. Democratic representation thus places in government not only spokesmen for the majority, but spokesmen for opposing minorities—an opposition—so that the majority may ever be renewed. Finally, underlying all of these requirements for democracy are the private rights of individuals and their associations, upon which the free development of majorities depends.

Majority rule, thus qualified and limited, remains an essential aspect of democratic politics. Its consequences are not insignificant. It produces responsible government, and not tyranny under the cloak of popular rule. Political leaders are allowed considerable discretion, yet they cannot diverge greatly or for long from what a majority will accept. The result of such majority rule is a political system more complex and sophisticated than earlier ages could have imagined.

Individualistic Pluralism and Democracy. Modern democracy arose in the eighteenth and nineteenth centuries in company with a heightened sense of individuality. That government derives its just powers from the consent of the governed was only one aspect of the political theory of the American and French revolutions; equally important was the fact that the governed were seen not as a mass of people but as individuals, each of whom possessed "natural and inalienable rights" to "life, liberty, and the pursuit of happiness," and to property. Many have argued, in reaction, that no rights exist independently of society and government; rather, private rights, social relationships, and political authority are all interrelated. They have pointed out, furthermore, that rights, in any specific sense, are extremely variable throughout history and around the world; therefore, if we desire to know what human rights are, we cannot find out simply by contemplating "the individual." In any event, there must be a power capable of defining these rights for any given time and place; and since the individual can hardly create his own rights, such power is logically, as it has been historically, government.

Yet, if government is the sole source of rights, then democracy is impossible, and benevolent despotism is the best that men can hope for. Democracy is a subtle interdependence of political leaders and the people. The people cannot hold down their side of the scale unless, as private persons, they have some independent powers; and the legal and political foundation for such powers are the rights people are presumed to possess. The argument against natural rights only proves that democracy is not inevitable. If the climate favorable to the recognition of fundamental private rights is a matter largely of historical accident, so then must be any democratic government. Most communities throughout history, however, have recognized private rights to be of equal standing with public authority. We need not be pessimistic about democracy on this account.

Not all types of rights are compatible with democracy: special privileges, for example, are not—as rights reserved to particular favored groups enabling them selfishly to control government. The right to an uninhibited use of one's property may also be turned into privileges dangerous to democracy. A further problem is that rights are meaningful only as opportunities to promote one's interests, and the same opportunities are rarely of equal use to all. In recognition of that, some democratic thinkers in defining the basic democratic standard have gone beyond the concept of rights, and have asserted that democratic procedures must embody a "belief in human dignity" and a "respect for personal integrity."

We have long passed the stage, in the Jeffersonian ideal, where we could preserve our individualism by remaining a community of small farmers. Jefferson believed, of course, that in a commercial and urban civilization persons become so mutually dependent that the good life is destroyed. The dependence that Jefferson feared is now an obvious fact of our lives. Contemporary emphasis upon the values of human dignity and personal integrity, therefore, are partly attempts to reperceive the social nature of man, and to prevent his isolation from his fellows. The contemporary counterpart of Jeffersonian individualism has come to be our social and political pluralism. The popular control of government now depends on the existence of nongovernmental power, widely dispersed among numerous entities. Today, these are not individuals, in general, but private groups and their leaders. More powerful than any individual could be, they are far more effective in keeping government responsive to the claims of the governed.

While the ultimate primacy of the individual and the openness of the order must still be maintained, contemporary liberal democracy recognizes that most political and social rights are exercised largely through associations. It also acknowledges the important right of individuals to join and quit freely the private groups and political parties they have created. This opportunity must be legally and practically available if democracy is present. Whenever the population, or any large part of it, becomes captive of a public or private organization, the result is dictatorship.

Rationality and Democracy. In the western world the search for the best political system most often has been for the most rational one. The term "rational" means agreeable to reason; and, broadly, a rational political system is one weighing the costs of ends and means, and displaying the prevalence of order, law, and harmony in relationships. Early democrats assumed that through democracy and majority rule—as opposed to accident and caprice, superstition and coercion —reason would prevail and men would be governed by law. Yet democracy has not escaped the criticism of being government based on popular emotions, whims, and fancies—rather than reason. It is often true that pluralities and not absolute majorities make decisions, for men have not agreed on what is the good life and often have radically different ideas about their welfare. Emotion plays a large part in all our lives; we often throw off one superstition or unreflective custom only to acquire another. Thus the debate has continued as to whether democracy is even compatible with rationality in political life, much less the necessary condition for it.

Democracy does serve the end of rational government, but it does so not in the simple and direct way that early democrats expected. We must understand, first, that rational action is not necessarily "right," and that it may not accord with perfect knowledge—for we have none. Reason demands only that we act consistently according to the best knowledge we possess, aware of its limitations and the constant need to improve it. Impulse and prejudice are opposed to rationality in this sense: impulse interferes with consistent action, and prejudice with improvement of knowledge. But it can be said also that prejudice, transforming knowledge into inclination to act, is necessary for consistent behavior; a person who never acts impulsively, therefore, will not have the new experience that can lead to new insights. These qualities of humanity are both opposed and necessary to rationality. Balancing tendencies to impulse and prejudice, the rational man is thus a self-critical man.

The core of rationality, then, is disciplined self-criticism. One becomes aware of the full nature of problems by seeking the most valid solutions to them. Rationality demands extensive cooperation in defining problems, examining relevant factors, and testing proposed solutions. In each area of human interest some methods of disciplined cooperation have been developed to promote rationality. In the realm of political life, the methods of liberal democracy serve this end. The process of building majorities within a free people assures that proposals and counterproposals will be discussed, evaluated, criticized, and supported. Democracy is, in fact, institutionalized self-criticism in public affairs, and the most intense form of it known to history.

In rational procedure, consideration of all relevant information must be concluded by decisions that can win the support of those concerned, and ultimately the problems of political life concern everyone. Political questions commonly ask, in effect, "what should be done here?" The answer supported by the largest possible majority, who have weighed proposals against their own experience, is the final test of the rationality of public policies at any time.

There is no expert in such rationality. No philosopher, no scientist, no student generation, no political leader, no self-chosen intellectual, no street mob, has the one rational answer to the problems of political life. The public in its diversity, working through their institutions, alone can develop answers to the extent these may be found. Each may have something to contribute to rational discussion, and on this assumption liberal democracy provides processes through which contributions may be elicited and fitted into political discussions the majority may approve. But as today's majority has no inherent authority tomorrow, neither is the reason of today necessarily that of tomorrow. Like reason itself, liberal democracy is a continuing process of seeking the most valid conclusions—the community's best insight into its objectives and the means of attaining them.

Of course, no existing political system is perfectly in tune with reason; and, subject to undisciplined impulses and prejudices, most men have limited ability to contribute to organized rationality. Political processes are often only partly effective, producing compromises and temporary expedients sometimes satisfactory to no one. It is easy to conclude that neither people nor institutions are anywhere perfect. We do not propose, further, that the validity of the populistic version of democracy be entirely set aside; it still most clearly idealizes democracy as a form of government—one that is the most difficult to realize. We have sought to show, rather, that liberal democracy offers far greater hope for rationality in public affairs. Acceptable government by the superman or the superclass has been demonstrated by logic and experience to be nonexistent. We conclude that majority rule—when majorities are forged in the forum of free criticism and represent the accommodations of a free people—is the best standard of rationality in public affairs we can have.

III. The Value of Democracy

The value of democracy has been a matter of controversy since ancient Greece, when men first came to reflect on their political experience. Throughout most of western history the consensus of learned as well as of ordinary men with regard to it has generally been unfavorable; only in the last century has democracy acquired any particular prestige, and even today it is challenged and misinterpreted.

The appeal of democracy, then, is not absolute. If we hold it to be of universal value, we are hard pressed to explain why it is interpreted in so many different ways or even rejected outright. In any case, liberal democracy is clearly related to the values and conditions that have appeared in modern western culture. Many feel these are basically sound and good, but there are also others who disagree and consider attempts to justify them not persuasive. There is no way of overcoming this difficulty with argument alone. We can only show what are the values of democracy evolved in western civilization and let the argument appeal to whom it may. What can be said against democracy will be treated in the latter part of this chapter.

Government Beneficial to Many. Undoubtedly the most general attraction of democracy has been its promise to ensure government beneficial to the greatest number. Its procedures reasonably guarantee that widely shared values will be respected and furthered. Although the people can in no immediate sense govern themselves, democracy gives them sufficient participation in political life, at crucial points, to permit them strongly to influence those who do govern. They exercise this influence continuously, furthermore, so that it is the values of today, not of yesterday, that dominate in political life; nor can the values of today be sacrificed in favor of some the people have not yet come to share, for the electorate can reject radical as well as reactionary advocates. They can insist upon receiving here and now what they most generally believe to be the good things of life. It has long been held that the most general interests should be served by government, and what the people at large think those interests to be is certainly worth consideration. They may be mistaken, of course, but dictators are not likely to do better. Only democracy compels rulers to give such consideration to the claims of citizens whose ideas are not the same as theirs.

Adaptable and Progressive Government. In the modern world, however, neither the wants and needs of men nor the conditions within which they live are static; adaptability is not only a virtue, it is a necessity. The status quo is a powerful force in any community, and no government can escape being partially rooted in it. Whatever may be said about "ideal" dictatorships or oligarchies, ruling in perfect goodness and wisdom, actual ones either are, or soon become, entirely rooted in the status quo, defending existing privileges and values against all change. Democracy, too, defends the status quo when the privileges and values it represents are acceptable to the bulk of the population. Yet democracy, in its modern liberal form, also creates channels through which attacks upon the status quo, whatever their justification, can be vented. No policies or vested rights are immune from criticism, for such criticism can always lead to change and reform, if those dissatisfied persuade enough others to follow them in their objection.

Only democracy among forms of government thus formally combines respect for traditional community values and opportunities for changing them. In practice, these rather antithetical characteristics lead to gradual or piecemeal reform, rather than radical and revolutionary change. In democratic politics diverse and changing ideas must be accommodated to one another, with new and old interests compromised. Radicals find this distasteful because there is not enough—or rapid enough—change, and extreme conservatives, because there is too much. But the net result, if the recent history of democratic communities is any indication, is a flexible and adaptable regime, and one of stable evolution in public policy. Democracies have accomplished enormous reform in this century, while retaining and even extending most of their traditional values.

Government Promoting Individuality. Democracy may well be most valued by its supporters because it promotes responsible individualism. Any majority decision is only a number of individual decisions brought to coincidence through discussions and leadership. The values and procedures of democracy begin and end with the individual, no matter what groups and collective judgments intervene in the process. However small his part in public life, it helps develop the individual's awareness of public issues. Men are both individuals and social creatures, of course, torn between asserting their personal worth and independence and merging themselves in aggregations for safety and a sense of purpose.

In modern communities men cannot find satisfaction of their needs in any one association alone. A diversity of associations is essential. These associations, however, must be compatible and cooperative to some extent; they must freely allow their members to come and go. An individualism that holds a man to be an isolated unit is self-defeating; to the contrary, individualism depends upon freedom being exercised in recognition of the liberty and needs of others, for none can stand alone. Only through democracy, indeed, can the conflict be reconciled between the individual and the social aspects of human life, as well as between the ideal and the practical.

IV. The Totalitarian Challenges

Democracy has never appealed to all men. Some have dissented from its aspirations; many more have objected to its cumbersome procedures. The old enemies of democracy, favoring aristocracy or monarchy as rule of the best, were frankly contemptuous of popular government. Few of these now remain. The very success of democracy during the last century, however, has produced its own peculiar enemies and difficulties. Today's enemies of democracy are products of the modern world. Like democrats, they also respond to the problems of contemporary life, professing to speak for the people and their aspirations. They appeal to much the same audience as democracy, sometimes even claiming to promote a "higher" democracy. Thus they beguile those unable to understand democracy or impatient with its limitations more than those flatly rejecting it. The most significant of these challenges, proposing alternatives to democracy both as fact and ideal, are communism and fascism. Indeed, the ideas of these totalitarian systems are so widespread and potent throughout the world that contemporary politics is incomprehensible without an understanding of them. They are not the only threats to democracy, to be sure, which is not easy to realize under any circumstances and in its own functioning must confront serious difficulties. We shall consider these after examining the totalitarian ideological challenges.

Communism

The strongest ideological challenge to democracy is communism, if only because such powerful and dynamic regimes as the Soviet Union and the Chinese People's Republic promote its extension by all available means. There are other explanations: the spread of communism reflects also the appeal of the ideology—its ideas and ideals— subverting many from liberal democratic values. There can be no simple explanation of this ideology, now the product of a century's revolutionary thought and experience, as affected by diverse personalities and circumstances. Despite some consistency, most original communist ideas were ambiguous at important points. Its modern adherents have thus been able to forge a theory for their purposes that follows basic communist doctrine, yet is disconcertingly adaptable to varying circumstances. To understand that ideology and its appeal as an analysis of social life and a guide to political action, we must examine its development from the writings of Karl Marx to the policies of contemporary Russia and China.

Marxian Communism. The modern age has been a revolutionary one, in all aspects of life, but also an optimistic one. Men have tended to assume that the changes taking place and those to come constituted "progress" leading to a glorious future. The industrial revolution, for example, getting under way in the eighteenth century, was a profound force for change. When its earlier phases produced appalling living and working conditions for many people, portending a widening misery for the growing urban working class, radical protests ensued against the new factory system. Some workers sought to destroy the machines they saw humiliating or displacing them. But most responses were not so reactionary; most thinkers called for reform and reorganization, and thus produced schemes for the betterment of society.

One of the most comprehensive of these, penetrating in its insights and total in its criticism of the existing order, was the "scientific socialism" of Karl Marx and Friedrich Engels, epitomized in the *Communist Manifesto* (1848). Contrasting their views with the idealistic and "utopian" socialism of such men as Robert Owen in England and Charles Fourier in France, Marx and Engels claimed to have a scientific program, reflecting their view of how the existing social order developed and how it must eventually fall. Marx assumed he knew how social reform would occur because he believed he had identified the characteristics of existing society and discovered its relevant law of historical change. The alleged law he termed "dialectical materialism," to be seen through history in the "class struggle."

Dialectical materialism is a frustratingly ambiguous concept. The dialectic has long been used as a method of analysis and argument. Briefly explained, in the dialectic a "thesis" is stated, then contradicted by an "antithesis," and the conflict is resolved in a "synthesis," which is presumably closer to the truth than its predecessors. The German philosopher Hegel had concluded that such a dialectical process is manifested in history and accounts for change. In both their ideas of themselves and in their actions, he saw nations as representing the theses of the dialectic, and thus as the actors in history, expressing "the march of God" in the world.

Marx accepted the Hegelian dialectic in form but rejected its idealism, which asserted thought and ideas as primary, and replaced it with a new materialism. "Materialism" again is a term meaning many things. In Marxism, it is intended to mean that ideas are not causes but effects—and the effects primarily of economic conditions. Marx claimed that a society's organization for production and distribution of food, clothing, and shelter—and particularly how the means of production are owned—determine fundamentally what men are and the importance of what they do. Economic systems and their social classes thus replace the Hegelian nations in the dialectic, and their opposition makes history what it is. As the dialectic insists there is room in society for only two significant forces, these are in irreconcilable conflict. According to the Marxists, therefore, if a person or group is to be meaningful in history, he must be identified with one or the other of these contending forces. Most persons are so identified, Marxists believe, and this is held to be the most important fact about them. In the Marxian dialectic the contending forces are economic classes—groups of persons with distinct positions in the organization of the economy. Thus, the fundamental concept of Marxism, both theoretically and practically, is the class struggle.

Capitalism and the Class Struggle. To Marxists, "capitalism" is the characteristic economy of modern times; the "bourgeoisie" and the "proletariat" are the economic classes in conflict; and "communism" is the new society to emerge out of revolution as the "synthesis." One must keep in mind, of course, that Marx's ideas about capitalism, economic classes, and the nature of the "good society" to come were products of the mid-nineteenth century in which he lived; however appropriate they may have been then, they do not accurately describe these phenomena today. Even some communists recognize this, though more usually they insist that Marx's analysis of capitalism is still relevant.

Marx used the term "bourgeoisie" to describe the dominant exploiting class of the capitalist economy. Exploitation is particularly pronounced, he asserted, because capitalism's central characteristic is the uninhibited pursuit of private profit, to which all ethical considerations are subordinated. The partial truth of this can be denied only by idealizing human beings. Marx, however, refused to admit any limits to the profit motive and greed within the capitalistic system. The bourgeoisie, then, have organized the modern factory economy as private property, and thus gained absolute control over the instruments of production in the modern world.

In the modern factory economy, as Marx saw it, the laboring class is especially at the mercy of its exploiters, having lost control of its tools. As defined in Marxism, the proletariat includes those persons who have nothing to sell but their labor power, and must do so at a price profitable to the capitalists. Class lines, Marx assumed, were becoming particularly rigid and opposed in modern capitalism; industrialism, given private property and the pursuit of profit, would have the effect of concentrating control of the instruments of production, thus dividing men more sharply than ever before into those who have and those who have not, while at the same time accentuating exploitation. Marx came to such conclusions partly by observations of how people in industrializing societies actually behaved in the early and mid-nineteenth century, and partly by the logical requirements of his own thought and values. The result was an economic theory of capitalism of an undeniable logical rigor, but of quite variable realism.

Marx took capitalism as a necessary stage in world development; from his perspective its task has been to create the highly productive modern industrial system. Only the subordination of all else to the pursuit of profit, apparently, could have brought about such radical economic and social change; and only the most complete exploitation of labor could have made available the necessary resources. Marx both admired and hated what the bourgeoisie had done. But he also thought that capitalism had finished its historic task and that its economy would soon destroy itself. The recurrent and ever worsening crises were signs, to him, of the intrinsic weakness of an economy based upon the pursuit of profit. Intense competition among capitalists, he thought, was driving increasing numbers of the bourgeoisie into the proletariat, at the same time that it rendered the latter more impoverished and miserable. Eventually production and opportunities for work would become so restricted that the infuriated proletariat would rise in revolution; and the bourgeoisie—what was left of it —would be too weak and demoralized to resist effectively. Thus, as the *Communist Manifesto* put it, the bourgeoisie would create its own "grave-diggers," and die of its own contradictions. Although this Marxist prediction is over a century old, capitalism has not yet perished for these reasons anywhere. To understand communism we must follow its argument further.

Politics as Superstructure. Marxist materialism, or economic determinism, yields very little that is explicit to political analysis. According to Marx, ideas, ideals, and all apparently noneconomic institutions are grounded in the needs of economic classes and have no independent value or meaning. They are, thus, the "superstructure" upon the "base" of economic life. Despite some mild qualifications of this extreme position, Marx and his followers persisted in holding that the economically dominant class is necessarily the politically and socially ruling class. Its influence, tending to preserve the sort of economy it has created, permeates all of society, creating even religious doctrines and ideas of family life appropriate to its needs. In consequence, the *Communist Manifesto* announced, "political power is merely the organized power of one class for oppressing another."

No governments, therefore, exist to promote the general welfare; all are in reality dictatorships, according to communist analysis. This is true regardless of their form; that is to say, democracies are no less dictatorships than are monarchies. Various forms of government are simply different ways in which the dominant class can most effectively maintain its power and economic regime. Given this opinion, it should be evident why Marx did not devote much time or energy to analyzing the subtleties of political institutions or procedures. Political activity within the legislative, administrative, or judicial agencies of any state is significant only as a means to something else. Progress, in the form of perfected economic functioning and realization of the full and rightful claims of the workers, can be achieved only through the overthrow of the existing state. This is the core of Marxist politics. In modern conditions, the "bourgeois dictatorship" must be replaced by a revolutionary "dictatorship of the proletariat."

One could still ask, of course, whether the proletarian dictatorship could be attained through democratic forms. Marx did remark that in Great Britain, the United States, and the Netherlands, the revolutionary transformation of society might be implemented peacefully through existing democratic processes. More characteristic, however, is a sentence in his major work, *Capital* (1867), in which he asserted that "force is the midwife of every old society pregnant with a new one." Generally, Marx thought that democracies, no less than other forms of government, would be unable to meet the workers' revolutionary demands. On the other hand, it seems that Marx hoped, and even expected, that the proletarian revolutionary movement would be democratic in some sense. The view of democracy he expressed, however, is populistic rather than liberal; as we have seen, this is a romantic vision, unrealizable in any complex modern community, whether promoting the interests of capitalists or workers.

Marx had little actual experience with democracy; his thoughts were dominated by his economic determinism. To Marx, absorbed in his abstractions, people were either "bourgeois" or "proletarian." Likewise, popular majorities were either properly proletarian and revolutionary—at least when economic conditions had sufficiently advanced—or the disguised instrument of the capitalists. Such an automatic assumption that popular majorities "really" and "naturally" manifest only proletarian characteristics, and therefore express themselves most effectively through a proletarian dictatorship, not only misses the whole point of democracy as a dynamic political order but is inherently destructive of it.

The Marxian Dream. Marx scorned the sketching of utopias. The community to come would emerge, he thought, as an original product of the proletarian revolution; it certainly could not be predicted in detail by those still enmeshed in bourgeois society. The determinism of dialectical materialism, of course, implies not only the inevitability of revolutionary change, but also that the characteristics of the future will develop not accidentally but dialectically out of the present. In short, whatever the proletariat negates in capitalism will be eliminated in communist society.

Primarily, of course, what will be eliminated is private property;

private ownership of the means of production will vanish in the communist society, communists assert, and property will be owned and controlled by all for the benefit of all. Just how this is to be organized, beyond depriving capitalists of their capital through heavy taxation and confiscation by the proletarian dictatorship, was never made clear by Marx. In actual communist regimes "ownership" of the means of production has merely been transferred from private capitalists to communist leaders and put to the service of their power. However, following the Marxist assumptions for the moment, the abolition of private property is seen as having vast implications for all aspects of human life. Private property was to Marx the sole foundation of classes and means of exploitation; after its elimination neither classes nor exploitation would remain. Convinced that classes exist only to exploit other classes, Marx concluded that the proletariat itself would eventually be "abolished as a class," lacking anyone to exploit once it disposed of the bourgeoisie.

The classless society resulting, according to Marx, will have still further desirable characteristics. The pursuit of profit accompanying capitalistic private property had prevented the workers from enjoying the full fruits of their labor. It had also, while leading originally to the creation of industry, ultimately prevented that industrial capacity from functioning most productively. Socialization of the means of production will thus, in the Marxist scheme, furnish both work and abundance for all. In these circumstances, Marx assumed, selfishness would disappear. Men would work because work was a psychological imperative, not only to obtain the necessities of life; and the fruits of labor could be distributed according to need. Not only would this represent a profound transformation of economic life, but a profound psychological transformation as well. Marx asserted, in effect, that only in communist society would the conditions be present for the realization of true individual freedom, which liberals had advanced as an ideal but could not fully implement.

In these circumstances, if Marx were right, the coercive institutions of prerevolutionary societies would obviously be unnecessary. In Engels' phrase, the state would "wither away," as the distinction between oppressed and oppressing classes became meaningless. So would such institutions as churches, which to Marxists exist to coerce through superstition. All that Marxists have assumed still necessary would be "the administration of things." This government, if such it is, would apparently be largely a matter of simple bookkeeping and completely noncoercive. For in the communist utopia, as Marx seems to have envisaged it, there would be no private interests in opposition; and science or objective knowledge would replace private subjective opinions and superstition. Here, at last, would all men form a harmoniously cooperating fellowship, in which each can nonetheless be completely himself. As Marx put it, "the free development of each is the condition for the free development of all." A more remarkable "heaven on earth," synthesizing modern liberal and humanitarian ideals and values, could hardly be imagined.

Modern Communism: Lenin and Revolution. The utopia of Marx, no less than his understandable criticism of the economic and social order of his day, has made its mark in the world—due in no small degree to Vladimir Ilyich Lenin, the leader of the Bolshevik revolutionaries in Russia who created the original seat of contemporary communist power, the First Communism. This power, together with Lenin's action-oriented interpretations of Marxism, gave to that doctrine a relevance in the twentieth century which it otherwise might not have had, although probably not the relevance Marx anticipated. Contemporary communist ideas are quite rightly termed "Marxism-Leninism."

Marx envisaged the communist revolution and its success as historically inevitable, and assumed that it would be a spontaneous uprising of the proletariat. His own role, and that of his followers, was largely limited to educating the workers to their proletarian mission of revolution and social reconstruction. Marx assumed a proletariat on the verge of birth and the revolution not far behind. By the end of the nineteenth century, however, the various disciples of Marx were bitterly disputing the proper Marxist interpretation of events. In fact, nothing was developing the way Marx had predicted. If the capitalistic order were nearing its collapse it was hardly obvious, nor was competition driving increasing numbers of the bourgeoisie down into the proletariat. Governments, not only in relatively democratic England but even in clearly autocratic Germany, were acting as something more than the armed guards of capitalism. Even worse, the working class was showing less interest in radical transformation of society than in immediate improvements in wages, and in working and living conditions; when it showed unity of purpose it was more often of nationalistic than proletarian inspiration.

Marxist theory was clearly open to revision, but the corrections split the socialist fellowship. At one extreme were the "revisionists," among them Eduard Bernstein, in Germany, and Jean Jaurès, in France. They largely abandoned rigid adherence to the doctrine of inevitable and violent revolutions, and endeavored to realize the Marxist ideals in peaceful evolution through democratic politics and education. From them sprang the social democratic movements of this century.

At the other extreme—equally revisionist, although vigorously proclaiming itself orthodox—was the Russian Bolshevik movement, led by Lenin, which explicitly rejected the name "social democrat" after 1917. Lenin, undoubtedly influenced as much by the repressive autocracy of Czarist Russia and its native revolutionary movements as by Marxism, radically altered the emphasis of Marxism. Under his leadership the seizure and stabilization of power by the Bolsheviks became the central interest of communism; and although the terminology of communist discourse and propaganda remained Marxist, it was Marxism seen, in Lenin's words, as a guide to action, not as dogma. Committed fanatically to revolution, and particularly to revolution in Russia, Lenin was not about to await the inevitable, or even merely to act a midwife to its coming. Consequently, he added to the rather speculative Marxist "science" of historical development a more immediately practical "science" of revolution, creating a powerful if not entirely consistent doctrine.

The Conspiratorial Organization. The Leninist science of revolution has two particularly important aspects. First, Lenin rejected the idea of the communist party as a broad popular association of workers and sympathizers with Marxist ideals. Because no effectively revolutionary proletariat yet existed anywhere, the party had to be its vanguard. Its task was to seize power and destroy bourgeois institutions, which Lenin assumed were suppressing the proletariat. As a revolutionary group, and not merely an educational institution, the communists had to form a centralized and disciplined conspiratorial organization, with membership restricted to those who would devote themselves unconditionally to the revolution.

Second, Lenin understood that conspiracy alone cannot make a successful revolution. The core of Marxist teaching was that the revolution depended less upon its leadership than upon appropriate economic conditions. Marx had specified these conditions rather narrowly. Adapting Marxist doctrine to the actual problems of his day, Lenin concluded that the conditions necessary for successful revolutionary action were a general popular discontent of some sort, and division and weakness among the defenders of the old order. The organization could then exploit these circumstances to create a communist revolution; that is to say, one dominated by the communists, taking their guiding principles from Marx and applying them expediently where the revolutionary potential was greatest.

The Revolutionary Dictatorship. The expropriation of the property of the bourgeoisie requires, as Marx had argued, the dictatorship of the proletariat. But although he was aware that some difficulties might arise throughout the transition to the communist society, Marx did not contemplate the necessity of a dictatorship of the party over the entire population, including the working classes—much less that of the party leaders over the party. Such a revolutionary dictatorship was established as a leading characteristic of communist regimes by Lenin and his successors under the convenient name of "democratic centralism." A euphemistic phrase, it means in communist jargon that once decisions are ratified—presumably by majority vote—they are not further to be contested by dissident minorities.

This dictatorship was required, if for no other reason, because from a Marxian point of view communism achieved its first victory—and later ones as well—under the most inauspicious circumstances. In the first place, the Russian economy the communists inherited was backward in both industry and agriculture; and it further suffered severely in World War I, the anti-Czarist revolution, and the civil war the Bolsheviks provoked. Second, they did not have the support of most of the population; even among factory workers the Bolsheviks could not always command a majority. Third, although Lenin anticipated numerous successful communist revolutions throughout Europe following that in Russia, he, and later Stalin, found that hostility to the new regime was virtually universal abroad, with only scattered support among working class movements and intellectuals. Thus, they had no choice but to build—in Stalin's slogans—"socialism in one country" in the midst of a "capitalistic encirclement," which of course posed both economic and defense problems. And finally among the revolutionaries, even those claiming Marx as mentor, considerable disagreement existed as to what should be done in the circumstances. These difficulties of 1917 have largely persisted.

Consequently, a communist seizure of power has been not the end of revolution so much as its beginning, and it has been so in two ways. On the one hand, dictatorship as the necessary means to complete the revolution, transforming the economy and the thinking of people in accordance with Marxist ideas, has seemed inevitable and proper to Lenin and his successors. No communist regime has ever been other than a dictatorship, despite the occasional pretensions to some liberal and democratic policies. For example, when Lenin tried after 1919 to install a militant communist economy, the results were disastrous to production and the stability of his regime. With characteristic flexibility he shifted to a "New Economic Policy," a tactical retreat permitting small-scale free enterprise; at the same time he began to organize party and government for a decisive degree of collectivization. He concluded that the party must remain a highly centralized and disciplined organization, through which alone the necessary control could be exercised over the entire community. Those who disagreed with either rigorous party discipline or his pragmatic policies he termed "doctrinaires" or "opportunists," purging them from power and the party. After 1929, Stalin continued Lenin's methods with heightened ruthlessness and barbarism, and no subsequent communist leaders have been able to avoid the precedent.

On the other hand, through their success in 1917 the communist revolutionary movement acquired a springboard onto the world scene. Previously, no Marxists or Leninists had power in any country. Communists thereafter asserted that however little the Soviet Union might resemble the Marxist dream, until after World War II it represented the sole foothold for communism in a hostile capitalist world. With the future of the movement depending upon its success in Russia, the First Communism had to be preserved and promoted at all costs. Most often the domestic costs were paid by foreign communist parties, and after World War II by the states of the Second and Third Communism—the communist regimes in Asia and eastern Europe, used by the Soviet leaders principally to strengthen Soviet power. The instrument was the communist party, effectively subordinated to an "international" movement dominated from Moscow, despite its nominal national independence. In this fashion, driven by the demands of the revolution and the ambitions of the Soviet leaders, and exploiting political chaos wherever it existed, communist dictatorships were exported by Soviet arms to other areas of the world.

Communism Consolidated. Experience thus taught Lenin and Stalin what Marx had not understood: that an efficient and despotic dictatorship was the necessary condition for the radical social reconstruction which communists envisaged. Only when the political means were firmly established—and no idealistic considerations were permitted to endanger them—was the Soviet regime able to resume its revolutionary program. Indeed, the elements of that program as instituted by Stalin—the "five-year plans," the increasingly tight governmental control over industry and commerce, the collectivization of agriculture, the increasingly coercive regimentation of the lives of Soviet citizens, the efforts to ensure loyalty to the regime through intense indoctrination in communist ideas associated with Russian chauvinism—can be understood only if seen as serving a dual purpose: the security of communist (party) power as well as the realization of communist (Marxist) values. And as the full Marxist utopia is unrealizable, at least in the foreseeable future, it is safe to conclude that the revolutionary dictatorship is an inherent aspect of any communist community.

Communist principles today have not changed, but the conditions to which they are applied have altered radically. In the Soviet Union the task of building "socialism in one country" was said by Stalin to have been completed in 1936. This meant that the communist dictatorship was then firmly established, as well as that control of the economy had been wrested from private hands and could henceforth be devoted to the building of the communist society, the ultimate goal. Of course, the party—which is to say largely the party's leaders —was still alone competent to determine what had to be done to accomplish that task; and this role of dominant leadership was clearly reserved to the party in the "Stalin Constitution" of 1936, as in all communist regimes since established.

Consequently, after 1936 and particularly after World War II, communism became much more aggressive. While Lenin and Stalin had been engaged in consolidating their power at home, their machinations abroad were essentially defensive. But Stalin and his successors were well aware that neither their power nor the ideal communist society could be secured in one country alone. The worldwide revolutionary struggle against the bourgeoisie had to be resumed and won if full communism were to exist anywhere. The enormous increase in Soviet power after World War II, and the establishment of the states

of the Second and Third Communism in Asia and in eastern Europe
—together with unstable world conditions—produced in consequence
the most powerful and persistent revolutionary force the world has
known.

This extraordinary expansion of communism, however, has not been
without difficulties. For a decade after World War II the Soviet communist bloc functioned with great unity; the post-Stalinist rebellions
in East Germany and Hungary were ruthlessly suppressed by Soviet
arms. But Yugoslavia had already made the first successful breach in
the satellite system, demonstrating that a communist regime could
exist even when opposed by Moscow. In the 1960's, unity of the bloc
was further weakened; and with other variations emerging in domestic order and policies, the communist movement ceased to be an unqualified monolith. Soviet power still dominates the communist
world, but displays increasing vulnerability. Although the Soviet invasion of Czechoslovakia in 1968 was much like that of Hungary in
1956, it differed in being condemned—not only in Czechoslovakia
but by many communists elsewhere in the world, some even in the
Soviet Union. Although Yugoslavia, once the only black sheep of the
communist realm, has been followed by Hungary and Czechoslovakia
in efforts to achieve moderate reforms and decolonization from the
Soviet Union, even these modest deviations serve to underscore the
durability of despotism generally in the communist world. In the east
European countries of the Third Communism, the leaders continue to
rule amidst a sea of communist-hating masses. As the bitter iron curtain jest has it, "When the Russians speak of friendship and fraternal
aid, all I hear is tanks."

At the same time, Communist China, the Second Communism, has
condemned the Soviet Union for alleged defection from the correct
principles of Marxism-Leninism and for its abandonment of the revolutionary struggle. The Chinese Communist leader, Mao Tse-tung,
asserted his own version of true communist principles in such programs as the "Great Leap Forward" and the "Great Proletarian Cultural Revolution." Both of these represented Mao's dislike of legal
and bureaucratic government, his faith in popular action, and his belief that revolution must be a permanent condition. The Great Leap
Forward was an attempt begun in the late 1950's to organize the
Chinese into vast communes, and to force the people of this predominantly agricultural society to industrialize by establishing "backyard

steel furnaces" and "street factories." By comparison, the social impact of Stalin's furious efforts to industrialize Russia in the 1930's seems modest. The results were nonetheless disastrous for both Chinese industry and agriculture, and Mao's leadership was challenged by those favoring more conventional approaches. In reply, Mao launched the Cultural Revolution in 1965 to wipe out all vestiges of "capitalism, feudalism, and revisionism." Large bands of youthful Red Guards, armed with platitudinous quotations from Mao, attacked in Mao's name many existing institutions, organizations, and leaders. Few of Mao's long-time associates in the Chinese Communist party survived this nihilistic rampage, and relations with the Soviet Union were brought to the verge of war. After three years of chaos the Red Guard's Cultural Revolution was called off; Mao's young supporters were demoted to return to work and study. Mao now turned to the army to restore order and authority, and to rebuild the badly-shattered communist party. Thus the future remains uncertain, whether of China's domestic order or of China's capacity to lead effectively a revolutionary new communist international movement. In 1970, Mao adopted a grandiose new title—"Supreme Commander of the Whole Nation and the Whole Army." Yet he has demonstrated far more success in destroying an old society than in creating a viable new one.

The Communist Strategy Today. Beginning with Marx, all communists have insisted on the unity of theory and practice in communism, so that principles, organization, strategy, and tactics are but different facets of the same thing. Furthermore, the movement is fundamentally international, permitting only minor variations in these factors among various national parties and regimes. With communism an effective and continuing revolutionary movement, as much at home as abroad, deviations in either principles, organization, or strategy represent weakness. For these reasons, communist leaders everywhere find embarrassing the divergencies that have lately emerged and struggle to overcome them. Against the challenge of Maoist radicalism, on the one hand, and of the revisionism of Yugoslavia and elsewhere, on the other, Soviet leaders have attempted to restore their authority and regain control of the movement. The invasion of Czechoslovakia in 1968 had that purpose, as have their subsequent efforts. Knowing that most communist leaders will still follow their lead, they have called world conferences of communist parties in an effort to obtain binding statements of common policy. Unhappily, from their view, the Chinese and their supporters do not attend, and the breach remains unrepaired.

In their challenge to the noncommunist world, communist leaders since Lenin have pursued a twofold strategy. In the first place, they are devoted to strengthen the economic and political foundations of communist society at home, especially through a highly industrialized, technologically advanced, and centrally controlled economy. This is both an end of the revolution and a means to it. Technological and industrial development are idols of the modern world, particularly to Marxists; other communist leaders have been only less ambitious than Stalin, who killed millions in his efforts to collectivize agriculture. Central control of the economy—jobs, food, wages, and prices—gives the leaders immense power over the people, and serves also to direct production to the needs of economic and military warfare. Although communist leaders regularly promise change in the future, the interests of the people as consumers have not been a primary consideration in communist regimes; most consumer goods are of limited variety and shoddy quality. The aim of all communist policy is the increased power of the leaders in the interests of the revolution.

Second, complementing the intensification of communism at home, communist leaders have intensified the promotion of revolutionary movements and conspiracies abroad. No longer primarily defensive, these leaders now seek to hasten the "inevitable" collapse of bourgeois power through attempts to exploit its difficulties and intensify what communists assert to be its "contradictions." In communist thinking these contradictions of the noncommunist world exist on three levels: first, the conflict between capital and labor within any one country; second, the conflict between the bourgeois states themselves; and third, the conflict between the "imperialist" powers and their colonial and other dependencies. These are called contradictions because, in communist theory, they are not simply conflicts of interests which can be reconciled within the framework of capitalism and liberal democracy; they will be irreconcilable until they are transcended in the victory of communism.

The communist leaders appear in essential agreement on how they hope to achieve this collapse of bourgeois power. They have normally attempted to avoid direct confrontations of forces between major communist and noncommunist powers, particularly since the Korean War. The Soviet Union so far has used its military forces directly only in suppressing rebellions in Hungary and Czechoslovakia, in border skirmishing with the Chinese, and in establishing a naval presence in the Mediterranean. When challenged by President Kennedy in 1962, Premier Khrushchev withdrew from Cuba the Soviet missiles that directly threatened American security. China has acted similarly, invading Tibet and warring with India on their common border, but generally behaving cautiously. They have preferred instead, with policies much in common, to extend their power and influence indirectly. It is possible that their present rivalry makes these policies more dangerous, as they struggle for dominance in the communist movement and compete in revolutionary zeal.

We must conclude that though some confusion and weakness may result from their lack of unity, communists will continue to exploit the three contradictions they have identified in the noncommunist world. The communist tactics within established communities are intended mainly to undermine any anticommunist front by intensifying controversy. To this end they organize communist parties, aimed at inhibiting the effective functioning of parliamentary politics rather than expecting to win control of governments through elections. These efforts have been rather effective in France and Italy, for example, forestalling there the formation of effective progressive parties or coalitions; they have not similarly succeeded in Great Britain, the German Federal Republic, or the United States. The communists also organize or infiltrate associations of industrial and agricultural workers to turn them from reformism—the search for immediate benefits —into instruments of class warfare. Ostensibly to promote various worthy causes, they form "communist front" organizations under varying labels to disguise communist domination. They also attempt to acquire "fellow travelers" and to support and infiltrate any movements tending to weaken the authority of the established government and order, stirring up whatever local disturbances they can.

While formally pursuing a policy of "peaceful coexistence," contemporary communists are actually most concerned with conflicts among bourgeois states and between them and their present or former dependencies. In exploiting these, communists have achieved their greatest recent successes. Except for the period immediately following World War II, when the states of the Second and Third Communism were established, their recent efforts have been devoted largely to breaking the unity of the anticommunist states, and to fomenting "anticolonialist" rebellions throughout Africa, Asia, and Latin America. With ruthless realism, their appeal has been largely to nationalistic "antiwestern" sentiments, rapid economic growth, and the fear of war —emphasized according to circumstances—which they have turned to their advantage in those areas. They have particularly benefited from prejudice against "imperialism"—associated with white, European, or American culture and power. They call movements they support "national liberation fronts," and when fighting breaks out it becomes a "war of national liberation." Usually they support communists, like the Vietcong; but sometimes they support noncommunists and even monarchists, as certain of the Arab states opposing Israel, with their primary purpose to destroy western unity and influence.

The major communist powers have also not hesitated when they find it expedient to subordinate the peace and national interests of their supporters to the interests of the so-called international revolutionary movement. Marxist theory holds that nationalism, along with other liberal values, is reactionary and that peace and plenty will come only through total communist victory. In sum, the communists endeavor to intensify sources of discontent everywhere, and to control and utilize the expression of that discontent, convinced that such incendiary activities will enhance their power in the long run. One need not look for any other purpose in communist policies—there is none. Milovan Djilas, a disenchanted Communist, stated it simply: "Power is an end in itself and the essence of contemporary communism."

In a world seething with poverty and discontent, a theory giving a simple explanation for such conditions and promising eventual peace and well-being easily finds support among frustrated and shortsighted masses and their ambitious leaders, and appears to justify almost any actions. To the ideology and promises of communism, furthermore, must be added the facts of Soviet and Chinese communist power. By their open and continued hostility to the long-dominant western states, these communist nations have shown their independence. The Soviet Union has also launched selected programs of technological development, as in outer space, with obvious if limited success. Thus, some people still struggling against their national backwardness, both political and economic, find communist doctrine convincing, particularly when the Soviet Union and China stand by with aid and direction. By contrast, others in various parts of the world have learned the limitations of the doctrine, and have discovered that communist aid and direction are a powerful form of imperialism. To be sure, with the communist bloc broken, its expansion has slowed. Incompatible with democracy in both theory and practice, communism nevertheless remains an impressive force in the world, challenging democracy on every front.

Fascism

Fascism offers the second significant ideological challenge to democracy in the modern world. "Fascism" is a term derived from the Latin word *fasces,* referring to the bundle of rods containing an axe carried before Roman magistrates as a symbol of authority. This emblem was adopted by Mussolini's regime in Italy, 1922–43, reflecting his desire to reestablish in that country the power and authority of ancient Rome. Although the term originally applied only to Mussolini's movement of belligerent nationalism after World War I, it has come to be used more generally, designating similar movements and some regimes elsewhere. It denotes the sort of regime resulting when some central ideas of modern political life—particularly those of the nation-state—are carried to an extreme and pursued with fanatical zeal.

Like communism, fascism is ambiguous at crucial points, and its manifestations are confusingly diverse. We should note that in political parlance, the word "fascist" is now often used as a term of abuse, applied especially to anyone to the right of the namecaller's views. The term "fascism" has also been frequently misapplied to what are really traditionalist, conservative, and anticommunist regimes. These are commonly less repressive, fanatical, and despotic than the regimes of their communist opponents. By their very conservatism, right-wing authoritarian systems cannot also be revolutionary. In the analysis of totalitarianism, indeed, the terms "left" and "right" lose direction. For example, fascism has always promised a total "new order" to produce a "new man"; to describe this revolutionary élan as a movement to the right of democracy is as much an error as portraying Stalinism as a movement to its left. Certainly, we can never be sure what to expect from fascism; we can only attempt to understand it in its principal manifestations.

Fascism first emerged in Italy, but during the 1930's some of its principles were accepted in varying degrees in Austria, Hungary, Japan, Romania, and Spain. In Argentina, Perón established a fascist dictatorship lasting from 1943 to 1955. Its principal and most virulent manifestation, however, appeared in National Socialist (or *Nazi,* a contraction from *Nationalsozialistische*) Germany under Hitler from 1933 to 1945. It has appeared as an occasional tendency among some elements in many other countries, including the Republic of South Africa, France, Great Britain, and the United States. Although no powerful fascist regime exists in the world today, fascist ideas are by no means dead, and challenge democracy no less than those of communism.

Fascism is in principle an authoritarian ideology and movement. Fascists, like communists, have been totally opportunistic in practice, denying or distorting any doctrine which threatened to interfere with the seizure and exercise of power by their leaders. Communism speaks in Marxist terms and claims to be the revolutionary movement of the proletariat; fascism speaks in national and racial terms. Promoting the unity and power of a national or racial group is the customary objective of a fascist movement, and fascist ideology is built around vague but potent nationalistic or racist symbols to which unqualified allegiance is demanded. To fascists, however, the highest expression of the nation or race is found in a leader and his elite party. A fascist regime, consequently, is necessarily a dictatorship, glorifying the authority of the leader, through which alone the community can find its unity and power. This, and the means of rule flowing from it, distinguish fascist from more common nationalist regimes, and even from those in which racial distinctions are significant.

Nationalism and Racism. National and racial differences have long been recognized by mankind. In western civilization, however, men have endeavored only in recent centuries to found political orders upon them, and most often even then with a moderation recognizing more universal values. Increasingly, however, sentiments of nationality, and occasionally of racial distinction, have become dominant themes and perhaps the most powerful forces in modern political life.

Fanatical and extreme nationalism, often called "integral nationalism," appeared a century ago. It found its most powerful voices first in France; although England did not lack for its jingoism, nor was the United States completely immune, as the yellow journalism of the Spanish-American war period indicates. French integral nationalists, such as Charles Maurras and Maurice Barrès, wrote in violent rebellion against the liberal principles of the revolution of 1789 and against the democratic republic of their day, which they saw as corrupt and petty. Instead they worshiped an "eternal France," fair and powerful, and demanded unity and sacrifice for the glory of the nation. Their cry found willing ears; leaders appeared throughout Europe, and eventually elsewhere as well, championing the special destinies of their particular peoples.

In countries where nationalism had become strong, but where that sentiment was outraged by the absence or weakness of a national political order, the advocates of fascism found the most fertile soil. Germany and Italy, for example, both possessing old and distinctive cultures, had come only recently—after 1870—to a national political unity. Both communities were emotionally affected by the national humiliation they suffered in World War I and the economic difficulties which followed it, and by the fact that substantial national populations were outside their state borders. Both, likewise, after that war had weak governments which reflected divisions and tensions within the countries far greater than they could overcome. As the jealous gods of nationalism were frustrated in these states, the reaction was violent. The call for national unity and the promise of national glory expressed by Mussolini and Hitler brought to their standards millions of the discontented—albeit for many different reasons.

Despite its emotional appeal, however, the nationalism of the fascists has had little specific content. It led itself automatically to the condemnation of liberalism for its individualism, of socialism and communist theory for their emphasis upon economic conditions, and of any sort of internationalism. Though fascists insisted everything should be subordinated to the nation, what they thought the nation was or what it should become remained vague. Mussolini, seeking power in 1921, promised only to rule so as to "ensure the moral and material greatness of the Italian people." Fascism could not be committed to a program, for it "builds the structure of its will and passion from day to day." Regardless of this vagueness as to the good to be served, however, Mussolini still insisted that "the State stands for the immanent conscience of the nation," and that "everything [is] within the State, nothing outside the State, nothing against the State." In short, individuals can find morality and worth only in obedience and service to the nation as organized by the fascists. To support these arguments great nationalistic celebrations were promoted, while blackshirted gangs terrorized those who objected. Despite all this, however, fascism in Italy was moderated in its thoroughness, if not its brutality—tempered undoubtedly by the stubborn individualism and sense of humor of the Italian people.

It was in Nazi Germany that nationalism rose to a brief peak of unbelievable fury, and fascism flowered. To Italian fascism Hitler added embellishments derived from his Teutonic background. The romantic Wagnerian operas, with their mystically inspiring music and legends of godlike heroes, set the mood, to which the exotically challenging nineteenth-century German philosophy, from Hegel through Nietzsche, added diverse but always antiliberal messages. Alongside this existed a widespread anti-Semitism—and often anti-Slav and anti-Latin attitudes as well—which gave to German nationalism a racist character generally lacking in Italy. The Nazi god was the *Volk*, a tribal Germanic population, which Hitler proclaimed to be the "blood-conditioned entity," and the "God-willed building stone of human society." "The individual is transitory, the *Volk* is permanent," and to its preservation all the institutions and values of society were but means. To that end there is nothing which may not be sacrificed; to the glorification of the *Volk* and the expansion of its *Lebensraum* (living space) were devoted the most impressive mass demonstrations and terroristic brutality of all time. Millions of Germans cheered these, apparently finding in the Nazi regime, and in its dramatic if perverse achievements, the manifestation of German honor and blood. Yet this "revolution of nihilism" achieved only the sadistic suppression and extermination of "inferior peoples," and the holocaust of World War II.

The Fascist Movement and Its Leader. Although fascism depends upon the existence of widespread nationalistic sentiments, a fascist regime can survive only through accentuating these sentiments, often to the point of hysteria. For the nation, the state, and the *Volk* as envisaged by fascists do not actually exist but are "ideals" to be realized through a revolutionary struggle. In the process all the conflicting traditions of western civilization must be destroyed. The "ideal" and what it opposes find full and clear expression in the words of one Nazi: "There has arisen blood against formal reason, race against purposeful rationality, honor against profit, unity against bourgeois security, the folk against the individual and the mass."

Carrying the revolutionary torch, expressing the blood and honor of the nation to come, is the fascist movement and its leader. "The community of the *Volk*," Hitler said, "[is] organized in the National Socialist movement," which is engaged in "stamping the Nazi *Weltanschauung* (ideology) on the German people." Quite naturally, any rival political organizations—not only active parties but even groups independent of fascist control—are eliminated as soon as fascists gain power. Into this revolutionary struggle are thrown all the modern techniques of coercion and propaganda. Although not possible without mass response to its leadership, fascism is nevertheless highly elitist in its actual operation. The mass of the population cheers and supports the regime, but this is its sole participation. Dominating the fascist community is the party, a militant and quasi-military elite.

If the fascist movement is the elite, however, it in turn finds its unity only in absolute devotion to one man, presumed to be the perfect representative of all that is vital and valid. Thus, the key aspect of fascism is the "leadership principle." Throughout Italy under fascism appeared the slogan, "Mussolini is always right." In Germany, more ominously still, Hermann Göring announced defiantly to the world: "If abroad it is believed that chaos threatens Germany, the German people responds with the single cry 'We all approve always of what our leader does.'" And from Nazi Germany's leading lawyer came the assertion that "our constitution is the will of *Der Führer* (the leader)." Rarely has personal infallibility been thus glorified and all traditional, legal, and rational limitations on political power been so totally set aside.

The Background of Fascist Elitism. Fascism's fanatical and elitist politics has deep roots. For the past century, the liberal belief that democracy could produce adequate political leadership was frequently attacked. Literary figures, such as Carlyle in England and Nietzsche in Germany, found the reality of history in the activity of dominant personalities, "heroes" and "supermen." The developing social sciences lent little support to the ideals of democracy; psychology pointed to the dominance of irrational and aggressive elements in human nature, and "intelligence tests" demonstrated pronounced inequalities in human capacities. Early in the century, Max Weber distinguished by their varying claims to legitimacy three types of authority: traditional, rational, and charismatic. The traditional form supports hereditary and aristocratic leadership based on practice and custom. Rational authority is observed when officials are selected by legal means through established institutions. Charismatic authority is supported by personal allegiance and devotion to a popular leader. The term "charisma" refers to the leader's exceptional and extraordinary qualities, which capture the imagination of others and make them want to follow him.

The unsettled conditions of the twentieth century, especially the aftermath of World War I, produced widespread insecurity in Europe; and insecure men feel the need for leadership with particular intensity. Large numbers of the discontented, rootless, and alienated in Italy and Germany thus responded enthusiastically to the charismatic and even messianic leadership offered by Mussolini and Hitler. Their appeal was not simply to the old and embittered—it was youth who embraced fascism with the greatest fervor. Nor did fascism's support come only from the middle classes, as communists have claimed; it cut across all class lines in offering, not just one more political program, but surrender to the national leader of an "army on the march."

Charismatic leadership is undoubtedly a vital aspect of political life in periods of radical change; the greatest leaders have all possessed that quality. Nonetheless an important difference between fascist dictatorship and democracy is in the way that coexisting traditional or rational forms of leadership limit charisma in responsible government. By contrast, the charismatic form is the essence of fascism; personal loyalty to the leader replaces allegiance to the country. Thus, the dictator is "always right" and his "will" becomes the constitution. Neither tradition nor reason, of course, could possibly justify those assertions. But when large numbers of people lose both their traditional faith and confidence in reason as means of ordering their lives, they are likely to offer themselves to fanatic and unscrupulous demagogues who fill their emptiness with myths of superior racial or national destiny. Where such manipulation is possible, fascism threatens; and both civilization and liberal government are challenged. Unfortunately these conditions exist in many states of the world today.

Totalitarian Dictatorship

However different in their arguments, justifications, or even manifestations, communism and fascism produce the same result: totalitarian dictatorship. Though totalitarianism had its roots in the messianic mass movements of the nineteenth century, it is truly a phenomenon of World War I and its aftermath. As Mussolini observed, "a party that governs a nation in a totalitarian manner is a new fact in history." The true novelty of these regimes—creating chaos to demoralize their opponents, at war with law and morality, and seeking total domination and politicization of all human activity—is perhaps hard to appreciate, inured as we have become to their existence in the past half century.

To be sure, authoritarian regimes, including dictatorships, have long filled the pages of history; but with few exceptions at least they were restrained by some acknowledged objectives and standards. They were governments responsible to something—if not the people —and they sometimes produced conditions in which democracy could arise. As traditionalist regimes for the most part, limited by the laws and customs they professed, they have not been threats to democracy. But the present age has seen traditionalist governments fall throughout the world. Increasing millions aspire to the benefits of modern life and to provide these, governments must be flexible, pragmatic, and capable of securing the support of large numbers of people. There are fundamentally two forms of government inherently pragmatic and founded on mass support: liberal democracy and totalitarian dictatorship. This is why they are in such basic conflict throughout the world—they are the ultimate alternatives in modern life. As we have already discussed the essential nature of democracy, we must do the same for totalitarianism.

The Struggle for Power. Whatever their differences, totalitarians see as the central reality of history a brutal struggle for power in which might equals right. In the end, after vanquishing their enemies in this ennobling conflict, they believe a perfect community will emerge, cleansed of all those individual and group differences that liberal democracy values. Whether nationalist, racist, or proletarian, the community sought is totally collectivist, much resembling the undifferentiated community of primitive life. We have noted before the persistence of this urge of men to find satisfaction and security in the close communion of values and emotions which a pluralistic liberal order may not provide them. Yet men are also persistently individualistic, and enjoy the benefits afforded by a diversity of values and activities. Liberal democracy provides the modern method of reconciling within man these two conflicting tendencies. Its efforts are imperfectly effective, to be sure; and the collectivist urge erupts in periods of rapid and disorienting change with movements of social protest markedly susceptible to primitivism.

Communism and fascism are extreme forms of the eruption of collectivist idealism in the twentieth century, but they are not its only manifestations. In various parts of the world there have appeared small bands of contemporary revolutionaries—new leftists, militant cultists, underground extremists, student anarchists, or whatever their labels—promoting counter-cultural and antiestablishment movements. Though presenting a superficially attractive idealism to some, perhaps because of their denigration of their own countries, and their rejection of reality, they have actually behaved much as the other totalitarians. Especially do they resemble the fascists in their elitism, and their opposition to free speech, free elections, and other institutions of liberal democracy. Their imperialistic bent, a mixture of arrogance and intolerance, is equally inherent of course in the ideologies of communism and fascism. Responding to the enormous social, economic, and political changes of our times, all such totalitarian movements envisage great communities of their own kind in which all divisive elements will be eliminated, and over which they will exercise an absolute and imperialistic power. To such mentality and purpose there can be only "brothers" and enemies; the whole world must be conquered therefore by the cause, if not for it.

An objective so extraordinary cannot serve as a rational goal. It functions only as a myth or vision, often of a lost innocence or greatness to be recaptured, and whether true or false is unprovable and irrelevant. The real value of the cause is its emotional impact, leading people to march unquestioningly and unendingly in search of power. To the drive for power—stimulated by the myth of the great brotherhood, class, or race—may be sacrificed the values of civilization together with anyone defending them. The sole virtues recognized by the totalitarians are unity and power; anything else is destructive of their myth or obstructive of their struggle for revolution against a refractory world.

Total Revolution. The symbol of the totalitarian myth and the expression of its virtues are found in its leader. The popular worship in their time of such men as Lenin, Stalin, Mussolini, Hitler, Perón, and Mao well demonstrates that doctrine or ideology alone cannot govern. And when the reality about such a political god is finally exposed, following the demise of his regime, the evidence always shows how much personal leadership was at its heart. We also acquire insight into the true atmosphere that surrounded the adulated "superman"—invariably, commonness and banality, petty intrigue and conspiracy, cruelty and ignorance, venality and ruthlessness are characteristic of the movement's top leaders. Quite similarly, in the revolutionary new left of today one finds repetition of the paramilitary organization, struggles for leadership, hero worship, cult of violence, and exploitation of martyrs—all strongly reminiscent of the early days in communist and fascist movements.

Totalitarianism in its natural form is dictatorship; the fascists recognize this and exult in it, while the communists attempt to disguise the reality with jargon about "proletarian democracy" and "people's republics." Of course, no regime is perfectly totalitarian if only because there are limits to human power and madness. But in principle, and so far as possible in practice, the dictatorship must be absolute and unqualified.

Totalitarian regimes rest fundamentally, therefore, on the means used to attract, sway, and coerce the wills of men. They appeal to the elemental lust for power and the excitement of militancy; they fully indulge the destructive impulses as the supposed prelude to grandiose creation. Totalitarianism employs intensive propaganda, mass demonstrations, and violence against popular and convenient targets, thus revealing a remarkable if perverse insight into human weakness. Used to repress "counter-revolutionary" thought and activity are censorship, closed frontiers, secret police, terror, torture, and purges, often reaching to the very top.

These methods of "government" play upon the aspirations, fears, and hatreds of men, isolating and terrorizing opposition and hypnotizing supporters. They are systematized devices and not the temporary expedients of particular leaders—the inherent and inevitable characteristics of totalitarian dictatorship. The dictator's terroristic repression is indeed much the product of his morbid fear and suspiciousness—the result of his achievement and exercise of great power without real legal or institutional support. Totalitarianism is a "total revolution," aiming simultaneously at a collectivism that corrupts the individual mind and an atomization that destroys the individual will. However familiar it has become, it always presents a chilling demonstration of political power unrestrained by law. Totalitarianism is probably doomed to failure in the long run, but in our time none of us can escape its consequences.

V. Problems of Contemporary Democracy

Virtue, it has been said by stern but realistic moralists, is its own reward. The democratic ideal may thus be similarly transcendent, along with justice, and be pursued for its own sake. There is much of this sentiment in the literature of democracy. The democratic governments of history arose as practical responses to particular problems. Democracy appears and survives, however, only when it represents a widespread preference, derived from a sustained conviction that political affairs can best be conducted through that form of government. The question to be confronted here is whether that conviction is still justified: is the choice of democracy realistic today? The rise and spread of totalitarianism has not been a mere accident, and such regimes may acquire considerable popular support. The very existence of totalitarian regimes indicates that our question cannot be answered definitively. Democracy is everywhere under attack and nowhere secure. At this point we can only consider some problems democracies must solve if they are to survive.

The Atrophy of Democratic Public Spirit

Although modern democracy is designed to protect a wide range of values and interests among its citizens, it equally presupposes a community underlying such diversity. But diversity can be tolerated only within a framework of agreement on basic values. When democracy arose, the values then shared defined a general community of persons, and in more specifically political terms, a public. Political responsibility was clearly given to the public. But recent signs appear to suggest that this public has disintegrated; since democracy very much depends on public-spirited activity, such signs signal a very real danger.

The Weakened Sense of Community. A striking aspect of political life today is the widespread apathy of so many. Even in the most spectacular elections, large numbers of persons abstain from voting, seeing the issues as insignificant. At the same time, many who do have a concern with politics do so from the standpoint, "what's in it for me?" Also obvious is a frequent lack of information among people about the nature and consequences of public issues they are expected to resolve. More recently there has been speculation on how the public may be sundered between an undemonstrative "silent majority" and a demonstrating vocal minority. Still other minorities have asserted their alienation from traditional democratic procedures because they cannot achieve immediately their various idealistic goals.

None of these attitudes bodes well for democracy. It cannot function upon a base either of the apathetic, selfish, and ignorant, or of the utopian, anarchistic, and revolutionary—much less upon a population polarized between them. Democracy is not primarily a matter of numbers alone. The power of majorities springs from their organization and morale, and from recognition of a common good which majority rule may serve. Only a broad sense of community transcending any majority—and frequently reuniting with it the minority—can make long-run decisions legitimate and effective.

It is difficult to get agreement today over what the public interest might be or what democratic citizenship implies. The individual values of liberalism and the specialization of functions inherent in modern technological society encourage man to take a circumscribed view of what goes on around him. The organization of our lives into great impersonal aggregations—urban metropolises, school systems, universities, and bureaucracies of industry, commerce, and government—further diminishes the individual. The average citizen is well aware that problems exist: he immediately suffers the consequences, for example, of polluted air and water, noise, strangling traffic, crowded schools, unemployment, inflation, strikes, crime, and breaches of order and peace. But he cannot easily determine solutions to these problems and agree with others how to achieve them.

A result is that many retreat into apathy; some engage in a frantic crusade to eliminate an especially trying problem; and others simply oscillate between these conditions. To be sure, apathy, cynicism, and alienation flourish in the totalitarian parts of the world; but in those parts of the world the only acknowledged problems are those authoritatively defined, officially publicized, and resolvable in greater efforts by "the people." Originally, democratic thinkers believed universal education would ensure a competent, informed, and public-spirited citizenry. But earlier expectations were adapted to a simpler agrarian way of life. The future of democracy, thus, depends upon our ability to develop ideas of education, community, and government relevant to present conditions.

Private Interests and Community. In the absence of public-spirited citizenship, democratic politics loses coherence and legitimacy. Public policy then advances not the common good, or even particular interests related to it, but purely private interests as limited only by mutual bargaining. In such a process, general though unorganized interests—such as those of consumers—often suffer. Still more disadvantaged are the interests of small and poorly organized groups. Often subjected to such a "tyranny of the majority" are racial minorities, when the majority is indifferent to discrimination; cultural minorities, when popular taste alone dominates; and economic minorities, those in pockets of poverty in the midst of general prosperity. Such minorities may add up to a large part of the population, yet divided they are relatively impotent. Their ultimate reaction to such disadvantage can be extreme: to respond to the leadership of militant demagogues and aspiring dictators. They are thus only led to emulate others, who pursue their own selfish advantage in a contest where the rules appear to aid those already favored.

The pursuit solely of private interests, therefore, is not a principle upon which free and democratic government can be founded. A government founded on such interests does not support a systematic concern for justice, freedom, or general well-being, or set standards of responsibility within which social problems can be solved. Indeed, democracy will not survive the unqualified dominance of interest politics, and the rejection of public responsibilities it implies. The selfishness of some and the resentment of others can combine to destroy both freedom and democracy. Popular government long benefited from the fact that a community of farmers and small businessmen made only limited demands upon it. Those conditions have vanished. The need now is to create and sustain a sense of community sufficient to support public-spirited government for large democratic states.

Democracy and Experts in the Welfare State

Democracy has always taken for granted the independence and competence of its citizens. It is today being challenged in this basic assumption. Our forebears viewed democracy from the perspective of a way of life in which persons were not drastically affected by what others did, required relatively little cooperation from others in the achievement of any of their purposes, and generally possessed the knowledge required by their activities. Citizens of contemporary communities, however, no matter what ends they choose to pursue in the highly urbanized and technological societies of today, cannot accomplish them apart from intense cooperation and exceptionally knowledgeable decisions. For these, they are very much dependent upon a high degree of organization, often governmental, and upon the guidance and assistance of experts. Neither sort of dependence is readily reconcilable with democracy.

Increasing Dependence on Experts. The first of these problems of dependence occurs because the categories of professions and highly skilled occupations have multiplied enormously in recent years, and have advanced in technical development to the point where only the specialist can understand what he is doing and why. The common man is today the nonspecialist, and everyone is that in regard to much upon which his life depends. Although the promise of the technological age is great, and its achievements already substantial, men as individuals have lost control of their own lives. Technical experts have thus come to play an increasingly prominent and essential role in managing our complicated society for the public good.

Though the place of experts in government has long since been recognized, the traditional democratic attitude was that they were to be "on tap but not on top." Despite occasional fears of a managerial revolution, our real concern must be that the governmental process may move so far beyond the experience, knowledge, and values of the citizen-at-large that effective democratic control will be lost. Even the popular representatives—politicians with their own kind of expertness—find it difficult to control and evaluate the work of the agronomists, economists, engineers, lawyers, statisticians, and other technologists throughout government. Yet without effective political control, public policy may come to reflect only the disparate technical ideas of the experts, with their product a technocracy far more dictatorial than democratic.

Increasing Dependence on Government. The second problem of dependence is that an urbanized technological society is necessarily one in which the role of government and other great organizations is crucial. The necessity of this was for some time concealed from liberal democrats by their faith in a natural harmony of human interests and activities, and a belief that even selfish actions ultimately promote the best possible interests of all. This view has generally been abandoned or limited in recent decades, due to experiences in wars and depressions. The rise of socialistic governments and welfare states has been brought about not by some devious conspiracy, but simply as the consequence of present-day social and economic organization—big government along with big business and big labor —coupled with the democratic idea of a generalized distribution of benefits. Many oppose socialism from genuine democratic convictions. Yet, the steady expansion of government services and regulation of formerly private affairs is generally the result of an honest attempt to resolve some of the difficult problems of modern life within democratic procedures and values—rather than destroying them outright, as do communism and fascism. If increased government control of social activities is one way of avoiding anarchy in those activities, and of remedying private tyrannies, it also tends to deprive citizens of their independence of government—in ideas and values as well as powers of action—without which the democratic aim of popular control of government has little likelihood of success.

The Military in Government. There is a third problem here. As professional experts, the military may also pose a threat to democracy. Democracies have traditionally recognized this possibility, and have in principle preferred a militia—a body of citizen-soldiers on temporary duty—to standing professional armies. As such casual forces are rarely practical, the alternative has been limited professional forces explicitly subordinated to civilian authority. For several reasons that subordination is not easily effected. In times of crisis, now almost continuous, nations are dependent on the leadership of their professional military forces against the dangers they confront. Another problem flows from the technological nature of modern warfare, requiring a great "defense industry," which acquires economic and political importance. The measure of secrecy necessary to matters of national security may prevent some of the public discussion of military affairs otherwise appropriate to democratic decisions. In these ways a large military establishment, however necessary, may weaken its control by even a solidly established democracy.

Where democracy is not well established, the military threat takes a different form. Inefficient and disorderly national conditions are not normally tolerable to military professionals, whether concerned solely with defense of the state or with their own political inclinations. They may be thus tempted to abolish the complex procedures of politics, and establish government authority by their own command. Military leaders can enjoy important advantages in taking over unstable nations. In nonwestern states, they are often among the best educated, modern-minded, and disciplined men; they control the most highly organized segment of the public forces; and they have weapons. While military coups and periods of military rule are frequent in much of Africa, Asia, and Latin America, they are not necessarily reactionary. The officers seizing power may well favor modernization, social reform, and an approach to democracy. In principle at least, this has been the case recently in such countries as Bolivia, Peru, Ghana, Indonesia, Pakistan, and Thailand. Through progressive reorganization of their national life they may be able to create conditions appropriate for democracy, though the road to this end appears long.

Democratic Freedoms and the Totalitarian Conspiracy

Democracies are especially challenged today by the totalitarian threat to peace and to their survival. The challenge is not merely one of adequate external defense, but also one of maintaining democratic procedures in the face of this implacable attack. Tensions and conflicts between political regimes in the world have always existed, and domestic politics have always been affected by the requirements of foreign policy. But the problem today is whether the tension is not so great and pervasive that democracy will die in any event—either struck down from outside, or committing suicide in an effort to defend itself.

Early in American history Thomas Jefferson insisted that a free country, in which error of opinion could be tolerated because reason was free to combat it, was the strongest on earth. "Every man," he said, "at the call of the law would fly to the standard of the law, and would meet invasions of the public order as his own personal concern." Clearly, Jefferson did not think that democratic communities needed dictators or censors to tell them what they stood for or what they needed to do, even in critical times. This has been the traditional democratic view, but many have come to question it.

The Problem of Democratic Defenses. It is not easy today to share Jefferson's faith that democracy is "the strongest government on earth." We have seen, on the one hand, too many regimes more effectively integrated by force, and even by violence and terror, than the democratic faith ever dreamed was possible. On the other hand, we have seen long-established democratic regimes threaten to destruct over increasingly polarized animosities. We have discovered that the general agreements of the past, supporting an earlier confidence, rested on traditions that are now rejected by many. Consequently we no longer take for granted that men generally will spring to the defense of public order as their personal concern, whether because of other personal concerns or because of other ideas about order. The capacity of democratic governments for united action seems especially tenuous today, unless it be to retreat from responsibilities or to decline initiatives. About the world many fledgling democratic regimes have fallen to military rule or other dictatorship. Democracy seems neither as natural nor as effective as Jefferson thought in the circumstances we have lately known.

In a world of violence and frustration, and of widely disparate aspirations, conditions, and needs—in which democratic peoples are heavily engaged but only imperfectly understand—what chance is there democracy can flourish? Clearly, much depends upon a resolute democratic political leadership. Jefferson also once observed, in a reflective moment, that the best constitution was one which placed in office the "natural aristocracy of virtue and talent." The people must be able to recognize and support such leaders, consequently, for in a democracy the ultimate responsibility is theirs. This obligation is difficult in the best of circumstances; in a period of crisis and division it becomes overwhelming.

Confronted with developing totalitarianism in the international arena, the people too often fluctuate between two extremes. At the one, they ignore the danger and permit it to grow, in the name of "live and let live," "peace in our time," or "their intentions are good." At the other, they fail to distinguish between responsible and subversive critics of current policy, and yielding to violent antipathy, demand "total war" against "world communism."

These tendencies are not encouraging, for in that sort of game the totalitarians hold all the high cards, and will win by playing the extremes against each other. Democrats cannot beat totalitarians at their own game. Democracy will survive only with means both appropriate to its own character and to the nature of the totalitarian attack.

4

Constitutions: Order and Freedom

"ONE country, one constitution, one destiny." Daniel Webster forcefully expressed the close relationship between a constitution and the political spirit of the nation-state. The term "constitution" and its derivatives are used to refer to one of our most important political concepts. The sort of order they identify has been at the core of western political life since ancient times. The term has come to be particularly important to those who recognize that it is largely through constitutional government that liberal democracy is secured. As the theory and practice of constitutions and constitutionalism are complex, we must probe further for their significance.

Constitution as the Framework of Politics. A constitution is usually viewed as the basic law of a political system. Yet it is often difficult to tell what that law is and how it is effected. It is not simply a matter of looking at some document called "the Constitution"; this may or may not be evidence that a constitution exists. When we become aware that governments are not alike, we reflect about politics. Our reflections require, however, that we delineate some types of governmental forms and procedures if we are to make comparisons. The identification of the fundamental—or constitutional—aspects of political order gives us that basic law.

Aristotle took the first step in constitutional analysis. In the perspective of ancient Greece, the constitution was to him not only an arrangement of offices but also the underlying way of life. Going behind the basic threefold classification of government by "the one, the few, or the many," he distinguished also the virtues and vices of each form to show in whose interest the community was ruled. He thus discerned six types of constitutions: monarchy, aristocracy, and polity (moderate democracy)—forms of rule according to law and particular civic interest; tyranny, oligarchy, and ochlocracy (extreme democracy)—lawless forms ruling in the interests of the tyrant, the wealthy, or the mob. Aristotle's subtle analysis has long been influential, but as all modern government is undertaken practically by "the few," the important distinction in constitutions is how these few exercise political power.

Constitutions of government are the product of historical development, and their very existence reflects the changing circumstances and purposes of political life. One of the most important characteristics of constitutional laws is that they substantially shape the distribution and exercise of political power. They are thus important facts regarding the power structure that is government. At the same time constitutions embody ideals; they are created by men seeking fulfillment of their needs and security for their values. A constitution, then, channels the exercise of political power—to stabilize it and to limit its scope to the needs of the community.

I. Constitutional Government

Although the importance of the constitution as a political concept has been fully recognized only in recent times, contemporary institutions that we call "constitutional" have a substantial historical development. They are the result of several thousand years of human thought and action, into which gradually has been built a pattern of political beliefs and practices. The constitutions of today would not be the "facts" they are were this not so, and we shall understand them better if we look first to their roots.

The Roots of Modern Constitutions

Although the conditions of contemporary political life are vastly different from those of classical Greece and Rome, our debt to that time is incalculable. All succeeding stages in the development of western civilization were strongly influenced by classical political thought and practice, which endeavored to cast political life in a mold of reason and law.

Greece: Political Philosophy and the Ideal of Justice. Most spectacularly expressed in the teachings of Socrates, Plato, and Aristotle, Greek political life introduced into our culture the spirit of rational criticism that is the foundation for constitutional politics. In the absence of this spirit, the basic elements of a political system tend to be arbitrary or mystical; but its presence encourages developing them into patterns of functions and responsibilities, methods of control, standards against which particular acts of officials can be evaluated, and powers necessary to accomplish some rather clearly defined goals. The history of constitutional institutions is largely therefore an elaboration of Greek political thought and logic. The tendency to a monolithic view of political life, however, limited the development of institutions to enforce these convictions. Law and justice remained the preferences of a ruling group and could not control the exercise of political power. The Greek contribution was primarily one of declaring aspirations.

Rome: Government, Law, and Rights. The Romans developed institutions that were to be a solid foundation for those of modern political life. The core was a massive and systematic body of law. Within Roman society and by its law, private affairs were defined in terms of rights, and public affairs in terms of power and responsibilities; furthermore, this law became increasingly technical and its administration highly professionalized. The result was that it came to serve as a control over the exercise of political power, establishing as one of the functions of government the protection of private rights. Rome succeeded in practice where Greece had failed. Quite explicitly in Rome did all authority flow from the law, which conferred powers as it limited power.

Roman law, expressing itself in terms of rights and responsibilities, ultimately gave rise to a new conception of citizenship. The Greeks had viewed citizenship as akin to family membership, intense and exclusive. But the demands of a growing empire brought the essence of Roman citizenship to be enjoyment of rights defined by law and protected by officials. Our modern conception of citizenship—as "equal protection of the laws"—is predominantly Roman. And this Roman view, together with their inventions in the realm of law, is basic to modern constitutions.

The Middle Ages: Order, Rights, and Law. The thousand years following the fall of Rome was a period of transition between the ancient and modern worlds. The general characteristics of political life during those centuries have been briefly treated previously. One of these was a multiplication of social organizations and a dispersion of power. Lacking a single center around which to integrate, the medieval social order was fundamentally pluralistic. From it emerged the institutions of modern constitutions, elaborated as ideas and practices concerning law and rights, political obligation and consent, representation, and public power as a trust.

In the medieval social order, the various corporations and classes were considered natural parts of the community; each performed necessary functions to which appropriate rights were attached. Therefore positions in society, with attendant rights and duties, were also thought of as natural to the community and beyond the power of any man to alter.

These rights and duties, and the social order they expressed, were considered to be rooted in law. Law defined the position, privileges, and responsibilities of every member of the community. None was outside the law and none above it. The medieval idea crystallized clearly: the purpose of government was to maintain law and order, to preserve the peace and administer justice, by methods the law provided. No better technique of controlling the exercise of political power—its subordination to law—has ever been devised. Even so, to distinguish what rule is law in every case is not easy in a society based on custom. Who can declare the law, and by what criteria, now became important problems.

For various reasons, monarchical government seemed the most natural to the medieval mind; and with his prestige and power as a great lord, the king became the most likely source of legal norms, through his ordinance and judicial decision. But neither preference nor power made any particular man king. Legitimate title was acquired through laws of succession, renewed in oaths of fealty from the nobles, acclaim by the people, and sanctification by the Church.

The king, then, was subordinate to the laws governing how a man became king. And to medieval thinking, the king was subject to other norms derived from revelation and reason, called "divine" or "natural" law. Against these, even the ordinance of a legitimate ruler had no authority; the king was always under the law, even if he alone had authority to define it. Hence, the beliefs in the existence of a "higher law," and that conformity to it alone justifies government, have been rooted in our constitutional systems since the middle ages.

The Middle Ages: Consent, Representation, and Trust. An interesting aspect of the medieval order was its confusion of private and public rights and responsibilities. The personal interest of a king or noble was totally merged with his public position; he could not resign one while retaining the other. Since public authority was thus a matter of personal status, voluntary acceptance of the position was deemed necessary. Consent thus became essential to political obligation. Through the medieval oath of fealty, therefore, a man became a vassal of a lord by placing himself under that lord's protection and pledging in return the customary services. As the free populations of the cities became important, they were brought within the political order through royal charters, analogous to oaths of fealty, granting them privileges and obligations. Such charters not only manifested the idea of consent to government, but as written documents stipulating fundamental law, they were prototypes of modern constitutions.

To the modern mind, consent to government demands at least continuing consent through representatives. In the middle ages, too, participation in government by at least some of the governed was also institutionalized from the manor to the Church. Charlemagne's edicts, promulgated in the late eighth century, indicated that tribal leaders and populations affected had given their advice. The practice was ultimately formalized in the great feudal councils of emperors and kings. In thirteenth-century England, participation to "council and consent" was even extended to commoners. Here the foundation was laid for modern representative government.

Although political authority derives from the "higher law," we also require a body of positive law, as rules appropriate to the practical needs of everyday life. To meet this need, the middle ages developed the idea of power as a trust. Explicit in medieval thought, it was institutionalized in coronation oaths. The king promised to rule the people justly, providing peace and order; in return the people promised to obey. Through trusteeship, it was possible to hold the king responsible in the broad objectives of government, but to give him at the same time freedom to pursue those objectives through varying circumstances. What we have done since the medieval period has been essentially to develop new instruments to control power yet promote a dynamic society.

The Features of Modern Constitutionalism

The middle ages shade gradually into the modern period; yet by the seventeenth century, political life had changed radically. New political ideas and needs were pressing for recognition and, during this and the two succeeding centuries, ultimately found institutional embodiment. The late eighteenth and early nineteenth centuries were, in fact, a spectacular age of constitutional development. There emerged new conceptions of the nature of political order, its foundation, its proper organization, and the relation between it and private persons. Expressed in patterns of procedure and policy they directly underlie the constitutions of the twentieth century.

Sovereignty and the State. Sovereignty as the core of political order is essentially a modern innovation, created in response to the need of a rapidly expanding European culture for an effective lawmaking power. Though the term "sovereignty" had existed in medieval usage, where it had meant little more than "superior," in the writings of Jean Bodin (1576) and after, it came to have a much more radical significance. Sovereignty became the concentration in a determinate person or group of the authority to create law. Rights and obligations acquired legal existence only as expressions of that sovereign's will. A legal term, "sovereignty" merely expresses the necessary conditions for the existence of law—primarily a unity of will.

As the modern form of political order, the state has been forged through the doctrine of sovereignty and cannot be understood apart from it. The state is not a sociological phenomenon discoverable in laws of nature, but a legal one manifested in positive laws willed by men. In consequence, as a realm in which the common positive law is created, the state depends upon the unified will, or sovereign power, which creates that law. Common citizenship in the modern state likewise has come to mean subjection to a common sovereign power.

The location of the sovereign power in the political order is of practical significance. Initially it was claimed in behalf of a king or prince, so that his unchallenged authority could create an effective legal order. In this form, sovereignty is indisputably clearly located, but with the disadvantage that the entire political order rests upon one man. Eventually, a more fundamental location for the sovereign power was sought. Some found it in the state itself; others sought to transfer sovereignty from the king to the people, hence the term "popular sovereignty." These formulations separate the state or the people from the government of the day, however, and raise the question of how either could act independently as sovereign. In such ideas there remains a unified legal order free of tradition and alien control, but the sovereign as a determinate body or person disappears. Thus sovereignty, once a very concrete concept, has become quite abstract.

Underlying all modern politics, nevertheless, is the idea that behind the visible agency of government there is a power that usually acts through that government and according to existing law, but cannot be limited to those means of realizing its will. It seems largely a matter of convenience or ideological orientation whether one refers to that sovereign as the "people" or the more legalistic "state." Sovereignty persists, despite our uneasiness with some of its implications, because we have not yet disavowed the revolutionary perspective which gave rise to it. Only the continuing concentration and liberation of authority expressed in sovereignty will enable us to live with the tensions inherent in the dynamic pluralism of modern life, with its rejection of custom in favor of continuing innovation. In short, sovereignty is the will to ordered change. Although often in conflict with the liberal ideal of individual freedom, sovereignty is really its societal counterpart. The concept of sovereignty, however, does not alone sufficiently describe modern political life. Sovereignty, expressing its most general characteristics, is in itself too abstract; we need to know how it is manifested, through what channels it flows, and what may be the practical limitations surrounding its exercise.

Constitution: An Explicit Grant of Authority. To modern thinking, quite evidently, the foundation of political systems is no longer a matter of myth or dim memory, nor is it a natural event. It is of human doing. As such, it must suit man's needs, values, interests, and capabilities. Consequently a constitution has come to be seen somewhat as a blueprint, a standard which both authorizes the work of governors and permits that work to be evaluated. A constitution is not necessarily democratic, nor even innovative; indeed, most have been well rooted in traditional practices. The modern idea of a constitution, however, is most perfectly manifested in the "We the people . . . do ordain and establish," of the Constitution of the United States. Thomas Paine put it well, more than a century and a half ago: "A constitution is not the act of a government, but of a people constituting a government, and a government without a constitution is power without right."

Fundamentally, then, a constitution is an enactment of, or a set of principles accepted by, the people who are to be governed under it, creating political authority and defining its proper methods and competence. To Paine, and late eighteenth-century opinion generally, it had to be a document, drafted by a convention selected for the purpose, and approved by the public in special elections before being put into effect. The first constitution so established for an independent government was that of Massachusetts in 1780; the American federal Constitution was similarly adopted a few years later. The practice of drafting a document has been dominant since throughout the world. Only Great Britain among the major powers, because of the unusual continuity of its regime, lacks an explicit constitutional document, although France from 1871 to 1940, and Israel more recently, were unable to agree on a complete constitution and proceeded under a number of "organic laws." Many of the fundamental laws and practices of these countries have been so well established, however, that the difference is essentially nominal. What is important is that law, recognized as such by rulers and ruled alike, should effectively condition the exercise of political power in the interests of stability and the realization of communal political values.

Constitutional Change. Modern constitutions characteristically provide explicit means for their own amendment. Thus, the idea of a constitution is related to that of sovereignty; for sovereignty implies freedom to create new powers and limit old ones, to adapt the constitution to changing circumstances and to the realization of newly recognized values. Deliberate provision of amending procedures expresses awareness of this, even though formal amendment is not the only or the most important means of constitutional change. Most alterations in constitutions take place through reinterpretation of the law by the courts and other public officials, especially where constitutional provisions are broadly cast; but the amending process is restrictive, as in the United States.

Yet neither this informal method, nor the formal process of amendment may be adequate to the need for change, in which case the traditional method of revolution remains even today the ultimate recourse. It has been the hope, not the certainty, of the framers of modern constitutions to avoid the necessity of such recourse through providing the opportunity of peaceful amendment. The American experience for the most part justifies that hope, but we must recall that the Civil War was necessary to secure the abolition of slavery and the preservation of the Union. The existence of amending processes is thus a general recognition that constitutions must change in time, but not a guarantee that they will be altered adequately.

Individual Rights against Government. A striking aspect of most modern constitutions has been the protection they have aimed to furnish to individual rights, equally for all men. The constitutions adopted in France and the United States at the end of the eighteenth century, and one then gradually being evolved in England as well, attempted to provide barriers against governmental interference with essential realms of individual freedom, and to curtail arbitrariness in the exercise of governmental powers.

One of the explicitly constitutional documents in English history is the Bill of Rights, set by Parliament in 1689 on the accession of William and Mary to the throne. Principally designed to guarantee the place of Parliament in the government of Great Britain, the Bill of Rights nevertheless did specify certain liberties of British subjects. Among these were the right to petition the government, trial by jury, reasonable bail and punishment, the possession of arms for self-defense, and a Parliament independent of the king.

The best illustration of this constitutional development, however, is to be found in the American constitutions adopted following the outbreak of the Revolution. The prevailing attitude was expressed by Thomas Jefferson, protesting against the omission of a bill of rights from the federal Constitution as proposed in 1787, a guarantee which, he said, "is what the people are entitled to against every government on earth, general or particular, and what no government should refuse, or rest on inference." Ten amendments to the Constitution were adopted in the first session of Congress, and in 1791 the Bill of Rights became a major example of the reservation of private rights in modern constitutionalism. Generally comparable was the French Declaration of the Rights of Man and the Citizen, 1789. Because of its form, more philosophical than legal, the Declaration has been a universally appealing expression of the liberal attitude toward government. We shall consider these documents later in the chapter.

Representative Government. Obviously, bills of rights do not enforce themselves, however useful they are as explicit statements of the rights to be secured. They must be supported by operating institutions that effectively control the exercise of political power and force officials to respect them. One of the most important methods of assuring that the rights recognized in law and cherished among the people are effective in practice has been representative government. We need not elaborate on it here except to observe that, when effectively functioning, representative government shifts ultimate political responsibility and power from officials to private citizens acting as an electorate, and thus ensures at least some correspondence between the acts of government and the values of the population.

Political Parties. For the community to exercise this political power, some sort of organization is necessary; private persons, dispersed both in space and in interests, cannot support effectively, much less control, their government. Consequently political parties emerged rapidly as central constitutional institutions within all modern political systems, even though not usually provided for in constitutional documents. They were from the first a practical response to the needs of democratic and representative government; in the complex politics of today, however, they have become a practical necessity. Through political parties alone can governors and governed be related sufficiently for the existence of effective modern government. Over the last several centuries political leaders have had to devote an increasing effort to organizing support for themselves and their policies, while, at the same time, private citizens increasingly interested in government have had to organize themselves to exert maximum influence. The modern political party is the result.

Checks and Balances. A political system embodies checks and balances if the performance of any function is not entrusted exclusively to any one person or agency, but a share in it or control over it is possessed by other agencies. Few of the American founding fathers believed that representative government alone would furnish good and just rule. The key to what was additionally necessary came to them out of their own English and colonial experience, supplemented by the philosophic and legal thought of their age, and by practical ingenuity in dealing with conflicting ideas and interests throughout the former colonies.

The American Constitution, consequently, embodies a particularly complex pattern of checks and balances—expressed in, but also as modifications of, the separation of powers and federalism. Some checks and balances are characteristic of every developed constitution, though with variations in numbers and subtlety. To treat the idea further we must discuss these more particular constitutional techniques.

The Separation of Powers. The separation of powers was considered so important in the late eighteenth century that James Madison and Thomas Jefferson wrote that its absence was the "very definition of tyranny," while the French Declaration of the Rights of Man asserted that a regime without the separation of powers has no constitution. To some degree a matter of common practical experience, especially for the American colonists, the doctrine received a classic and persuasive statement in the interpretation of English government in *The Spirit of the Laws* (1748) of the French philosopher, Montesquieu. In sum, Montesquieu found the secret of political liberty in a constitutional organization dividing the functions of legislation, administration, and adjudication among different persons or groups. Only if these powers are kept distinct, thought Montesquieu, can the rule of law be maintained.

Neither in Montesquieu's statement of the doctrine, nor in its application in the state and federal constitutions in America, was the separation of powers rigorously applied. It was modified out of practical necessities and in the spirit of multiplying checks and balances. The American Constitution, for example, assigns the legislative power to Congress, but the House of Representatives and the Senate divide it. Furthermore, the authority of the President to veto congressional enactments and to recommend legislation gives him substantial participation in the legislative process. The President's primacy in the executive function, on the other hand, is limited by Congress' control over revenues and appropriations, and the requirement that the Senate approve ratification of treaties and many appointments—to mention a few of the formal controls available to Congress.

Of course, Montesquieu and other advocates of the separation of powers recognized that the cooperation of the three powers is essential for effective government, and believed that only in justice could the legislative, executive, and judicial powers work in harmony. Since such harmony has not always been forthcoming, the separation of powers has not been universally adopted in modern constitutions, and has been criticized even in its principal home, the United States.

Federalism. Another innovation of the late eighteenth century is federal government. Confederations and alliances, associations for limited purposes of independent political units, had been known since antiquity; but the federal system established in the United States in 1789 was a remarkable and original variation on the older theme.

Federalism is similar to the separation of powers, since it creates a division of powers and responsibilities; but the division is essentially territorial, based upon a distinction between general and local interests. By a federal constitution two spheres of government are established: one, a general government for the whole community; the other, several regional governments, with authority only over their more limited areas. Both derive their legitimacy from the same source, the constitution, and neither is the creature or the agent of the other.

The range of responsibilities of each of the levels of government is determined in constitutional law, and is not subject to change at will by either set of authorities. However, within their proper competence both the central and the regional governments possess all powers not specifically denied them in the constitution, as by the provisions of a bill of rights. This distinguishes a federal system from a confederation, in which the "central government" acts in domestic affairs only through the member states, not directly on the population. But similarly to a confederation, on the other hand, in federal regimes the member states are specifically represented in one or more aspects of the central government.

The precise patterns of federal regimes, however, vary considerably. In the United States, for example, the Constitution assigns "delegated" powers to the central government; all others, or "residual" powers, are reserved to the states. In the Canadian federal system, on the other hand, delegated powers are assigned to the provinces, with the central government possessing an extensive residue. In the Canadian and other more recent federal constitutions, also, areas of "concurrent" powers have been specified in which both levels of government may act, although in case of conflict the acts of the central regime are superior.

In the German Federal Republic since 1949, the central government has the larger share of authority, and much exclusive legislative power; but the administration of most federal legislation is left to the states (*Länder*). Federalism combines a measure of unity with a measure of diversity; it is appropriate for those peoples who want unity but not uniformity. It is an important constitutional institution in that it limits political power by relieving a community of complete dependence upon any one government to accomplish its needs.

Judicial Review. Constitutions cannot be self-effecting and therefore must be enforced by some agency if they are to be truly superior to momentary political demands. There has been little willingness of constitutional framers to follow the British principle of parliamentary supremacy, which allows Parliament to change constitutional arrangements at any time with an ordinary law. Thus, Great Britain has no judicial review, in the sense that the courts have no authority to test the constitutional validity of the laws.

In the United States, by contrast, we find the earliest and also the most extensive development of the power of judicial review. In a practice written into American constitutional law by Chief Justice Marshall, the courts have become the central and ultimate interpreter of the Constitution, with their decisions overridden as a rule only by constitutional amendment. Marshall argued that the Constitution is the fundamental law; any statute or administrative act incompatible with the Constitution is not lawful, and the courts must refuse to enforce it (*Marbury* v. *Madison,* 1803). To the extent that the constitutional law is clear, and a particular inferior rule clearly in violation of it, Marshall's reasoning is hard to controvert. But constitutional law is often not clear on important and emotionally charged issues, and its interpretation is not solely a judicial but a political function. Few countries have been willing to emulate American practice.

The power of judicial review as it exists elsewhere usually takes a rather different and limited form. In states with federal systems— such as Australia, Canada, and Switzerland—of necessity in constitutional stipulation or practice a supreme court or its equivalent must be capable of resolving disputes over the division of powers; of reconciling differences between federal law and that of the states, provinces, or cantons; and of resolving controversies between these component units.

Still other states, particularly those in Europe that are reacting to experience with dictatorial regimes, have sought to protect new constitutional systems adopted after World War II with special constitutional courts or councils. Austria, France, Germany, and Italy are among those establishing such special bodies. Since they vary in their nature and utilization, it is difficult to assess their effectiveness so soon; but clearly they have supported democracy and constitutionalism.

Parliamentary Government. In this discussion of the features of modern constitutions, we should not wish to leave the impression that all political systems adhere to the principle of separation of powers.

Parliamentary government—with Great Britain its outstanding example—has as a distinguishing characteristic that its executive, cabinet, and ministry, are drawn from Parliament and are not independently elected. As this is a method also of ensuring the responsible exercise of political power, it deserves mention here. Most of the new constitutions adopted in the twentieth century have instituted the parliamentary system, though the presidential system with an independent executive has recently had some popularity.

Parliamentary government appeals to those with democratic sympathies because it founds the government upon a majority in the representative assembly, which in turn is founded upon a majority of the electorate. It appeals also to those concerned with efficient government because it appears to weld into an operating unity the electorate, representative assembly, and government. Yet long experience demonstrates once more that to function properly and harmoniously parliamentary government must also have the right political environment; and this is not to be had simply for the asking.

In governmental forms, it is possible to combine various features of the separation of powers, the federal, and the parliamentary systems into effective constitutional government. Switzerland, for example, has produced a type that defies classification. The Swiss Federal Council, or executive, is elected by the representative assembly, but is maintained on an essentially nonpolitical basis with extraordinary stability. Even though councilors recommend legislation, they do not resign if their proposals are defeated, but adapt themselves to the decision of the legislature and continue their administrative tasks. This arrangement is probably suited only to such a relatively small country, without critical internal or foreign problems, and capable of substantial self-discipline. Other democratic regimes as they emerged in this and the last century are, however, largely variations on the parliamentary system.

II. Contemporary Constitutions

Most of the constitutions in the world today are products of the last several decades. Only the United States has a written constitution nearly two centuries old. Yet both the Constitution of the United States and the ancient but largely unwritten constitution of Britain have been substantially modified in recent years. Both the new constitutions and the altered old ones reflect the special political circumstances of the last part of the twentieth century. To illustrate contemporary constitutions we shall first discuss briefly those of four important regimes, and then indicate some of the principal trends in constitutional development today.

Four Major Constitutions

In the creation of constitutions throughout the world in this century, as well as in political life more generally, four states have been particularly influential: Great Britain, the United States, France, and the Soviet Union. Well-established regimes, compared with most countries at the present, their constitutions warrant special note.

The British Constitution. Great Britain offers the only example of a major country with a constitution that is not written—which is to say that there is no single document, or set of them, undertaking to order the basic organization and proceedings of British government. There is, indeed, no difference between constitutional and ordinary law, as respects the legal methods of their enactment or alteration. Yet there are fundamental laws and practices according to which British government operates; they appear in diverse guises.

The law of the constitution—those rules the courts will enforce—is supplied from several sources. First, there are the great charters and other historic agreements—such as Magna Carta of 1215, the Petition of Right of 1628, and the Bill of Rights of 1689. These constitutional landmarks were the products of major political crises and manifest the terms of their settlement. Second, there are certain statutes of Parliament—such as the Act of Settlement of 1701, regulating succession to the throne and the tenure of judges; the Great Reform Act of 1832, which reorganized representation in the House of Commons; and the Parliament Acts of 1911 and 1949, limiting the powers of the House of Lords. Third, there are certain principles of the common law, derived from court decisions, which have defined the royal prerogative and many of the basic civil liberties, such as freedom of speech, press, and public meeting. Of course, an act of Parliament enjoys supremacy over any other constitutional rule and provides the formal method for altering the British constitution.

In addition, the British have developed a substantial body of constitutional customs, called "conventions." They include such practices as the annual meeting of Parliament, the sovereign's selection of the leader of the majority party in the House of Commons as Prime Minister, the Prime Minister's resignation when he loses the support of that majority, the collective responsibility of the ministers to the Commons, the exercise in practice by ministers of the royal prerogative, and so on. Obviously, these principles are very much at the heart of the parliamentary system; yet though they are regularly observed, they are nevertheless not rules which the courts will enforce. The conventions of the constitution derive their authority from the fact that parliamentary government would not function apart from them; they are closely interwoven with the law, with each element assuming the existence of the other; and they are strongly supported by the forces of tradition and public opinion. This latter is of greatest importance; with such support the slenderest customary rule can be maintained, but without it even the law may fall into disregard.

The Constitution of the United States. The United States possesses the oldest documentary constitution now in effect. America's experience with constitutions began in royal charters and the compacts of the colonists, familiarizing the Americans with documents setting forth authoritative rights and powers. The colonial period ended in a revolutionary break with the homeland, requiring the explicit establishment of new independent governments both for the former colonies and for their union. This experience, plus the rationalistic temper of the period, led to the general drafting of constitutional documents.

Unlike most later written constitutions, that of the United States is a relatively brief document, almost deceptively simple in its provisions. The American founding fathers never lost sight of the fact that they were framing an instrument to endure, and to fill it with minute specifications would soon render it obsolete. For this reason, and because they had many diverse ideas and interests to compromise, the Constitution deals in quite general language. That there have been great controversies over the interpretation of its provisions is not the consequence of faulty draftsmanship, but of the close relationship of any constitution to a changing social life.

The Constitution provides for its formal amendment, although the process is somewhat complex and difficult. Amendments are proposed either by Congress, through a two-thirds vote in each House, or by a national convention called by Congress at the request of two-thirds of the states. Amendments must be ratified by three-fourths of the states, either through their legislatures or in special conventions, as Congress may direct. Twenty-six such textual alterations have been made. Most earlier amendments limited the central government's powers respecting the rights of private persons and the states; others have merely altered particular procedures, as the election of the President and Senators, and succession to the presidency in case of death or disability. Only a few amendments—such as the Fourteenth, protecting basic national rights against state action; the Sixteenth, authorizing a national income tax; and the eventually repealed Eighteenth, or prohibition, amendment—have worked to enlarge the powers of the national government. Of course, the Thirteenth, abolishing slavery, and the Nineteenth, extending the suffrage to women, instituted dramatic political changes. But if formal amendment were the only means of constitutional change, the national government would today have less power than was inherent in the original document of 1789.

In extension of the original provisions, however, much more in the way of laws and practices has developed to round out the whole constitutional system. Certain acts of Congress have implemented the Constitution, such as those establishing the major executive departments and agencies, organizing the federal courts, ordering presidential succession, and the provision of the civil service and social security systems. Further, there are legal principles developed through judicial interpretation that have given broad meaning to various provisions of the Constitution, such as the commerce clause, tax powers, and the concept of due process of law. Finally, there are also customary practices which have grown up around the Constitution. Here, outside the legal rules, are important and relatively stable procedures respecting the political parties, selection of the President and Vice-President, congressional elections, the role of the President's cabinet, and other such governmental arrangements. Understanding the American Constitution in practice requires considering all these later developments.

The French Constitution. France has the distinction—a rather dubious one, all things considered—of having undergone more frequent and drastic constitutional changes than any other state. This fact reflects not a constant improvement in document writing, but rather the inability of the French people, after overturning the old regime in 1789, to reach agreement for any extended period on the fundamental character of their political institutions. More than a dozen constitutions, some republican and some monarchical, were adopted between

1789 and 1946; but none provided France with adequate and stable political institutions. In view of this history, uncertainty is justified as to the permanence of the most recent, adopted in 1958.

The most durable settlement in modern France followed the Franco-Prussian War and lasted from 1875 until 1940. Due to a continuing controversy between monarchists and republicans—but even more to disagreements among the monarchists as to who should be king—no comprehensive constitutional system could be adopted. Several "organic laws" established an intentionally temporary republic with an elective president, a bicameral legislature, and ministers whose responsibility to the assemblies was clarified only when President Mac-Mahon failed in 1879 in his attempt to make them responsible to him. This "constitution" was all that the Third Republic was to have—"a scaffold of chance," as Hanotaux described it; but out of it grew an assembly-dominated parliamentary system that succumbed only to the invading German armies early in World War II. After liberation, most Frenchmen voted overwhelmingly in favor of a new constitution. Despite their intentions, nonetheless, the Constitution of the Fourth Republic diverged remarkably little from the lines of its predecessor. Perhaps for that reason it was greeted with enormous indifference and lasted but twelve years.

The apparently interminable Algerian rebellion, which broke out in 1954 and aroused animosities and posed problems with which the government in Paris was unable to cope, brought an end to the Fourth Republic in 1958. Insurrections among the army and police that threatened to spread led to the appointment of General Charles de Gaulle as Premier with emergency powers, including that of preparing a new constitution. Its final draft was submitted to a popular referendum and received the approval of more than four-fifths of those voting, with few abstentions. This unusual display of agreement among the French seems to have been less a verdict on the Constitution than a demonstration that General de Gaulle offered the only leadership under which the nation might unite.

The Constitution of the Fifth Republic retains many features of preceding regimes—such as universal suffrage, representation through a bicameral parliament, and a ministry that must have the confidence of the National Assembly. The traditional individual rights of the Declaration of 1789 and the complementary "economic and social principles" of the 1946 Constitution were reaffirmed. However, it was designed throughout to provide a vehicle for General de Gaulle's leadership through the presidential office.

In effect, the Fifth Republic under De Gaulle until his resignation in 1969—after a defeated constitutional referendum that he chose to interpret as a vote of no confidence—was very much a limited monarchy, even if the king were called "President" and popularly elected. The objective, of course, was to give France a new political stability. De Gaulle insisted in 1964 that after five years' experience his Constitution could be pronounced a success, but admitted that there were still critics—"who find the bride perhaps too beautiful and who suggest changes which, in fact, would upset the system from top to bottom."

Thus the constitutional system continues to be a matter of controversy, reflecting the diverse political interests and concerns of the French people. Efforts to consolidate the regime invariably raise opposition to it. Nonetheless, it survived the serious crises of the May, 1968, revolutionary uprisings, and De Gaulle's precipitous resignation followed by the election of Georges Pompidou as President in June, 1969. While it is not possible to evaluate the intrinsic durability of the Constitution, it is evident that the French tradition of writing a new constitution to suit varying political moods and exigencies will not be easily discarded.

The Soviet Constitution. The Soviet Union has had three documentary constitutions. The first, proclaimed in 1918 for the Russian Soviet Federated Socialist Republic, announced the objectives of the socialist revolution and described the gross structure of the government. A second was issued in 1924, marking the new federation of the Union of Soviet Socialist Republics and the improved stabilization of affairs following the civil war. The third, or Stalin Constitution, was promulgated in 1936, after a campaign of "popular discussion." One might well wonder why the well-entrenched dictatorship required a basic charter at all, much less a new one. The answer appears to lie in the ambition of the regime at that time to acquire a new liberal respectability, both at home and abroad. The Soviet Union, so it was claimed, had achieved "socialism," the first step to communism, and the Constitution was officially hailed as the "most democratic in the world."

In form, the 1936 Constitution contains much of the content usual in such documents. It provides a federal system, an elaborate arrangement of organs of government along parliamentary lines with definition of powers and accountability, and popular elections—all of which would appear to support a regular system of democratic and representative government. It also includes an extensive list of individual rights—not only the classic substantive rights of British, American, and French tradition, but an additional number of social and economic ones, far beyond those guaranteed at the time in the liberal democracies.

Yet there is an air of unreality about the Soviet Constitution. It made no change in the source or control of political power; indeed, Stalin emphasized that the Constitution preserved unchanged "the dictatorship of the working class" and "the present leading position of the Communist party." Equally, the "rights" described in the Constitution are without any means for their implementation; they do not create claims that are upheld by the courts and enforced against the government, nor is representative government available to those who do not choose the Communist party. In short, the Constitution established few if any limits on the power of the Soviet rulers, the leaders of the Communist party; rather it was dictated by expediency as an instrument of their policy. The document may be something more than a scrap of paper, if viewed as a political document and a social and economic manifesto of communist aims expressed in a strange combination of communist and liberal terminology. But since it is neither controlling law nor convention, it is only formally a constitution. One may learn something about Soviet government by reading the Constitution, but the realities are on a different plane. We may reasonably doubt that a new constitutional document, allegedly in preparation since 1962, will alter this situation significantly.

This brief treatment of four major contemporary constitutions should make evident the limited significance of constitutional documents. Obvious similarities in crucial concerns are to be found in British and American political life, yet the latter alone has one great historic document. The former, having a much smaller and less complete body of constitutional law, has developed its constitution largely through practice and convention, although this method has played a substantial role in the political life of the United States as well. Existing in both systems, however, is a universal disposition to maintain the continuity of a set of effective fundamental rules. This spirit has been weak in France and completely lacking in the Soviet Union; consequently constitutional law—impressive documents notwithstanding—has been either unstable or ineffective. The Soviet Constitution coexists with a complete dictatorship that one could barely suspect from a reading of the document. Clearly, the distinctions among governments that constitutions express are far more profoundly rooted than in sheets of parchment!

Major Constitutional Trends

The constitutions of the present, even in the newly independent states, are largely built upon those of the early modern period. Formally, this has not been a period of great innovation. Yet within the framework of older ideas, there have been developments in both fundamental political objectives and in governmental procedures, so that contemporary constitutions reflect many new features.

Contemporary Western Constitutions. The constitutions of a century ago reflected the limited political objectives of the period. In recent decades, however, governments have been charged with a role in the development and functioning of the economy. Education has become a growing public responsibility; and public works today involve, not merely buildings and monuments, but highways, airports, hydroelectric systems, and slum clearance. Even more challenging is the leading part government is expected to play in promoting public health, welfare, and full employment; protecting consumers; reducing racial, sexual, linguistic, and religious discrimination; preventing urban blight; limiting the birth rate; and so on—thus requiring radical transformations in community cultures and mores.

The newer constitutions have sought to reaffirm the primacy of private individual rights, yet at the same time to qualify them in the interests of general public purposes. For example, in the case of the basic freedoms of expression, rights have been reaffirmed to prevent their exploitation by the enemies of constitutional democracy; or, in the guarantee of private property, rights have been qualified to prevent their obstruction of broad social needs. The demands of contemporary government have also led to the elevation of the executive to a position far above that of his predecessors. Special efforts have further been made to add to the continuity of executive office, reinforcing against the ministerial instability formerly characteristic of several European regimes. At the same time that the executive has become more intensely the personal leader of the country, he has also become more impersonally institutionalized within a complex of secretaries, councils, committees, and bureaus, which both limit and add to his powers.

The rise of the executive to leadership is probably necessary—certainly undeniable—yet in the traditional constitutional systems it has not produced dictatorship; and checks and balances have still been maintained. If representative assemblies are no longer the core of modern government, more than ever they are the forum for criticizing government policies and exercising controls over the executive and his subordinates. Judicial controls have also enjoyed a renewed favor in recent years; we have earlier mentioned the institution of special constitutional tribunals to guarantee the maintenance of the constitutional order. Finally, federalism remains a significant method of controlling political power. The simplicity of earlier federalism, assuming that a national community could be split across its middle, has largely vanished. The "new federalism" involves much more cooperative action by central and local governments, extending national power but also strengthening local authority. At the same time, even long-established regimes have sought to decentralize public power in certain ways and gain some of the advantages that federalism offers. A survey of the Italian, German, and French Constitutions—of 1948, 1949, and 1958 respectively—and of recent American and British practices, will provide numerous illustrations of the several generalizations offered above.

Constitutions in New Nonwestern States. The adoption of a written constitution has almost universally accompanied the independence of the new states. This was not an imposition by the former colonial rulers; the leaders of these new countries wanted such constitutions as status symbols recognizing their political coming of age. Most showed only limited inventiveness, however, adopting constitutional systems often resembling those of the former colonial rulers, and retaining little of their countries' indigenous cultural and political characteristics. For example, most of the states of former French Africa adopted constitutions à la française; the Constitution of South Vietnam in 1956 was based on those of the United States and the Philippines.

Broadly speaking, these new constitutions were well-intentioned: they incorporated the traditional western ideas of civilian rule, through elected representative institutions, within a framework of public liberties. They very commonly sought to spell out important social changes of their time. Thus, the Indian Constitution of 1949 abolishes "untouchability"; the Japanese Constitution of 1947 has guarantees that include "choice of spouse," "academic freedom," and "cultured living." They are also notable as asserting the dominance of the executive, registering distrust of legislative power, and some jealousy of judicial authority. Such executive primacy reflects not only the expectation of strong leadership, of course, but the traditional deference accorded the ruler.

Formal institutions and processes can be more readily adopted, however, than the attitudes, habits, and values essential to their functioning. In all but a few of the new states, there have been lacking the basic social, cultural, economic, administrative, and political foundations necessary to the effective operation of their adopted constitutions. Some states, particularly in southeast Asia, possessed established cultural and political communities differing greatly from the western regimes superficially introduced into them. Others, especially in Africa, simply had no cultural or national community corresponding to the territorial boundaries they inherited from colonial systems. Except for a few states, therefore—such as India, the Philippine Republic, and Tunisia—the western-style constitutions have broken down. In Pakistan, for instance, the Constitution of 1956, which took nine years to frame, was abrogated in 1958; a second Constitution of 1962 was suspended in 1969; in 1971 as a committee was convened to prepare a third, the country was racked by civil war. Similarly, in its short period of independence, Ghana has had new constitutions in 1957, 1960, and 1969.

If we insist, as we must to preserve the integrity of our terms of analysis, that a constitution is present only if it controls the exercise of political power, we must conclude that the so-called constitutions of most new states in Africa and Asia are, if anything, largely "promissory notes on the future," in Professor Robert C. Bone's expressive phrase. The good intentions and sense of responsibility of leaders are not in themselves a constitution, nor are the purely *de facto* limitations on their power. Remembering that constitutional institutions emerged in the west over many centuries in circumstances that no longer exist even there, we simply cannot predict what sort of constitutions, if any, the new nonwestern states will create and maintain in the future.

Principles of Constitutionalism

We may now see that constitutional government, or constitutionalism, is government limited by a fundamental law. It does not mean government in any state where some document labeled "the Constitution" may be found. In many countries the constitution has little to do with constitutional government: such constitutions, at best, are declarations of independence and statements of intentions; at worst, they are façades behind which leaders conduct absolute rule. These "constitutions," far from controlling the rulers, are really instruments of their power. True constitutionalism, on the other hand, requires the presence of a constitution with a system of effective restraints on political power. Constitutions are not only important political facts, but are basic standards for evaluation. Whether or not a constitution is present, as truly fundamental law, is one of the most important judgments to be made about any political regime.

Constitutional Objectives. Properly, the most immediate and obvious objective of constitutionalism is the limitation of arbitrariness by defining and controlling the scope of official behavior. The constitutions in systems marked by such limitation, further, have sought to provide rational government—founded in common consent, serving the general welfare, and protecting diverse interests. More recently, they have also sought through constitutional forms to make governments effective instruments for progress.

The importance of the immediate goal of constitutionalism—to limit arbitrariness in official acts—should not be underestimated. The security of citizens depends on whether their rights and responsibilities are determinate, known to them, and effectively maintained. In constitutional government, they have been defined and implemented traditionally through "the rule of law." Modern constitutionalism has not been willing to found politics on reason alone. Instead, it has emphasized consent of the governed, and a constitution has come to be thought of as expressing this consent. The dynamic character of western culture, especially in recent times, has also obliged us to adapt to constitutional as well as social change. Increasingly, we have appraised constitutional institutions for their ability not only to protect diverse interests, but to promote diversity and progressive change as well. To retain popular loyalty and continuing consent to government, a constitution today must be an effective instrument for the advancement of society's interests.

Constitutional Mechanics. In constitutional government, a constitution is a system of devices that divides political power in the community. Such devices take two forms: those dividing power between government and governed, and those dividing power among officials. Our historical survey above gave a number of examples of institutions that do so divide power, directly or indirectly. In such institutions, officials act under rules and through machinery controlling what they do; no one is the sole judge of the legitimacy of his acts or unlimited in the exercise of power. Thus it is ensured that what government does, and how it is done, will be the expression of a broader public opinion than that of the rulers themselves.

Unlike the pseudoconstitutions of totalitarian and dictatorial systems, an effective constitution includes methods of dividing power within the government itself—systems of checks and balances, for example. Citizens are thus confronted, not with an integrated government against which they are defenseless, but with one in which many centers of power exist. To determine, then, whether a true constitution is present, one must consider: first, if the terms of public authority are limited by fundamental law receiving general support; and second, if through these rules and their machinery the exercise of political power is divided within and without the government. Both answers must be affirmative.

Constitutional Dynamics. In today's fast-changing world, neither the objectives nor the methods of a political regime can be interpreted in static terms. A feature of modern life is the advocacy and pursuit of progress; thus, the essence of the modern state lies in its legislative power and not its laws. Constitutions today must provide security in the midst of change; they must be flexible if they are to be successful. Constitutional government is indeed especially appropriate, experience shows, in periods like ours—dominated by large and heterogeneous national communities, and by scientific and technological revolutions rendering so much from yesterday obsolete. The irrational reaction to such insecure conditions may be dictatorship. But government by arbitrary commands, coercion, and terror can be an efficient instrument for only limited purposes and times.

Constitutional government alone can serve the broad objectives and utilize the diverse capacities through which a people's future can be built in freedom. Its power rests on its discipline; it is government according to rules, based on discussion and cooperation. As in science and technology, this discipline is ultimately more fruitful and powerful, as well as more acceptable, than one of commands and purges. Scientists and artists are particularly crippled in their achievements by bureaucratic dictatorship. Constitutionalism is unusually relevant, therefore, in a world which science and technology continue to shape, and which only free art can inspire. Thomas Carlyle once wrote of the ease with which constitutions can be built; "but the frightful difficulty," he said, "is that of getting men to come and live in them!"

III. Civil Liberties

As we have seen, democracy rests upon the basic propositions of government by the consent of the governed, and of possession by the governed of certain inalienable rights. Yet there are two conflicting forces here. Every person by his nature seeks to express himself without restraint; but each society seeks to oblige the individual to conform to its broader needs. How do we permit the maximum area of freedom for the individual and at the same time maintain the restraints essential to the welfare of the community? To strike a balance is not easy.

The discussion of this problem leads us, first, to clarify some terms. The words "freedom" and "liberty" are essentially synonymous, with the former derived from the Germanic and the latter from the Latin sources of the English language. Usage has given "freedom" a wider philosophical connotation, and "liberty" a more specific and limited one, though they are virtually interchangeable. "Civil liberties," broadly, are the freedom and the opportunity to do certain things without restraint from government; limitations are considered justified only when required by public welfare or to prevent abuse of liberty, though they imply no absence of restraint by individuals. "Civil rights" are positive acts of government intended to protect individuals against discriminatory treatment by government officials or other persons. Civil liberties fulfill the ideal of freedom; civil rights fulfill the ideal of equality. These concepts of necessity interrelate, as neither freedom nor equality can be much enjoyed without the other; the terms "civil liberties" and "civil rights" are thus often used interchangeably.

Government and Civil Liberties

Liberties and rights are the concrete result of significant historical experience; they are neither abstractions nor philosophical concepts, though they are sometimes so treated. Emerging in the western political tradition, they are therefore often not recognized outside it. Those who are beneficiaries of the ideals of the British, American, and French revolutions have come to know civil liberties best as realities. Yet the idea that governments serve freedom by protecting fundamental rights has now traveled around the world.

The Kinds of Civil Liberties. There is no authoritative statement of what the civil liberties are. The closest the world has come to a general expression of what they ought to be is found in the Universal Declaration of Human Rights, adopted by the General Assembly of the United Nations in 1948. Proclaimed as "a common standard of achievement for all peoples and all nations," it nevertheless has no restrictive effect on governments and stands only as a declaration.

The Declaration contains thirty articles, beginning with the proposition that all persons are born free and equal in dignity and rights, and are entitled to all rights without distinction of any kind. Article three states: "Everyone has the right to life, liberty, and security of person." Other articles affirm the prohibition of slavery, torture, and cruel treatment or punishment. A number of rights are enumerated: privacy, movement and residence, nationality, exit from any country, and asylum in other countries; also, rights to marriage and family, property, freedom of thought, conscience, and religion, peaceful assembly and association, participation in government, equal access to public service, and genuine elections. Procedural rights include the right to recognition and equality before the law, remedies for violation of rights, presumption of innocence in penal charges, and fair public trial. The Declaration states that no one is to be subjected to arbitrary arrest, detention, exile, or retroactive penal charges. Other articles define so-called "economic and social rights": social security, work, protection against unemployment, equal pay for equal work, just remuneration, trade union membership, rest and leisure, adequate standard of living, special care for mothers and children, education, and participation in the cultural life of the community.

Of special interest is article nineteen: "Everyone has the right to freedom of opinion and expression; this right includes freedom to hold opinions without interference and to seek, receive and impart information and ideas through any media and regardless of frontiers." Although framed in generous dimensions, this article does not use the specific terms "freedom of speech and press"; the many governments that engage in press and media censorship or control them outright are obviously not inhibited by it. Yet the Declaration has had value as a statement of norms and aspirations, and as a guide for some of the new states in the preparation of their constitutions.

A more specific international instrument is the European Convention on Human Rights; prepared as a treaty by the Council of Europe in 1950, it has been ratified by fifteen of the west European states, and thus imposes among themselves international obligations. Though modeled somewhat after the Universal Declaration of Human Rights, the Convention constitutes a more precise and qualified statement of the political and civil rights it guarantees. Further, it contains no enumeration of "social and economic rights," leaving these to accomplishment in other ways. The rights and freedoms specified were considered to be those established through long democratic usage and recognized in the common heritage of the west European political tradition. They include the right to life, liberty, and security of person, to own property, to marry and found a family, to respect for private and family life, and to a fair hearing on any criminal charge. The Convention also undertakes to secure freedom from inhuman treatment, slavery, retroactive criminal law, and discrimination—as well as freedom of thought, conscience, religion, expression, peaceful assembly, and association.

The European Convention, which went into effect in 1953, created a Commission and a Court of Human Rights, which in some cases may hear appeals from state courts. Their operations have not proved to be significant: many claims have been trivial; few cases have been heard on such appeals; and no state has been declared in violation of the Convention. Yet this display of concern by west European governments for basic human rights is important, as is the precedent of attempting to protect them on a regional international basis.

The Crucial Civil Liberties. In practice, civil liberties exist within the context of democratic constitutionalism. One may expect that they will differ somewhat in time and place, as historical experiences vary, but in modern democratic governments they have come to display an essential core. Characteristically, then, the substantive civil liberties protect these freedoms. First, freedom of the individual—seen as a right to life, to personal liberty, privacy, and security, freedom of movement and domicile. Second, freedom of conscience and religious practice—including also freedom from religious tests and conformity. Third, freedom of speech, press, and expression generally. Fourth, freedom of property, its possession and use—including the right to buy, sell, and contract, and equal access to such other practical valuables as jobs, education, public benefits and facilities. Fifth, freedom of political activity—including the right to peaceful association and assembly, petition of grievances, as well as to vote and take appropriate part in government.

Such rights are termed "substantive" because they specify conditions of liberty or advantage desirable for their own sake as the very essence of freedom. A sixth and distinctive category of liberties may be termed "procedural." These work in the main to guarantee substantive rights against interference and to protect people against arbitrary action in the administrative and judicial processes. Broadly they are associated with such concepts as "rule of law," "due process of law," and "equal protection of the laws," which limit the ways in which officials may proceed against an individual or his property, as well as providing more specific protections of his liberty—including rights to due notice and fair hearing, compensation for expropriated property, action for false imprisonment, writ of habeas corpus, and similar access to the courts. Those procedural civil liberties bearing on criminal charges include a presumption of innocence, right to jury trial, to confront one's accusers, legal counsel, protection against self-incrimination and double jeopardy, right of appeal to higher courts, and so on.

The procedural perspective presented here is that of the common-law system; specific procedural rights vary in other legal systems and are rarely so generous to the accused. The distinction between substantive and procedural rights, one may also note, is not absolute; without the support of procedural rights the substantive cannot survive. All substantive and procedural rights are essentially negative in character as stipulations of what government may not do to the individual or how it may not act. In recent years the enumeration as civil liberties of various "economic and social rights"—such as to work, rest, food, medical care, and shelter—or of such "human rights" as freedom from fear and want, however, constitute positive stipulations and stand very differently from restraints imposed on government. They are not generally amenable to judicial enforcement, nor even, practically, to administrative implementation, as far as the individual is concerned. Such statements of positive rights are more nearly aspirations to some broad ideas of social justice; their fulfillment depends upon a country's wealth and public policies.

Civil Liberties and the Constitutional Order. The rights of men are claimed by some as natural and inalienable; others see them as only concessions by government; and to still others they are policies relative to particular conditions and orders. Whatever their source or foundation, civil liberties take form only where they can be defended as well as defined. In modern government definition usually takes the form of a declaration or bill of rights to be protected as part of the fundamental law in a documentary constitution.

Yet this is not always the case. In Great Britain, with the oldest and strongest tradition of civil liberty, there is no such declaration. In English law, the rights of the citizen do not depend upon a formal guarantee of any constitutional component. Contrasting the English constitution with those of other states nearly a century ago, Professor A. V. Dicey proudly concluded: "freedom of person is not a special privilege but the outcome of the ordinary law of the land enforced by the courts." The marked respect for individual liberty so early characteristic of English law, indeed, was registered in the Magna Carta of 1215: "No free man shall be taken or imprisoned or dispossessed, or outlawed, or banished, or in any way destroyed, nor will we go upon him, nor send upon him, except by the legal judgment of his peers or by the law of the land." There are well-established limits to all rights in the British system, of course; but they rest in substance upon the proposition that the citizen's liberty results, as one observer put it, "from the principle that he may say or do what he pleases, provided he does not commit breaches of the substantive law or infringe the legal rights of others." Thus British civil liberties are a product of centuries of historical precedent, of assorted judicial rulings and parliamentary statutes, and of attitudes widely shared by the British people.

Although some specific rights were enumerated in the body of the

Constitution of the United States as drafted in 1787, the Bill of Rights was added in the form of the first ten amendments in 1791. Considered an integral part of the Constitution, it contained the most far-reaching guarantees: "Congress shall make no law respecting an establishment of religion, or prohibiting the free exercise thereof; or abridging the freedom of speech, or of the press; or the right of the people peaceably to assemble, and to petition the Government for a redress of grievances." (First Amendment), and "no person shall be . . . deprived of life, liberty, or property, without due process of law; . . ." (Fifth Amendment). The declaration of rights in such broad and unqualified terms has meant, however, that they could not always be maintained as written; and as statements of somewhat abstract principle, they have required extensive interpretation. This situation, along with the emergence of the practice of judicial review, brought to the courts the function and responsibility of redefining American civil liberties. The result of such judicial interpretation has given those rights a markedly legalistic cast, and led to the popular view that the Supreme Court is the principal guardian of American civil liberties. Although legislative and administrative interpretations have not been unimportant, the Supreme Court as a rule has ultimately decided what governmental restraints on basic rights will be allowed.

Another widely influential statement of civil liberties is the Declaration of the Rights of Man and the Citizen, adopted by the French National Assembly in 1789. A document of seventeen clauses following a preamble, and based upon the American Declaration of Independence, 1776, this Declaration came ultimately to be an integral part of French constitutional theory and practice. Resolving "to set forth in a solemn declaration the natural, inalienable, and sacred rights of man," the document stipulated that "men are born and remain free and equal in rights," and that "the natural and imprescriptible rights of man" are "liberty, property, security, and resistance to oppression." The Declaration recites most of the conventional civil rights; but of special interest are its statements that "Liberty consists in the power to do anything that does not injure others," and that "the law has the right to forbid only such actions as are injurious to society." These typically reflect a continental European viewpoint giving considerable latitude to the realm of personal behavior. The French Constitution of 1958 in its first sentence states: "The French people hereby solemnly proclaims its attachment to the Rights of

Man . . ." and speaks subsequently of the judicial authority as "guardian of individual liberty." Though constitutional arrangements thus give judicial protection to civil liberties, it must be emphasized that in a society where liberty has often been used to attack public authority, rights against the state tend to be narrowly interpreted where the public security is concerned.

In the German Federal Republic, by way of final example, the Basic Law ("Bonn Constitution") of 1949 contains in its first nineteen articles a statement of basic rights. These are generously stated in considerable detail, with a concluding specification that "Should any person's right be violated by public authority, recourse to the court shall be open to him." The Constitution further provides that when a basic right may be restricted by law, the law must apply generally and not solely to an individual case; and "in no case may a basic right be infringed upon in its essential content." "Whoever abuses freedom," it also stipulates, "in order to attack the free democratic basic order, forfeits these basic rights." The framers of the German Constitution were still sensitive to their totalitarian experience and discarded the older legalistic view that laws would enforce themselves. Throughout, the Constitution shows a determination to ensure that both law and the courts be able to deal effectively with political threats to the democratic system.

Civil Liberties and Government Procedures. Whatever the particular techniques attempted to define and protect civil liberties, it should be clear that no bill of rights can in itself guarantee what liberties will be effectively maintained. Declarations of principle can be influential, but they cannot define the precise nature of civil liberties. Even specific constitutional provisions are likely to fail in this respect because of lack of flexibility in changing conditions. Consequently, the liberties that people desire and governments recognize continually must be redefined in day-to-day politics under the influence of public opinion and in the operations of the executive, legislative, and judicial institutions.

Thus, civil liberties cannot be independent of the political and legal machinery of government; only those liberties exist which are effectively protected by government. Civil liberties are not the foundation of a constitution but a fundamental aspect of it, manifested as much in the procedures of the constitution as in any bill of rights. As a good example of how totalitarian states say one thing and do another, the 1936 Constitution of the Soviet Union contains a chapter on "Fundamental Rights and Duties of Citizens," which speaks of freedom of speech, press, and assembly—rights which are to be exercised, however, only "in conformity with the interests of the working people [the dictatorship], and in order to strengthen the socialist [communist] system." Even within these limitations, they are still not enjoyable or enforceable rights, which would be incompatible with communist dictatorship. Indeed, persons who write and distribute unofficial "self-publications" (*samizdat*) are subject to heavy penalties.

No rights can be enjoyed absolutely, of course, however democratic the state. "My freedom to swing my arm," Justice Holmes once said, "stops where the other man's nose begins." Limits to civil liberties have always been necessary to preserve public order and peace. Further, in recent times the powers and responsibilities of governments have expanded, as much by popular demand and need as by official imposition, so that the requirements of public order and peace are more invasive than ever before. In the interest of some social good, limitations on individual freedom barely conceivable a century ago are now commonplace. This is particularly evident with property and economic activity; but it extends even to the use of such democratic liberties as speech, press, and assembly if in our great urbanized communities life is to be peaceful. The rewards of freedom are also its perils.

Civil Liberties Today

Modern western culture, after a long evolution with much uncertainty, has embraced the ideal of freedom for all men more completely than any other in history. In upholding the ideal of liberty and creating conditions within which it can flourish, western societies have moved almost steadily forward. Yet civil liberties are not widely enjoyed throughout the world; in many political systems other ends are valued far more highly than freedom for the individual. Even in democratic societies, liberty must be balanced against other social goods.

Civil Liberties in Practice. "Nature hath put this tincture in our blood, that each would be a tyrant if he could." Daniel Defoe long ago observed how natural it seems to some to repress the liberty of others. In the totalitarian states, the twin blankets of an official press and a government censorship seek to insulate the people against reading, seeing, or hearing anything but what the state wants them to. In the Soviet Union, for example, Lenin made the communist position clear from the beginning, as he asked: "Why should freedom of speech and freedom of the press be allowed? Why should a government which is doing what it believes to be right allow itself to be criticized? It would not allow opposition by lethal weapons. Ideas are much more fatal than guns." Stalin made it emphatic in 1927: "We have no freedom of the press for the bourgeoisie. . . . But what is surprising in that? We have never pledged ourselves to grant freedom of the press to all classes, to make all classes happy. . . ." In this respect nothing has changed in half a century. A Russian underground "self-publication" relays the words of the Leningrad party secretary to a Soviet mathematician in April, 1970, before he was jailed: "If you think that we'll let everyone say and write just what they like, that will never happen. We do still have enough power not to let people commit acts which will harm us. Never will there be any concessions at all in the sphere of ideology."

Elsewhere in the communist world, the Soviet pattern is observable with only minor variations. The Chinese Communist regime not only imposes a barrier against information from the outside but conducts a high-pitched and aggressive propaganda program through the press, radio, films, and wall newspapers. In eastern Europe, the regimes have not usually published a government newspaper, such as the Soviet's *Izvestia;* but all papers are directly supervised by the government, receive the bulk of their news from government press agencies, and provide party views only on all subjects. In recent years, severity of censorship has been marked in East Germany and Albania, and modestly relaxed in Yugoslavia (though writers are still jailed for being too critical) and Czechoslovakia (until the Soviet military occupation). In all these countries the core of the censorship system continues to be the secret security police, with power of arbitrary arrest and imprisonment. Moreover the Soviet Union and Poland have again adopted official policies of anti-Semitism, under the guise of anti-Zionism. Compounding this intolerance is the Soviet Union's persistent refusal to honor the right of a citizen to exit from his country; instead an illegal effort to leave is a serious offense. East Germany and Cuba offer other examples of the state as concentration camp.

In countries outside the grip of totalitarianism, also, the most basic rights go unprotected. Only a few illustrations are offered here. In some parts of the Arabic Middle East, the United Nations reports, Africans are still bought and sold as slaves—some while on holy pilgrimage to Mecca. There have been major massacres in recent years of Chinese in Indonesia, Biafrans in Nigeria, Moslems in India, Bengalis in Pakistan, and Negroes in the Sudan. Overt racial or religious discrimination—often accompanied by violence and riots—is practiced against Asians in east Africa, Chinese in Malaysia, Irish Catholics in Northern Ireland, and Basques in Spain.

More subtle, but still insidious, are repressions practiced in countries which try civilian political offenders in military courts—as in Algeria, Greece, and Iraq. Emergency Provisions of the Indian Constitution (Part XVIII) have been employed with supplementary legislation for years at a time to suspend rights, justify preventive detentions, and outlaw organizations. South Africa has long maintained a policy of racial segregation (*apartheid*), which requires ever more repressive restrictions, detentions, and imprisonments in the interest of public security. Political prisoners are a reality in much of the world.

Civil Liberties in Free Societies. No civil liberties are ever exercised without limits even in the freest societies. The problem, of course, is where to set limits. Much of the significant controversy over civil liberties in free societies turns on the issue of freedom of expression, and we may examine it by way of example. A long recognized exception to free expression is found in laws against slander and libel: speech or writings that defame the character of another; bringing him into contempt, hatred, or ridicule; injuring him in his calling or profession; or imputing to him criminal behavior. Since whispering campaigns and character assassinations do occur in politics, the definition of what is not "protected expression" is important. In the British tradition the attitude is still conservative, with the standards for slander and libel extremely strict; attacks there on personal reputation do not occur in politics as freely as in the United States or France. The United States Supreme Court has ruled, however, that slander and libel do not apply to comment about public officials or figures, unless malicious intent is proved, because such comment is in the public interest (*New York Times* v. *Sullivan*, 1964). In American public affairs, officials and active citizens are required to be thick-skinned.

In contrast to slander and libel, which are generally enforced by civil actions for damages, obscenity is punished by criminal prosecution and deprivation of public services, as use of the mails or entry through customs. Definitions of "obscenity" and their application have long aroused much disagreement. In the United States the Supreme Court has ruled that obscene publications are not within the constitutionally protected area of free speech and press. It has also defined the "obscene" by the standard "whether to the average person, applying contemporary community standards, the dominant theme of the material taken as a whole appeals to prurient interest" (*Roth* v. *United States*, 1957). The "obscene" is thus defined narrowly to be materials "utterly without redeeming social value." As the result of changes in public attitudes, standards, and declared interests—materials, books, films, and theater heretofore repressed have become freely available in the United States, subject only to restriction for the protection of children, and of adults who do not wish sexually explicit material in their mail.

The American Commission on Obscenity and Pornography, further, asserting in its 1970 report that obscenity does not cause antisocial conduct, reached the conclusion that "there is no warrant for continued governmental interference with the full freedom of adults to read, obtain or view whatever such material they wish" and recommended generally that laws interfering with that right be repealed. The British position in practice is also now close to the American; in 1969 the Committee of the Arts Council, a quasi-official body, recommended repeal of laws prohibiting obscenity. Only Denmark has done this, however; amendments to its penal code in 1967 and 1969 removed all prohibitions in the distribution of obscene materials to adults. Israel has penal laws against obscenity; but courts have applied the *Roth* definition as above and erotic materials are widely available. Much the same standard now prevails in West Germany, Sweden, and other north European states. By contrast, Australia not only bans pornography, but maintains a rigorous censorship that excludes many books, films, and other materials circulating freely elsewhere. The Irish Republic censors books and films under a law prohibiting works that have a tendency to corrupt; among the many books banned are George Orwell's *1984*.

A further restriction on expression has been the offense of blasphemy. A misdemeanor at English common law, blasphemy consists in irreverently ridiculing or impugning the doctrines of the Christian faith, Jesus Christ, or exposing the Scriptures to contempt or ridicule. The offense of blasphemous libel is also punishable; an English conviction was upheld as recently as 1922. In the United States, statutes have defined the offense in many states; but in both countries the law has fallen into disuse. In 1965, the Finnish government prosecuted an author and a publisher for blasphemy because of antireligious words in a book. Finally, virtually all countries have imposed restrictions on expression in wartime. Censorship is commonly imposed to protect military plans, troop movements and morale, and other information believed to be of value to an enemy. There is usually little objection raised to such practices in the midst of war; controversy may arise, however, when governments use a plea of military security to cover information that is nonmilitary.

Most immediately and generally significant for politics has been the restriction of expression by sedition. In law, sedition is the effort to disturb the peace and tranquility of the state. Sedition was originally an English common-law misdemeanor—taking the form of seditious libel, meeting, or conspiracy. It thus covered wide areas of political expression and behavior. Seditious libel is largely what remains of the offense in England today, and it is narrowly interpreted. It allows the freest public discussion and criticism of government, but still penalizes language directly intended to incite public disorder—such as riot, rebellion, insurrection, physical force and violence—or to subvert the police or the armed forces. French officials have similar powers and used them against the violence of students' and workers' strikes in the Paris disorders of 1968. The American Sedition Acts of 1798 and 1918 imposed severe restrictions on seditious speech. More recently, the Smith Act of 1940 made it unlawful to teach, advocate, or distribute information advocating forcible overthrow of government or to have membership in an organization that does so. The law was sustained by the Supreme Court, upholding the conviction of some top Communist party leaders (*Dennis* v. *United States,* 1951). The Court modified its interpretation somewhat later by holding that punishable advocacy of revolution must be accompanied by active participation in illegal activities (*Scales* v. *United States,* 1961). As a last example, there is a guarantee of freedom of expression in the Italian Constitution; but the penal code defines the crime of "contempt" (*vilipendio*) as disrespectful statements or actions concerning the state, the head of state, the Church, the Pope, the armed forces, the police, and so on.

Liberty and Responsibility. The idea of civil liberties—of individual rights limited only by the minimal necessities of peace and order, and the preservation of the similar rights of others—is one of the great achievements of western political thought. Totalitarian communities do not honor the idea in theory or practice; for they deny the value of individuality, upon which it is based, and the constitutional restraints on official power, which are necessary to its preservation. Only a small number of states—the constitutional democracies—have realized the ideal of civil liberty in practice. Yet that liberty has been threatened in ways that could scarcely have been foreseen even a few decades ago. These are threats raised not by reactionary governments nor repressive societies; in recent years the atmosphere of social self-consciousness, particularly in the United States, is so pervasive as to make concern for individual rights nearly universal. The threats are raised instead by the abuse or misuse of rights.

The protection of civil liberties compatible with civil order has been made substantially more difficult in the democracies recently by the use of confrontation as a form of expression. The confrontation produces behavior ranging from the outrageous to the illegal, thus ensuring wide publicity and intense reaction. The tactic assures that dissent will not be ignored, but it also exacerbates conflicts and inhibits their rational solution. In extreme form confrontation is a revolutionary tactic rather than an exercise of freedom of speech and assembly; when conducted through aggressive mass demonstrations, as it has been practiced, with some of its participants engaging in violence, it frequently provokes some counterviolence by police or public, as it was calculated to do. A nineteenth-century French sociologist, Gustave Le Bon, pointed out that persons transformed into a mob feel, think, and act quite differently from what they do as individuals, yielding to instincts that if acting alone they would have kept under restraint. A mob, he said, "descends several rungs in the order of civilization."

Mob tactics, appearing in the past decade, have been employed most commonly in the very states most hospitable to the protection of individual rights—in France, Great Britain, Japan, the Netherlands, Sweden, the United States, and West Berlin. Street mobs led by militants and radicals have attacked government officials, public buildings, private property, and disrupted traffic, public meetings, and the normal activities of schools, universities, and government offices.

Claiming to protest over issues ranging from war and foreign policy to educational procedures and assorted social ills, they were not seeking a judicial or political test of a claim that a particular policy or law is unconstitutional, undesirable, or imposed on the majority against its will. They simply proclaimed this to be so, on occasion making "nonnegotiable demands" that called for the surrender of responsible authorities and attempting to silence all who disagreed with them. In some cases, the sequel to such demonstrations has been severe rioting and bombing, and bringing death and injury to persons, destruction of property, and other clearly criminal acts.

Such tactics are those not of persons devoted to civil liberties, but of persons determined to abuse them. They are also self-defeating. Closing a university does not make it a better educational institution, much less change a state's foreign policy. Screaming obscenities at public officials does not make them more reasonable or moral. Bombing a public building cannot eliminate police forces. As Leon Trotsky, a real revolutionary, observed, "Every policeman knows that though the Government may change the police remain." The politics of confrontation—manifesting no respect for common sense, law, or authority—is an attempt at coercion. And the new radicals who practice it must surely know that civil liberty in consequence is threatened, both by themselves and by the reactions from society their behavior elicits. Taking disputes out of the streets and into peaceful legislative chambers was one of the great accomplishments of democracy.

Another threat to liberty today is raised by those who misuse freedom of expression and thought. The great tradition of academic freedom, for example, has been for centuries the right of qualified teachers and students, proceeding in detached and objective scholarship, to discover and disseminate the truth within their discipline, and to permit others the same freedom. Academic freedom rests upon individual integrity, honesty, and dedication, and has its justification in permitting the profession of scholarship to be conducted autonomously and without interference from the outside. In recent years, however, some have sought to reverse this tradition—aiming to politicize institutions of higher learning, to convert them into agencies of social change. At the same time some have sought to use academic freedom as a defense against retaliation for such misuse of academic privilege and university autonomy. No major university—from Berkeley, Berlin, Cambridge, Columbia, to the Sorbonne—has escaped these efforts.

Numerous observers have also remarked another feature of contemporary academic life, the "mass consensus of intellectuals." For instance, a Carnegie Commission survey in 1969, asking for political self-description of over 1200 American political scientists, brought this response: left, 13.8% ; liberal, 58% ; middle of the road, 16.2% ; moderately conservative, 8.4% ; and strongly conservative, 0.7%. Faculty members in other social sciences showed similar inclinations.

The growing politicization of the intellectual world is not confined to the social sciences, nor even the universities and colleges. Lionel Trilling, a literary critic, has been writing for some time about what he first termed "the adversary culture." And as an American sociologist, Daniel Bell, recently observed, "the protagonists of the adversary culture, despite their sincere and avowed subversive intentions, do substantially influence, if not dominate, the cultural establishments today—the publishing houses, museums, galleries; the major news, picture, and cultural weeklies and monthlies; the theater, film, and the universities." Such intellectual like-mindedness cannot be healthy. And it has bred a new intolerance totally out of place in academia.

"Men are qualified for civil liberty in exact proportion to their disposition to put moral chains upon their own appetites," wrote Edmund Burke. "Society cannot exist unless a controlling power upon will and appetite be placed somewhere, and the less of it there is within, the more there must be without. It is ordained in the eternal constitution of things that men of intemperate minds cannot be free. Their passions forge their fetters." In each nation the history of civil liberties manifests the balance which has there been struck between liberties and responsibilities; it is the history of how much freedom men have actually learned to live with. Nowhere has the final chapter yet been written.

5

Interests and Opinion

"A MAN'S skin sits closer to him than his shirt." And so men think more carefully, as a rule, about their own immediate concerns than about the general welfare; they are more likely to perceive their special interests in politics than those of the general public. Thus we now seek to provide a vantage point from which to observe the political process at closer range and more narrowly conceived—that is, the interaction of men in the day-to-day activities of achieving political goals.

Perhaps the most useful approach is through a twofold perspective toward popular political activity. On the one hand, in traditional democratic thought man is seen acting formally as a citizen and voter, motivated by a sense of civic duty and by appeals to his rational judgment of the public interest; he associates with others through a political party; and his political opinions are registered by votes in elections and plebiscites. He is, in a sense, acting thus as a public person. On the other hand, modern political science has come to consider of great importance that man may also be seen acting informally as an individual and as a member of diverse groups and categories, manifesting a variety of interests and idiosyncrasies. His political opinions are thus partly assessable through polls and interviews, furnishing data for sociological and psychological analysis. This is man acting as a private person in his relation to government. In the present chapter we shall employ this perspective, returning in the following chapter to man as a public person.

I. Interests and Their Organization

Man, being a gregarious creature, is always found in groups of some sort. The kinds of groupings that can be made because of man's differential characteristics—according to whether he is left-handed, long-headed, or leaf-eating—are not relevant to our purposes; for men do not ordinarily associate on the basis of such characteristics alone. Of greater concern to social science are those groupings which reflect that men have values, ideas, and interests; that they are ambitious, yet weak except when cooperating with others; and that they seek through combining with others to promote their purposes. Though all such groups—whether familial, religious, social, vocational, economic, or other—may have some significance to the governmental process, political science is especially concerned with interest groups.

Interest Group Defined. For present purposes we prefer to simplify rather than complicate attempts to define the variously used term "interest group." We shall employ it to describe any collection of persons with common objectives who seek the realization of those objectives through political action to influence public policy. Still more simply, an interest group is any particular group that wants something from government. Other terms inevitably come to mind. "Pressure group" is employed by some writers in an invidious sense to label political groups whose methods or objectives they deem questionable or reprehensible; other writers use it merely as a synonym for "interest group." Yet "pressure group" is not so neutral a term, and suggests methods which are not always employed; groups may persuade as well as pressure. Our preference is for the term "interest group," and for separate judgments on tactics and ends. "Lobby" is also a well-worn political term, employed in some instances to denote interest groups or their agents. It seems preferable, however, to employ "lobby" in its original sense as an attempt directly and immediately to influence the decisions of legislative and executive officials. Individuals, corporations, and other bodies—as well as organized interest groups—may undertake lobbying.

Interest Politics and Their Importance. The realm of interest politics—the various ways in which individuals add their informal influence to their formal impact upon government—is a broad one. The representation of interests is unquestionably an important and central phenomenon of modern politics. In our previous discussions we have generally assumed that private interests are the foundation of the state, which exists entirely to promote them. And if the state is to be effective in this purpose, it is clear that those interests must possess ways of expressing themselves and influencing the development of public policy. Otherwise, they will be ignored—as is often the case in communist regimes, where, despite the claims of theory, only those interests acceptable to the party and its leaders are promoted. In the ebb and flow of political activity in the liberal democratic regimes, on the other hand, representatives of diverse private interests exercise influence, contend for dominance on issues involving them, and participate actively in the formulation and execution of public policy.

Yet in the recognition of the place of interests in modern politics some extremely important considerations are often overlooked. We are inclined to accept too simple a view of what these interests are, who has them, and how and under what conditions they are manifested. The whole picture is more than an enlarged version of those parts which we can bring into clear focus. Consequently, students of political life have historically assumed, with some oversimplification, that the active forces in politics are *either* the community as a whole (or its leaders), *or* the various social groupings comprising it, *or* the many individual persons who, as citizens, make up the commonwealth. The great political theories which have informed the western imagination have endeavored to combine all of these perspectives, yet always to accord one of them particular dominance.

In recent decades, the dominant theme in political analysis has been the second of the above perspectives. Philosophers and political scientists alike have tended to doubt both the real existence of "the community as a whole," and of individuals with interests taking action independent of group association. They have seen politics as the manifestation of conflicting group interests and the controversy or bargaining which such conflicting interests produce. According to this view, the individual, insofar as he is politically important, is relegated to acting as a member of such groups; and the community as a whole is manifested only in the rules of the game upon which the various groups have generally agreed.

The Formation and Organization of Interest Groups. Sociologists give a great deal of attention to the nature and structure of groups generally, and have demonstrated how complex and multiformed they are. We need not survey that ground here; but even so, we shall be obliged to adopt a fairly abstract view of groups for the purposes of analysis. Interest groups arise under many different circumstances, as when a number of people share common concerns or problems, whether in bird-watching or the conservation of natural resources; when they seek common objectives or support common causes, as prohibition or international peace; when they engage in common activities, as coal miners or stamp collectors; when they are gathered in a common location, as downtown merchants or suburban homeowners; when they are producers or consumers of common products or services, as naval stores or ferryboat commuters; and so on. The point is that interest groups come into existence because such experiences produce shared attitudes and a conscious mutuality of purpose; they induce reciprocal relationships; and they may encourage concerted action to make some political demand.

Although we have ample demonstration that men necessarily compete for the attainment of their ends, it is equally important that they also cooperate. Within any given group, the extent to which they do can vary enormously. Many interest groups are entirely unorganized; a collection of taxpayers, or consumers, or people who share a common skill, language, or religion may have only a vague sense of common interest, and the most limited sort of interaction. Yet they are not necessarily politically unimportant. They may have some self-chosen leaders and spokesmen; and even if they do not, political leaders, government officials, legislative representatives, or others may make decisions or take action with the specific group very much in mind.

Economists are aware of the phenomenon of consumer sovereignty —the power of entirely unorganized consumers to refuse to purchase everything offered in the market, whether ahead of or behind current tastes, and thus pronounce against their producers punishing economic judgments. There are full political analogies to this behavior; politicians, too, must compete for "consumer" support. Public policy is distinctly affected when groups of people behave—even if most spontaneously—in a certain political way; while this is true in any political system, it is especially so in a democracy. Many significant groups, then, particularly in the simpler societies, may not be organized. And important groups in advanced societies may choose to re-

main unorganized and to refrain from conscious concerted action because their members may feel that their influence is greater if their
attitudes are not too easily predictable—or, no less important, precisely because they are getting what they want from government!
Similarly, groups that have achieved their goals may disband their
formal association.

Clearly, a number of factors do encourage the members of a group
—or some of them—to organize and thus form themselves into an association. Most important, perhaps, as government extends its regulatory activity, raises its levels of taxing and spending, and penetrates
ever more deeply into the realm of private interests, the group may
feel obliged to organize in order to defend its position. Second, as
men become more specialized in their functions and activities, and
develop refinements in their interests beyond the concern of political
parties, they seek to promote their objectives through separate organizations. Thus, they may conclude that, in a society of many highly organized groups, the unorganized are not receiving their share of attention and government is not responding to their wants; they hope
to intensify their influence by organizing, designating leaders, disci-
plining members, and conducting sustained and persistent programs.
Third, the complexity of government and society has made the representation of group interests—the conduct of public relations, propaganda, and lobbying, for example—a highly specialized process requiring expert leadership and management available only to the
organized group.

The formation of an association within an interest group—the formalization of membership, agreement upon objectives, selection of officers, and so forth—may have various consequences, not all of which
are necessarily intended. Organization attracts the attention of other
associations, and of some individuals outside the group; their opposition to and competition with the newly organized group's aims may
be intensified. The fact that an association is formed does not automatically increase its strength; members may then expect the organization to exert all necessary efforts and may discontinue their own.
On the other hand, some associations have a wider support than the
size of their formal membership would indicate; they may have numerous adherents or fellow travelers. In a formal organization, leadership and control tend to fall into the hands of a minority, in an oligarchic pattern common to such bodies. At the same time, leadership

is often more moderate or more extremist than the membership; and, because it is not truly representative, may not best serve group interests. Organization generally promotes greater similarity of attitude among members, though, and increases their loyalty to group interest. Pronouncements by officers, meetings, conventions, official journals, and the use of propaganda, symbols, and slogans—all work to standardize thinking to some degree and emphasize the need for cooperation, discipline, and concerted action.

The Classification of Interest Groups. Various proposals have been made for the classification of interest groups, yet no single system appears adequate to reveal every significant feature. Professor Gabriel A. Almond, however, has developed one that distinguishes four kinds of structures. The first contains *institutional* interest groups, or organizations commonly existing to perform functions within government itself, which by their nature accumulate important vested interests to promote. Examples include government departments, such as the treasury or ministry of agriculture, armed services, central banks, or other bureaucratic groups. The second contains *nonassociational* interest groups, or those based on class, kinship, religion, or other traditional characteristics, whose basis of communication is often informal and intermittent. The third contains *anomic* interest groups, or those largely spontaneous in character, such as demonstrators, protest marchers, street mobs, or rioters. Such groups tend to break into the political arena suddenly and may aim at a show of force or violence. Of course, such groups may be deliberately organized or abetted, and their spontaneity, entirely a pretense. The fourth contains *associational* interest groups, or those formally organized to represent the interests of particular persons and to enjoy the advantages that such association provides in dealing with other political structures.

Associational interest groups, which are highly developed in the advanced societies of the western world, have been variously distinguished in other ways. They have been classified as self-interested, for example, the National Association of Manufacturers, or disinterested, for example, the Council for the Preservation of Rural England—with the difference, of course, based upon whether they promote particular and private, or universal and public interests. A difficulty immediately arises with this classification, however. Can we say that the Navy League, for instance, which seeks a strong navy and a high level of naval preparedness on behalf of national defense—certainly a public interest—is not also promoting the private interests of naval officers and shipbuilders? Many groups are at the same time self- and public-interested. Again, interest groups have been classified as to those interested exclusively in public policy, such as the League of Women Voters, and those concerned with a variety of functions, for example, the National Grange. Still other classifications have distinguished groups as offensive and defensive, economic and noneconomic, elite and mass, unitary and federated, and so on. Finally, it is common to classify groups according to the kinds of interests with which they are concerned—such as business, labor, agriculture, professional, veteran, civic, or religious. Within any such class, it should be noted, groups may compete among themselves; the interests of small business may be in conflict with those of large, cattle ranchers may oppose sheepherders, and one taxpayers' group may be in controversy with another.

What of the distinctions between interest groups and political parties? In the broadest terms, a party is also an interest group; yet there is justification for seeing that they have fundamentally separate as well as certain similar roles in the political process. It is traditionally asserted that the basic difference arises over whether a political association offers candidates for office and is thus willing in some sense to assume responsibility for its influence on public policy; a political party meets such a test and an interest group does not. The distinction is undoubtedly clearer within a state having a biparty system, where the two major parties not only offer candidates for office but take positions on most of the main issues of public policy. Where a multiparty system exists, or a number of minor parties operate, the difference between party and interest group is narrowed; a political group may well give rise to a new party, and small parties may revert to interest group status.

The American Prohibition party emerged largely from various prohibitionist groups, and has generally remained a one-issue party. The British Labour party was an outgrowth of the trade union movement; this has been the case, indeed, with many socialist parties. After World War II associations such as the German *Bund der Heimatvertriebenen und Entrechteten* (League of the Homeless and Disfranchised) and the French *Poujadistes* moved from interest group to party status and back again within a few years. In Israel, which has a political system including more than two dozen parties, many of the smaller ones are in fact little more than interest groups. Nevertheless, there is always a main difference: a political party submits its claims periodically to the stern and objective test of an election, whereas an interest group does not; unlike a party, it never assumes responsibility for the operation of the government.

The Variety of Associational Interest Groups. Interest groups are by no means a contemporary phenomenon alone. Even in medieval times, interests were represented by estates, by guilds of professional men and artisans, by cities, and by large property owners. Yet these were hardly voluntary associations; due to social and religious circumstances, individuals did not choose the groups of which they were members—indeed, they were the virtual prisoners of them. It is difficult to say precisely when or where nonparty political associations first appeared. They are clearly a concomitant of industrial societies and in their modern form could only become significant in liberal democracies, necessarily accompanied by representative government, a party system, freedom of organization, and a general recognition that there may be diverse ideas as to what government should do. In Britain, their origins are marked in the foundation of such bodies as the Society for Supporting the Bill of Rights (1769), National Union of Working Classes (1831), Howard League for Penal Reform (1866), Trades Union Congress (1869), and National Anti-Vivisection Society (1875). Comparable entities were also organized in the United States, including the American Temperance Society (1826), National Anti-Slavery League (1833), American Medical Association (1846), Modern Language Association (1883), the American Federation of Labor (1886), and Sons of Norway (1895). Each of these organizations illustrates something of the character of interests and causes which then were concerns of public policy.

In the twentieth century, associational interest groups have emerged more widely, wherever democratic and representative government extends. Though now quite universally encountered, their nature, diversity, and role in any particular country are related to political circumstances. In the United States, notorious as a nation of joiners, they number in the thousands, in bodies as varied as the American Sunbathing Association and the People Against Unconstitutional Sex Education. In Great Britain, their number and variety are no less—reflecting again the Anglo-Saxon proclivity to embrace causes and organize—demonstrated in associations ranging from the Licensed Victuallers Defence League to the Lord's Day Observance Society. In Latin countries, such as France and Italy, where the sense of public-spiritedness is less developed, interest groups tend for the most part to be self-interested; yet thoughtful people in these countries behold with some wonderment civic-minded societies in which human behavior nonetheless apparently makes it necessary to organize a National Society for the Prevention of Cruelty to Children, as in Britain, or a Society to Maintain Public Decency, as in the United States. Interest groups in France are much more likely to aim at protecting "acquired rights," styling themselves "Society for the Defense of the Rights of——" (taxpayers, banks, peasants, mongrels, or whatever may be). In states with strong authoritarian and bureaucratic traditions, such as Germany and Japan, interest groups have heretofore been inhibited, though they have begun to flourish under current regimes. The attitude toward such groups generally in the autocratic governments of the nineteenth and early twentieth centuries was repressive, denying them the opportunity to operate openly. Eventually, they were either stifled outright or converted into underground and revolutionary conspiracies, ultimately forming many of the extremist groups of the political world. In general, too, the presence of a multiparty system—in which the several parties reflect many narrow economic and ideological interests—also discourages interest group organization.

Any general survey of political associations quickly demonstrates how preponderantly they do reflect economic interests. This is probably an indication not so much that man's objectives are primarily and mainly economic—important as those are—but that economic affairs are widely regulated by government and that economic means are as well the most obvious and immediate to man's goals. The realm of business is characterized by a variety of organizations, and these are found, much alike, in all industrially developed states. We encounter, for instance, the Confederation of British Industries, the Federation of German Industry, the Swedish Export Association, and the National Council of French Employers. Agricultural interests produce such bodies as the American Farm Bureau Federation, the National Association of Swedish Farmers, the (Finnish) Union of Agricultural Producers, and the Dairy Farmers of Canada. Labor is invariably represented in such national organizations as the Confederation of Mexican Workers, the (French) General Confederation of Labor, and the German Workers' Union.

Professional groups are illustrated by associations such as the (British) National Union of Teachers, the Australian Dental Association, and the American Bar Association. Veterans' groups are equally ubiquitous—the American Legion, the Canadian Legion, the French Union of Associations of Combatants and Victims of War, and the (Australian) Returned Services League. Consumers undertake to protect their interests through such bodies as the (French) National Federation of Consumer Cooperatives, the (Japanese) Federation of Housewives, the (Swedish) Cooperative Union, the (Australian) Housewives Association, and the (American) Consumers Union. In the category of civic associations, we have the examples of the (American) National Congress of Parents and Teachers, the (British) Hansard Society for Parliamentary Government, and the (French) Association for the Protection and Improvement of Historical Paris. Many other western countries have their counterparts to these bodies; they only illustrate the ways in which individuals, through many different kinds of groups, enlarge their participation in public affairs and promote the various civic, economic, and vocational interests they share with others.

II. Interest Groups in the Political Process

The range of techniques which interest groups may employ to promote their ends is extensive; we can examine them here only in summary fashion. In general, organized groups have two principal alternative strategies: to influence government, with its organs and officials, directly; or to influence the public—through individuals, political parties, and opinion media—and so exert an impact on government indirectly. Many groups, of course, undertake to do both, hoping thus to ensure their optimum effectiveness.

The selection of strategies and techniques for any group is by no means arbitrary; it is distinctly conditioned by group nature, membership, means, and aims. The kind of government within which operations are undertaken is also important—devices usefully employed in a presidential system may not be effective in a parliamentary one. The nature of the party system and the whole national political climate are also decisive. Group activities are welcomed in some countries or accepted as a matter of fact; in the totalitarian states they are rigorously controlled or suppressed.

Interest Groups and Government. First of all, in representative government, groups are much attracted to the legislative institution. Here important decisions of public policy are made, and the opportunity is broadly presented to obtain or oppose not only legislation generally but the all-important tax and appropriation measures as well. The legislative process offers many different stages when any particular bill may be critically affected; hence the importance of lobbying —persuasively communicating with individual legislators, committee chairmen, and other parliamentary officers.

Lobbying may well involve attempts to apply pressure on such persons, but this is by no means the only or even the most effective technique. Providing legislators with information, statistics, and research studies is common, and there may be opportunity to testify in committee hearings. Nor should it be supposed that all lobbying is unwelcome. Legislators frequently depend on it to assist their decisions; without the contact provided by group agents they could well lose touch with important group needs. Other methods utilized by groups in this realm include seeking the election of some of their own members to the legislature, supporting or opposing the election—or reelection—of others, organizing pressure from the constituencies, and so on. Some legislators are amenable to the influence of favors and gifts, and a few even to blackmail or bribery—though corrupt practices, if not unknown, are nearly everywhere illegal.

Executive and administrative officers are also the subject of organized group attention. The executive is ordinarily an important source of legislative proposals and also has the power to reject enacted bills. The administrative organs of government are active in enforcing laws and determining important aspects of public policy, as well as spending, regulating, purchasing, and similar matters. Obviously, interest groups will seek access to administrators to make their views known, to furnish information, and to assist in policy making—sometimes even to make it. Other methods applied in this sector include influencing the selection of administrators, participating in advisory committees, publicizing administrative actions to call attention to grievances or abuses, and encouraging legislators to do the same. Administrative officials are also sometimes offered valuable inducements for their favor by "influence peddlers." The extent of the success of such "peddlers" largely turns on the prevailing business mores as well as on the rectitude of officialdom.

Judicial institutions may also be the target of interest group activity, though where judicial independence is secure, judges are usually protected from it. Nevertheless, groups as such are not denied the ordinary opportunities to secure their ends, where appropriate, through judicial procedures and claims for justice. Judicial rulings can be highly important, obviously, in the interpretation and enforcement of law, most especially so where courts have the power of judicial review. Political groups may also promote their objectives by assisting plaintiffs or defendants in particular cases of litigation or, if occasion affords, by acting as *amici curiae* (friends of the court) to provide additional legal arguments and briefs. They may exert some influence on judicial selection, whether appointive or elective; they may also publicize judicial decisions and praise or criticize them. Two well-known American interest groups, the American Civil Liberties Union and the National Association for the Advancement of Colored People, have had considerable success in advancing their objectives by litigation.

Interest Groups and the Public. Interest groups focus their attention on individuals to affect their attitudes, opinions, and behavior. We have already noted that they are concerned with influencing their own members, and have suggested the common means so employed; this must be a continuing process if the cohesion of the association is to be maintained. They are likely also to attempt to reach potential members and sympathizers—all persons with similar self-interest who might be induced to accept membership or to act in concert with the organization. They may even seek cooperative action with other organized groups, either because they share some related interests or are able to provide each other mutual support. Inevitably, too, organized groups seek to influence the influential—those whose role or function as civic, social, or business leaders, professional men, authors, journalists, or celebrities puts them especially in a position to influence others.

We have already referred to certain similarities between political parties and interest groups. It might be expected that they are mutually dependent to some degree. Influence with political parties offers avenues of access to the organs of government, and party support of particular interests can be highly effective in securing them. In consequence interest groups often collaborate with parties, sometimes merging themselves into the larger group for purposes of influencing its program, endorsing its candidates, participating in election campaigns, and obtaining office for the association's members. Such groups may provide campaign contributions and other financial assistance, as well as attempt to deliver the votes of its members.

Finally, organized interest groups not uncommonly seek to obtain support for their objectives by informing and winning over public opinion. Since this is a subject we shall be examining later in the chapter, we need only mention here some principal devices utilized. Groups may advertise their views, disseminate them by programs of public relations and publications, and conduct propaganda. Some groups, indeed, attempt to impress their views or wants upon the public by demonstrations, picketing, strikes, and even mob violence.

National Variations in Interest Group Roles. Associations are found operating in all free societies, but they do not everywhere customarily employ to equal extent or with equal effectiveness all of these techniques. In the United States, they have long had a significant role in the political process, for the American machinery of government as well as certain other national characteristics seem definitely to encourage them. The federal system, allocating many important functions to the fifty states, centers much political power in the state party systems and allows groups great effectiveness at this level. The separation of powers also decentralizes the election process, with comparable effect. The vast number of elective offices—giving a very popular quality to American government—and the high cost of elections create official sensitivity to group demands; so does the decentralization of executive authority at national and state levels, where there are many independent establishments and regulatory boards. The operation of a biparty system in a country of America's continental proportions—heterogeneous in its interests, ethnic origins, and regional characteristics—leaves large room in its politics for additional political associations. No less important, as a consequence of the foregoing factors, is the impossibility of exerting tight party discipline over legislators and elected officeholders.

Different circumstances prevail in other countries, though we can only touch briefly upon these. In Great Britain there are quite as many groups as effective as in the United States; differences in the two political systems, however, accord British groups a somewhat altered role. To mention a few of the differences, the executive originates all important legislation; hence the cabinet and ministers generally constitute the sensitive points at which groups seeking or resisting particular legislation may aim. At the same time, the ministries have long considered it routine to consult with interested groups when preparing legislation, making policy, and drafting regulations. British political parties, as well as governmental administration, are also more highly centralized than American; their leaders are among the most influential to which groups seek access. The party system keeps M.P.'s under distinctly close discipline, and thus free of many pressures of the lobby; at the same time, it is common practice for M.P.'s to be agents of organized groups—especially business associations, trade unions, and civic societies—and to speak for them inside the House of Commons, offer amendments they may desire to bills, and ask parliamentary questions of ministers in their behalf. The extent alone of group organization in Britain, even though less attention is given to the mass electorate and public opinion, is ample evidence of the effectiveness with which special groups work within the parliamentary system, either as component elements within the major parties or as bargaining and consulting units outside them.

France is another country in which interest groups flourish. Under the Third and Fourth Republics, indeed, given the tentative character of government majorities, the weakness of coalition cabinets, and the ever-splintering and undisciplined parliamentary party system—not to mention a persistent venality in certain sectors of political life—all combined to make government, and politicians generally, inordinately vulnerable to powerful interest groups. Indeed, one may well ascribe much of France's continuing political instability to the ineffectiveness of its government machinery to contain, reconcile, or resist the importunate claims and clamor of many narrowly organized and uncompromising but powerful groups. Popular dissatisfaction with the Fourth Republic and support of the new Fifth were in no small measure a reaction to weak governments, strangled by interests.

By sharp contrast, in Sweden, also a country with a multiparty system and highly organized interest groups, conflicting group interests are conciliated largely by open negotiation and a politics of compromise. Sweden is, of course, a relatively small state with a highly homogeneous population; and, with the pluralistic character of its society generally accepted, groups habitually make mutual concessions and aim at something like an equilibrium among themselves. The result is that parliamentary and administrative organs have well-established means for official or informal consultations with group agents. Indeed, in this atmosphere of moderation certain organized groups are even delegated authority to perform some administrative functions for the state.

As a further contrast, in the underdeveloped countries, interest groups tend as yet to operate quite differently from those in the industrialized western states. These countries have cultures which are partly western and partly indigenous, and still in the process of change; their politics are commonly monopolized by traditional ruling families, a ruling class, or a single national party. Illiteracy and other factors impede communication between government leaders and the masses of the people. The most important classes are likely to include the wealthy landowners, religious leaders, bureaucrats, and army officers, who exert their influence through institutional and non-associational interest groups. The conduct of politics is thus dominated by these cliques, and the masses—mostly poorer peasants—have no significant representation. Hence, their interests may be expressed largely through anomic groups, and their political activity limited in the main to participation in sporadic demonstrations, riots, revolutionary uprisings, or other violence. Government reliance on the army to repel such disorders enhances the role of the military, which may thus come to be the principal center of politics and power itself. While this is not a precise pattern for interest politics in all of the new nonwestern states, it can be seen with individual variations in many countries of Latin America, Africa, and Asia where associational interest groups have not yet achieved importance.

Interest Group Effectiveness. A number of factors determine the relative success of particular organized groups. Size is an important criterion; larger groups will ordinarily enjoy advantages over smaller ones. The American Legion could be expected to exert more pressure than the American Association of University Professors. Yet size can be deceptive. The National Congress of Parents and Teachers is one of the largest associations in the United States, but not the most powerful by any means; its members are associated only on the most tenuous basis. Hence, cohesiveness counts; a group whose members accept discipline, whose votes can be delivered, or who otherwise act in close concert can be very effective even though small. Funds are also important—not that groups can usually buy what they want from government—but they thus enlarge enormously the variety of techniques which they may employ.

Qualities of leadership deserve consideration in gauging group success: efficiency, ingenuity, skill, and persistence. Group objectives also make a difference. It is generally less difficult to promote public causes (or what appear to be such) than limited private interests. It is usually easier for groups to operate defensively than offensively; given the character of government machinery, as a rule it is easier to obstruct than achieve. Finally, tactics and techniques determine success. They must be appropriate to the ends sought. Enemies are loudly attacked, but friends must be whispered to. Excessive pressure, display of funds, or strident propaganda can easily boomerang. In some societies, such as in France, demonstrations of violence are not uncommon and may even be effective; in the entire contemporary world, indeed, political tempers seem to have shortened, and political disorder is no longer unusual anywhere. It should not be overlooked that the effectiveness of particular groups may depend upon what political party controls the government; fluctuations in public sympathies and in the temper of the times may also affect the success of competing groups.

Interest Groups in Totalitarian States. So far, we have discussed interest groups in free societies, but a few words are in order concerning totalitarian regimes. No matter what the monolithic unity claimed for their people by the modern one-party dictatorships, it should be obvious that they do have heterogeneous and conflicting interests. No modern industrial society can be turned into a one-class, one-interest, one-people state without repressive force. We traced earlier the ways in which western social and political development made the undifferentiated community an impossibility for modern times. Yet the establishment of completely integrated and unified societies is precisely what dictatorial leaders seek. What, then, of interest groups and their role in the totalitarian state?

Basically, the totalitarian formula is to create a comprehensive system of government and party monopoly designed to encompass all possible bases of group interests, subordinating all possible activities to political control. Thus, organized groups are taken over and potential groups are given official organization; voluntary societies outside this rigid structure are forbidden. The party supervises associations and provides their leadership. Even religious groups, if tolerated, are thereby sanctioned. Any form of group expression is highly limited; all media of communication—publication, broadcasting, even public meetings—are officially controlled to insure conformity and prevent dissent. At the same time, all of these media are employed by the regime to instruct groups and individuals in what, presumptively, their interests are. Of course, the party must maintain an awareness of the more important group interests that are self-generating, and to some degree placate them. Those which cannot be "educated," appeased, or repressed, finally, are commonly liquidated.

Some illustrations of this pattern may be seen in the Soviet Union. Certain obvious latent interest groups exist: party and government officials, military officers, the managerial elites, the police, and professional men, artists, and intellectuals. Being special beneficiaries of the regime, however, most of these have a distinct interest in its perpetuation and fall readily into groups that have long been coordinated or created by it. Other elements in Soviet society with less stake in the regime—such as workers, peasants, and students—are gathered into various overlapping associations; these dispense certain benefits and services, thus forcing some level of attachment to them, and also serve as important institutions of control. Newspapers, periodicals, and books—whether general or for the particular group only—are produced under license and censorship, so that the expression of dissent through the official media is virtually impossible. "Self-criticism" only is allowed, which is to say that complaints in performance or administration may be aired if they do not constitute opposition to or obstruction of the regime or its policies. The communist leadership is nevertheless always alert to mass restlessness, for the expression of even small discontents may reflect major disaffection. It can also be ruthless in dealing with recalcitrance. When substantial peasant groups stubbornly sought to resist the collectivization of agriculture in the 1930's and did not respond to "reeducation," they were liquidated with bloodshed and starvation. Similar treatment was meted out to various ethnic minorities in the U.S.S.R. at the end of World War II.

Anomic groups do appear in the Soviet Union and other totalitarian states. Some of their performances are a sham, of course, organized by political authorities to appear as spontaneous outbursts of popular approval or disapproval, as may be desired. But despite government efforts to prevent or conceal actual hostile demonstrations, isolated outbursts of restlessness, discontent, and resistance occur at intervals in the U.S.S.R.; substantial rebellions have flared in communist China, Czechoslovakia, East Germany, and Poland; violent revolution broke out in Hungary in 1956. Though these were repressed—in Hungary and Czechoslovakia, with Russian military forces—they demonstrated the presence of deep antagonisms which can find no other avenues for expression.

Criticism and Control of Interest Groups. Even in democracies, groups are often an object of suspicion and concern. Rousseau, whose *Social Contract* (1762) helped inspire the French revolution, devoted much of his argument to emphasizing the danger of particular interests to the public interest, "the general will." Men should be dependent, he asserted, not upon narrow groups but upon the whole—united in a total solidarity of the free and equal. James Madison, too, in the tenth essay of *The Federalist*, expressed a concern over the dangers resulting from the expression of group or factional interests. He saw their effects as "adverse to the rights of other citizens, or to the permanent and aggregate interests of the community."

What, in sum, are the principal grounds for fearing evil consequences from groups in the political process? First of all perhaps is the feeling that they permit the "part" to prevail over the "whole," and in so doing distort the democratic process. To see, or appear to see, "group interests" triumph over "the general interest" results in the conclusion that organized groups enjoy inordinate power. Then, too, their methods often make them appear sinister. So many of the terms applied to discussion of them—"lobby," "pressure boys," "influence peddlers," and even their exposure by "muckraking"—have an odious sound. In this realm of "anonymous government" the plutocrats, the unprincipled, and the corruptors seem to enjoy special advantage. Again, interest groups are not always democratic in their organization, and unscrupulous leaders may exploit the funds and the power of the organization in selfish and irresponsible ways. Unlike political parties, interest groups generally cannot be held to account for their policies; their leaders cannot be turned out of public office and punished at elections. Finally, it appears that, though selfish and narrow interests effectively organize, some important and socially significant ones go unrepresented. The battle between producers and consumers, for example, is notably uneven.

Nonetheless, interest groups hardly ever succeed in having everything their own way; controls of various kinds impose limits to their operations and effectiveness. No group ever commands the total loyalty of individuals, except in rare instances. Most persons have common cause with many groups, and may support several. Whatever the basis of organization—whether economic interest, social class, or religious, ethnic, or occupational lines—no association gets very large before its members begin to divide again on other bases. Groups also compete with each other, a situation which encourages discretion and compromise. Those with extremist ends ordinarily engender their own extremist opposition, and these sometimes cancel each other out entirely.

There are institutional controls upon group power. Though without complete efficiency, most political party systems ameliorate group influence if only because parties must offer broad programs and organize majorities. By their aggregate efforts they moderate many demands. The machinery of government itself does the same; if it is at all broadly based and supported, it offers concessions but not surrender. The weighing and mediating of group interests is indeed at the heart of the governmental process.

There is the possibility, finally, of formal control. This generally takes the form of publicizing and limiting campaign contributions and prohibiting undue influence, inducements, and threats. In the United States, Congress and some state legislatures have required the registration of group agents and declaration of the amounts collected and spent to obtain passage or defeat of legislation. Such efforts have not been especially effective. They relate narrowly to the legislative process, and even there the exertion of influence takes forms far too delicate to be captured within a statutory clause. Such restrictiveness can quickly begin to restrain freedom of speech, press, petition, and association. It should not be overlooked that the only really efficient controls of interest groups are those applied by the totalitarian states; these, however, patently destroy the representative and democratic process.

Group Functions Are Important to the Democratic Process. As Professor David B. Truman observes in his study of interest groups, *The*

Governmental Process, "The persistence and the dispersion of such organizations indicate that we are dealing with a characteristic aspect of our society." Truman's work well demonstrates the importance of a behavioral approach to group theory—examining what in fact groups do—as well as the importance of the group itself. As we have earlier emphasized, it is unrealistic to attempt to eliminate the group from our analysis of political life, or to conclude that interest groups, their conflicts, or their methods are bad in themselves. Rather, such associations perform demonstrably important functions compatible with and necessary to democratic government.

First of all, the interest group helps to overcome the individual's insignificance, politically speaking, in a mass society. Few men at best can have more than a limited participation in the political process, and most, if only because of their lethargy and apathy, have almost none at all; the group serves to enlarge men and frequently to represent them in areas where political parties cannot. Second, the political interest group may perform a valuable informing and advising function. In complex technological societies, governments continually require more and more expert and technical advice to assist their processes. Often group organizations alone are able to supply this. Third, there is the important "checking" function which the interest group performs. As groups are in fact a fixture of our society, we had best accept their inherent contributions to their own control—their mutual restraining influence. Fourth, particular interests are always to some extent segments of the general interest. However difficult to decide what the general interest really is, it must somehow be compounded of the parts, high and low, broad and narrow. The most characteristic activity of the group is in fact nothing other than its effort to identify its needs with those of all.

The conclusion seems unavoidable that groups have the essential task of insuring that private interests receive public attention. It is important that this be done as openly as possible and in the presence of strong and effective government. Because there is never complete agreement on what is the general interest, the government of the day must be able at intervals to effect a reconciliation of narrower interests into broad policies and enforce them to the public benefit. Thus we may see the value of group moderation and reasonableness, and the need for resolving interest conflicts regularly, before they become extreme. "A democratic society is able to survive," Professor E. E.

Schattschneider has observed, "because it manages conflict, usually at the point of origin. . . ." If this management fails, the political process is either reduced to a kind of continual "cold" civil war—eventually bursting into a real one—or so weakens political society that dictatorship is produced and one group forces its solution on all others. We cannot eliminate self-interest, of course. But when interest groups are reasonable in their aims and moderate in their methods, their responsible political activity will also contribute much to the realization of the common good.

III. Public Opinion

Even brief inquiry into the meaning of the familiar term "public opinion" demonstrates how ambiguous it is. Writers as eminent as Bentham, Bryce, Lowell, and Lippmann have not been able to establish agreement on a definition of it. The subject has continued to attract the attention of historians, political scientists, sociologists, and psychologists; but in their attempts to define and study it, "public opinion" has acquired even more disparate connotations. After a group of social scientists several years ago endeavored to agree on its meaning, some concluded that there was no such thing; others, that it was an imprecise term; and still others, that an effort should be made to measure it even if definition were impossible.

The problem is obviously an important one. David Hume observed two centuries ago, and few have since disagreed, that all government is founded on opinion. Today, however, trouble arises in connection with efforts to determine what such opinion is—who holds it and what it concerns—and how it is related to government and political life so that it may carry the adjective "public." The problem is especially intriguing and important in democracies, which are often said to conduct government by public opinion—and this in a fairly immediate and direct way.

The Nature of Public Opinion. When men began to reflect upon the importance of public opinion in political life, conditions then prevailing greatly simplified their ideas about that opinion and their attempts to identify it. The important political communities of the last century possessed traditional political values far more than those of today. These were well understood and were shared by most of those private citizens who were politically active. Public opinion was very largely the opinion of this group—actually the informed middle classes—concerning the relatively few and simple problems which arose in the day-to-day conduct of government. The term "public opinion" thus referred both to a fairly distinct and homogeneous group of people and to the relatively limited number of issues and of standards which they recognized—largely as a matter of tradition— as affairs of public interest, not just of private concern. Furthermore, the members of this public shared much the same media of communication, enabling them to express and inform themselves, and thereby to maintain something approximating a widely held opinion reasonably related to the actual political problems of the day. Government controlled by this public opinion was not difficult to maintain and was generally beneficial in its consequences.

More recently, however, this traditional sort of public has broken down, and its public opinion along with it. What we now have, it would appear, is either a great variety of publics, or no public at all! Expanding democracy has tried at least to make influential citizens of all persons, at the same time that many of the traditional political values and opinions which gave coherence to earlier public opinion have either disappeared or have been drastically modified, being "undemocratic" or out of step with changing social and economic conditions. Communications media, which once effectively served the public of old, have proved incapable of serving with equal effectiveness the more extensive citizenry of today. Regardless of the apparent potentialities of contemporary media of mass communication, the democratic public is not as well provided with means of informing itself and, through exchange of ideas, of developing a public opinion which can be communicated to the organs of government and to political leaders, as was the more limited public of several generations ago. And to make matters worse, the problems of contemporary politics are far more difficult and diverse than those confronted by that earlier public. The modern democratic community is hard pressed to function as a public, identifying its common problems and reasonable approaches to them, and thus creating a public opinion which can effectively control government. The great public of modern democracy sometimes seems to exist only in a babble of unrelated demands and protests, and the meaning of the term "public opinion" is thereby reduced to a frustrating ambiguity.

Actually, neither our traditions nor our communications processes, patterns of leadership and social organization in the private realm, have collapsed completely. Public opinion is much more difficult to identify than in the past, however, both as to who expresses it and as to what it concerns; and thus the relation between it and government is much more complex. For a working definition of public opinion, therefore, we consider useful that of Professor V. O. Key, Jr., who employed the term to mean "those opinions held by private persons which governments find it prudent to heed." It is not necessary that the "public" in this sense be all of the people or even a majority; and governments may or may not be concerned to act upon, ignore, or even alter that opinion. But politicians know they must reckon with public opinion; it sets some bounds to what they can do and to some degree they are even positively directed by it. For some time social scientists have endeavored to understand better what public opinion is in the confusing conditions of contemporary social life; they have traced the processes through which opinions appear and change, and how communications media affect them. They have surveyed the population to discover what opinions are held on various issues, and how they are related to one another. A brief indication of the results and their political implications will conclude this chapter.

The Foundations of Opinion. To discuss the elemental foundations of opinion is to raise far more questions than can be answered. Nevertheless, the possession of any particular opinion, we may observe first of all, depends upon the nature and character of its possessor; those who seek to influence opinion never write upon blank slates. We must begin with the thinking process, the study of which falls largely within the area of psychology. The mental process is complex, even in its simplest forms. The way one thinks is bound to affect the conclusions reached. Individuals, as a consequence of heredity, environment, and experience, acquire predispositions of many sorts: to be liberal or conservative, optimistic or pessimistic, imaginative or inhibited, and so on. The ways in which a person may confront any particular situation can range from rigorously logical thought to completely emotional response. Some persons find thinking, other than of the simplest sort, a painful process; others indulge in it as a pleasure. Differences of opinions, at all events, are bound to result.

Also of importance are the terms in which one thinks; these are made up, of course, of words, symbols, and images. Walter Lippmann emphasized that these take the form of stereotypes or "pictures in our heads," and though they are the currency of our mental transactions, they may well be counterfeit in reality. That is to say, they are highly subjective, impressionistic, oversimplified, and inaccurate; they tend to give much that is false and distorted to our thinking—we are obviously not thinking very precisely if we are using in the main such tokens, for example, as "fascists," "communists," "Madison Avenue," "Africans," "neocolonialists," or "military-industrial complex." The kinds of stereotypes with which we are individually equipped are determined in many ways: by family influence, religious faith, peer groups, formal education, ideological beliefs, national traditions, and the entire culture which we share.

What one thinks about also significantly conditions opinion. Generally people do not think much beyond whatever is familiar and comprehensible to them—immediate objects, persons, and events. Others are capable of abstraction. Education, of course, greatly enlarges one's view of the external world. Self-interest, whether actual or supposed, also directs mental activity. Associations are obviously important; ideas, attitudes, and emotions have a high contagion among those interacting within a group. Even the character of the group, whether it is a deliberative assembly or a mob, is important. The ancient Goths, so runs the apocryphal story, debated every matter twice—once drunk and once sober—to ensure that their discussions had both vigor and discretion!

The Formulation of Opinion. We may now examine something of the techniques available purposely to influence or change the opinions of others. Generalizing broadly, we may distinguish three approaches: propaganda, appeal, and education. The term "propaganda" acquired currency with the establishment by Pope Gregory XV, in 1622, of a Congregation for Propagating the Faith, a body devoted to the foreign mission work of the Church. Economic and political propaganda developed in importance in the nineteenth century; the twentieth has seen it become a major instrument in the struggle for men's minds.

The term has long since outrun any commonly accepted definition. To describe propaganda as any attempt to influence the thinking and behavior of others, is usage so broad as to be almost meaningless; to limit it to the dissemination only of lies and untruths is unduly restrictive. The term is better used, we think, to describe attempts to manipulate opinion, largely by emotional appeal, through concealment of origin and purpose or of falsity in content. In essence, the propagandist is concerned only with achieving an effect or end; he chooses to implant opinion through emotion, prejudice, and irrationality; he fabricates, distorts, and selects only those truths which support his cause. Propaganda may be undertaken by an individual and is resorted to by some groups; its present advanced development arose out of government use in modern warfare. It has now become a disturbingly effective weapon and an instrument of control in the hands of the totalitarian states. Conceivably, propaganda can be for good ends as well as bad, but good ends risk being tainted by the propagandist's lack of scruples and his inevitable disrespect for his chosen audience.

A second device, appeal, may be described as an attempt to influence opinion by a call for aid, sympathy, or support—through reference to advantage or interest, and without concealment of source or intent, or claim to whole truth. Appeals seek to direct interest, win attention, and induce self-identification with their particular purpose. They may well constitute special pleading, but they allow their audience an opportunity to consider the source. The appeal is widely used in public relations, publicity, and advertising by commercial enterprises and interest groups; electric power, oil, steel, and other large companies frequently advertise in support of "free enterprise," "private ownership," or "government economy." Political parties, public officials, and governments make extensive use of the device in its simplest form: "Vote Labour," "Post Early for Christmas," "Keep Washington Green," "Buy U.S. Savings Bonds."

A third principal means for influencing opinion is through education. It involves the entire process of pursuing the truth wherever it leads and disseminating or receiving its results with full freedom. Of course, not all that transpires in the schools is necessarily education. At the elementary level, for instance, in the interests of patriotism, children may be subjected to some indoctrination about the American revolution or foreign nations; in the interest of nutrition, to appeals to drink milk; and as first steps in the learning process, to memorize "the facts" in geography and arithmetic. At the same time, the process of education is not confined to schools; governments, groups, and enterprises may seek to educate particular audiences.

The three techniques described above may well be intermingled in practice, but they are still distinguishable in motive. Propaganda thrives best when accompanied by censorship as reinforcement to prevent contradiction with fuller information or truth. Education flourishes least in the presence of propaganda and censorship. It will not do to say there can be no distinction between education and propaganda because the whole truth may never be known or cannot actually be presented on any one issue. The difference remains in their object: the latter aims away from objectivity, and the former toward it. The effectiveness of propaganda is thus heightened by giving it the appearance of appeal or education. Election campaigns are commonly conducted by a combination of all three methods, though the proportion of education is ordinarily much too modest.

The Media of Mass Communication. During the present century, four means of mass communication have been developed: the print media (mainly newspapers and periodicals), radio, television, and motion pictures. The technology of their production makes possible the communication of information with unprecedented uniformity and intensity. But it is almost entirely a one-way communication; virtually the only notable response audiences can make is to cease to read, listen, or watch. Precisely what impact these media exert on the masses of people is much debated. Undoubtedly they influence public thinking, but they are also equally influenced by it—they are as much product as producer of mass opinion.

The press is the most ubiquitous and politically significant source of news and opinion for the average individual. Though performing a quasi-public function, the press in the democracies is privately owned and controlled; its freedom from governmental control is a hallmark of full civil liberty. Newspapers have been of special importance because of their traditional concern to inform public opinion. Since there is no limit, theoretically, to the number of newspapers that can be published, a free press is generally believed to be the means of offering the widest range of political expression. And most western countries, except for the smallest, have a hundred or more daily papers. Yet their range of opinion is not nearly that broad. Financial considerations have steadily shrunk the number of daily papers and now practically limits them one to a community, except in the largest cities. Most papers depend heavily on the several standard news and wire services for much of their content beyond local news. Newspapers are often standardized in chain ownership by a single proprietor. Much of the press is partisan, without necessarily being the mouthpiece of particular political groups; and since many papers are also valuable business enterprises, they are likely to be conservative in their outlook. Thus, even where a free press exists, papers are subject to "censorship" by community taste, their publishers, to some degree by their advertisers, and by the limitations of their reporters—who can only be in one place at a time, work under deadline and space limitations, and so on. Even what is considered "news" is likely to be measured in terms of reader interest rather more than by its importance. The newspaper reader is thus given what must be a somewhat limited and selective view of the outside world.

One should not overlook other factors, however, which mitigate some of the newspapers' shortcoming. The publication of books ever widens and that of inexpensive paperbacks significantly extends the circulation of serious quality works. In countries such as the United States, Great Britain, and the German Federal Republic, from twenty to thirty thousand new titles are published annually; even a small state like Denmark can produce some five thousand titles a year. News magazines circulate widely; farm, labor, and other special interest papers do also. The trade and business press in the United States alone runs to over two thousand publications; house organs and corporation magazines number over seven hundred. Circulating internationally are scholarly, scientific, artistic, and technical publications numbering more than thirty thousand. Popular and "little" magazines—of comment, prose, and poetry—come and go but the medium flourishes. The underground press claims a readership of some three million in the United States.

There are still other counterweighting factors that positively affect the role of newspapers. Much of their partisanship is confined to editorial opinion and is clearly separated from the news columns. The larger contemporary newspapers are likely to be at least fair, if not completely objective, in their approach to politics and political differences; purely one-sided news accounts tend to lose circulation and advertising. Though a paper may oppose particular candidates or parties, it often also gives them free publicity that aids their cause. There are limits to the influence of advertisers; they are primarily buyers of circulation rather than content. True enough, very little of the mass press serves near the level upon which public opinion might ideally be informed and educated, yet a free press cannot publish much above the demands of its average readers and survive. People get the kind of newspaper they want. And Oscar Wilde's wicked observation is hardly consoling: "Newspapers have degenerated," he said. "They may now be absolutely relied upon."

After World War I, radio broadcasting became a major medium for communication of music and speech. Though its role has varied somewhat over the years since then, radio flourishes today as the most inexpensive source of entertainment and information. There are some 13,000 radio stations and 620 million radio sets over the world, though about half of each are in the United States. Domestic radio broadcasting has largely been devoted to entertainment: music, drama and humor, sports, and public events; it has had far less concern with politics than the press. Whether it is privately owned as in the United States, publicly owned as in France, or both, as in some other countries, has not made much difference in its effect on public opinion. Where radio broadcasting is not conducted by public authority, it is regulated by it, and thus is "censored" in ways a free press is not—with the justification of public interest in the use of a limited number of broadcast channels. Practically limited to broadcasting short immediate bulletins of news, weather, markets, and so on, radio tends to avoid controversy and discourages reflection. Its greatest contribution in the domestic political sphere is its ability to give political leaders, especially national ones, access to national audiences. To be sure, this role has been taken over increasingly by television. Internationally, radio broadcasting for propaganda purposes was begun in the 1920's by the Soviet Union, soon followed by Fascist Italy and Nazi Germany. World War II saw the practice developed as an important weapon of psychological warfare by all belligerents. Today it is common for countries to broadcast to audiences beyond their frontiers. The Voice of America, the BBC, and Soviet radio, for example, all transmit around the clock in some forty languages.

Though the medium of television is considerably more costly than radio, it continues to expand in more than a hundred countries, most having one- or two-channel systems. Of the more than 230 million TV sets in the world, over a third are in the United States. Much of television's promise has gone disappointingly unfulfilled; even the best contributions of educational television reach limited audiences. Where government owned, the medium is commonly subjected to bureaucratic programming in the government's interest. Where commercially owned, programs tend to be controlled by advertising sponsors, and aimed at attracting mass audiences for merchandising.

The political role of television depends in part, of course, on how much time is allocated to politics and politicians, and whether it is made available for purchase. Politicians have found that television as a medium for campaigning must be met on its own terms. The television camera vividly discloses aspects of personality and character in ways that can damage the political acceptability of some and vastly enhance it for others. Possession of a positive television personality or image that appeals to mass audiences has now come to be a major political asset. Indeed, few contemporary politicians can hope to aspire to high national office without some mastery of the medium, and some have already appeared who are well able to exploit it. Television has therefore become a necessary accessory to political life today.

How television can meet its responsibilities in opinion formation is far more complicated than choosing between the alternatives of "give the public what it wants" and "give the public what authorities think it should have." Television journalism, because it tends to concentrate on what can best be treated visually, shown dramatically, and reported instantly, has tremendous emotional impact. But, in its high selectivity, it generally lacks breadth and depth; it is better at stirring up feelings than informing opinion. Even a half-hour news program is the equivalent in words of only six columns of newsprint. Bias may be introduced by the attitudes of its newsmen and commentators, and their blurring of the distinction between news and opinion. Furthermore, as is the case with radio, telecast channels are monopolistic or semimonopolistic, and are subject to conditioning, intimidation, and censorship by both private and public authority. Television makes some significant contributions through its coverage of party conventions, news conferences, political debates, and legislative hearings; but only on such occasions as great national elections or epic manned moon landings does the medium demonstrate its full capabilities.

Motion pictures have undoubtedly exerted the least impact among the media upon public affairs; devoted mainly to entertainment, relatively few films have political significance. At their best, they constitute an art form with strong emotional and dramatic appeal, and at their worst, formula-bound banalities of a fictional and escapist world. Motion pictures have long been subjected to considerable censorship, not primarily for political reasons, but because of the preoccupation of the form with crime, violence, and sex. With current standards of permissiveness, such controls have largely disappeared in much of the western world. The era of the regular once-a-week cinema audience is also gone, most of it captured by television. Films are now aimed at particular rather than general audiences. In recent years, half or more of filmgoers are in the 14-to-25 age bracket, and want films that entertain and relate to social and romantic perspectives of the young. Box office demand, and not political and ideological predilection, is the impelling influence in the film industry. As one Hollywood cynic long ago concluded, "If you want to send a message, call Western Union."

Our conclusions must be brief. Of the communications media only newspapers and television provide much political information for the mass of the people, and even their influence in political affairs is limited. The news media are best seen as mutually supplementary, and, taken together, convey much information about what goes on in the world; they help those interested to form some reasonable opinion. If these media partly distract mass attention from politics, they also demonstrate popular apathy toward it. At least, democratic audiences are free to choose, even though few people read more than one paper or hear more than one commentator. But where media are free, we cannot expect much raising of their taste and content levels above that of their consumers. At the same time, political and opinion leaders, and other elites generally, are able to achieve a considerable face-to-face communication, and have recourse to books and journals of opinion with smaller but more influential circulation. Indeed, virtually every significant group has its own influential publications. But we simply have not solved the problem of developing media— whether in public or private custody—to inform public opinion adequately. Juvenal long ago asked the question: "*Quis custodiet ipsos custodes?*" ("Who is to guard the guards themselves?") Yet as Britain's *Guardian* observed editorially, "What people read and hear and see helps to make them the people that they are, whether we think of the cultures of nations or the characters of individuals. Dictators know it. Free people may take it too lightly."

The Measurement of Opinion. Executive and legislative officials, and politicians generally, have long been concerned with gauging opinion to determine public needs and to anticipate political behavior. A number of traditional methods are employed today; they include talks with people, comments of the press and other media, legislative debates, reports of field agents, letters and petitions, representations from interest groups, exchanges in election campaigns, and votes cast in elections. Except for the latter—which do tell which candidate the voters wanted to elect, or in the case of referendum measures, for example, whether the voters support, say, new bonded debt—none of these methods is an accurate opinion indicator and can in fact be entirely misleading. Not surprisingly, political leaders, social scientists, and even interested citizens have long been concerned to obtain more precise information about popular thinking in public affairs.

From the beginning of this century, a number of American newspapers and magazines conducted straw votes in an effort to forecast for their readers the outcome of elections. These operated from a chance sample of voter preference provided in unofficial ballots returned to the publisher or by interviews with the man-in-the-street. For some years *The Literary Digest* attracted much attention to its straw votes on presidential elections; it sent return postal cards to persons on mailing, telephone-directory, and automobile-registration lists, and successfully predicted a number of times which candidate would win. In 1936 over ten million "ballots" were mailed out; on the basis of more than two million returned, a victory of Landon over Roosevelt was indicated. Landon subsequently received the electoral votes of only two states, and the magazine did not long survive this disaster, a result of its unrepresentative sampling. Meanwhile, considerable success in market research employing the principles of statistical analysis, proved its commercial utility in measuring various kinds of consumer demand and buyer preference. The polling organizations of Gallup, Roper, and Crossley—later joined by others in the United States and abroad—began to apply these techniques to forecasting the outcome of elections and reporting popular views on various issues. Though with varying margins of error, they enjoyed success for a number of years. Then in 1948 the polls confidently predicted a victory for Dewey over Truman, a polling debacle which widely shook confidence in their scientific character.

Although the statistical procedures involved in opinion surveys are too complex to be discussed here, the methodology of polling—the sampling process—rests on the simple proposition that an accurate sample demonstrates the character of the whole. The public opinion polls are conducted by obtaining individual opinions from a cross section of the universe being examined; according to mathematical probability, these will reflect the views of the entire population. Census and election statistics are used to determine what constitutes a correct sample—according to age, sex, residence, economic status, education, party affiliation, and the like—of the group being surveyed. The sample may be small; ordinarily less than five thousand people are consulted in a national poll.

Of course, polling involves human activity as well as mathematical operations, and in the process small defects may be magnified into large distortions. The statistical procedures are subject to errors in sampling and subjectivity in question-framing. Interviewers may bias responses or misinterpret them. Respondents may not always do as they say, and sometimes change their minds. Where polling is conducted on a pro and con basis, it tends to conceal gradations in opinion, the intensity with which opinions are held, and their stability—and thus their likelihood of being subject to change. Someone must decide, finally, upon the meaning of the data collected. In view of these circumstances—and we have not exhausted the list—scientific polling encounters a variety of difficulties in its practice. When a high percentage of those polled respond as "undecided," as in the presidential election of 1948, or when the contest is an extremely close one, as in 1968, the pollers may fail to predict the outcome—or do so with such hedging and indecision that the prediction is little more valuable than a shrewd guess.

An Evaluation of Polling. We hardly need point out that public opinion polling is not regarded with entire enthusiasm in some quarters. It has been decried by politicians, investigated by parliamentary bodies, and criticized by academicians. Its exponents insist that the polls help to preserve democracy by extending means to ascertain the will of the people. They thus serve to explore areas of ignorance and misinformation that require attention. Polls are used by, and are most useful to, political parties and their leaders, it is claimed, in revealing minority as well as majority opinion. The results may also serve as a check on exaggerated claims by interest groups. In practical terms, politicians have employed privately-commissioned polls in recent years to probe public attitudes, determine their chances of winning should they become candidates for office, and see how voters respond to particular issues; a showing of strong support in such polls may help to win financial backing. It has even been argued that the polls may be a better reflection of opinion than elections themselves! At any rate, there is certainly recognition of the utility of polling as one of the tools of the social scientist in his study of human beings, entirely apart from its more sensational employment at election time.

The views of critics are aimed, to be sure, at much of the journalistic use of the polls rather than that of furthering knowledge of human behavior. Leaving aside criticisms of methodological inadequacies, these critics are much concerned whether, in any real sense, public opinion is being measured at all. As Professor C. H. Cooley put the matter many years ago, "Public opinion is no mere aggregate of separate individual judgments, but an organization, a cooperative product of communication and reciprocal influence." It is not at all clear that in view of extensive popular ignorance about many public matters, the sampling of such opinion in oversimplified terms, out of context, without consideration of alternatives, and in the absence of any deliberation, is especially meaningful. Thomas Carlyle, not much a democrat, once asked: "How can I believe in the collective wisdom of individual ignorance?" To be sure, we cannot have too much information about popular thinking; but if such information is to be taken as eliminating the need for the decision-making process, private as well as governmental, it is also dangerous. Opinion must be created, of course, for it does not arise spontaneously; and there is further concern that polling may discourage courageous and independent leaders from contributing to this creative function. There should be no doubt, certainly, that constant preoccupation with the dead center of opinion, emphasizing what may well be the uninformed and the mediocre, must offer a threat to an enlightened society. Finally, it might be argued that polls devoted to predicting elections may undesirably condition their actual outcome; and even if they do not, they are only predicting what will soon be known for certain anyway. Indeed, the British politician Aneurin Bevan complained, "Opinion polls have taken the poetry out of politics."

Public Opinion and Democracy. The formation of effective public opinion in a democratic society requires, as Professor Bernard Berel-son has cogently stated, "that the electorate possess appropriate personality structures, that it be interested and participate in public affairs, that it be informed, that it be principled, that it correctly perceive political realities, that it engage in discussion, that it judge rationally, and that it consider the community interest." It ought to be apparent, as he also points out, that this is a very high ideal, and often unlikely of attainment by the mass of the people. We have ample indication that a very great many people, confused and frustrated in their attempts at understanding or influencing the many complex issues of public policy, have simply abdicated this function. Crucial to the whole process of creating adequate opinion is its leadership, and we may ponder whether today's democratic societies receive enough of the positive direction they require from either their political leadership or the popular communications media.

We have observed that the foundations for opinion are complex and its formulation subject to much manipulation. The individual is assaulted with so many strident appeals for his attention, often for trivial purposes, that he tends to acquire immunity to all—even those deserving his consideration. Despite the technological excellence of our media of mass communication, they function more as indices to the common level of popular interest than as significant contributors to opinion. The wide extension of literacy in the past century has not produced a corresponding elevation in popular taste.

Thinking about public opinion today is thus very much in a state of flux. Whether there is anything in contemporary societies worthy of being called "public opinion," and if so what it might be; what is, and what should be, the role of the various opinions held throughout populations in the political process—these are questions not easily answered. Relatively few assume, or have assumed, that the sort of opinions collected by polls ought to be directly and immediately translated into public policies; and the inevitably large number of "don't knows" in itself precludes this. This is not to say that government is better conducted in ignorance of mass opinion than with knowledge of it. But we must continue to emphasize the quality of opinion; and we may wonder whether we have properly allocated values in a society where we spend as much on tobacco and advertising as on the public schools. The central problem of liberal democracy is the creation of popular majorities upon which the exercise of government authority must depend. Although we need to hear the voice of the people, it is not always a finished expression of the general interest; it must be filtered through and weighed by a number of agencies and institutions. To the discussion of these, we shall devote the next several chapters.

6

Parties and Voters

"GOVERNMENTS, like clocks, go from the motion men give them," wrote William Penn; and men put governments in motion in many different ways. In the previous chapter we considered how individuals exert informal influence and pressure upon government and its policies. We shall now adopt the traditional perspective toward popular political activity and examine the role of individuals more formally organized for participation in political affairs. Once again it must be emphasized that we are not thus revealing distinct or disparate processes; on the contrary, they are interwoven and involve the very same people. The emergence of political groups is a normal occurrence in the democratic context and, if moderate and responsible, they can contribute much to the reconciliation and satisfaction of interests. Interest groups also help to shape and express opinion and relate the individual to society at large. All of this is equally true of political parties, which are another kind of group—too well known to require much formal introduction, but not always so well understood. About few entities, perhaps, arc there so many erroneous stereotypes.

I. Political Parties

Political parties are modern contrivances, and as is the case with many recent phenomena, our knowledge and understanding of them are limited. Most parties operating today are less than a hundred years old; many are creations of the last few decades; and all tend to alter in character with time. They are also difficult to compare. Each party system has its own national setting and differing governmental form, history, and tradition, which uniquely shape its features. Thus, the term "political party" is used to describe political organizations with substantially disparate forms and purposes. In order to conclude what parties are, we had best first examine how they developed.

An Outline of Party Development. The modern political party has its origins in seventeenth-century England and the quarrels of Royalists and Parliamentarians. With the establishment of parliamentary supremacy after 1689, members of Parliament divided into Tories and Whigs—in disagreement less on fundamentals than in degree over matters of royal prerogative, support of the established church, and economic policies. For the next century and a half these groups, joined by traditional and personal loyalties to certain leaders, were more nearly political factions than parties in the modern sense. The extension of the suffrage after 1832, however, required members of Parliament to broaden their appeal to larger electorates and get out the vote. To win a body of supporters, therefore, and ensure that they were registered, candidates organized local political associations. Thus in the course of the nineteenth century, the name "Whig" gave way to "Liberal" and "Tory" to "Conservative," and both parties became instruments for joining mass support to political leaders in Parliament. At the turn of the century, the Labour party appeared on the scene, and by 1922 had replaced the Liberals as the second major party.

Within American colonial government, Whigs also opposed Tories. The American founding fathers, after separation from Great Britain, hoped to avoid faction and party; they are not mentioned in the Constitution, many of whose features aimed at preventing their rise. Yet the contest over constitutional ratification divided citizens into Anti-Federalist and Federalist. With some realignments, a continuing basis of division produced ultimately the Democratic party in Jackson's time and the Republican party in Lincoln's. Like their English counterparts, these parties were obliged, as the nineteenth century proceeded, to seek mass support; given the many different levels of American elections, they acquired an even more elaborate organization.

On the European continent, slower development of representative government and restriction of the suffrage largely limited political association to parliamentary factions. In 1848, however, popular discontent exploded into widespread European revolutions. Liberal constitutions, extended suffrage, and more popular parties were the result.

In many countries, labor unions, workingmen's clubs, and student societies began the formation of socialist organizations. These emerged as socialist parties once working-class suffrage was granted, and though utopian ambitions for remodeling society were in some cases abandoned reluctantly, most such parties sought their goals by parliamentary means. Where parties and political activity were repressed, however, underground revolutionary conspiracies often formed. These were widespread in central and eastern Europe. In Russia, for example, no political parties were legalized until 1905; yet the Bolshevik faction of the Social Democratic movement had already committed itself to revolution.

World War I toppled the old citadels of privilege and repression in the eastern half of Europe, but its chaotic aftermath furnished no solid ground upon which to establish normal systems of parliamentary government and parties. The Bolsheviks in Russia rode to power on waves of popular discontent and political confusion; they monopolized rule for the Communist party and eliminated all others. In Italy, Germany, and other countries reacting to communism, the democratic parties quarreled bitterly among themselves; and in their division were swept away by the fascist movements. These, like the communist parties today, originally combined parliamentary with revolutionary means in their quest for power; but once they gained power the fascists also abolished party competition, free elections, and parliamentary government.

Other states attempted a still different path. Lacking the political experience to develop a workable system of competing parties on the one hand, but seeking to avoid totalitarian dictatorship on the other, various countries in Europe, Asia, and Latin America sought political order and national integration by means of "single national" parties. These commonly arose as nationalist movements which, after a period of revolution, provided politically inexperienced people with a sustained and unified government leadership. Thus another kind of party was created. With the retreat of colonialism after World War II, many such dominant parties, which began as independence movements, have taken over political life in the new states. It appears that these will be an important fixture of the political scene for decades to come.

The Nature of Party. The preceding sketch of party development should at least serve to demonstrate how diversified in meaning is the term "political party." It has been applied equally to eighteenth-century factions, caucuses, and political clubs; to informally organized groups of parliamentary leaders and supporters; to formally organized popular movements and their leaders; to confederations of militant labor unionists and socialists; to revolutionary conspiratorial movements; to political elites in totalitarian states; and to nationalistic movements integrating government and popular masses into political community.

What all these disparate entities have in common, of course, is that they are groups trying to gain or hold political power. While there is nothing necessarily wrong in applying the term "political party" to all of them, with no more discrimination than this, the term is not very useful. By restricting our connotation, perhaps we can restore our perspective. Political party was originally associated with representative government and developed in its conventional sense along with the idea of democracy. It described a voluntary association, concerned with government office and public policy, and providing means to organize majorities necessary to free government. As party stood for only a "part"—one side in a political contest—it necessarily recognized the existence of other parties.

Thus, the term's longest usage was limited to describe a fairly specific pattern of political behavior—a group of people organized to gain office for their leaders and to exercise political power in competition with other similar groups. This seems the most useful definition of the term. Unfortunately, like many another word in the vocabulary of representative government—"election," "plebiscite," "legislature"—it has been borrowed for use in nondemocratic and antidemocratic contexts. We can only offer the *caveat,* therefore, that when it is employed with the qualifying adjectives "revolutionary," "single national" or "totalitarian" it is describing political bodies with quite different purposes and methods from those of conventional democratic parties.

The Bases of Party. Much literature has been devoted to accounting for the bases of party division. People are divided by temperament and inclination, and any significant degree of commitment to party involves a measure of emotional response. Studies have also shown that party preference commonly accords with family tradition and social status; relatively early in life one acquires unconsciously stereotyped ideas about parties which thereafter condition the image that they project. Habit and custom, and the individual desire to appear generally consistent, all reinforce a continuance of party ties.

Yet socioeconomic factors, interrelated with the psychological, are probably of equal importance. We refer to our earlier discussion of interests: men have certain values and ends which they seek to promote and protect. These may be class, economic, vocational, religious, sectional, ethnic, or still other. We have seen that support of these gives rise to interest groups of many kinds for the influencing of public policy. But the supreme method to this end is manifestly through outright control of government; by organization on bases broader than those of interest groups this becomes possible, and party provides the principal vehicle for that purpose. People commit themselves to party, then, because they see it as a direct means for promoting self-interest, or the general interest as it appears to them, however variable or irrational their conception of these may be. Party may subsume some special interests but it overrides certain others. Aside from the additional objective of putting candidates in office, it is generally obliged by its greater size to promote a larger common denominator of interests, leaving to interest groups the task of filling in the interstices that remain.

These factors are roughly reflected in the kinds of parties which may be encountered and account generally for three main types which are to be found in a competitive and democratic context. First of all there are the *pragmatic* parties; these may well promote interests but are largely unconcerned with doctrine and ideology. Their policies and programs alter considerably with changing times and circumstances; they tend to emphasize the personalities of their leaders rather than distinct principles. The American Democratic and Republican parties, the British and Canadian Conservative parties, and the Australian Liberal party—indeed, most contemporary liberal parties —are all bodies with these characteristics.

There are, second, the *doctrinal* parties; these are value-oriented, pursuing some particular principles or viewpoint. Parties based upon socialist ideologies, such as the Netherlands' Labor party and the Norwegian and Belgian Socialist parties, are common. Religious doctrine accounts to a large extent for the Austrian Christian Democratic party, the French Popular Republican Movement, and Israel's *Mizrachi* (Spiritual Center) party. Other examples of doctrinal parties are

India's *Swatantra* (Freedom) party and South Africa's Nationalist party.

Third, there are *interest* parties; these are most commonly encountered in multiparty systems, though they also appear as minor parties in biparty systems, and reflect the determination of a large interest group to undertake formal political action. Interests may be ideal or material, or a mixture. The American Prohibition party is an example. Agricultural and rural interests have produced the Australian Country party, the Canadian Social Credit party, and the Swiss Farmers' party. Ethnic or sectional interests, often interrelated, are reflected in the organization of the Irish Nationalist party in the United Kingdom, the *Volkspartei* in Italy's Tyrol, and the Swedish People's party in Finland.

Political parties are not found in all political systems. In 1971, for example, some twenty-two states were under military government; nine had royal regimes; and a dozen others because of small size, limited development, civil war, or other circumstances simply had no parties.

The Biparty System. The three major types of party systems found within popular government—biparty, multiparty, and one-party—produce quite different results. They not only point to significant differences in the way political power is organized in various societies, but provide one important basis for the classification of contemporary political regimes. In a biparty system, two major parties vie in the political contest, attracting between them the overwhelming measure of electoral support. One or more minor parties may exist along with a biparty system, but they receive only marginal support. The two major parties alternate at intervals in the roles of government party and opposition.

Dualism in party division has often been incorrectly considered— by American and British writers at least—to constitute the natural and normal form of political cleavage, with other arrangements as deviations from it. Yet the two-party system is anything but common beyond the United States and Great Britain. It appears now to have been established in the German Federal Republic, if the pattern of recent elections is sustained, as well as in Austria. It may also be seen in the Liberal and Nationalist division in the Philippines. Two parties, Labour and National, have alternated in control of New Zealand's government. The biparty system is least common, occurring in less than two dozen states.

Great Britain presents the classic biparty structure. Here, according to the customary view, a party of stability and order opposes one of movement and reform. Both Conservative and Labour parties are unified in their organization, closely controlled from their centers, and disciplined at the parliamentary party level. Both are truly national parties, and have come close to excluding minor parties and independent candidates from Parliament. In recent years, however, the tightness of the political contest has closed much of the difference between them, so that despite their traditions, their fundamental disagreements are modest and both have become essentially pragmatic.

In the United States, the Democratic and Republican parties are also pragmatic rather than doctrinal; they are parties of broad program rather than sharp principle. They are not national parties in the British sense, and have considerably less national organization and centralized control; rather, they are loose associations of state parties which cooperate, more or less, every four years in presidential elections. Elections are conducted entirely by the states; and the electoral system produces results, on occasion, where one party controls the presidency while the other controls Congress. There is, indeed, some truth in the observation that these two political labels barely conceal what is really an American multiparty system. Certainly, Republican parties are rather different things in the Carolinas, Colorado, Connecticut, and California, just as are Democratic parties in Massachusetts, Missouri, Minnesota, and Mississippi.

We pointed to development toward a biparty system in West Germany. This had been unexpected because under the imperial regime and the Weimar republic, Germany had a multiparty structure—reflecting class, religious, and ideological distinctions—until it was suppressed by the Nazi dictatorship in 1933. In the first postwar *Bundestag* election of 1949, some ten parties sought representation, following the earlier German pattern. After the general election of 1969, however, only one minor party remained in the *Bundestag*—the Free Democratic, with 5.8 percent of the votes and 30 seats. The Christian Democratic Union acquired 46.1 percent of the votes and 242 seats; the Social Democratic party 42.7 percent of the votes and 224 seats. It seems likely these two major parties will continue to monopolize the political contest in Germany.

The biparty system has several consequences. It requires both parties to propose a national program and undertake organization on a national scale. It encourages pragmatic rather than doctrinal parties; since winning the election allows control of the government, both emphasize ability to govern. The system discourages extremism as both parties moved toward the middle to attract a majority of the electorate. It has the final effect of offering the voter a clear-cut choice between alternative governments, if not always distinctly differing programs.

The Multiparty System. Where there are three or more major political parties in the electoral contest—and more than three is quite likely where pluralist division occurs—a multiparty system exists. There may be no alternation in control of government; one party may be dominant and so situated that it participates in most coalitions organized in the parliamentary body. Or electoral support is so dispersed that fragmented groups move in and out of ever-changing coalitions, as various parties form different combinations from one issue to another.

It is not possible to say precisely what produces a multiparty system, or to conclude that it constitutes some kind of deviation. It is, indeed, twice as common as the biparty system; more than forty examples of it may be found among modern states. The theory that a multiparty pattern is produced by the electoral system is unsupported by the evidence—a matter to be discussed further in the chapter dealing with the legislature. It seems to arise in states with deeply ingrained and complex conflicts in interests and ideas, whose differentiation is too great to be resolved into only two opposing sides. Yet even multiparty systems not infrequently display one major fault line; in France, for instance, with half a dozen party groups normally in competition, the major cleavage between Right and Left is the most substantial and long-standing.

The cleavages in multiparty systems vary with national circumstances. Australia displays a three-way Labour-Liberal-Country party division. In Canada, a basic twofold division between Liberals and Conservatives has been broken somewhat in recent years by the emergence of minor parties—in the 1968 election, the New Democratic party (socialist and laborite) and the Quebec *Créditiste* party (rightist and nationalistic). The Scandinavian countries have tended to a four-way division of agrarians, conservatives, liberals, and socialists—with some additional minor, including Communist, parties. Israel demonstrates the extreme division of two dozen parties; here *Mapai* (Labor party), a dominant "national" party historically, leads every government coalition and is supported by a third of the voters. The wide incidence of multiparty systems is demonstrated by their presence, in addition, in Belgium, Finland, Ireland, Italy, the Netherlands, Switzerland, and Venezuela, among others.

The dispersal of partisan support and organization has several consequences. Some groups may organize only in certain sections of the country; some parties may not offer national programs. Where governments are formed by coalition of several parties, they are weakened by the fact that the withdrawal of any member of the coalition may destroy it from within. It is certainly more difficult to assess party responsibility in these circumstances. Where one party is substantially stronger than the others, and controls or dominates the coalition over a long period, the excluded parties may be inclined to irresponsibility and extremism. Indeed, some parties, especially the communists, may choose to occupy a position of permanent opposition. Finally, while the multitude of partisan views which arise from a multiparty system will certainly not oversimplify public opinion on political questions, they may well overcomplicate it.

The One-Party System. The one-party system is often equated with totalitarian government, but to do so misrepresents the political arrangements of a number of states. We have already pointed out that the communist and fascist states have totalitarian political regimes, but the single totalitarian "party" is a very different sort of thing from what we are now talking about. However, there are states which are not totalitarian, nor necessarily on the road to becoming so, in which we may observe the phenomenon of the "dominant" party largely monopolizing political activity and government control. These states are emerging from absolutism, dictatorship, or colonial rule; and their leaders are aiming at least at something like what we earlier described as populistic democracy. Where such "national" parties are directed to democratic purposes, they deserve consideration within the context of democratic party systems.

The political leaders of these states face prodigious tasks. They are seeking simultaneously to create a new state, a new nation, and a new society among a people generally divided, poor, and illiterate. They must quickly improvise elaborate domestic and foreign policies. The operation of a delicately balanced biparty system is clearly beyond the immediate ability of such people; the operation of a multiparty system portends disintegration and chaos. Inevitably, the nationalist movement—which was organized to overthrow absolutist or colonial rule, and which is enthusiastically hailed for the achievement of liberation—offers the only auspices under which the masses may be united and governed with some measure of popular consent.

Most regimes of this sort are quite contemporary, but there are some older examples. Dr. Sun Yat-sen devoted great effort to establish a united and democratic China under the tutelage of the *Kuomintang* or Nationalist party. But the quarrels of the war lords and Japanese invasion led his successor, General Chiang Kai-shek, to adopt increasingly dictatorial methods; and, after further civil warfare, mainland China finally succumbed in 1949 to communist military conquest. Turkey took a different direction; on the ruins of the old empire, Kemal Atatürk sought to reconstruct and westernize his state through his Republican People's party. His successor, General Ismet Inönü, continued the program and ordered the organization of an opposition Democratic party in 1945, which five years later was elected to office. Nevertheless, the increasingly repressive character of the resulting Menderes government raised widespread resistance. In 1960, the Turkish army deposed the government; but under a new Constitution popular elections were subsequently held, and a half-dozen parties have now developed.

Despite the long traditions in Mexico of revolution and violence, a one-party system has succeeded in recent years in establishing political stability and moderation. Politics are monopolized by the *Partido Revolucionario Institucional* which, claiming inheritance of the 1910 revolution, has supplied Mexico with its presidents and congressional majorities from Plutarco Calles in 1924 to Echevarría Alvarez in 1970. Opposition candidates and opposition party labels appear in elections; but though force and fraud are not unknown, the PRI has won the overwhelming support of the people.

Another important example of the dominant or "umbrella" party is seen in India. The Indian National Congress, created in 1885, operated originally as an interest group. Under Gandhi's leadership, it began agitation for national liberation, which won Hindu mass support and resulted in Indian independence in 1947. Overnight the Congress became a political party, continuing to supply the government and political leadership of the country. Beginning with the first election in 1952, under Nehru's leadership, the Congress won three-fourths of the seats in parliament; others went mainly to small political groups breaking away from the dominant party. The decline of unity has continued, however. And in 1970, the party split into a socialist New Congress and a conservative Old Congress. But in the 1971 parliamentary elections, the New Congress won two-thirds of the seats and became again the dominant political force.

More than a dozen one-party systems exist, most of them among the newer Asian and African states. In these countries the one-party system has been born largely of necessity, each in its particular national circumstances. Even the most charismatic political leader must have some organization through which to conduct and coordinate his regime. The one-party system does offer means to infuse some popular quality into government and to begin political training of the politically inexperienced masses. If stable and moderate government can be maintained, if leaders are steadfast in their loyalty to democratic ideals, and if the people can acquire some degree of political sophistication, a political opposition and alternative government may in time emerge. The danger of the single-national party is that its democratic forms can conceal authoritarian government. The absence of an opposition confronts the dominant leaders with neither rivals nor checks; all too easily they suffer the delusions of indispensability and omniscience and drift into unqualified dictatorship.

II. Party Organization and Function

We have shown that both parties and party systems vary substantially among different countries. Our discussion of several remaining aspects of party must therefore be quite generalized and brief, to avoid what could become an almost endless task, the narrow description of individual parties.

Followers and Leaders. Membership is of obvious significance to the party: from it come voters, workers, contributors, lieutenants, and leaders. The dismal imbalance of too few Indians and too many Chiefs is fatal for party success. Each party has its own concept of membership, but two general patterns prevail, informal or formal. Among the pragmatic and conventional parties, membership is largely informal; they may encourage official membership and payment of dues, but do not require it. Thus the members of the party are those who decide they are and vote for it. In many American states, one must register as a party member to participate in its primary elections, but no further commitment is involved.

The highly doctrinal parties, however, and some of the "interest" type—especially labor, socialist, and communist—commonly establish formal admission to membership, attested by enrollment on the membership lists, acknowledgment of party doctrine and rules, and payment of regular dues. These differences reflect real distinctions between the parties themselves. The conservative or pragmatic parties appeal with program rather than doctrine; their financial support comes mainly from a limited number of donations; and they aspire to votes from the independent and the unorganized. The doctrinal parties attempt to furnish ideological training to their members, are more dependent on financial support from the rank-and-file, and aim at success through the disciplined solidarity of a specific membership. Whatever the conception of membership, there are also differences in the extent or intensity of participation within a party. Most persons are no more than sympathizers, fellow travelers, or adherents of a party—more or less consistently voting for its candidates. Others may be supporters or members, declaring their allegiance to it and encouraging others to a similar commitment. A still smaller number will be militants, actively engaged in party work, publicity, canvassing, and meetings.

Political parties are agencies for the recruitment of leaders, as well as followers. The leaders of successful parties hold office and exercise governmental power—the essential purposes for which parties operate—so that the means by which they establish their superior position within the party are of interest and importance. Various formal procedures are employed, but broadly speaking there are three possibilities. Party leaders may be appointed: the chairman of the Democratic and Republican national committees are named, practically speaking, by the presidential candidate; the leader of the British Conservative party designates its national chairman. Leaders may be chosen by co-option within a party caucus; this is the case in both the British Parliament and the American Congress. Third, leaders may be elected by delegate convention or popularly, though the latter method is practicable only at the precinct, branch, or local association level. Party conventions, for example, elect the leaders of the Canadian Conservative and Liberal parties and the national executive of the British Labour party. The more democratically inclined a party is, the more emphasis it ordinarily places on democratic selection of leaders. Yet such methods are not always as democratic in fact as they may appear in form. The very nature of party introduces a measure of autocratic or oligarchic control; the higher the level, the more likely is co-option of leaders by an inner circle.

Party Organization. As may be expected, there is great variance in the structure of parties, not only from state to state but also among those in any one country. Party organization is shaped by the form of government and the levels at which elections are held, as well as by the kind of membership and degree of centralization which a party seeks. Organization begins locally, as at the precinct, ward, or municipality in the United States; the local association in Great Britain; or the commune in France—with party caucuses, committees, or branches. These will be gathered into constituency organizations within whatever area officials are elected to office; this may be at the county or provincial and national legislative district level. Party organs at this stage have quite important functions: to nominate candidates, see to the registration of their adherents, collect funds, and conduct campaigns for the election of their candidates. In federal governments, at least one more stage of party organization exists for the state, province, or canton; and in countries such as the United States and Canada these may well constitute the significant centers of party power.

At the national level, generalizing broadly again, the party normally has several other organs of importance. Most convene an annual or biennial congress or delegate convention representing the lesser units (though this is quadrennial in the United States) for the purpose of choosing national officers, discussing and adopting resolutions and programs, and proclaiming election manifestoes or platforms. Less formally, these convenings are intended to attract popular attention and publicity, to inform and invigorate the party workers, and to permit the leaders and workers to meet and talk shop. The party congress may choose a national committee to act when it is not in session, and provide funds and staff for a national headquarters, central office, or secretariat. The amount of power actually exercised by such an agency depends on the party and its degree of centralization; commonly, it collects and distributes party funds, conducts studies and publishes literature, assists candidates in their election campaigns, and in some cases gives official approval to party candidacies.

Another party organization of significance at the national level is the parliamentary party organization, which is the caucus of party members in the national legislature. This body, though it may not appear so in form, is likely to be the most powerful and important of the national organs. Its members have legislative seats and votes; it contains much of the national party leadership; it determines what the party will actually do in support of or opposition to various public policies; and, in the parliamentary form of government, its members may become ministers of the government. Then, too, parliamentary party members have not merely some mandate from the party; they are the elected representatives of their constitutencies. For this reason, there is always something of a hiatus between the national party congresses and party executives on the one hand, and the parliamentary party organization on the other. Though the former may be given status as the highest party authority, real power is exercised by the parliamentary body.

Party Functions. It should be evident by now from the attention we have given to what parties are and how they organize that they perform functions vital to the governmental process. The selection and support of candidates for office is the unique and exclusive function of party, and all of its activities follow from that function. It is certainly not difficult to imagine how chaotic would be the process of conducting representative government if millions of voters arrived at the polls with no candidates nominated among which they might choose. The party has the parallel function of formulating programs and policies. In general, the acceptance of an agreed program is what all the candidates of one party have in common and offers the basis upon which they seek the voters' support. In this way, the party offers its interpretation of what a majority of the voters want.

The two general functions just enumerated point to the party's immediate aims: it undertakes, if successful, to operate the government and effect its policies, or in a multiparty system at least to join with other parties to this end. Alternatively, a party which is unsuccessful criticizes the party in control by opposing its programs and proposing alternatives, thus keeping public acts and policies subject to scrutiny. In this manner, elected government officials can be held to account, for parties can be obliged to accept political responsibility for what they do. It may be seen, then, that party provides the bond of loyalty and discipline which leads government officials to cooperate within and between organs of government, or a means by which differences between them may be given orderly mediation and adjustment. This is important both for the executive and the legislative institutions.

For the electorate, the party also performs additional important functions. It informs the voter of the issues in public policy and their alternatives. Election campaigns, especially, induce the voter to weigh the issues and cast his ballot. In some states, such as India and Turkey, parties may undertake an even greater tutelary role: to re-shape the country along modern and western lines. In still others, parties may seek to hold their adherents by performing services not really political at all; in Israel, for example, parties operate insurance companies, housing developments, and welfare institutions. Finally, the party raises a standard to which majorities are invited to rally and calls for the uniting of individuals who are otherwise divided to make common cause. In this way parties may make an important contribution, if not too narrow in their appeal, to the transcendence of sectional interests, thus promoting national unification.

An Appraisal of Parties. Political parties are made up mostly of ordinary people. Not surprisingly, they often display certain human fallibilities. As voluntary associations they obtain both their followers and leaders largely through appeal to self-interest. They are rather easily denigrated, of course; such criticism is aimed, in the main, at defects in their efficiency, responsibility, and attachment to the national interest. While they are often short of ideal in these respects, let us consider why and to what extent.

First of all, their efficiency is criticized on the grounds that they do not perform their chosen functions with full effectiveness. They do not always choose the best candidates, it is said, nor clearly define and differentiate the really important issues; they subject the voter to propaganda rather than education, and appeal to his prejudices and fears. Parties are mercenary organizations, furthermore, collecting and distributing large sums of money in secretive and suspicious ways.

As a rejoinder, it may be said first that these criticisms are as much

—perhaps more—a reflection upon the electorate as upon the parties. Parties nominate for office men they believe can be elected, who are willing to do the hard work of campaigning for and serving in political office, and who have demonstrated their allegiance to the party and its program. These may not always be the best candidates, but it is difficult to see how they could otherwise be selected. It is further the case that parties choose the issues which they believe are of popular concern and conduct their campaigns at that level to which ordinary voters will respond. Indeed, the very art of political polemics, as *The Economist* points out, "is first to oversimplify the issues, for true clarity's sake, and then to exaggerate them, for the sake of effect." Voters certainly can raise the level of political discussion by choosing to ignore irrelevant issues and refusing support to those who engage in emotionalism, personal malice, and appeals to bigotry. The mere mention of money in politics causes apprehension, implying that place and favor are being bought and sold. But it is obvious that political campaigns are exceedingly expensive affairs. Even so, in the United States, more money is spent in selling soap than on presidential election campaigns.

In the matter of party responsibility, much criticism arises out of a misapprehension as to what parties ought and can do. There are those who imagine an ideal party as something of a political army— under discipline, centralized in control, whose leaders and members obey all commands unquestioningly, and who subscribe to a precise and comprehensive program ideologically distinguished from that of all other parties. Yet it is not clear how such organizations could be at the same time democratic instrumentalities—responsible to the public, adapted to the configurations of local and sectional government, sensitive to changing circumstances and varying group needs, and amenable to compromise and adjustment with opposing parties. Most advocates of responsibility seem to have in mind that parties should have entirely distinguishable programs and in office should perform according to a definite electoral mandate, doing exactly and only what they said they would. Some see as ideal the British parliamentary party organization, whose leaders are generally able to discipline their backbenchers in voting. But even those parties are not so responsible as they may appear on superficial examination and exact their discipline at a price in other disadvantages—a matter we shall discuss in the chapter on the legislature. Democratic government is not government by plebiscite. Parties cannot itemize complex issues of public policy in the electoral programs; nor can voters decide them —their function is to choose between groups of men who will conduct government and to assess the overall results of their choices.

With respect to the attachment of parties to the national interest, people tend instinctively to fear that the part may dominate the whole. The Marquess of Halifax in the seventeenth century insisted, "The best party is but a kind of conspiracy against the rest of the nation." Somehow, the ideal persists that what is wanted is not government by party, but government in the national interest. Yet parties exist because of differences of opinion over what programs and policies will best serve the national interest. The contest for power is inseparable from politics, and party interest is an interpretation of national interest. Professor William Goodman has thoughtfully pointed out that "parties do not create the power struggle nor do they either intensify it or make it more immoral. They simply mark out certain confines in the political sphere and direct the power struggle into distinctive channels." It is entirely proper to be critical of politicians and political parties as they may individually perform, but one cannot rightly be cynical about the need for them. Parties are the only effective means yet devised to permit popular participation in the decision-making process of government. Parties are truly the connecting link between government and people.

III. The Electorate

In the conduct of elections, universal suffrage is today so commonplace that it is hard to believe how recently it has been realized. Yet democratic practice has always run somewhat behind its professed ideals. To be sure, in many a newly created nation-state today, the vote has been given overnight to an entire electorate which had never cast a ballot before. This is not the way, of course, in which the suffrage developed in the older democratic states; there the opportunity to vote, originally possessed by the few, was only gradually extended. Poor and nonpropertied men fought for it in many countries of the western world. Thus, there has been struggle, but even so, a bestowal of the right has been as common as the conquest of it.

The Development of the Suffrage. Even after the adoption of the Constitution of 1789, perhaps one man in fifteen in the United States qualified to vote; that white manhood suffrage was established by the middle of the nineteenth century was one of the unique achievements of this country, demonstrating the practicability of popular government for the first time. Notwithstanding the Civil War and the Fifteenth Amendment, Negroes were effectively disfranchised in the southern states during the following decades as one of several forms of discrimination against them. In Great Britain, after the Great Reform Act of 1832, only one man in twenty-five voted; and, by the beginning of this century, one-third of the adult males were still ineligible. The revolution proclaimed the ideal of manhood suffrage for France in 1789, but only restricted electorates were allowed there until the establishment of the Second Republic in 1848. Even so, these privileges were extended only to the metropolitan territories; the position of the British and French imperial territories was another thing. In most of the states of western Europe, manhood suffrage was not established until near or after the turn of the present century. Woman suffrage was granted in only a few American states before 1900, and not achieved nationally until 1920. Britain extended the vote with some qualifications to women over the age of thirty in 1918—though ten years later they won equality with men. France did not enfranchise women until 1945; Italy, until 1946; and Greece, until 1952.

Theories of the Suffrage. There is no practicable way in which the people can "govern"; rather, through the conduct of free elections they can choose governments that are popularly representative. In effect, the people are drawn upon to constitute an electorate, which becomes something like an organ of government itself. Who is entitled to participate in the electorate? To answer that question, there are two general theories: the vote is either a right or a privilege.

In ancient Greece and Rome, and among the Germanic tribes, the vote was considered to be an attribute of membership in the community. Though citizenship then had greater exclusiveness than it does today, the suffrage was considered the inherent right of the citizen. Later, in the middle ages, when systems of representation began to develop, the vote was seen as the privilege of status and ordinarily attached to the ownership of land—an idea persisting until quite recently.

The democratic movement revived a form of the older theory; and as an accompaniment to the ideas of the social contract and popular sovereignty, the vote was claimed to be a natural right. First advanced by the Levellers in seventeenth-century England, this view was entertained by some leaders of the American revolution, for instance, Paine and Jefferson, and by Rousseau and Condorcet in France. Yet throughout the nineteenth century, a substantial body of opinion continued to oppose placing any governmental power in the hands of the "poor and ignorant masses"; the suffrage was a privilege appropriate only for those with education and property, who alone could properly speak for the whole community. Nor were these ideas immediately and everywhere abandoned in the present century. And reversing the concept of who should be privileged, prior to 1936 the Soviet Union confined the electoral privilege to workers, peasants, and soldiers; other persons—for example, those who employed labor, private businessmen, clergymen, and members of the former Czarist police—were all excluded.

Even today, no single conclusion embraces the various democratic views concerning suffrage. The wide extent of modern suffrage has been mainly the result of political expediency: the hope of political parties and their leaders to secure greater support from a larger electorate. Some view suffrage as an office or function conferred by the state upon all persons capable of exercising it. To others it is a political right, if not a natural one, and like other such rights to be withheld only for most exceptional reasons. It is now generally recognized, however, that the vote must be widely extended on an equal and universal basis as the only practical means of ascertaining the wishes of the majority and of ensuring that government will respond to the will of those being governed. Universal suffrage, then, is essential to the effectiveness of representative government and to the self-respect of the democratic citizen; if restricted on some differential basis, the result is to create a group of citizens denied the means of full political expression. Universal suffrage promotes not only an atmosphere of equality but, exercised through free elections, one of liberty as well. Important also, it promotes legitimacy in government—a sense of responsibility and obligation among both rulers and citizens —by providing the essential ingredient of consent.

Defining the Electorate. The widespread establishment of universal suffrage has worked to standardize the qualifications for voting among contemporary democracies, though individual national variations remain. As might be expected in this nationalistic world, citizenship is everywhere required, as evidencing the voter's attachment to the political community. In the nineteenth century, some American states allowed aliens to vote on the ground that it was desirable to draw the then large immigrant population into the political community without delay; but this practice generally ended with World War I. Because Great Britain recognizes citizens of the Commonwealth states as "British subjects," those who reside in Britain are allowed to vote there if otherwise qualified; this seems to be a uniquely British practice, however. All states set minimum age requirements as well; these vary from eighteen to twenty-five, with the tendency in recent years to enfranchise at the younger age. A residence requirement is also normally imposed; this is especially important in the United States, where one must be a citizen of some state or of the District of Columbia to vote. In an increasingly mobile population, however, residence requirements of even a few months will permanently disfranchise many migratory workers, and for occasional elections, those who move from time to time, with some distortion to the representativeness of elected officials. In many countries, required residence is not more than the lapse of time necessary to be entered in the periodically revised electoral register, which establishes what persons are legally qualified to vote in each locality.

Sex is rarely a basis for qualification today, though Switzerland did not grant national woman suffrage until 1971; a few other states exclude women from the electorate. In the development of woman suffrage, we have striking testimony to the speed with which social attitudes have changed during the present century. No more than fifty years ago, most men—and most women, apparently—were opposed to women voting. The arguments of opponents of woman suffrage appear today as museum pieces of Victorian—and sometimes medieval —attitudes. Woman, they said, was simply not a political animal! To give her the vote would unsex her and distract her from her proper functions of keeping the home and bearing children. The votes of women at best would only duplicate those of men and increase election costs needlessly; at worst, they would be dictated by their husbands, controlled by their church, or cast in ignorance. As clinching arguments, it was often asserted that women ought not to vote because they did not perform military service, and at all events should not risk threats to their virtue that might attend appearance at political meetings or polling places. In the face of such masculine casuistry, it is small wonder that women leading the suffragist movement occasionally felt provoked to violence.

Disqualifications in Voting. All states disqualify certain persons from voting—most commonly, those convicted of serious crimes and the mentally incompetent. Many disqualify illiterates and, if literacy tests are fairly administered, do so reasonably as long as all persons may have had access to free elementary education. Although some new states in Africa and Asia face difficulties in this regard, in the long run literacy is certainly an essential to modern democratic citizenship. Few countries still continue to disqualify persons who own no property or pay no property taxes. It would be a rare person today who does not pay taxes in some form or another or who, because he owns no significant amount of property, goes unaffected by government and public policy.

IV. Elections

An election offers the voters an opportunity to decide who are to take office and conduct government. Because most countries with representative government have parliamentary systems, their elections are confined to the choice of members of parliament, or additionally in some instances of a provincial or local government representative. Countries with presidential systems of government also elect the chief executive. In the United States alone a large number of administrative and judicial officers are also popularly elected at state, county, and local levels as well. As a result, American elections have a special complexity, frequency, and elaborateness unknown elsewhere; this method of choosing public officials has consequences beyond the realm of the election process which we shall discuss in later chapters.

Nominations. Voters are normally limited in an election to choosing between candidates who have been formally nominated; thus the nomination process is a significant part of the entire electoral procedure. We have already observed that this is commonly a function performed by party. Yet inevitably, party and public interest here conjoin, and some state regulation of the process may result. There must be some formal determination of whether a candidate meets the legal qualifications for office; and the date for making nominations, the payment of filing fee or election deposit, the submission of nominating petitions, and so on, are also matters commonly established.

Generally, parties are free to select their nominees by whatever methods seem appropriate to them; most commonly, selection is by special committee or caucus of the party organization within the constituency. In some of the American states, and in those of the German Federal Republic, party conventions are employed. Rarely is nomination considered a popular prerogative; the Swedish Social Democratic party, however, permits a decision of a district nominating convention to be appealed by mail ballot to the party members. The United States is unique in the use by most of its states of the direct primary method of selecting nominees. Here, in effect, the nominal members of the party choose its candidates through an officially conducted election. In some states an open primary prevails, which permits any voter to participate in the selection of any party's candidates. Such procedures may give a more popular quality to the nomination process; but at the cost of making elections more confusing and campaigns more expensive, weakening party responsibility, and encouraging divisive contests within the party's ranks.

Election Campaigns. From country to country, election campaigns vary in their length, elaborateness, and expense; but all involve variations on certain well-established techniques. Undoubtedly the most efficacious method of campaigning is through direct contact with the voters and organizing to ensure that supporters turn out at the polls. It is also advantageous for a candidate, in advance of the election, to establish a wide acquaintance in his area, join organizations, deliver speeches, and otherwise make himself and his views well known—a practice the British describe as "nursing a constituency." During the formal campaign, the candidate holds as many meetings and rallies as possible; even if attended only by the party faithful—and sometimes not many of these—they may produce some publicity. Candidates usually distribute party literature and posters, and buy what advertising space they can. In a number of European elections, the candidate is authorized to mail post-free a copy of his "election address" or a manifesto to each registered voter.

The local candidate for national office expects some assistance from the national party organization, as well as the local association. This may take the form of literature, funds, and sometimes campaign speeches delivered by national party leaders on the candidate's behalf. The major parties will also conduct some nationwide publicity and perhaps make use of radio and television facilities where the latter exist. If these media are state-owned, it is the practice to allot a limited amount of broadcasting time equally among the parties—or in some ratio related to the number of their candidates—for use by the national leaders. In the United States, commercial radio and television time can be purchased locally as well as nationally; and it has come to be one of the most important means of electioneering, although a very costly one. In the 1970 election, political broadcasts on radio and television cost over $50 million.

Money in Elections. We have remarked before the popular suspicion which generally surrounds the subject of money in politics. Money is a form of power in the political realm no less than in others. While parties make extensive use of the volunteered services of their leaders and workers, they also require funds, especially for election campaigns. Most people do not realize how expensive these operations are; yet a well-organized campaign requires money for salaries, office equipment, travel, printing, postage and telephone, rental of halls, purchase of advertising space, and—where available—expenditures for radio and television time. Lately, American presidential campaigns have involved outlays in the neighborhood of $100 million. A recent German election campaign cost more than $20 million. In Britain, the relatively short seventeen-day campaign for parliamentary elections has involved expenditures of something like $10 million.

Parties are obliged to tailor their campaign to fit their treasury. But they are driven to expend sufficient funds to reach the mass of the electorate, and the costs of doing so are not purely a matter of choice. In the countries just mentioned, this means appealing to an electorate of some 35 million in Britain and Germany, and perhaps 120 million in the United States. To conduct an advertising program of any kind on this scale must be expensive. Furthermore, parties campaign competitively; and are thus also driven to attempt to spend as much as their principal competitors. These necessary funds must come from somewhere. The most common sources are party dues; levies on candidates or office holders; money-raising events, such as banquets and social affairs; in some countries, from party newspapers, cooperatives, and other business enterprises; and from contributions. It is the latter resource which raises the particular problem of undue influence and corruption. Large contributors, interest groups, business firms, labor unions, and others, may well expect favors and privilege in return.

These concerns can scarcely be waved aside, of course, but there are mitigations. By their nature, parties cannot concede endlessly to narrow interests. Some contributors see their party's success as quite sufficient compensation for supporting it. To relieve parties of any obligations, however, it has been suggested that campaign expenses should be met from public funds; yet it has not proved easy to devise a practical means of doing so. More important, taxpayers have not warmed to the idea, critical though they may be of other fund-raising methods. To equalize the role of money in elections, Britain imposes a limit to expenditure by or on behalf of individual parliamentary candidates, but subjects national party organizations to no restrictions. In the United States, federal and state legislation have made various approaches to regulation: some limiting total campaign expenditures, some limiting the amount of individual contributions, and some requiring a post-election account of what has been spent. Most countries have no restrictions at all. In any case, the central problem of political finance goes unresolved.

The Administration of Elections. In unitary states, the administration of the electoral system is in the hands of a central government official, such as the Minister of the Interior in France and the Home Secretary in Britain. In the United States and most federal systems, control rests with state or provincial authorities. Immediate administration of elections in both unitary and federal states is conducted by local officials: a county board or city clerk in the United States, a "returning officer" in British counties and boroughs, and the departmental prefects and subprefects in France. Usually local government employees preside at the individual polling places, though in the United States this function is commonly entrusted to bipartisan precinct boards, on the assumption—not always warranted—that corruption will thus be prevented.

An electoral register is essential to the conduct of efficient polling. Its preparation is a task for local government officials in most countries, and they revise it annually on the basis of local records and canvasses. With a permanent system of registration, the individual need make no effort to get his name on the voters' lists, and thus is qualified whenever elections occur. The American states, on the other hand, usually require individual personal registration, and this sometimes repeated at intervals. Thus only those may vote who have taken the initiative to qualify. For the election day, polling places are set up in town halls, schools, and other accessible buildings. Except in English-speaking countries, elections are commonly held on Sundays, when all school buildings are available and teachers can assist in clerking and tallying.

There are several principal methods of voting. Where the "Australian" ballot is used, the voter marks an official ballot paper containing the names of all candidates and deposits it in the ballot box. Voting machines, so widely used in the United States, are not employed elsewhere; indeed, with the short ballot they are scarcely necessary. In many countries, the parties supply ballots which name their candidate or candidates; the voter encloses the ballot of his choice in an official envelope and places it in the ballot box. Where much of the electorate is illiterate, as in some Asian and African countries, a ballot box displaying an identifying sign or symbol is provided for each party; the voter need only recognize the party box of his choice and deposit his ballot paper in it. Each country has, finally, in its particular electoral laws, provisions which make certain practices illegal; these commonly forbid treating, intimidation, personation, and bribery. In sum, the essentials of effective election administration must ensure that only the legally qualified participate, that their vote is secret, that the ballots are honestly counted, and that voting is free of corruption.

Nonvoting. Nonvoting is a phenomenon which necessarily attracts attention when elections are discussed. Considering the efforts that went into the achievement of universal suffrage and considering the efforts as well which political parties expend to turn out the vote, it may seem a matter for proper concern when many citizens fail to exercise the voting privilege. In recent national elections, the turnout of voters was on the order of 72 percent in Great Britain, 77 percent in France, 87 percent in West Germany, and 92 percent in Italy. At recent presidential elections in the United States, by contrast, the proportion of potential voters participating was 60 percent in 1956, 64 percent in 1960, 61 percent in 1964, and 60 percent in 1968. The presidential elections are high-water marks in American voting; in other elections, especially local ones, participation sometimes drops to as low as 10 percent.

What causes nonvoting? The greatest factor is always indifference; and most likely to be apathetic are those with the least education, those in the lowest income levels, young persons, and women. Inability of various kinds also prevents voting; conflicting hours of work, absence from the polling area, recent change of residence, illness, and family responsibilities are obvious causes. Also, some people profess to see no real choice between the parties or live in a district where the election result is a foregone conclusion. All these circumstances prevail generally however; hence other reasons must account for the lower level of American voting. For instance, personal and periodic registration requirements and weekday elections reduce participation. The unwieldy American "long ballot" and the frequency of primary and regular elections also do the same. Particularly, the situation in the southern states substantially reduces the national average; indeed, in half of the American states, 70 percent or more of the potential voters have participated in recent presidential elections.

Remedies for nonvoting need to be related to its causes. To be sure, nothing much can be done for those who through mischance are unable to reach the polls on election day; however, nonvoting in the United States would be considerably reduced by simplifying registration and absentee balloting procedures, and by respecting the voting rights of all citizens. But what of the indifferent—are they sorely missed on election day? A number of countries have laws which make voting compulsory—Austria, Brazil, Italy, and Peru, for example—but impose no penalties for failure to do so. Others, such as Australia, Belgium, and the Netherlands, however, seriously undertake their enforcement and regularly fine offenders. Obviously, such laws transform a right or privilege into a legal duty. But voting is scarcely an end in itself; it ought to involve a considered choice, and the value of the vote of the least interested and least informed is most questionable. Some may well have no choice to express in the political order, and this is not necessarily damaging to it. The conscripted voter is likely to be an incompetent one; still worse, he may feel as coerced as the citizens in a totalitarian state, where sometimes 99 percent of the eligible voters voice confidence in their leaders. A high level of election participation is not necessarily a measure of democratic health, for it can reflect declining cohesion and political disarray. In a stable democracy, many may feel the outcome of an election will not make much difference. In any event, the level of popular voting is not an index of popular influence on government.

Even so, those who do not value their vote might be reminded that a relatively small number of voters can exert significant influence.

The British Labour government of 1950 was organized with a majority of only five seats; the Conservative government of 1964 with a majority of only four. The American presidency was shifted from Republican to Democratic in 1960 by less than 120 thousand votes, and from Democratic to Republican in 1968 by less than 500 thousand. The German Social Democrats organized a government in 1969 with a two-seat parliamentary majority over the Christian Democrats.

V. The Totalitarian Party

We introduced the concept of "party" as an instrument of totalitarian dictatorship earlier in our discussions; we shall make further references to it in later chapters as it relates to the organs of government. Our treatment here will only undertake to emphasize that the term "party" associated with totalitarianism is really a misnomer; though such usage is so common we are obliged to employ it, it is certainly misleading. Let us be clear: true parties are instruments of democratic government which institutionalize the contest over office and policy. The totalitarian party, on the contrary, refuses to be a "part" of the "whole"; it must either stand outside the democratic context, whose political order it seeks to destroy, or monopolize political power entirely.

The Totalitarian Party as Revolutionary Force. The purpose of the totalitarian party, whether communist or fascist, is to effect revolution. It may work underground to destroy a political order by intrigue, infiltration, violence, and coup d'état; or it may operate in part on the surface among the parliamentary parties, with its object always to disrupt their functioning. The choice of methods is determined by circumstance and strategy, but in any case parliamentary operations are always an expedient.

As a revolutionary conspiracy, the totalitarian party need not be large. Its leaders can function more effectively with a relatively small band of disciplined militants serving as the conspirators in their struggle for power. The Bolsheviks, for example, numbered about 24,000 at the time of the collapse of the Russian monarchy in 1917, and only later did the party acquire numbers. If the leaders undertake to compete in the popular political contest, a mass following becomes necessary. The totalitarian party then takes the form of a private army, with at least some of its members drilled and armed to wage political warfare. The choice of such tactics led Mussolini to expand his original fascist militia, and Hitler his storm troop units, into parties of the millions. In France and Italy as well, the Communist parties are mass movements, whose followers can be summoned into the streets by the party leadership for demonstrations, strikes, and riots.

The Totalitarian Party as Standard-Bearer. Once the totalitarian party seizes power, its very success obliges alteration in its role and methods. The attackers must become defenders, though of a beachhead which must continually be extended. The party is now the standard-bearer of permanent revolution, the rallying point for those who join its "marching column," and the perpetuator of the new ideology. With other political groups outlawed or destroyed, membership in the party becomes a privilege and the principal means of advancement; its militants become a political elite. The character of the membership also undergoes some change. With the consolidation of the dictatorial regime, many radical and zealous members—too well practiced in the destructive arts—are rendered superfluous, if not downright dangerous, and have to be purged. In the ranks, the virtues of dependability, discipline, and conformity prevail. As a matter of expediency, some further additions to party membership may be made from those adults whose abilities are of special value; but generally recruitment thereafter is through the youth organizations, where political reliability is better established by previous innocence, youthful ambition, and thorough training.

Once in power, the party must devote itself to establishing a new totalitarian order; whether as the "vanguard of the working people" for the communists or as the "supermen" of the Nazis, its members acquire the task of indoctrinating and controlling the masses, inspiring loyalty by precept and example, and promoting a spirit of self-sacrifice. As Professor John S. Reshetar observes in his study of the Soviet Communist party, "admission to its ranks has involved oppressive obligations, unexpected personal compromises, and untold risks." It also carries rewards, of course, though of varying duration; through party membership lies almost sole access to preferment and prestige, to career opportunities, and ultimately, to the levels of real power.

The Totalitarian Party as Superbureaucracy. The totalitarian party in power has a second major function: to organize and direct government. To do so, the party becomes a superbureaucracy, coordinating and energizing the administrative process. As dictatorship destroys institutionalized power, and the legislature, courts, and the law cease to provide restraints upon the administrative machinery of government, power can be controlled only through the party and its centralized command. In order to encompass total control of society the dictatorship vastly enlarges the government's administrative structure, as well as paralleling it with the elaborate machinery of the totalitarian party. These structures must be knitted together at various points, and every instrument from internal espionage to terror must be employed to keep the bureaucracy functioning. We have seen that elections or plebiscites are continued by the dictatorship, and these too must be managed by the party. As the Soviet Communist leader Molotov once pointed out to Sir Anthony Eden, "The trouble with free elections is that you can't be certain about the outcome." The purpose of the managed election is not one of inviting popular electoral choices, but of staging a mass "educational" campaign, promoting a sense of popular solidarity and political identification with the regime.

Even within the government of a dictatorship, politics of a sort occurs: choices must be made at various levels between alternative policies, the measures for their administrative implementation, and the men to be given office and authority. And dictatorship destroys neither ambition, competition, nor opportunity for rewards. The quest for these, however, must take place entirely within the totalitarian party, which frequently seethes with intrigues, particularly among the ranks of the secondary leadership. On occasion, the violence of these contests erupts into the open. Since there are few ways to withdraw gracefully from the totalitarian political contest, there are displayed at intervals the self-denunciations, "cleansings," "treason trials," and "blood purges" by which the politically inept, the inefficient, the unreliable, and the inconvenient—in a totalitarian state it can be as dangerous to know too much as too little—are removed. However monolithic and unified the totalitarian party appears to be, it never meets the demand of the dictatorial regime for total efficiency; as it grows in size and weight it suffers the ills affecting all bureaucratic organizations.

7

The Executive

TRADITIONALLY, the major branches for the conduct of government have been distinguished as the executive, the legislative, and the judicial. Montesquieu in particular popularized the idea, not entirely original with him, writing in his *Spirit of the Laws* (1748) of "those three powers, that of enacting laws, that of executing the public resolutions, and of trying the causes of individuals." He concluded, too, that such a separation of powers within a threefold government structure was essential to maintain liberty and avoid tyranny.

Of course, to look at government, even in gross structure, only as a three-way grouping of institutions into executive, legislative, and judicial branches is in many ways unsatisfactory. From one perspective, indeed, the functions of government may be broadly distinguished as rule making, rule enforcement, and rule adjudication; yet by no means do these correspond identically to the actual functions of the legislative, executive, and judicial organs. Nonetheless, a comparative introduction to governmental institutions, with an awareness of such problems, can be usefully undertaken by examining in turn the three traditionally distinguished branches of government. We may thus begin with the executive. In the simplest sense, an executive is concerned with enforcing the law and administering public policy.

I. *The Development of the Executive*

The history of the executive is the history of the development of political authority, for the executive is above all the essence of government. From the early patriarchal family emerged the warrior-ruler-judge, and as political societies increased in size and complexity, political headship and leadership were asserted and recognized as significant forms of social control. To be sure, it was many centuries —after the middle ages—before any rulers comparable to the modern executives emerged. Yet how this came about deserves attention.

Early Kingship. The institution of kingship was widespread in ancient societies. It was already well established in the city-states of what now is known as the Middle East over 4,000 years ago, when the ancient Sumerians began to write. A clay tablet of this era, on which are inscribed some of the earliest laws that have been found, indicates that the king, among other things, dismissed corrupt officials, standardized weights and measures, and looked after the needy. Tax collectors then, as now, were necessary, as well as unpopular.

Although the character of kingship in these ancient lands—Israel, Mesopotamia, Egypt, Crete, and elsewhere—differed in details, there were many similarities. Royal succession was commonly hereditary, but dynastic lines were frequently broken by court intrigue, palace revolution, assassination, foreign conquest, and other circumstances. These early kings came to administer empire over wide areas, and their responsibilities were likely to be broad. To them were usually attributed divine powers, and their priestly functions were important. They served also as chief lawgivers and judges. Despotic as these rulers tended to be, they were not absolute in their authority. Popular resistance did now and again assert itself effectively, and despotism was partially tempered by practical difficulties of communication and control. Even this early the germ of the idea of modern constitutional government was emerging: that the law applies alike to the ruler and the ruled.

Greece. The early Greek tribes were ruled by hereditary kings who claimed religious sanction for their exercise of authority, and combined the functions of general, priest, and judge. As the influence of the rising class of nobility increased, however, government by a landed aristocracy succeeded that of the Homeric monarchs. In turn, these aristocracies gave way widely in the seventh and sixth centuries B.C. to rule by tyrants, who often justified their seizure of power as a means of providing security in times of stress. Such tyrannies might last for decades before their excesses brought about the tyrant's expulsion, and his replacement by some form of oligarchy or democracy.

The outstanding example of Greek democracy, Athens, had no executive branch of government in the modern sense. General political powers were vested in a popular assembly, the *Ekklesia,* composed of the entire citizenry, and assisted by a Council of several hundred, chosen by lot from all the citizens. While the Assembly exercised control over all magistrates and determined general policy, the Council acted somewhat as an executive committee, concerning itself with the detailed supervision of civic affairs.

The government of Sparta differed from that of Athens in many ways, reflecting important differences in the philosophies of the two communities. Sparta was organized to achieve maximum military efficiency, and though there was no separation of powers, the executive position stands out more distinctly. Spartan government was monarchical in form and oligarchical in fact. Two hereditary kings performed religious, judicial, and military duties; but the main executive authority rested in the five *Ephors,* or overseers, who were elected annually and actually governed. Their selection was democratic in form only, however, and a limited oligarchy kept the city-community under the discipline of an armed camp.

If the experience of ancient Greece made no practical contribution to the evolution of the executive institution, it definitely influenced political thinking. The word "tyrant" came to acquire strong moral implications: tyrants ruled irresponsibly, without accountability to their subjects; they disregarded the customary laws and monopolized and abused power. The ideal ruler, so Plato taught, was one who perfected the art of statesmanship, and was wise and just. Aristotle, as well, contrasted the rule of king and tyrant, with the distinction between them based essentially on their moral character.

Rome. Rome began its history as a city-state and, though ruled by kings in the early period, established a republic in the sixth century B.C. Full executive authority, formerly possessed by the king, was vested in two consuls elected for one-year terms, who exercised military and judicial powers. Acting in an advisory capacity was a Senate, composed of several hundred elder statesmen appointed for life and representing the wealthy patrician families. An assembly of citizens exercised legislative powers.

The expansion of Rome, first over the Italian peninsula and then to more distant Mediterranean lands, placed great strains on the republican government. To be sure, an elaborate system of provincial administration had been created, but provincial governors tended to become increasingly independent, and generals commanding far-flung armies were difficult to control. In the first century B.C. changes were instituted, after a period of civil war and military dictatorship, centering military, legislative, and administrative powers in an emperor. Theoretically, political power continued to remain with the Roman people, and republican forms were preserved, but surface appearances were practically obscured by the deification of the emperor. Thus his absolute power came to constitute a model of splendor and centralized authority to which innumerable subsequent rulers would aspire for centuries.

During the period of the Roman republic, numerous dictatorships were established through the concentration of power in the hands of one man. Unlike the Greek tyrannies, however, the dictator was appointed by the Senate for a limited period of time to deal with a particular crisis; he was obliged to respect the basic law and answer for his exercise of office at its conclusion. Despite the interludes of dictatorship and tyranny, the law steadfastly recognized the existence of basic rights enjoyed by all Roman citizens and the idea remained that "the laws govern the magistrate."

Feudal Rulers. In the mingling of Roman and Teutonic political experience which followed the collapse of the Roman empire in the fifth century, the institution of monarchy continued in western Europe, though on a somewhat different basis. Whereas the Roman owed allegiance to his emperor as the embodiment of the authority of the state, the Teuton, bound by kinship to his fellows in a tribal organization, recognized the authority of his king on a personal basis as a leader or military chieftain. From the combination of Germanic and Roman attitudes—and which was the more influential is arguable—there thus grew up the intricate relations of personal allegiance that constituted the feudal system. An attempt was made, indeed, to revive the Roman concept of emperorship by conferring the title on Germanic rulers after A.D. 962 under the Holy Roman Empire, but western Europe was actually ruled thereafter by many kings rather than a single emperor.

The nature of feudalism, more a civilization than a system of government, prevented the development of any idea of exclusive authority over a particular area. In the absence of any strong central government the king was only an overlord, sitting at the apex of an intricate hierarchical organization. Feudal kings were not despots, ruling by their own fiat, but only a part of a whole system. Their authority was shared with their underlords, the free cities, the medieval estates and, not unimportantly, the Church. They had certainly to reckon with the power and influence of bishops and popes. An increasingly significant restraint on kingly power was the law, which rested largely on a customary basis rather than on statute, with the king himself expected to observe it.

Absolute Monarchy. The fifteenth and sixteenth centuries saw national monarchies in western Europe rise to a position well beyond that of feudal kings. Several factors account for this situation. For one thing, the pretensions of the emperors of the Holy Roman Empire to overlordship of all Europe were never successfully asserted in practice. The Reformation shattered the claims of central religious and secular authorities—popes and emperors—to rule a unified Christian world. With the decline of feudalism, many circumstances permitted and encouraged strong national leadership under a single ruler. Absolute monarchy offered a means of drawing together larger areas under centralized control to provide order and security against both internal dissension and external attack. Only in England, among the important European states, was there to be a substantial variance in this pattern. The idea of absolutism, which was to continue dominant in the next two centuries, arose from the practical necessity of releasing the authority of the ruler from feudally imposed limitations by emperor, church, and nobility. It asserted that the monarch could not be bound by legal limitations of any sort.

Constitutional Monarchy. The successful assertion of monarchical absolutism had the effect of bringing kings into sharper conflict with the middle classes, who had originally been willing to support the doctrine to escape the clutches of the nobility. The excesses of the absolute monarchs and their courts—their propensity to dynastic-interest war, secret diplomacy, financial extravagance, and other unpopular practices—invariably encouraged demands for their restraint or even overthrow. Of course, some kings exercised their power with benevolence, but others, disregarding the political and commercial interests of the growing middle classes, turned support to enmity. Inevitably, some rulers now sought to ally themselves with the aristocracy against the commoners in self-defense, and did so successfully.

The achievement of effective limitations upon royal authority and the establishment of constitutional monarchy came first in England.

With the accession of the Stuart kings in the seventeenth century, a struggle commenced between King and Commons over conflicts of interest and principle. Against attempts of the Stuarts to assert their absolutism and sanctify their rule by divine right were opposed the rights of Parliament and the supremacy of the common law. After a series of quarrels, civil war broke out, and in 1649 Charles I was beheaded. The restoration of the monarchy eleven years later led only to renewing the duel between Crown and Parliament over constitutional issues. As a result, James II was forced to vacate the throne in 1688, and a new line of monarchs was installed. To ensure that kings would not henceforward overreach themselves, Parliament in 1689 enacted the Bill of Rights, which served as a constitutional document defining the monarch's position—now king only by act of Parliament —and asserting the rights of English subjects. Theories of absolutism and divine right were definitely rejected; the supremacy of the law and the sovereignty of the nation over the will of the king were assured.

The French revolution, coming a hundred years later, struck another blow at monarchical absolutism. Following the vicissitudes of the Napoleonic period, France installed a constitutional monarch in 1815. By the middle of the nineteenth century, the institution of constitutional monarchy was established in Sweden, the Netherlands, Belgium, Sardinia-Piedmont (extended later to all Italy), and Denmark.

The essence of constitutional or limited monarchy—all that remains of hereditary rule—is that the king's power is distinctly restricted by fundamental law or constitution. He serves as titular head of state, but without political power. The king (or in some countries, a queen) reigns but does not govern; instead, he is used as a convenient symbol of the continuity of authority and the unity of the state. "The king," as Edward VII stated, "never expresses any opinion on political matters except on the advice of his responsible ministers." In the classic phrase of Bagehot, the constitutional monarch enjoys three rights: to be consulted, to encourage, and to warn; but his acts must be those of responsible ministers, not his own. The king may exercise some personal influence, but it must avoid partisanship, and be exerted with tact and discretion.

II. Modern Executives

The working executives in the principal modern states may be broadly classified into three major types: parliamentary, presidential, and dictatorial. Our purpose in classifying is to get at significant realities. In politics things are not always what they seem, nor what they are labeled. Form and fact may well be at variance. Thus, a parliamentary type of government may operate with the head of state, the titular executive designated "president." A state may also have a parliamentary or presidential type of executive in form, and yet be governed by a dictatorial executive in fact. Indeed, even a king may be a dictator.

The Parliamentary Executive

The parliamentary executive—sometimes designated as the "cabinet" type—is the most widely adopted form in systems of representative and constitutional government. It developed first in England by a process of historical growth, was adopted on the European continent, and spread extensively. Its wide incidence may be explained by several factors: the transplantation of English institutions throughout the British Commonwealth, the extent of European political influence, and the fact that the parliamentary executive is compatible with either monarchical or republican forms of government.

Essential Features of the Parliamentary Executive. The essential features of the parliamentary executive include a titular head of state, who may be a "constitutional" and hereditary monarch—as in Great Britain, Sweden, Belgium, the Netherlands, or Japan—or who may be a president, commonly some elder statesman chosen by an electoral body for a fixed term of years—as in Finland, Germany, Ireland, Italy, and Austria. In either case, his position in government is essentially without political power. His principal function, beyond ceremonial duties, is to designate the political executive and to see, in short, that there is a government. The political executive—variously called prime minister, premier, or chancellor—is the leader of the major party in the parliament, or someone able to organize a coalition of several party groups; and he continues in office with his cabinet as long as he enjoys the support of a parliamentary majority. General elections, for the lower and popularly representative house of parliament, are held at intervals and provide a popular mandate to continue or replace the existing government. These features may now be examined in the British parliamentary executive.

The Executive in Great Britain: The Crown. Because the British constitution is not a documentary one, no fundamental single law describes the English executive. Its character cannot be accounted for as conscious choice; it can be explained rather as the result of English history, chance, and practical experience. Though its essentials may be duplicated in other countries, it may be seen nowhere else— even within states of the Commonwealth—with exactly the same details. Some of its aspects are, indeed, far too subtle to be captured in constitutional clauses. A description of it requires attention to the several institutions that comprise the executive: the Crown, the Monarch, the Prime Minister, and the Cabinet and Ministry.

We have seen that, until the seventeenth century, the principal executive in England was the king. For the most part, he performed the executive functions personally, or saw them performed under his immediate direction. Gradually, however, the royal functions were institutionalized and in the process their actual exercise was increasingly transferred into other hands. This did not mean that the executive powers were diminished, but rather that the king enjoyed steadily less personal discretion in their application; indeed, once the exercise of Crown powers was securely in the hands of responsible ministers, Parliament was quite willing to see the Crown's authority extended.

Thus the Crown today has come to represent the totality of executive authority in British government, as well as the office of monarchy. Although Crown powers relate primarily to the executive and administrative processes, they have legislative and judicial character as well. Laws are enacted by the "Crown in Parliament"; the authority of the courts is also drawn from the Crown. These Crown powers are derived from two sources: the royal prerogative and acts of Parliament, with the former defined by common law and the latter, of course, by statute. The Crown is thus an abstraction, "a convenient working hypothesis" to explain the changed constitutional situation whereby the executive powers are now exercised by the king's ministers.

The Monarch. The king (or queen, in the present reign) is a person, and by nature mortal; a monarch may abdicate, become incapacitated, or die. Yet there is never an interregnum in Great Britain, for Crown authority is never suspended; the Crown, like a corporation, enjoys a legal immortality. Then why not dispense with the king entirely and employ only the symbol? As a matter of fact, kingship is not essential to the operation of a parliamentary executive. Royal functions are, indeed, performed by a regency when the monarch is underage or incapacitated. But if there is no king, someone must be found to take his place in a somewhat similar office of government. A republic with a parliamentary government, such as Italy or Germany, does just that; it substitutes the office of a president for that of a king.

A king or president is therefore necessary to the operation of parliamentary government—and the British prefer a hereditary monarch for the job. Kingship is the most ancient institution in British government, its continuity broken only once in a thousand years. The present sovereign, Elizabeth II, is descended from the Saxon King Egbert, who ruled in the ninth century. Coming to her office as queen regnant by inheritance, she has not been obliged to enter any political competitions, and has not been a member of any political party. She enjoys, in consequence, a position of political neutrality, free of partisan strife, and is uniquely able to claim to represent the entire nation in a way an elected politician scarcely ever can.

Queen Elizabeth's main political function as a twentieth-century monarch is to appoint a Prime Minister, and while this responsibility ordinarily offers little opportunity for the exercise of discretion as long as there is a strong biparty system, sometimes there may be a choice, as when no party enjoys a majority, or when the majority party in the House of Commons has designated no leader. In the 1924 parliamentary election, for example, none of the parties— Conservative, Labour, or Liberal—won a majority of seats in the House of Commons. King George V chose the leader of the Labour party, Ramsay MacDonald, to be Prime Minister. Again, in 1963, Harold Macmillan suddenly resigned the prime ministership because of illness. After hurried consultations among Conservative party leaders to determine which of some four or five candidates would be most acceptable as a successor, Mr. Macmillan recommended Sir Alec Douglas-Home. The Queen's selection of the latter was impartial, and on the best available advice, of course, but no one could choose for her.

Constitutionally, the Queen as reigning sovereign has many other duties. She appoints all important officials of the government: ministers, ambassadors, military commanders, and judges; she is head of the established Church of England and appoints its bishops; she issues administrative rules in the form of Orders in Council; she summons and dissolves Parliament, assents to legislation, makes treaties, and declares war; she is head of the Commonwealth and appoints governors-general in its members. All of these acts are performed as Crown powers on the advice, to be sure, of ministers who are responsible for them. Even so, Queen Elizabeth is here not merely a figurehead. All major policy decisions and appointments are discussed with her; she sees all important state papers and receives firsthand reports of all significant developments respecting the work of the Cabinet, proceedings in Parliament, and the affairs of empire and Commonwealth governments. She is entitled to be fully informed of the nature and implications of all actions taken in her name. In a reign of some length, therefore, a British monarch sees a number of governments come and go, and acquires a unique overview, both of public affairs and those who engage in them.

The Prime Minister. The office of Prime Minister evolved slowly. The title was initially one of reproach, used to describe that minister of the king who was first in royal favor. It began to achieve real importance only in the eighteenth century, after George I ceased to attend cabinet meetings. Sir Robert Walpole is often described as the first Prime Minister. But it took another century, to the time of Sir Robert Peel, before that office acquired essentially its present-day form. For decades thereafter, although the term "Prime Minister" had come into general use, there was still no such office in the government, strictly speaking; the Prime Minister obtained official status and salary by taking the post of First Lord of the Treasury. In 1905, a royal warrant gave him precedence as the fourth nonroyal person of the realm, but not until 1937 was he given by statute a salary to go with the office of Prime Minister alone. Long before this, however, the Prime Minister had become the real head of the government. Even today, there is still no constitutional document or basic statute prescribing and defining his powers; they rest largely on constitutional convention—that is, custom and usage—developed out of the workings of the whole parliamentary system.

We have noted that the reigning king or queen designates the Prime Minister. The latter comes to this office ordinarily because the voters have elected the members of the party which he leads to a majority of the seats in the House of Commons. Only in unusual circumstances will the monarch be able to exercise discretion in the matter. On being invited to form a government, the Prime Minister organizes a Ministry chosen from his party in the two houses of Parliament, and from these a smaller group who constitute the Cabinet. The monarch then issues their formal appointments; and the government continues in office until it is no longer supported by a majority in the Commons or the Prime Minister chooses to resign.

The Prime Minister thus has no fixed term of office. He may be dismissed only by the Sovereign; but the latter would not take such a step unless the Prime Minister had lost his majority and another party leader was able to command one. Today, it is virtually impossible for this to occur—given the rigid division of the Commons membership between two parties, and the strict political discipline maintained over each of them—until a general election has intervened and the voters have altered the party balance in the House. Clearly, a Prime Minister is in a powerful political position. Not only is he the acknowledged leader of his party, and thus the leading member of Parliament, he is also head of the government, selecting and removing all members of the Cabinet and Ministry.

The Prime Minister has a broad range of duties, falling into three classes, arising out of his relationships with the Queen, the administration, and the Parliament. First of all, he advises the Queen in the performance of the powers of the Crown and keeps her informed of the state of affairs in the government generally. Second, as the "keystone of the Cabinet arch," he presides over that body, and supervises the work of the Ministry and the various departments of government, so that the activities of the executive branch are coordinated. Third, as a member of Parliament—since 1902 always in the House of Commons—he is the principal spokesman of the government before it, promoting the government bills which make up its legislative program and defending the Cabinet's policies. The Prime Minister also recommends the dissolution of Parliament and thus chooses the time for a general election.

The Privy Council, the Cabinet, and the Ministry. Before the eighteenth century, the principal advisory and administrative assistance to the king was provided by the Privy Council. In time this body became too large to offer advice effectively, and many of its members ceased to have any political responsibilities. Even so, it continues to have legal authority, though substantially altered functions. The Privy Council today is composed of some three hundred members. In addition to all present and past Cabinet members (for it is only through the Privy Counsellor's oath that a member is officially sworn to loyalty and secrecy as Her Majesty's Servant), the Council contains a number of persons accorded the distinction as a reward for important public service. As a body, it has only formal functions: the promulgation of Orders in Council and the giving of official effect to other executive acts.

The Cabinet originated as a gathering of the most important members of the Privy Council, and for most of its history was unknown to the law. Though its existence was finally recognized in the Ministers of the Crown Act, 1937, it is a conventional organ, composed of those ministers whom the Prime Minister invites to serve with him as a deliberative council. Though in the earlier history of the Cabinet the Prime Minister played a role described as "first among equals," his position today is far stronger than that. While the selection of Cabinet members rests with him, the choice of his Cabinet colleagues involves a number of considerations. The ministers heading the principal departments must be included because of their importance—hence, the Chancellor of the Exchequer, the Foreign Secretary, and the Ministers of Defence, Home Affairs, Social Services, Trade and Industry, and Environment. For practical reasons, too, the Cabinet must contain some effective debaters and several members of the House of Lords. Other choices rest on such varied factors as political obligation, administrative needs, and personal convenience. As a result, the size of the Cabinet, though not fixed by law, can scarcely number fewer than eighteen.

Thus, the Prime Minister's selections are not entirely unrestricted, and the alternatives available to him are not nearly as many as those of an American President. Once organized, the Cabinet is collectively responsible for its acts and policies. In shaping and leading this team the Prime Minister must display a large talent for leadership. He may go a considerable distance on his own discretion, but he must always carry his Cabinet with him. Now and then a dissident member may be dropped, or an ineffective minister replaced, but harmony and mutual trust are indispensable. Whatever internal differences may arise, the Cabinet must present a united front to the outside.

As the central institution between the executive and legislative branches, the functions of the Cabinet are most important. First, its members collectively decide broad matters of policy involving foreign affairs, finance, and other matters of concern to the entire government. Second, the Cabinet formulates the legislative program which is annually placed before Parliament; and its individual members lead in introducing, defending, and overseeing enactment of the legislation. Third, the Cabinet coordinates and delimits the authority of the various departments of government.

The Ministry is composed of the Cabinet members, other senior and junior ministers, law officers, and government whips—all the politically chosen officials of the executive branch, who together constitute Her Majesty's Government. All members of the Ministry, some seventy to one hundred persons, are selected by the Prime Minister and may be removed at his discretion. Most of them are members of the House of Commons, for it is before this body that principal accounting must be made for the policies and acts of government. There must also be some who are members of the House of Lords, because the upper chamber requires spokesmen for the Ministry as well.

The Parliamentary Executive in France and Germany. Two interesting variations of the Cabinet type of government are illustrated in the political systems of France and Germany. In contrast to the British system, both of these are provided for in documentary constitutions adopted since World War II, and both reflect previous unsuccessful parliamentary experiences, rather than centuries-old accumulations of custom. In the France of the Third Republic (1871–1940), the existence of a multiparty system, extreme ideological differences between the major political groups, weakness of parliamentary party discipline, frequent political scandals and crises, among other factors, all rendered the French Cabinet unstable and weak. Formed always by coalition of a number of parties, French governments could adopt programs that were only provisional compromises over a limited number of issues, and were frequently and easily pulled apart from within or overturned by one of the two houses of Parliament. During this seventy-year period, the average life of a Cabinet was nine months, producing a situation of instability barely mitigated by repeated reappointment of many ministers. Of course, proposals were made for strengthening the executive, but the memory of two Napoleons and the fear of an all-powerful ruler always obstructed their acceptance.

The Constitution of the Fourth Republic (1946) contained several provisions intended to give new stability to the Cabinet and greater scope for leadership to the Premier. These included a limited power of dissolution for the Premier, a cooling-off period before votes of no-confidence or censure were taken by the National Assembly—to which house alone he was now accountable—and the establishment of a broad basis of support for a Cabinet before it was installed in office. Even so, experience with the wartime Vichy dictatorship of Marshal Pétain restrained efforts—especially those of General Charles de Gaulle—to create an executive with effective powers. And again, the habits and atmosphere of the Third Republic continued to prevail in politics; French governments turned over even more rapidly—on the average every five months. Inevitably, the governments of the Fourth Republic proved increasingly less able to cope with France's serious domestic and foreign problems. In both the Third and Fourth Republics, legislative superiority over the executive led to their description as systems of "assembly government" rather than "cabinet government." Mounting frustration with such executive instability—and with a National Assembly which could not govern but could prevent the Cabinet from doing so—led to widespread support for General de Gaulle's proposal of a new constitution, and its adoption in 1958.

The new Fifth Republic displays a governmental system with a curious blend of features from both the parliamentary and presidential types of executive, as well as a style reminiscent of Napoleonic plebiscitary government. The President was initially chosen by electoral college, but a constitutional amendment of 1962 provides for his election by popular vote for a seven-year term. He is intended, however, to be much more than a titular head of state, and is given power to act as arbiter between the government, the parties, and the Parliament. The Premier and members of the Cabinet are appointed by him; but on accepting office they must resign their seats in Parliament, if they are members of that body, and ministers may be appointed from outside it. The President is further empowered to dissolve the National Assembly, though not more than once a year. On the other hand, the government may still be forced to resign by a vote of censure passed by an absolute majority of the National Assembly. Thus, an attempt was made to apply both the principle of a limited separation of powers, which in the Gaullist view is essential to executive stability, and the principle of ministerial responsibility, which in French tradition is essential to representative government.

Whether any or all of these institutional reforms can, in the long run, overcome France's long-standing political habits remains in question. President de Gaulle chose to resign abruptly in 1969 after his government was defeated in a legislative referendum; he was succeeded in a popular election by a political associate and former Premier, Georges Pompidou. The French distrust strong governments and disdain weak ones, so the present regime may be only another temporary solution to the vexing problem of reconciling liberty with authority in that country.

If in France the executive has often been weak and unstable, in Germany, by contrast, the tradition has been to overconcentrate authority in the executive and make him formidably strong. Even after putting aside autocratic rulers and an authoritarian dictator, the German preference for a stable and highly concentrated center of authority is demonstrated in the Bonn Constitution, adopted in 1949, and in the politics of the German Federal Republic. The federal President is elected for a five-year term by a special federal assembly composed of the members of the *Bundestag* and an equal number of representatives of the *Land* (state) Diets. He has the usual role of a republican head of state, with nominal rather than real powers. All his political acts are countersigned by the Federal Chancellor, who is the political executive, chosen by the President because he commands a majority in the *Bundestag*. Thus, the essential principle of parliamentary democracy—ministerial responsibility—is maintained.

Beyond this, however, virtually all arrangements operate to make the office of Chancellor considerably more stable and dominant than that of an ordinary prime minister. The Chancellor alone is specifically authorized to determine general policy. He chooses and dismisses the ministers, who need not be members of Parliament, but may be high-ranking civil servants or experienced *Land* politicians. The Chancellor is under no obligation to consult his cabinet colleagues, and in practice does so far less than do British and French prime ministers. What is unique in the German arrangements is the constitutional provision that the *Bundestag* may vote its lack of confidence in the Chancellor only by simultaneously electing his successor by a majority vote of its members—a so-called constructive vote of no-confidence. Thus, a Chancellor is virtually irremovable unless a majority opposing him is equally united behind another leader, or until a general election alters the political composition of the legisla-

ture. For this reason, Germany has had no problem of cabinet instability; and the first Chancellor of the Republic, Konrad Adenauer,
held the office without interruption during four terms for fourteen
years until his retirement in 1963 at the age of 87. Since then, to be
sure, the office has passed among Chancellors more frequently.

The Parliamentary Executive in the New Nonwestern States. The
widespread political awakening since the two World Wars has produced a host of new independent communities in Africa, the Middle
East, and Southeast Asia. After long periods of colonial government
—which is essentially a form of authoritarian rule—these countries
are attempting, generally after only short periods of transition, to
begin the conduct of self-government with the paraphernalia of western parliamentary institutions. As might be expected, it is proving to
be a difficult undertaking, for parliamentary or any other type of popular representative and constitutional government is a matter not
only of form but of spirit. Yet neither the indigenous traditions of
these countries nor their experience of colonial rule, for the most part,
have fitted their peoples for such a task.

Among the serious obstacles is the fact that the mechanisms of
popular elections are entirely novel to these new states. Since the voters are mainly illiterate and often unable even to spell their own
names, elections are difficult to administer and their results are at
least of partly questionable significance. Political parties tend to be
organized around personalities, are highly hierarchical, and may well
have had as their principal experience not the conduct of government
but nationalistic agitation or conspiracy for independence. In some
instances, parties reflect ancient tribal or regional differences and act
as divisive rather than unifying agencies. And the new national leaders who assume the prime ministership and other ministerial offices
may have little experience with the idea of political cooperation and
collective responsibility. They also tend to be hostile to the existence
of a parliamentary opposition, seeing it as dangerously obstructionist
or downright treasonable. The art of compromise is frequently unknown in such societies, as is acceptance of the principle that the
arena of politics is a place for the necessary display not only of moral
courage but also of moderation and restraint. In certain other societies, the idea of compromise is so ingrained traditionally that complete government inaction results if unanimity cannot be obtained.
All such countries have seen the conduct of effective governmental

administration complicated by the absence of any counterpart to the western middle class and the lack of an adequate supply of trained administrators, civil servants, scientists, technicians, and teachers. When it is considered, further, that great strains are imposed on these still frail and inexperienced governmental systems by the attempts of their leaders to effect thoroughgoing economic and social revolutions, immediate or even long-run success seems uncertain.

At best, considerable experimentation with and modification of western institutions will probably be necessary, as well as decades of political experience and education, to produce viable and stable governmental systems. At worst, we should not be surprised if military control and dictatorship, or intervals of such rule—which have already been instituted in many of them—are to be part of the making of such states, unpleasant though that prospect may be.

An Evaluation of the Parliamentary Executive. It might be expected that, given its widespread adoption, the parliamentary or cabinet type of executive has important advantages in its favor. It does produce, especially in its effective British form, a close union between the executive and the legislature, because the former is in effect a governing board drawn from the latter. A positive executive leadership of the legislature is both provided and accepted, and not left to chance. When a breach occurs between the two, it can be resolved; indeed, either a new ministry must be appointed or a new legislature elected. Once more, then, the executive and legislature move off on the same foot. There is, as well, always a clear distinction between the government majority that leads and the opposition that criticizes.

The tenure of the executive is not fixed, but rests instead upon the continuation of majority support in the legislature. Thus the parliamentary system creates an executive which is an excellent vehicle through which to express a popular mandate. And its policies tend to stay closely attuned to public opinion, for it has no calendar lease on office. Because the cabinet's powers are dependent upon a minimum degree of legal definition, its authority may be adjusted to the demands of the times; when necessary in emergency, political authority can be quickly centralized. Finally, the cabinet in the parliamentary system represents a considerable accumulation of political experience; its members reach their positions only after long apprenticeship in a parliamentary career. When a government loses office, its members then enter the opposition, where they remain within direct observational range of the conduct of public affairs and can hope, at least, for an early return to office.

Of course, the parliamentary type of executive displays certain disadvantages too. For one thing, the lack of a fixed tenure of office for the cabinet creates a degree of uncertainty—both for those within the government who must plan their program without knowing what time is available for carrying it out, and for those outside who must adjust their affairs to the new government's policies. Certainly, the advantage of some expectation of continuity in policy for a definite period is lost. In the absence of a separation of powers setting apart the legislative and executive branches, there is a lack of means to prevent one branch from overextending itself. The principal restraint upon the executive must be effected by its accountability to parliament; it is difficult to create others by law. Although some limitations may be imposed—the forces of custom and public opinion are most important in Great Britain—they cannot be counted upon to apply effectively everywhere. Thus, a common consequence has been failure to achieve an equilibrium between the two branches of government. In Great Britain and West Germany, the executive has enjoyed a dominance over the parliament to an extent that there are complaints of "cabinet dictatorship." In France of the Third and Fourth Republics, on the other hand, the executive was so dominated by the parliament, often acting arbitrarily and irresponsibly, that effective orderly government was impossible.

Clearly, the parliamentary type of executive is most effective when supported by a stable majority, and this is likely to be found only in countries having a strong biparty system. Most countries which have instituted the cabinet system have been hampered in its operation by their multiparty systems, and cabinets have tended to be indecisive and unstable. Various efforts have been made to resolve this problem by the application of mechanistic devices, such as cooling-off periods and "constructive" votes of no-confidence; but these have not succeeded in providing an adequate substitute for political stability, traditions of moderation, and reasonableness. This failure of the parliamentary system to produce stable and recognizable leadership has led to popular support for dictators and authoritarian government as a means of providing it. Ironically, many countries have chosen the parliamentary in preference to the presidential system, fearing the latter type of executive to be so powerful that it might become dictatorial; yet their failure to operate the cabinet system effectively has in many instances led to its easy conversion into a dictatorship.

The Presidential Executive

An American contribution to political invention is the presidential type of chief executive, originated in the United States Constitution of 1789. It has had nothing like the widespread adoption of the parliamentary type of executive, however, having been instituted only in such Latin American states as Costa Rica, Mexico, Uruguay, Chile and Colombia, and in a few other states immediately associated with American political experience, such as Liberia and the Philippine Republic. A form of the presidential type of executive may also be seen in many new African states, formerly French colonies, such as the Republics of Senegal, Chad, Ivory Coast, and Niger; here the executive position more nearly resembles the American than the French. It seems unfortunate that the presidential features and advantages have not been more widely appreciated. Among others, as a means of providing a strong and stable center of power within a newly created state embarked upon the difficult task of self-government, it might well prove less difficult to operate effectively than the more delicately adjusted parliamentary system.

Essential Features of the Presidential Executive. Essentially, the presidential system of government provides a chief executive who is not a member of the legislature, is chosen for a definite term of office, who holds a wide, popular mandate resulting from his election, and is largely independent of the legislative branch for the conduct of his administration. The president's formal powers are defined in a documentary constitution. The fact that his office combines the roles of both chief of state and political leader of the government provides a dual enhancement of his prestige and authority; there is no dispersal of fundamental executive authority and the power to exercise it. These features are demonstrated in the American presidency.

The American Presidency. The framers of the American Constitution in 1787 were obliged to undertake a substantial task of pioneering when they came to the problem of providing an executive for the new system of government. Given the still-vivid memories of the controversies with their former king, George III, the institution of monarchy, even with a set of responsible ministers, was popularly discredited. The inadequacies of a leaderless central government, with executive functions undertaken by legislative committees, had been fully demonstrated by experience with the Articles of Confederation since 1781. Although a single executive was feared by some as a possible opening wedge for monarchy, the alternative of a plural executive was opposed as being inefficient—lacking unity, secrecy, and dispatch. Agreement ultimately prevailed on the necessity for a single executive, modeled somewhat on the well-known office of governor in the individual states, though with considerably more power. The method by which the President was to be selected offered further difficulties. His election by Congress, it was argued, would place him too deeply in debt to the legislature and would impair the principle of separation of powers; election by the people, even in face of the limited suffrage allowed at the time, appeared to offer the still more dangerous possibility of mob rule. A compromise was found, therefore, in a system of selection whereby presidential electors, chosen in each state as its legislature should prescribe, would select the President. Thus, the Constitution provided for a President, relatively independent of both Congress and the people, indirectly elected for a fixed term, and vested with the full executive powers.

Nomination and Election of the President. The rise of the great national political parties was to short-circuit the indirect method of selecting the President intended by the Constitution. Within a few years after 1789, the parties began to offer specific candidates for the presidency and vice-presidency, and to place on the ballot a list of electors pledged in advance to cast their state's electoral vote, if chosen, for the nominees of their party. Well before the mid-nineteenth century, the major parties also began to hold national conventions in which to nominate their standard-bearers, and thus introduced a further extension of party control.

Briefly, the election of the President today still includes the constitutionally prescribed forms, if diverging from their spirit. Party control of the nominating process is complete, and election is virtually on a popular basis, as the electors are so chosen. In the summer of a presidential election year, delegates from the state party organizations meet in national convention and choose their presidential and vice-presidential candidates. On election day in November, the voters in each state cast their ballots for the list of electors of that party they wish to support. Approximately a month later the group of electors which has been chosen meets at their state capital, casts the state's electoral vote (equal to the number of the state's Senator and Representatives in Congress—or three in the case of the District of Columbia), and forwards the results to Congress. Of course, the outcome of the election has long since become well known, but certain formalities remain. In January, Congress canvasses the states' electoral votes and announces as elected the two candidates who have received the electoral majority. If no candidate has a majority, the Constitution provides, the House of Representatives chooses a President from the three names highest on the list; in the same circumstances, the Senate chooses a Vice-President from the two highest candidates. The President and Vice-President (elect) take office on January 20.

The election is thus not strictly by popular vote, because the majority of electoral votes, not popular ones, is decisive. A presidential candidate gets the entire electoral vote of each state he carries. The preference of the voters is not usually, but may be, affected by this stipulation. In three cases a popularly preferred candidate failed to obtain the office: Presidents John Quincy Adams (1824), Hayes (1876), and Harrison (1888) received fewer popular votes than their principal opponents. Twelve other presidents won with only a plurality of the popular vote. For example, Lincoln (1860), Wilson (1912), and more recently Truman (1948), Kennedy (1960), and Nixon (1968) lacked a majority of the popular vote but obtained electoral majorities. Though numerous changes in this system of election have been proposed, including abolishing the electoral college procedure and substituting a direct popular vote, none has achieved necessary acceptance in the form of a constitutional amendment.

The Office of President. The President's term of office is fixed at four years. The Constitution originally raised no obstacle to his re-election for further terms, but long-standing tradition and political practice prevented any President from obtaining a third term until 1940. Subsequent reaction to Franklin D. Roosevelt's election to a third and fourth term led to advocacy, at least in partisan quarters, of a formal two-term limitation upon the office. The Twenty-second Amendment, added to the Constitution in 1951, provides, therefore, that "no person shall be elected to the office of the President more than twice." As is the case with all civil officers of the national government, the President may be removed from office "on impeachment for and conviction of treason, bribery, or other high crimes and misdemeanors," and a President is allowed to resign. None has resigned or been removed, however, though several have died in office.

The formal qualifications for holding the office are few. The Constitution stipulates only that the President must be a "natural-born" citizen, at least thirty-five years of age, and a resident of the United States for fourteen years. In practice, however, the nominating conventions, the prevailing political atmosphere, and the voters themselves erect other prerequisites for achievement of the presidential office. These customary qualities, though varying in any particular election year, ordinarily require conformance to what is known as the principle of "availability." The common characteristics displayed by presidential candidates suggest that in order to be accepted as wholly "available" a candidate had best be a family man in his early fifties, of Anglo-Saxon stock, Protestant, college-educated, a veteran of military service, and serving successfully in public office, usually as governor of a politically pivotal state. Candidates without these characteristics have been at a disadvantage, though recently, religion seems less important, and more candidates have been cutting their political teeth in Congress. If a President is removed from office, resigns, dies, or is unable to perform his duties, the Constitution provides that the Vice-President succeed him. A law governing succession to the presidency beyond this point, adopted by Congress in 1947, provides that if there is neither a President nor a Vice-President, the office passes in turn to the Speaker of the House of Representatives, then the President pro tempore of the Senate, and thereafter to cabinet officers in the order of their precedence.

The constitutional enumeration of the President's executive authority is set forth in brief and general terms. Article II states that "the executive power shall be vested in a President"; that he "shall take care that the laws be faithfully executed"; and that he shall take an oath to "preserve, protect and defend the Constitution." He is made commander-in-chief of the armed forces; he is authorized to make treaties with the concurrence of two-thirds of the Senate; he is given power to appoint, with the consent of the Senate, diplomatic and consular officers, justices of the Supreme Court, and all other officers whose appointments are not otherwise provided for; he may grant pardons and reprieves for offenses against the United States. Finally, he may "require the opinion, in writing, of the principal officer in each of the executive departments, upon any subject relating to the duties of their respective offices."

Even more modest provision is made in the Constitution concerning the President's relations with other branches of the government.

He is authorized to give Congress information from time to time on the state of the Union, and may recommend measures for their consideration. He may call special sessions of Congress; if the houses disagree as to a time for their adjournment, he may determine it; and all bills and joint resolutions passed by Congress must be submitted to him for approval. We can see that the bare constitutional provisions concerning presidential authority, important as they are, give limited insight into the nature of the office and its actual powers. A discussion of the office in its broader aspects must be reserved for a later part of this chapter.

The President's Cabinet. The Cabinet of the American President is similar to its English counterpart in that it is composed of the principal department heads of the executive branch, but there the resemblance practically ends. Members of the Cabinet are appointed individually as secretaries of the eleven major departments; their principal functions are administrative; they may not be members of Congress, though they may be chosen from that body's membership. Collectively, the Cabinet members have consultative and advisory functions, though their responsibilities here are what the President cares to make them. He may consult them much or little; some Presidents, indeed, have preferred to seek advice from lesser officials or other persons with no official status at all. Of course, the Cabinet is available as an instrument through which to determine executive policy and to achieve administrative coordination, but it is not always employed to do so. The promotional responsibilities of its members are commonly stressed; President Lyndon Johnson once said of his Cabinet that it "consists of nine salesmen and one credit manager."

The Constitution does not provide for a Cabinet, nor do the statutes. Rather, the Cabinet arose informally in response to President Washington's desire for a body of advisers when the Senate refused to lend itself to this purpose (in any event, it soon became too large for such a function), and subsequent Presidents continued the practice. The basis upon which its members are selected accounts for still other reasons why it differs from the British Cabinet. Some of its members may well be outstanding leaders within the President's party, but this is not a primary requirement. As often as not, such appointments are made to reward party service or pay election "debts"; to give representation to principal geographical sections of the country or highly organized interest groups; and to obtain some members, even of the opposition party, who enjoy influence in the houses of Congress. The President's selections must be approved by the Senate, but usually go unquestioned; he may remove his appointees at any time. The members of the presidential Cabinet are thus the subordinates of the President rather than his colleagues. He is free to accept or reject their advice; and, in case of any differences, he may always have the last word.

Other Presidential Executives. The most extensive experience with the presidential executive outside the United States has been in Latin America. These states, winning their independence from Spain, for the most part in the first half of the nineteenth century, adopted constitutions which reflected their aspirations as much as their own traditions. Hence they looked in most cases to their sister republic to the north as a source of models for their political institutions. There was not, of course, blind copying of American arrangements; many of their institutions and ideas of democratic government were influenced by those of France and other countries. All of the states undertook to establish in some degree the separation-of-powers principle, though after a century of political development and constitutional revision, government in Latin America now commonly reflects the trend of indigenous experience toward a dominant executive branch.

Some comparisons of the presidential office in North and Latin America may be briefly noted. All of the Latin-American constitutions provide for the popular election of a president; five- or six-year terms of office are allotted in many cases; and most countries prohibit re-election, though in practice the restriction is not always observed. A vice-president is commonly elected at the same time as the chief executive, and provision is frequently made for the removal from office of both officials by impeachment.

Presidential power is everywhere supreme, mainly as a consequence of constitutional authorization, but also because of political tradition and practice. In much of Latin America, the major task of government is simply to maintain order. Weak administrations are quickly overturned, and a *caudillo*, or military chief, commonly assumes the reins of power. Most of these presidents enjoy, therefore, substantial emergency powers, and authority to initiate legislation and even to govern by decree. They may declare a state of siege and suspend constitutional rights; they may collect and spend taxes; they may appoint local governors; and in many other ways they may exert relatively complete authority. In practice, too, if not by constitutional stipulation, both the congresses and the courts are politically subordinated to the president. Although strictures may be raised at such violations of the ideals of limited government and constitutionalism, it must be pointed out that in an area characterized by chronic political and economic instability, inefficient and corrupt officials, political feuds and terrorism, any political regime is bound to be sternly tested.

An Evaluation of the Presidential Executive. On balance, the presidential type of executive has fewer advantages in principle than the cabinet type, but those it has are none the less persuasive. Certainly, the office of the presidential executive has met the test of time in the country of its origin, demonstrating its capability of bringing forward national leadership within the framework of the constitutional system. Comparatively, it seems obvious—despite the fear expressed by such foreign observers as John Stuart Mill and James Bryce that great men were not likely to become presidents—that the occupants of the office are entirely the equal, in general ability and practical capacity to govern, of the heads of governments produced by the parliamentary systems of Great Britain, France, or Germany. The president's fixed term of office assures a position of executive stability, particularly advantageous during times of crisis. The executive is separated from and independent of the legislature so far as his selection, basic powers, and terms of office are concerned. Such a situation has considerable merit, of course, in the eyes of those who believe in the desirability of a separation of powers and oppose an excessive concentration of governmental authority in any one place. The legislature is also independent of the executive in the same fashion; and thus each has important means of restraining the other against possible excesses. The presidential system offers greater opportunity in form, at least, for popular choice in the selection of the executive, permitting the voter to identify himself more closely with the national political leader. Generally, the system has the distinct merit of providing a stable executive even without the presence of stable legislative majorities.

The principal disadvantages of the presidential type of executive largely reflect the merits of the cabinet type. No direct executive leadership of the legislature is provided, since the latter is a coordinate, not a subordinate, body. As a consequence, the president is

often obliged to make extraordinary efforts—summoning all his resources of patronage, prestige, and personal influence—to accomplish
the enactment of a unified legislative program. Not uncommon, either, is the display of legislative jealousy of the president's prerogatives. Unlike the cabinet executive, who achieves that position as a
result of a long and successful career as a party leader in the legislature, the presidential executive frequently has had no such experience; indeed, he may well not have extensive knowledge of any part
of the national government's processes. Further, the executive and legislative branches may fall under the control of different political parties and thus produce the possibility of a deadlock between them
over certain important issues. Such a situation, which may be avoided
in the cabinet system, can make most difficult the accomplishment of
positive government action. A sometimes unsatisfactory feature—
because the executive has a fixed term of office—is that elections and
changes in government take place only at stated intervals, when there
may be no crucial political issue to be resolved, or may even occur in
the midst of war or crisis, when any change for the time being is undesirable. It is not possible in the presidential system, either, to produce a change of executive when circumstances might definitely require it, because a president, once chosen, is practically irremovable
until the end of his term of office. It should be noted, finally, that the
presidential system as such does not preclude the establishment of
dictatorial government. The president not uncommonly exercises dictatorial authority in many Latin-American states where democracy
has never flourished.

The Dictatorial Executive

The features of the dictatorial type of executive have been displayed in
twentieth-century political regimes as divergent as those of Mussolini,
Hitler, Franco, Stalin, Tito, Mao Tse-tung, Perón, Nasser, and Castro.
Which are the most typical and representative it is not, for several
reasons, easy to say. Each dictatorship, while demonstrating a number of characteristics in common with others, has had unique features: some have been motivated by the extremist doctrines of the political right, others of the left; and the length of their regimes and
the extent of their powers have varied. Not all dictators are
totalitarian—some undertake to monopolize political power without
dominating all aspects of society. Many contemporary dictatorships,

indeed, might well be characterized as modernizing oligarchies. Conducted as a rule by military juntas, whose leader may either take office as head of state or exercise control through a "revolutionary council" or "national liberation committee," these military dictatorships usually do not seek the maximization of state power or the personal aggrandizement of the leader. Discarding representative institutions, they seek such goals as efficiency, stability, financial responsibility, and economic modernization through the concentration of authority. They ordinarily claim to replace the rule of dishonest and irresponsible politicians, unreformed and inefficient traditionalists, or the chaos of no effective central authority. Furthermore, they usually propose to conduct "caretaker" regimes until their goals are reached and normal civilian authority can be restored. In recent years, Argentina, Brazil, Greece, Indonesia, Libya, Mali, and Pakistan have been ruled by such systems. Although a government by military dictatorship may seem to mark the complete destruction of democratic values and procedures, the real alternatives for many of these new or chronically unstable states seem to be strong, if arbitrary, government or no government at all. And it may be noted that military dictatorships have been more restrained in their domestic and international policies, and thus less tyrannical and dangerous, than civilian ones pursuing extremist and totalitarian ideologies, often to fatal stages of paranoia. Hitler's Nazi terror took at least six million lives; Stalin's Communist terror cost twenty million or more.

Considerably more significant, then, is the phenomenon of totalitarian dictatorship, which directly confronts and opposes the values and procedures of democratic government. Totalitarianism achieves the ultimate degree of dictatorship; it involves the imposition of personal political force through other than conventional political institutions. Since generalization about totalitarian dictatorship is difficult, we can most usefully examine it in its original home, the Soviet Union. The Russian Bolshevik revolution produced the first major modern dictatorship, and half a dozen men have largely monopolized political power there for more than fifty years. This political system not only commands one of the world's superpowers, but serves as a prototype for many states in the Communist bloc. Not least important is the fact that dictatorship in Russia appears as firmly entrenched as ever.

The Soviet Dictators. The Soviet dictatorship, like that in many other countries, was originally the product of political crisis in a state where representative government had never been established; it was ushered into existence by force, along with skillful agitation and propaganda; and it is maintained by such means under the aegis of a revolutionary political party. This first Communist dictatorship was established by V. I. Lenin in November, 1917, when he grasped power from a fumbling provisional government attempting to maintain order and conduct an unpopular war after the collapse of the Czarist regime. Lenin, a militant and professional revolutionary, and leader of the small but well-organized Bolshevik movement, stepped into a virtual political vacuum, created a government, and successfully maintained his authority through the four years of counterrevolution and war which followed. By 1921, organized opposition was largely liquidated; and though Lenin's rule was supported by personal prestige and a certain measure of popularity, he used forceful measures without hesitation to maintain himself. By the time of his death in January, 1924, the contest had already begun for succession to his power.

The grim struggle which resulted took place largely behind the scenes, of course, but its outcome was clear. Of the principal contenders, Trotsky, the commissar for war, had won a reputation as an orator and political theoretician; Zinoviev, leader of the Communist International, had a large personal following; Stalin, the other leading contestant, had become general secretary of the Soviet Communist party in 1922, and had created a well-established position within the party bureaucracy. By combining his control over the party organization with a series of astute and ruthless political maneuvers, Stalin was able to draw the reins of power into his hands. Trotsky was dismissed from the government, then exiled, and finally even written out of Russian history books. All other possible opponents of Stalin, real and imagined, were similarly eliminated in the years following, a process which culminated in the wholesale party purges and executions from 1934 to 1939. By 1941—of the seven men who had constituted the membership of the Politburo, or top party organ, in 1924—Stalin alone was alive. Trotsky had been murdered; Tomsky was reported to have committed suicide; Zinoviev, Kamenev, Rykov, and Bukharin had been shot.

Stalin himself, characteristically of most of the modern dictators, was a man of obscure and humble origins. Born Joseph Djugashvili in Russian-occupied Georgia in 1879, his life began in poverty. Failing to complete his training for the Orthodox priesthood, because of his expulsion from the seminary, he early adopted the life of a political revolutionary, and was arrested and imprisoned by the Czarist regime a number of times. He became one of Lenin's lieutenants after 1905 and served as a commissar in the first Bolshevik government, but attracted little public attention until the contest for power began shortly before Lenin's death. Stalin's position of primacy remained unshaken through the political and economic crises of the 1930's, World War II, and the years thereafter until his death in 1953.

Once again several aspiring successors began to vie for position: Malenkov, Chairman of the Council of Ministers, and apparently Stalin's intended heir; Beria, head of the security police; and Molotov, the senior "old Bolshevik" and foreign minister. However, a more effective competitor for power, Khrushchev, who became principal party secretary nine days after Stalin's death, again demonstrated the strategic utility of that office. Within the year, Beria was arrested and executed without public trial for a long list of crimes. In 1955, Malenkov was suddenly demoted and replaced by Bulganin as Chairman of the Council of Ministers; another two years saw Molotov also removed from the center of power. Bulganin in turn fell into disfavor in 1958, and was replaced by Khrushchev, who then became the one front-rank leader. Once more the Soviet system demonstrated how collective leadership tends to give way inexorably to one-man rule, and why the problem of succession in a dictatorship produces crises, rather than an orderly transfer of power.

Nikita Khrushchev was born of a miner's family, in 1894, in the southern part of what is now the Russian republic. Working as a sheepherder and miner when young, he joined the Red Army during the revolution, and later received some modest education in party schools. He then worked as a party organizer, rising rapidly to high posts in the Moscow organization. By 1938, he was the Ukraine's party boss; and the next year, a full member of the Politburo. He had various political and military duties during World War II, including, after 1944, the direction of the brutal and bloody Ukrainian purges that continued during the next three years. In 1949, he returned to Moscow, where he was soon to demonstrate his superior skill at ruthless political in-fighting and his success in outmaneuvering all opponents who stood in his way.

Khrushchev's fall from power came late in 1964, when he was unceremoniously ousted in sudden disgrace from government and party offices, without tears or cheers from a bewildered populace. A *Pravda* editorial blamed the deposed leader for "harebrained schemes, immature conclusions and hasty decisions and actions divorced from reality, bragging and phrase-mongering, commandism, unwillingness to take into account the achievements of science . . . armchair methods, personal decisions, and disregard for the practical experience of the masses." New leaders again divided the top positions, as in 1953; Leonid I. Brezhnev became general secretary of the Communist party; Alexei N. Kosygin became premier; and Nikolai V. Podgorny continued as president. Several of Khrushchev's closest associates were removed from top posts at the same time. The turmoil surrounding this upheaval not only damaged the prestige of Soviet leadership at home and abroad, it demonstrated the political dangers raised by a great power that has no orderly process for a change of government.

In the years following, the U.S.S.R. has returned to another phase of "collective leadership"—rule by the fifteen-man (since 1971) Politburo, continuing Brezhnev as party boss at the head. At the close of the Twenty-fourth Party Congress in that year, Brezhnev was reconfirmed in the top job as general secretary. Born in 1906, he joined the party at his Ukrainian home city of Dnieprodzerzhinsk in 1931. A metallurgical engineer, he served as a political officer in the army during World War II, and later became a protégé of Khrushchev's. He rose through various party and political offices to become a full member of the Politburo in 1957. With a reputation as a doctrinaire communist and colorless bureaucrat, Brezhnev served as nominal head of state from 1960 to 1964.

No one can predict the future of the Soviet collective leadership, but a look at the past suggests that such collegial periods of rule tend to be transitional until a new dictator or dominant member emerges. The present Politburo, an elderly team of bureaucrats and technicians trained during the Stalin era, has aimed at perpetuating the status quo, avoiding the crude tyranny of Stalin, and the egregious blundering of Khrushchev. But the leadership is aging and conformist— applying such repression as needed to keep things as they are— apparently without plan or practice for liberalization. Since Soviet society cannot be kept at dead center indefinitely, when so many serious problems persist, it seems likely that unexpected changes in the Kremlin must continue.

The Dictator: Status and Powers. Some of the significant common characteristics of the totalitarian dictator can be illustrated by example from the top Soviet leadership. First the dictator gains his political position through means of violence, conspiracy, or maneuver. As the brief background descriptions of the top party leaders in the U.S.S.R. indicate, none was chosen by election, either party or popular, to hold power. None came to the top according to any previously determined rules or within the framework of established political institutions. Rather, the dictatorial accession to power is marked by the breakdown of the existing political order; the dictator's power thus rests upon his ability to assert it, rather than upon any claim to legitimacy.

Second, the dictator's exercise of power is primarily dependent upon his position within the dominant ruling party or oligarchy rather than in an office of government. In the Soviet Union, the reins of political power are held not by a president or prime minister, but by the man who controls the Communist party. Four men alone Lenin, Stalin, Khrushchev, and Brezhnev—have been able to do this for any considerable number of years. Through more than a quarter of a century of absolute rule, Stalin held a governmental post but part of the time. Until 1941, when he became chairman of the Council of Ministers, Minister of War, and Commander-in-Chief of the Soviet armies, he had held only party office. Khrushchev, likewise, took office as Chairman of the Council of Ministers only after he was politically well-entrenched, and Bulganin had committed the error of intriguing against him. Fundamentally, then, executive authority, regardless of where it is formally located, stems from party leadership; even collective rule requires an arbiter.

Third, the totalitarian dictator forcibly maintains a one-party system and eliminates all opposition to his rule, whether from within the party or without. Lenin began by using the Bolsheviks, a comparatively small but highly organized and disciplined political group of agitators and revolutionaries, to seize control of government in Russia. Once established, he did not hesitate to unleash the "Red Terror" in applying the most extreme measures against his counterrevolutionary enemies. The monopoly of political activity was formally conferred in the 1936 Constitution, which defines the Communist party as "the leading core of all organizations of the working people, both public and state." Those within the party are given no immunity from violence. The savage purge trials ordered by Stalin in the 1930's to liquidate possible centers of political opposition reached well into the group that had surrounded him most closely. Before his death, there were indications that in his mounting pathological suspiciousness, an even greater purge was being prepared. Although Khrushchev and his successors have shown less tendency toward bloodthirstiness by curbing the secret police and closing many of the forced labor camps—if only because the highly developed Soviet industrial state can no longer be ruled by despotic terror alone—they have not abandoned terror as a political weapon. Frequent threats are delivered in the U.S.S.R. to warn "spies, bourgeois nationalists, fascist collaborators, deviationists, diversionists, hooligans, revisionists, and antisocial elements" that no opposition centers will be tolerated. Intellectual "dissidents, slanderers, or parasites" are still sent with or without trial to corrective labor camps, prisons, and mental institutions.

Fourth, the dictatorial executive employs a body of trusted (but carefully supervised) political lieutenants who serve as an advisory staff and occupy the most important and strategic positions in the party and government. No dictator ever rules alone in solitary splendor; he must surround himself with a group of able lieutenants who, functioning in some respects as an executive's cabinet in a democratic government, can individually assume directing and administrative functions, and collectively assist in determining policies. In the Soviet Union this agency is the Politburo of the Central Committee of the Communist party. Organized in 1919, and known between 1952 and 1966 as the Presidium, it has usually contained a dozen members and several candidate members. This self-perpetuating group constitutes the leading summit of the party, at which are decided questions of the highest concern, both foreign and domestic, in governmental policy. Its members also hold some of the highest governmental posts in the Council of Ministers, thus keeping a close grip on the armed services, the labor unions, the security police, the information media, and the constituent republican governments, as well as their influential party jobs.

Fifth, as leader of the state, the dictator is endlessly publicized and given an artificial popularity through the manipulation of all devices that create opinion. In the earlier years of his rule, Stalin made only infrequent public appearances and his speeches were rare, intended as documents to be studied by party functionaries. He never engaged in the oratorical flights and dramatic displays that were the stock in trade of Hitler and Mussolini. During the 1930's, however, he began to appear more and more in the forefront; by World War II, his name, his portrait, and his statue were on view everywhere in Russia. Thereafter, the name of Stalin was employed in the Soviet press only with accompanying praise and adulation. Such phrases as "the beloved and wise leader," "the great leader and teacher," "the steel colossus," "the towering genius of all mankind," were invariably used in reference to him.

Sycophantic adulation can reach its limits, and Khrushchev's agility in outmaneuvering his rivals was well demonstrated in the skillful manner by which he set out to put a new face on the dictatorship. At the Twentieth Party Congress in 1956, the dead Stalin was subjected to scathing criticism; Khrushchev himself denounced his late master as a sadistic tyrant. The cult of personality, now discredited, was to be replaced by the cult of party. Nevertheless, the change was really one of style rather than practice. Through his control of the party press— some 150 newspapers—Khrushchev kept his name and face steadily before the people. Where Stalin was taciturn and aloof, Khrushchev was garrulous and gregarious. He visited with peasants, talked to workers in the street, and appeared as a typical family man. His visits abroad—to China, India, Great Britain, the United States, France, and elsewhere—brought him immense additional publicity, outside the Soviet Union as well as within it. Although he was not obliged to submit to popular elections, he behaved at times very much like a candidate for office in a democratic state. The purpose of all such devices of flattery and adulation is not so much to appeal to the personal vanity of the dictator as to solidify popular support for the political regime of which he is the symbol—a part of the propaganda undertaken to convince the public of the dictator's benevolence, wisdom, and competence. Yet Khrushchev himself seemed to have fallen victim to it; his own personal and erratic style of rule was denounced as a new "cult of personality."

Finally, we should note that the dictator's powers are not to be defined in terms of legal authority, as in the case of the democratic executive. On the contrary, they are subject to no institutional or constitutional checks but are determined at the will of the dictator himself. Practically, of course, there are limits. A dictator must exercise some self-restraint or his recklessness can destroy himself and his regime; he must be capable of reckoning what the traffic will bear. In his exercise of authority and influence he must always carry some of his political lieutenants and most of the party organization along with him. Because he has the whole machinery of the state at his command, however, he is in a position to monopolize the agencies that mold and manufacture public opinion. Persuasion is preferred, but there is no reluctance to employ coercion. Nor are dictators, however ruthless and fanatic, devious and blundering, hated by all. In 1971 a spontaneous outburst of sorrow in Haiti followed the death of "Papa Doc" Duvalier. It also appears that, among the communist dictators, Tito is widely admired and respected by the Yugoslav people. To deal with any recalcitrant minority who may still remain unconvinced, there are elaborate systems of espionage, secret police, concentration camps, and military forces. Thus, the dictator's power is most difficult to challenge; his removal is accompanied by conspiracy and violence, leaving uncertainty at best and at worst turmoil in its wake for some years.

Executive Organs in a Dictatorship. The Communist dictatorship in the U.S.S.R. has established an elaborate complex of institutions and offices of government which give formality to the exercise of political authority, though they are not the actual centers of it. There is no concept here, in theory or practice, of a separation of powers. Governmental organs are the tools to be used by the Communist party, a façade to conceal the true source of power and window dressing to emulate the representative institutions of the democratic systems. Thus, the 1936 Constitution provides for a Presidium of the Supreme Soviet, as one of the "highest organs of state power"; reconstituted in 1966, the Presidium is composed of a chairman, fifteen vice-chairmen, a secretary, and twenty members. The duties of this organ include the convening and dissolution of the Supreme Soviet, issuance of decrees, interpretation of laws, exercise of the right of pardon, declaration of war, ratification of treaties, and an extensive appointing power. The Presidium—functioning as a sort of collective presidency, and combining the exercise of legislative, judicial, and executive rules—has no prototype in western political institutions. It is the principal law-issuing body, and since its composition usually includes several members of the party Politburo, it operates close to the apex of authority.

The more immediate administration of affairs is assigned to a

Council of Ministers. "The highest executive and administrative organ of state power," according to the Constitution, this agency coordinates and directs the work of the various ministries of the state. Theoretically subordinated to the Supreme Soviet, it nonetheless prepares most of the legislation to be approved by that body, and—more importantly perhaps—issues the wealth of decrees, regulations, and ordinances essential to the day-to-day conduct of the government. The Council of Ministers is composed of the heads of various ministries and state committees, several other high officials of comparable rank, and some members of the Central Committee, numbering altogether several score members. Thus we see here another example of the interlocking relationships between party and governmental organs, as well as the means by which the top party leadership can control and coordinate a vast bureaucracy.

An Evaluation of the Dictatorial Executive. The advantages claimed for dictatorial government rest upon a frame of values so fundamentally distinct from those assessing democratic forms that few bases of comparison really exist. In the main, the claims run somewhat as follows: dictatorship is necessary to provide the government required by modern crisis conditions. When existing political and social institutions of a state fail to function with full effectiveness, it is argued, the only solution is vigorous rule imposed by force to provide swift and direct action, unimpeded by the slow-moving and inefficient machinery of democracy. Dictatorship also claims to have a monopoly of truth and the only correct blueprint for the future. Further, dictatorship makes possible the authoritarian control of the citizens' lives, forcefully eliminating the dissensions and conflicts of democratic politics and enforcing a reconciliation of class, economic, racial, religious, and other interests. In this way, the dictator copes with competing interests, but within limits, and without a legislative opposition. It is asserted as well that authority enforced from above by the dictatorship strengthens the state militarily, socially, and economically, so that the government may gain a totalitarian command of all the state's resources, human and material. Finally, such a system claims to recognize the real inequality of men to participate in the political process. In a dictatorship, power rests in the hands of a natural leader, who has demonstrated his ability by successfully seizing it.

Against any such claimed advantages, however, must be balanced some real and important disadvantages. The exercise of political power in a dictatorship lacks freely given consent by those who are ruled; it has no basis in law, regardless of retroactive pseudolegalisms. Dictatorship need make only the most limited responses to popular demand; it is not held to account for its exercise of authority; it may ruthlessly silence any criticisms. Obviously, too, the exercise of political power subject to no restraint is inevitably corrupting, for both ruler and ruled. Because the reconciliation of interests by the dictatorship is an enforced one, it is, therefore, apparent rather than real. The compromise and adjustment of interests are effected by the sacrifice of minority rights—in extreme cases, by the liquidation of the minority itself. Further, dictatorships do not in practice produce real administrative efficiency; they may appear to because of their ability to conceal waste and blundering, and to withhold the truth about their operations. But these can never be hidden indefinitely. Again, dictatorship subverts all individual liberties, since the only freedom, if it can be called that, is one of supporting the regime in the manner prescribed by the government. If its authority is to be maintained, the dictatorship can scarcely allow the exercise of fundamental democratic rights. Finally, the tenure of a dictator is usually terminated in disorder; succession involves a struggle, often to the death, by the contenders for power. The system is thus incapable of developing constitutional government because it rejects the concept either of a supreme legality or of stable institutions with real authority.

In sum, exponents of dictatorship argue that the end—that is to say, the necessity of creating effective political authority—justifies any means, however violent or immoral. Its opponents, on the other hand, insist that the means employed inevitably condition the ends achieved—so that illegal and immoral means only result in producing a corrupt and corrupting state.

III. Executive Functions

In early governments there was no conception of executive functions, as such, distinguished from legislative or judicial ones. All powers of government rested in the same hands. As the performance of governmental responsibilities became more complex, however, a division of labor and a specialization of function began to develop. Further, as a means of imposing some restraint on arbitrariness and of limiting governmental authority, responsibilities in the realm of policy determination and adjudication tended to be conferred on separate organs —legislatures and courts. Neither the legislative nor the judicial functions, though, can ever be mechanically distinguished or wholly divorced from that of the administration of policy; executive functions inevitably resist any precise compartmentalization, even in such systems of government as that of the United States, where the constitutional framers intended to impose a sharp separation of powers. The lines of demarcation arising from this somewhat artificially conceived three-way division of government functions, therefore, are invariably blurred in modern democratic states, and intentionally obliterated in dictatorships.

Symbolic and Ceremonial Functions. The importance of symbolic and ceremonial functions is often underestimated, particularly in democratic societies, which emphasize the ideal of social and political equality for all citizens; yet experience indicates their indispensability as human nature calls for some personification of the abstraction which is the state. The civic loyalty of many persons attaches far more readily to an individual than to an impersonal institution. The highest governmental authority requires not only dignity but some distance between ruler and ruled if overfamiliarity is to be avoided. As President de Gaulle observed, "There can be no prestige without mystery." A nation expects someone acting in its name to express national sentiments by appropriate means and to give tangible recognition to nationally accepted values. If some peoples prefer less emotionalism in the realm of government, none has proved to be so politically sophisticated as to dispense with symbolism and ceremony altogether.

The British offer the carrying out of ceremonial functions as one of the principal justifications for their hereditary monarchy, even though its powers have ceased to be of political importance. The titular head of state and others in the royal family can be usefully employed to spare the Prime Minister, the working executive, a considerable burden. Moreover, it is the general British view—and one which represents long experience—that their monarch performs these ceremonial functions far more effectively than would a plain citizen temporarily elevated to high office. Queen Elizabeth symbolizes both the British state and the unity of Commonwealth and empire, acting as a tangible tie binding together Commonwealth citizens in all parts of the world. Her personal presence lends dignity to, and represents the national interest in, such occasions as the opening of Parliament, the patronage of charitable undertakings, the review of military formations, the visiting of disaster-stricken areas, leadership in religious and patriotic celebrations, and the initiation of a large variety of national enterprises. "On the whole," Sir Winston Churchill once suggested, "it is wise in human affairs and in the government of men, to separate pomp from power."

In its earlier history, as a struggling young republic determined to reject monarchical trappings, the United States sought to de-emphasize such activities and expected a minimum of such performances from its presidents. But symbolic responsibilities have accumulated, and the President as the working executive now has ceremonial duties to perform. His personal appearance before Congress to deliver his State of the Union message, entertaining at diplomatic receptions, the inspection of military forces, attendance at Veterans' Day ceremonies, and his issuance of Thanksgiving proclamations, for example, all evidence popular demand for his presence or performance. The greeting and entertainment of foreign heads of state and other important official visitors have come to take so much time that he must limit the number of such visits.

In the totalitarian state, the symbolic and ceremonial functions of the dictator take on a special significance. Here the appeal to unquestioning obedience and undeviating loyalty—and the formation of the people into unbroken and disciplined ranks—focuses all attention on the exalted position of the national leader. At the same time, the mass rites over which the dictator presides are considered important as a means for inculating an individual sense of identification with the regime. Mass activity is in effect offered as a harmless substitute for democratic participation in the governing process; hence the continual marchings, wearing of uniforms, mass calisthenics, chanted slogans, and party rallies. The individual is thus encouraged to believe he is sharing in the glory and superhuman strength of the dictator.

Political Leadership. The histories of governments indicate that some of them may operate without effective leadership for a considerable period—particularly in times marked by the absence of stress or crisis—by drawing upon a momentum gained earlier, but such cases and conditions are exceptional. Indeed, numerous examples of weak and unsuccessful government—such as the United States under the

Articles of Confederation, the Russia of Czar Nicholas II, the French Fourth Republic, and the German Weimar Republic—all show notorious deficiency in bringing forward or sustaining effective leadership. By contrast, periods of national greatness are often identified with an Emperor Napoleon, a Czar Peter, or a Chancellor Bismarck; even in democratic states, where popular sentiment is inclined to be suspicious of truly positive leadership, the statesman's laurels are belatedly granted and to only a few—a Gladstone or a Churchill, a Jackson or a Lincoln. Yet however widely the control of political power may be distributed, the necessity for leadership remains. In fact, without it democracies tend to paralysis as quickly as other systems. Leaders must reflect national aspirations, organize them into practical programs, and show how they may be accomplished.

One of the great merits of the cabinet type of executive, as developed in Great Britain, is its effectiveness in encouraging—indeed, requiring—positive leadership. The process by which the British Prime Minister reaches that office is arduous and selective. He must expect to undergo a decade or two of service in the House of Commons, learning to speak and to negotiate persuasively. He will serve an apprenticeship as minister in one or more cabinets, demonstrating sufficient qualities of administrative efficiency to bring his appointment to one of the major departments of government. To make the last step to the prime ministership, he must become the choice of his colleagues to lead his party, whether in office or in opposition.

The situation of the American President in this respect is rather different. The method by which he is nominated and elected, and the popular interpretation of what qualities an acceptable presidential candidate must display, neither require nor assure that the President will necessarily have either natural or practiced ability as a political leader. Although a presidential nominee must somehow have identified himself with his party, he cannot be said as a rule to have become its national leader until he wins the presidential office and is able to employ its patronage and influence. Of course, an incumbent President is in a position to assert national leadership of his organization in a way that the various party chiefs in the states and in Congress cannot. He reaches a wider audience, as Professor Max Beloff observes, if only because "he also has more interesting and important things to say." The President's party leadership provides him a major means of exerting a unifying influence over the government—

primarily the executive branch—and encourages collaboration with the individual state administrations controlled by the same party. It is worth noting that the outstanding American presidents have been strong party men; the less successful have been those who have seen the party organization break from their control, or who never mastered it at all.

In the modern dictatorships it is through the party, we have noted, that the dictator asserts and exercises his political leadership. Indeed, the dictator tends to place more emphasis upon his role as party leader than upon his official post in the government. Mussolini as *Il Duce* of the Fascist party, Hitler as *Der Führer* of the Nazi party, and Stalin, "the great leader and teacher" of the Communist party, were in each case stressing the prime basis for their popular appeal. The dictatorships make a fetish of leadership, proclaiming always as their especial virtue that they direct the destinies of the incompetent masses by placing the state under the control of the "true aristocrat." Undoubtedly, though, that a dictator has first become the master of a party organization is a most significant factor in his success as a popular leader. The years he devotes to organizational work, to winning the loyalty of a dedicated band of adherents, and the struggles with factionalism, underground intrigue, or "cold" civil war, all give him an exceptional schooling.

Policy Formation and Legislative Leadership. It is a common American belief—arising from a misconception of the true functioning of government—that the power of policy formation properly and necessarily belongs only to the legislature. Legislatures, so this simplified version of the governmental process goes, make laws and policies; executives merely carry them out. This view is hardly realistic. In these times, the executive can adequately discharge his responsibilities only if he himself first formulates and initiates policies—many of which, to be sure, may subsequently be presented to the legislature for criticism, modification, acceptance, or rejection. There are several reasons why this must be the case. First, the executive head of the government often has the only adequate sources of information that permit policy proposals which envision the whole national interest. Second, rapid changes in the course of events are produced by economic fluctuations, international crises, and war, so that the executive is constantly required to act upon matters over which a legislative decision would come too slowly. Modern legislatures are thus obliged increasingly to enact their legislation in general terms, leaving to executive determination the immediate application of principles to individual times and circumstances. Third, several of the most important government functions—those related to foreign and military affairs, especially—require a large exercise of administrative discretion. A legislature is scarcely organized to negotiate international agreements or to command military forces.

The British parliamentary executive is definitely organized to assume responsibility for policy formation. The Cabinet, under the leadership of the Prime Minister, has distinct and undivided responsibility for all matters of policy, both legislative and administrative. Not only does the Cabinet formulate plans for the conduct of the government's business, but it prepares and presents a legislative program to which most of the time of Parliament is devoted. The British tendency, indeed, is to look upon the parliamentary function as one primarily to promote or criticize the effecting of Cabinet policies.

Although some of the largest areas of the American President's discretion are in the fields of foreign and military affairs, which are discussed below, vastly important areas of domestic affairs also belong to him. American experience, like British, has conferred upon the executive a considerable amount of policy-making authority—well beyond that associated with the performance of narrow administrative functions. Part of this authority derives by implication from the Constitution, but considerably more is conferred by act of Congress. Although Congress may not delegate its legislative power to the President, strictly speaking, it may still grant him extensive policy-making functions, provided always it establishes some defined limits within which the President is to act.

The exercise of the policy-making function in a dictatorship is essentially confined to the dictator and the narrow group around him. By its very nature, dictatorship precludes any wide sharing of authority, and leaves to the executive complete freedom of action. To be sure, after the establishment of dictatorships in Fascist Italy and Nazi Germany, the national legislatures were not abolished—and in the Soviet Union one was created—but in no sense was policy formation turned over to them. Rather, composed of hand-picked members, they have been employed as a convenient stage fixture before which the dictator can appear, creating the illusion of popular representation without granting its substance. In any event, executive decrees provide the most important form of legislation in a dictatorship, and the legislature need not be consulted at all.

Supervision of Administration. In the supervision of administration the executive releases the initial energy which, conveyed to the machinery of government, makes its wheels turn. Although the functions of policy formation and administrative management are closely related, as we have suggested, it is one thing to decide what to do and another to do it. The latter responsibility is clearly that of the administrative branch of the government which, headed by the chief executive, looks to him as the ultimate source of inspiration and authority. Only in a very limited degree is the chief executive an administrator himself. Given the large demands on his time and energy, only a portion of them can be devoted to the problems of administrative management; actual performance rests with his subordinates. The chief executive must solve the most difficult problems, and of necessity they are difficult, for the easy ones are disposed of at lower levels.

The British Prime Minister has in the Cabinet an admirable instrument for the supervision of administration. Composed of the principal majority party leaders, it controls the executive branch and coordinates its various ministries. Given the Prime Minister's central position, he need not go far to make his influence felt. Within the Cabinet is decided what legislation is needed to effect particular policies, while individual cabinet members see that their departments carry them out in appropriate relation to the government's program as a whole.

The American President, like the British Prime Minister, is concerned as chief executive to oversee the performance of administrative functions. The Constitution stipulates that he shall "take care that the laws be faithfully executed," and vests in him "the executive power." This delegation of authority is made in such broad terms that the Supreme Court has concluded that the President is responsible not only for the enforcement of acts of Congress and treaties, but also for "the rights, duties and obligations growing out of the Constitution itself, our international relations, and all the protection implied by the nature of the government under the Constitution." The President appoints most important officers of the national government; except where Congress has provided otherwise in a few instances, he also removes them at his discretion. He issues rules and regulations for the civil, diplomatic, and armed services; and, in many areas of concern even to ordinary citizens, he promulgates codes and orders. The President's powers of administrative supervision are no less than those of the British Prime Minister, but he is subject to a greater degree of legislative check in the exercise of some of them.

For the dictatorships, the problem of administrative supervision is even greater than for democratic states. Obviously, if the aims of the dictatorship are to be realized, there must be the most complete conformity to the leader's policies throughout the administration from top to bottom. A less obvious reason, however, originates in the magnitude of government machinery, which must perform not only normal state functions but extends its control to the economic, cultural, social, and even personal life of the individual. It is noteworthy that aspiring dictators usually level their guns at the bureaucracy, the red tape, and the inefficiency of the democratic system; yet when they come to power themselves, they invariably bring into existence an even more monstrous apparatus for the performance of state functions.

Diplomatic and Military Powers. Diplomatic and military functions have always been among the most important of executive duties, in earlier history as exclusive prerogatives of the monarch, and today as responsibilities practically amenable only to a single authority. Both functions are vitally related to the security of the state; they require decisiveness, dispatch, consistency, and a measure of secrecy in their performance. To no small degree the exercise of the one function is complementary to the other. The principal diplomatic powers are those of sending and receiving diplomatic representatives, including the power to recognize new governments, determine foreign policy, and negotiate and ratify treaties and agreements. The major military powers include those of commanding the armed forces, declaring and waging war, and proclaiming a state of martial law. While these powers are usually considered in democratic states as too momentous to be turned over to a single individual, their monopolistic exercise by the executive is an unvarying characteristic of dictatorship.

The control of diplomatic and military affairs has always been among the prerogatives of the British Crown, but has long been exercised in the monarch's name by the Prime Minister and Cabinet. Although Parliament possesses some ultimate check upon policies in these areas through the general operation of the principle of ministerial responsibility, it has not gained anything like the direct share in their determination enjoyed by the American Congress. The broad lines of foreign policy are shaped by the Cabinet under the influence of the Prime Minister and the Foreign Secretary. While the latter selects most nominees for diplomatic appointment, the most important are chosen in consultation with the Prime Minister. Treaties and other international agreements are negotiated and ratified solely by executive authority; strictly speaking, no parliamentary approval is required for ratification, but it is the practice to lay important treaties before the House of Commons in advance of such action, so that any objections may be raised and aired.

The American President has chief responsibility for the formulation and execution of foreign policy. By constitutional authorization he appoints diplomatic representatives, receives those from abroad, and negotiates and ratifies treaties. Yet the President's authority is not absolute. The Constitution provides that he can ratify a treaty only with the consent of two-thirds of the Senate, and that body has been inclined to be most assertive of its right to approve. His appointment of ambassadors, ministers, and consuls also requires consent of the Senate.

The President does enjoy exclusive command over the armed forces, however; the Constitution designates him commander-in-chief of the armed services, and of the National Guard when the latter is called into federal service. Under this cloak of authority, the President can appoint officers, issue and enforce regulations, and make almost any disposition of the armed services he sees fit; but the Constitution still reserves to Congress the formal power to declare war and to appropriate funds necessary to conduct military operations. In wartime, Congress confers additional authority on the President so that he may effectively defend the country, to such an extent that he has it within his discretion to command practically all resources of the nation.

Totalitarian dictatorships invariably emphasize alteration of the international status quo, and incline toward national aggrandizement and militarism, so the dictator's preoccupation with diplomatic and military affairs may be expected. The diplomatic service of a dictatorship functions largely as an intelligence agency, as well as a propaganda corps, for the regime. Both become completely coordinated for the dictator's purposes; interference from other sources cannot be permitted. The usual devices of supervision over the diplomatic service are adequate for his purposes, but the dictator's control of the armed services is a much more difficult problem. Mass armies in the modern state may well come to constitute centers of power in themselves—particularly in states where traditions of effective civilian control are lacking—and, in domestic controversies over influence and power, can obviously get out of hand. To win and hold the personal loyalty of the military forces, therefore, the dictatorships have resorted to devices ranging from generous rewards to ferocious purges of the high commands. The lower ranks in the forces dare not be neglected either, as the Soviet army's use of political commissars and the Nazi systems of youth indoctrination suggest. But whatever the precautions, the relations between the dictators and their armed services are frequently uneasy.

Judicial Functions. A few functions commonly conferred upon the executive have a judicial character. The executive is commonly authorized to appoint judges. More immediate to the administration of justice, however, the executive is usually authorized to exercise clemency in the application of legal punishment. This takes the form of power to grant reprieves and pardons, as a means both of mitigating possible severity of judicial sentence in the interests of justice or mercy, and of rectifying judicial error when the liberty of the individual is at stake. Of course, these considerations are largely disregarded in a dictatorship.

In Great Britain, the power of pardon is a prerogative of the Queen, but is actually exercised by the Home Secretary. The latter may also reduce sentences, fines, and terms of imprisonment. Judges are appointed in the name of the Crown and derive their authority from it. The higher judges may be removed from office by Crown authority, but only after a formal request from Parliament.

The American President is authorized by the Constitution to grant reprieves and pardons to offenders against federal law, except in cases of impeachment. He may also grant an amnesty, which is the pardon of a whole group. The President appoints all federal judges, but they may be removed from office only after conviction following impeachment by Congress.

Since dictatorships do not maintain an independent judiciary, the exercise of judicial functions by the executive has considerably less significance. In the Soviet Union, for example, judges are closely supervised by the administrative apparatus and the Communist party, both as to their political reliability and the performance of their duties. The Presidium of the Supreme Soviet exercises the right of pardon, according to the Constitution, and the further power, partaking somewhat of judicial review, to annul decisions and orders of the councils of ministers, both all-union and republican. Cases involving failures of party discipline, ideological heresy, or "treason," are subject to trial and punishment, with neither appeal nor pardon allowed.

IV. The Growth of Modern Executive Power

One of the striking aspects of modern government is the constant tendency toward aggrandizement of the executive. In the extreme, the process has been consummated in the creation of dictatorship. Yet in such countries, no sharp break with precedent can be marked. Dictatorships, as we have noted, have generally been instituted where there has been little previous experience with representative institutions, where the legislature has held little or no real share in the political process, and where executive supremacy has long been traditional.

The appearance of similar tendencies of executive expansion in states where democratic institutions have been firmly established, however, is more noteworthy and, from some points of view, more worrisome. Several centuries of British constitutional controversy were devoted to establishing the principle of parliamentary supremacy over the monarch as the embodiment of executive power. Yet the present century has seen executive authority again grow apace. Through the Defence of the Realm Acts of World War I and the Emergency Powers (Defence) Act of World War II, adopted to give the Cabinet full powers to prosecute the war effectively, Parliament surrendered a large segment of its legislative authority. Though most of these extraordinary powers were relinquished after the end of hostilities, the executive nevertheless gained on balance. Further, the nationalizing of large portions of the British economy under the control of public corporations and the continuing tendency to allow the Cabinet to legislate by means of administrative rules and orders, have brought a renewal of complaints against a "new despotism."

In like manner, the political disputes between American colonists and the English king were most bitter over the pretensions of royal authority, leading the framers of the American Constitution to elaborate a variety of arrangements to prevent an excessive concentration of power in the executive. Yet there has been a substantial and continuing enlargement of the powers of the American presidency. The mobilization of the nation during two world wars brought tremendous augmentation of the President's authority—powers to control transportation, communications, manpower, foodstuffs, and raw materials. Almost as important in enlarging the scope of this office were the authorizations of the New Deal years, when the President was given substantial new power to levy war upon the economic depression. And urgent as the need was for vigorous executive action, no President who used his full authority during these crises escaped frequent charges of "dictatorship."

In still another example, we see in France of the Fifth Republic an expansion of the President's powers to such a degree that it is questionable whether parliamentary government is truly continued. The power relationship between the executive and legislative branches is distinctly shifted to the advantage of the former. The President makes a personal choice of the Premier, and cabinets are far less subject to parliamentary control than was the case with previous regimes. The President's power to dissolve the National Assembly is increased, and at the same time that body's right to delay action on the budget or other major pieces of legislation is reduced. An unprecedented clause in the Constitution gives the French President power to assume virtually unlimited authority to govern in time of emergency. To be sure, there seems little alternative to these constitutional innovations in France, reflecting as they do a reaction to the inability of the executive, in the declining years of the Fourth Republic, to govern at all. Thus, we find at the present that the executive in Great Britain, the United States, and France—to take but three examples—is, historically considered, at the apex of its powers. What, then, is the significance of these developments?

The Demand for Positive Leadership. Essentially, the continuing extension of executive activity is an accompaniment of the extension of all governmental activity. Modern government has been obliged to discard its earlier negative role in the community, the modest night-watchman's function, and is now held responsible for providing positive leadership; because the executive alone of the three branches can perform this function of leadership with any degree of effectiveness, the results seem inevitable. Much of the executive's increased power is the result of legislative conferment of discretion upon him. Wherever legislative action is inappropriate to determine policy dependent upon narrowly technical findings, or where a high degree of flexibility in policy is necessary, or where the situation to be regulated is subject to frequent change, legislative bodies are inevitably inclined to leave a large share of policy application, even policy determination, to executive discretion. Moreover, the accelerated frequency of war and international crisis in the present century has tremendously increased executive authority. There seems here again no alternative to placing in his hands responsibility for the security of the state when it is threatened or attacked, since total war requires nothing less than the mobilization of all the state's resources at the executive's command. We should not overlook, too, the fact that all attempts to cope with modern economic crises have further extended executive power. It has become commonplace to allow the executive a wide choice of means to resuscitate the national economy when it verges on collapse. Most new functions of government fall upon the executive, and the expansion of these, requiring as they now do the services of millions of government employees and the expenditure of colossal sums of money, also tends to enhance the power of the executive who commands them. Finally, the executive assumption of the role of representative and spokesman for the nation as a whole, standing above the obvious discords produced in the multimember legislative body, assures him a central position in, and unrivaled influence over, the governmental process.

8

The Legislature

THE second traditional branch of government for our consideration is the legislative. At the outset, three significant aspects must be observed. First, the term "legislature" has long been used to designate a body of persons who propose, alter, and make laws. Actually, however, various organs of government may perform or participate in this function, so the modern legislature does not monopolize the activity. Besides, it now undertakes a number of additional functions in the governmental process. Nonetheless, lawmaking—a very great power in itself—is the principal and primary preserve of the legislature, and all of its activities relate in some manner to that process. Thus it is much more limited in its scope of action and responsibility than the executive branch.

Second, a most important aspect of the legislature lies in its representative character; fundamentally the legislature represents the people. It is intended primarily to be a source of popular views respecting public policy, rather than expert ones. We expect that the legislature will represent a broad range of experience and knowledge, reflecting the extensive diversity of personality, interest, and judgment of the peoples themselves. All efforts at devising acceptable systems of democratic representation are therefore necessarily directed at securing a recognizable reflection of public opinion and assuring a wide popular support of public policy. At the same time, the structure of the legislature also reflects a certain distrust of popular opinion— the unpredictable passions of the people—and various devices invariably are applied in the attempt to limit possible excesses and abuses in the exercise of legislative authority, and to protect other values.

Third, the legislature has been the indispensable organ of democratic government. The alternatives to representative assemblies have long seemed to be only two: a system of direct democracy, which is scarcely practicable in modern times—or a system of absolutism, which is the obvious negation of popular government. Hence, the growth of modern democracy has been indissolubly linked with the extension both of legislative authority in the governmental process and popular participation in the election of legislators. Yet indispensable as the representative assembly was to the eighteenth- and nineteenth-century development of democratic government, in the present century its competence, efficiency, integrity, and even its representativeness have been increasingly criticized. Of course, democracy did not invent the representative assembly; it merely adapted it to newer objectives. We thus have the paradox that, although the representative assembly is the most characteristic feature of democratic government, it did not originate as a democratic institution and is increasingly found wanting in the contemporary democratic process.

I. The Development of the Legislature

The modern legislative assembly, dating only from the seventeenth century, is manifestly of more recent origin than the organs of the two other major branches of government. Legislatures in the modern sense could come into existence only after there was a relatively advanced differentiation of governmental functions and a considerable degree of popular political sophistication. Of course, from the time of the ancient empires, consultative bodies of some kind, created to advise and assist the ruler, were commonplace. Such bodies were not representative in the modern sense; they did not "stand for" all particular interests and individuals. However constituted, they were generally presumed to express the consent—often required—of the people to certain acts of the ruler. In addition, they broadened the base of influence and information that contributed to the determination of the ruler's will.

Greece. Although the ancient Greeks did not develop what we today would consider to be representative government, they did have various legislative institutions and were not unfamiliar with the function of representation. The greatest advance in such institutions came during the classical age in Athens. The popular organ, the *Ekklesia* or Assembly, brought together all adult male citizens who would attend

—six thousand or so from all classes of society. Most of these assembly discussions were dominated by a few leaders, it appears, but all members were entitled to be heard and to vote.

The Assembly heard all important discussions of policy: control of foreign relations; treaties, alliances, questions of peace and war; apportionment of funds for public enterprises, temples, statues, roads, ships; pronouncement of ostracism, whereby leaders suspected of tyrannical ambitions were sent into exile; and election and supervision of magistrates. Ten times a year, all state officials were obliged to appear before the Assembly to account for the performance of their duties. The senate, or Council, of Five Hundred, was composed of citizens thirty years of age or over chosen by lot for one-year terms, fifty each from the ten Athenian tribes. This body, functioning somewhat as an executive committee of government, heard reports, received foreign envoys, prepared measures for the Assembly, and issued decrees effecting Assembly decisions. The Council's functions, therefore, were more nearly administrative than legislative; it was a body significant more for its influence than for its authority.

Rome. Roman experience did not carry the representative process substantially farther. Well before historic times, the Romans must have accustomed themselves to convening popular assemblies composed of all men of military age. Through the period of Rome's development from monarchy to republic, an assembly, or *Comitia*, was variously constituted on the basis of civil, military, or tribal organizations. The functions of the *Comitia* were not too precisely determined, and changed with the times. Opposed to this democratic element in Roman government existed an aristocratic element, the Senate. Herein both the wealthy and the politically wise elements of the community were given representation. Appointed originally by the king as an advisory council, the members were later chosen by the consuls or censors from among the ex-magistrates. As Rome extended its empire and engaged in long struggles with its enemies, the Senate came increasingly to occupy a central role in the political process, slowly absorbing more and more of the powers of government as the only body capable of administering the complex affairs of state. With the beginning of the Christian era, the power of the Senate began to recede, however, as the absolute authority of the emperors increased, though it continued as a consultative body long after the popular assemblies had lost any significant functions.

The Middle Ages. The parliaments and councils which developed in medieval Europe were slow to achieve influence. Whether they owe their origin to Teutonic tribal institutions, to the practices of religious orders and church councils, or otherwise, is a matter of scholarly dispute. The government of the Germanic tribes described by the Roman historian Tacitus included an assembly of freemen, known as the folkmoot, which discussed and decided all important questions. As the tribes were combined into large kingdoms, these popular assemblies were replaced by councils of chieftains advising the king.

Rudimentary parliaments did not emerge until the fabric of European feudal society was thoroughly woven, and only the later middle ages saw the development of representative—though certainly not popular—institutions. Among the earliest, an Icelandic folkmoot or *Althing* functioned in the tenth century, and a representative *Cortes* was convened in Spanish Aragon in 1133. The French Estates General appeared in the thirteenth century. So also did the English Parliament. There developed in Anglo-Saxon times a court of wise men, the *Witenagemot*, which had a variety of duties. This assembly of the chief men of the state served as an advisory council to the king and participated in functions we would today describe as legislative and judicial. After the Norman conquest this assembly was shaped by the Norman rulers into the *Magnum Concilium,* or Great Council. Composed initially of the great nobles—lay and clerical—after the middle of the thirteenth century, Parliament included with increasing frequency knights from the counties and burgesses from the towns who were summoned by the kings to "council and consent" with respect to the business of the kingdom. These medieval bodies, even so, possessed no true legislative powers, but were convoked irregularly by the kings to approve taxes and to consult on matters of high policy. They did not represent the population as a whole; they represented the recognized estates, or classes with established legal and economic status, such as the clergy, the nobility, or the burgesses.

National Legislatures. The emergence of monarchical absolutism in Europe inevitably brought decline or reduction to impotence of most incipient national assemblies. After 1614, the Estates General of France was not convened again until 1789, on the eve of the revolution. The Russian national assembly was not summoned after 1649; soon thereafter the German Diets were reduced to insignificance. Perhaps such an eclipse was a necessary step in the evolution toward modern legislatures, as the absolute monarchs devoted themselves to the struggle against the privileged estates and their institutions. National unification of the many feudal units was a prerequisite to the existence of truly national parliaments. The augmentation of monarchical power next brought the rulers into direct conflict with the middle classes; as the extent of governmental activity and expense increased, bourgeois demand for a share in its control, commensurate with their growing economic interests in the nation, became inevitable.

In a history of uneven development, England led the way. The thirteenth-century summoning of knights and burgesses to Parliament introduced representation of commoners that could later be substantially broadened, and the power of Parliament was augmented as well. In the sixteenth century, having forced the King to assent regularly to its petitions as a condition for the granting of taxes, Parliament was able to exercise an influential share in the lawmaking process. In 1689 it deposed one monarch and bestowed the crown upon another, asserting its ultimate supremacy as spokesman for the nation. In France a legislative assembly was created after the revolution, in 1791, but a full parliamentary government was not to be securely established until—after a number of false starts—the Third Republic emerged in 1871.

The institution of republican government in the United States also constituted an important landmark in the development of modern legislatures. In an extreme reaction to monarchical rule—and encouraged by experience with the colonial assemblies as balance-weights against the English kings and colonial governors—the Americans sought initially to make their legislative bodies the paramount organ of government. Indeed, under the ill-fated national government of the Articles of Confederation, Congress was made the sole organ of government, to the exclusion of either a separate executive or federal courts; even under the Constitution of 1789, Congress was still intended to be the popular and most conspicuous organ.

By the early part of the nineteenth century, modern parliamentary institutions had been installed in some of the smaller European countries, the Netherlands, Switzerland, and Sweden. By the close of the century, they had also emerged in Italy, Germany, Austria-Hungary, and Japan, though in these countries they lacked sufficient power and influence to control the executive. And not until 1906 was an elected body with a small share in the governing process, the *Duma*, convened in Russia—soon to be swept away by the 1917 revolution. In non-European areas, also, there were some gains; national parliaments emerged in Canada, South Africa, Australia, and New Zealand, as these portions of the British empire gained autonomy. In Latin America, by contrast, the development of effective legislative institutions proved less successful.

II. Modern Legislatures

With this brief history of the development of the legislative institution, we can now usefully describe the general character of several national legislatures before turning to an analysis of legislative organization, functions, and problems. This description will give us some specific bodies to comment upon when we reach the discussion of the latter topics.

The British Parliament. The Parliament at Westminster, Britain's national legislature, easily deserves first attention here, not only because of its great age and continuous development, but because of its influence the world over in shaping the character of modern legislative bodies. The Queen in Parliament, as the formal term describes it, possesses the supreme legislative authority in the United Kingdom. Since the British have no documentary constitution, there are legally no limits to parliamentary authority, though there are traditional and practical ones, to be sure. Parliament can pass, amend, or repeal any law for all of the countries of the United Kingdom—England, Scotland, Wales, and Northern Ireland, though there is also a separate Northern Ireland parliament which may legislate on certain matters.

The composition of the second chamber, the House of Lords, derives from the medieval principle of representing the great estates of the realm. Its membership may be divided into two principal groups. In the first group are the Lords Temporal, which include a few Princes of royal blood; some nine hundred hereditary peers; the Lords of Appeal in Ordinary—that is, at least nine eminent judges who are appointed for life and who perform the judicial functions of the House of Lords; and the life peers and peeresses, some two hundred persons of "eminence and authority," also appointed to serve for life. The second group includes the Lords Spiritual, consisting of the Archbishops of Canterbury and York and twenty-four Bishops of the Church of England, who serve for the length of their ecclesiastical office. Peers receive no salary for their service, though they may claim some modest expenses for attendance in the Lords.

By no stretch of the imagination can the House of Lords be considered a democratic body; at best it represents a very narrow segment of the British population and its interests. Yet it is not merely the preserve of hereditary and aristocratic privilege. Its unrepresentative character is, indeed, largely mitigated by two factors: first, constitutional limitations prevent the Lords from exercising anything like equal power to that of the House of Commons; and second, by custom the actual work of the Lords is performed almost exclusively by "first-generation peers" and the life peers and peeresses—individuals who have been ennobled themselves rather than having inherited titles. These individuals have been honored in recognition of generally distinguished careers in the military, diplomatic, or civil service; or in the House of Commons, business, or the professions—thus bringing to the House of Lords a considerable knowledge and experience of public affairs. Peers with hereditary titles, and also without other qualifications, are neither obligated nor expected to attend. Most apply for "leave of absence," indicating they do not wish to participate in the work of the House.

Despite its formal membership of well over a thousand persons, the Lords as a working body is much smaller. In recent years its average daily attendance is about two hundred and fifty. A highly independent body, it is led by so-called government peers, individuals who are members of the ministry and are present in their official capacity. The Lord Chancellor, an important member of the government, presides; though unlike the Speaker of the Commons, he is partisan, speaking and voting on measures before the chamber. The daily sittings of the Lords last for only a few hours and debate is quite free; otherwise procedure is similar to that of the Commons.

The House of Commons is composed of 630 members, elected by universal suffrage from single-member constituencies with an average population of some 80,000 people. Members of this house have a term of office for the life of a Parliament—a period not exceeding five years—since the law requires a general election at least that often; the members are paid for their services. As individual seats may become vacant in the interim, they are filled at by-elections. With a few exceptions, and excluding members of the House of Lords, any British citizen who is of age may be elected to Commons. An interesting difference between the British and American qualifications for legislators is that there is no local residence requirement for a parliamentary candidate. The British view is that better candidates are obtained when they may be drawn from the nation at large, and that both voters and M.P.'s are encouraged to think more of national than of local interests.

The presiding officer of the Commons is the Speaker. Formally, his office is filled anew with each Parliament; actually the choice of a new Speaker is necessary only when the incumbent retires. The majority party will then put forward its candidate, but on his achieving the office, he will sever his party connections. Unlike his American counterpart, he will thenceforward perform his functions with entire impartiality. Thereafter, he will be rechosen as long as he wishes to serve, and ordinarily has no difficulty in being reelected to the House from his own constituency. His chief duty is to preside over Commons debates; he grants recognition to speak, makes rulings, announces votes, and keeps members in order and addressed to the subject under discussion. The importance and prestige of his office are very high, because he symbolizes the powers and dignity of the popular house of the Parliament.

The Commons has only a small number of standing committees, and except for the Scottish and Welsh Committees, they do not specialize as to subject matter the way American committees do. Their role in the legislative process is far more limited, since they receive bills only after they have been approved in principle by the House; they have no authority to undertake wholesale revision of bills—much less to throw them out entirely—and thus may concern themselves only with details of draftsmanship. Because nearly all bills are introduced by the Cabinet, these leaders are unwilling to permit other centers of legislative power to be organized.

The houses of the British Parliament do not possess coordinate powers. It is to the House of Commons alone that the Cabinet answers for its political responsibility; the Lords cannot overturn a government. Further, the Lords' function in the legislative process is definitely restricted by the Parliament Acts of 1911 and 1949; accordingly, they have no power at all over money bills—that is, taxation and appropriation measures—and can interpose a delay of only one year to the adoption of other public bills, if the Commons should pass a desired bill twice. The Lords' principal contributions to the legislative process, therefore, are to serve as a revising body to improve—but not obstruct—legislation, and to provide a more leisurely forum in which to debate important issues for which Commons' time is lacking. What is said in the Lords is distinctly more important than what is done there, and the Commons is the real center of legislative power.

The United States Congress. The creation of a bicameral American Congress was obviously inspired by the two-house British Parliament, though the framers of the Constitution had further practical reasons for choosing that form. They wanted to prevent any organ of government from becoming all-powerful—hence the objective of having one house to serve as a "check" on the other; and they were obliged to resolve a controversy over whether Congress should represent the states equally or according to their population—a bicameral legislature could do both.

The Senate was intended as an "upper house," rather than as a "second chamber." The Constitution stipulated that it should be composed of two Senators from each state, and that no state should be deprived of equal representation in the Senate without that state's consent. Since large states and small alike have an equal vote in this body, its base of representation is undemocratic to that extent, though no longer is the Senate more representative of rural than of urban areas. Further, the Constitution originally provided that Senators were to be chosen, not by the people, but by state legislatures. The Seventeenth Amendment (1913) required the Senate to be popularly chosen, as was the House.

The one hundred Senators are elected at large from their states for six-year terms, approximately one-third at each biennial election. It is thus a continuous body whose composition will not change considerably as a result of any one election. The constitutional qualifications for a Senator are not highly selective: one must have attained the age of thirty, been nine years a citizen of the United States, and be an inhabitant of the state from which he is chosen. Senators and Representatives receive equal salaries and liberal allowances for expenses, with somewhat more generous allowances for Senators, in view of their larger number of constituents.

The presiding officer, the President of the Senate, is the Vice-President of the United States. Because of that body's tradition of full and free debate, and because he is not himself a Senator, the presiding officer has nothing like the powers of the Speaker of the House of Representatives. He thus has much less opportunity to assist his party in the legislative process. Because, too, the Senate is a comparatively small body, it does not require the elaborate organization and rules of the lower house. Its sixteen standing committees are centers of real power, and several of them can be included among the most influential bodies within the machinery of American government. Further, party discipline is considerably more relaxed than in the House. In all respects, the individual Senator counts for much more than the individual Representative.

The House of Representatives consists of 435 members elected from single-member districts into which the states are divided, containing an average of over 400,000 people. The House is intended to be directly representative of the people; seats are apportioned among the states according to their population as determined by each decennial census—with each state having at least one Representative—and election is by those persons who qualify in their states to vote for the "most numerous branch" of the state legislature.

To qualify for a seat in the House, the Constitution requires only that a member be at least twenty-five years of age, seven years a citizen of the United States, and an inhabitant of the state from which he is elected. There is no legal requirement that he must also be a resident of the congressional district, but custom has long insisted upon it. In this respect it is clear that the American party organizations and the voters are willing to support only a "local man," who must serve first the interests of the district. The fact that the term of office of the Representative is only two years further reinforces his obligation to be immediately responsive to the opinion of his constituents; otherwise, his congressional career will be brief.

In view of the size of the House—a body in which few individual members can expect to play a leading role—it has a more elaborate organization and more restrictive rules than does the Senate, both of which aim to ensure, as the House *Manual* says, that "a majority may work its will at all times in the face of the most determined and vigorous opposition of a minority." And, majority dominance begins at the top. The Speaker of the House enjoys extensive authority, not only from the rules of procedure, but because he is an influential leader of the majority party. As a frankly partisan officer, he has been elected to his office by the majority party; and if party control of the House changes as the result of an election, he will be replaced. This is not to say that he uses the power of his position arbitrarily; in the performance of his function as presiding officer to grant recognition, put votes, make rulings, and keep order, he observes the House rules —which duly regard the right of the minority to be heard. To further the program of the majority, there are additional components of the party organization: the caucus, to make decisions on policy matters; the majority floor leader, field general and strategist of the majority forces; the whips, who function under the floor leader to marshal party members for crucial votes; the steering committee, which is headed by the floor leader and operates to supervise the majority party's legislative program; and the majority members of the House Rules Committee. The minority party, of course, organizes in similar fashion.

The House is also organized by an elaborate committee system, through which its work is primarily performed; indeed, the principal functions of the House as a whole are to take action upon its committees' recommendations. There are several types: the select committee, created to consider some special question, of which type the committee of investigation is best known; the conference committee, appointed from members of both houses to reconcile differences between them when they disagree over a bill; the joint standing committee, to deal with matters of common concern to the two chambers, such as the printing of documents; and the standing committee. The last is the most important, organized on a permanent basis according to subjects of legislative action—for example, agriculture, armed services, foreign affairs, judiciary, and ways and means. The House has twenty-one of these committees, whose size ranges from nine to fifty-one members, constituted on a bipartisan basis roughly reflecting the strength of the two parties in the whole House. All bills introduced in the House must be referred to the relevant committee, which exercises powers of life and death over legislation. Memberships in the more influential committees, therefore, are eagerly sought.

A comparison of the functions of the two houses of Congress reveals a striking fact—that the upper house is manifestly the more powerful of the two. Among the upper chambers of the world, only the American Senate enjoys this distinction of superiority. From the viewpoint of legislative authority, the houses stand virtually even; and although the Constitution specifies that "all bills for raising revenue shall originate in the House," this has had little practical significance, since there is no limit upon the Senate's power to amend such bills. Shifting the balance in the other direction are the constitutional arrangements for several special Senate powers: it has the responsibility of trying impeachments, of consenting to the President's ratification of treaties, and of consenting to the appointment of thousands of officials of the federal government. Yet important as the latter two functions are in securing for the Senate a share in the executive control of patronage and foreign affairs, they do not alone account for the Senate's paramount position. Reasons are also to be found in the following factors: the Senate is a smaller, hence more select, body and tends to attract abler and more experienced men; its members have longer terms, and may see both Presidents and House members come and go; and its members are in a position to speak for their entire state. These factors, then, combined with equality in legislative responsibility, make the Senate a national forum of unrivaled influence.

The French Parliament. The French have a long history of attempts to achieve a satisfactory equilibrium in government with a responsible and representative parliament as its base, demonstrating how difficult the problem may be for a nation torn by dissension over its fundamental goals, and how little the problem may be solved by alterations in the mechanics of government. The Parliament of the Third Republic (1875–1940), following the autocratic government of the Second Empire, was composed of two houses: the Chamber of Deputies, popularly elected, and the smaller Senate, indirectly elected. The houses enjoyed equal powers, practically speaking, with respect to both legislation and control of the executive. Though Parliament predominated among the organs of government, the two chambers functioned—undoubtedly more enthusiastically than intended—as a check upon each other, thus reflecting the dominant republican desire to avoid an overconcentration of political power. An ever-widening division among the French people, drawing them toward either the political left or right, however, made parliamentary operations increasingly ineffective. By the close of the 1930's, Parliament was widely held in low esteem within the country and blamed for much of France's ills, especially the weakness of the executive.

At the end of World War II, the French electorate voted over-whelmingly to replace the governmental system of the Third Repub-lic. Under the leadership of parties of the left, a constituent assembly thereupon offered a first draft constitution providing for a unicameral parliament, but this was rejected in a popular referendum by a nar-row margin. A second draft constitution, largely resembling the first, reestablished a second chamber, though one with extremely restricted powers, and this draft was adopted in another close popular vote. The new Parliament of the Fourth Republic (1946–58) was thus at least bicameral in form. The successor to the old Chamber of Depu-ties, the National Assembly, was soon behaving as disappointingly as its counterpart in the preceding regime. At the same time, the other significant constitutional feature of the Fourth Republic—the ar-rangements to give greater stability to the ministries—proved entirely unsuccessful, and Parliament continued to make the life of French governments brief. As a result, in the face of an increasingly confused political situation, fiscal weakness, and insurrection in Algeria, the re gime was abandoned and a still newer one created.

The Constitution of the Fifth Republic (1958) substantially changed the structure and function of Parliament. Once again it has bicameral form, but is removed at the same time from the center of political power. The size of the National Assembly is now related to population—one deputy for each 93,000 inhabitants—and elected from single-member districts for five-year terms, with a runoff election a week later if no candidate is chosen by a majority in the first. As a result of the election of 1968, the Assembly contains 487 deputies, in-cluding ten from overseas *départements*, and six from overseas territo-ries. The second chamber, now restyled the Senate, consists of 283 members elected indirectly by local electoral colleges for nine-year terms. The powers of the new Senate are placed somewhat between those of the Third Republic and the Council of the Republic of the Fourth. It still is denied any power to overturn a cabinet; and if the two houses disagree over bills submitted to them, and a government-requested joint committee cannot reconcile the differences, the Na-tional Assembly may decide the matter definitively. Other limitations in the process of government imposed upon the present Parliament restrict the length of yearly sessions, the power to legislate, and the opportunity to control the executive. The National Assembly may also be dissolved.

Other National Legislatures. A brief examination of a few other representative bodies will indicate some of the variations in structure. The parliamentary functions in the German Federal Republic are performed by a Federal Diet, or *Bundestag* (sometimes itself designated as the Parliament), and a Federal Council, or *Bundesrat;* they may also be collectively described as a parliament. The *Bundestag* is popularly chosen by a combined system of direct election from single-member districts and proportional representation. Members of this body, which is subject to dissolution, are elected for four-year terms; it performs the usual parliamentary functions, but shares some of them with the second chamber. The *Bundesrat* represents the ten *Länder,* or states, composing the Republic; each *Land* has at least three members—and some of the larger have additional ones—to produce a total membership of forty-one. These members are appointed by and drawn from their state governments. They may introduce bills and exercise a suspensive veto over those passed by the *Bundestag.* As the delegates are bound by the instructions of their individual governments—and are essentially officials of their state administrations, rather than legislators—they must coordinate the administrative and legislative processes within the federal system. The *Bundesrat* has no control, however, over the executive, a situation which tends to minimize its partisanship.

A legislature influenced by the British Parliament, but reflecting its own national circumstances, is the Canadian Parliament. It is a bicameral body containing a House of Commons and a Senate. The House has 265 members, popularly elected like those of Great Britain at least every five years; the Senate has 102 members apportioned among the ten provinces. The second chamber had inevitably to take a form different from that in Britain. For one thing, Canada had a federal system of government, and the Senate was intended particularly to protect provincial interests. For another, Canada had no hereditary peerage with which to constitute a House of Lords. In consequence, its Senators are appointed by the Governor-General on the nomination of the Prime Minister, serving to age seventy-five; they must be property owners and at least thirty years of age. Although the Senate has formally the same powers as the House of Commons, in practice it is a much less active and influential body. Indeed, so unimportant has its contribution been to the governmental process that Canadians have frequently discussed reforming it substantially or abolishing it outright. Since about one-third of Canada's population is French-speaking, either the French or the English languages may be employed in the debates of its parliamentary houses, though by no means are most of the members bilingual.

One of the more unusually constituted legislative bodies is the Parliament of Norway, the *Storting*, which might be described as a unicameral chamber with certain bicameral modifications. Containing 150 members—50 from the towns and cities, and 100 from rural areas —the *Storting* is elected by a scheme of proportional representation; this scheme, among other things, supplies an alternate member available to replace each elected one, should the latter enter the cabinet or otherwise vacate his seat. Following each quadrennial election, the *Storting* selects 38 of its members to constitute the *Lagting*, or Upper Section, with the remaining 112 making up the *Odelsting*, or Lower Section. For certain purposes, including constitutional amendment and financial legislation, the members sit together as the *Storting*. For others, they sit in separate sections under their individual presiding officers. A bill intended to become formal law is introduced in the *Odelsting*, and if passed, is sent to the *Lagting*, which may approve or reject it. If, after passage again by the Lower Section, the Upper Section rejects the bill a second time, both bodies are convened in joint session, where the bill may then be passed by a two-thirds vote.

A last generalization—about Latin America—will conclude this section. Here, the national congress is definitely subordinated to the executive, even when dictatorship does not prevail, and regardless of constitutional stipulations. Legislators representing different parties may sit in the houses, and may well have been more or less the choice of the voters in a popular election. In the sessions of the legislature, personal and political differences between members, indeed, may lead to bitter debates and even violence. If these circumstances seem to offer refreshing contrast to the unquestioning unanimity displayed by legislatures in the fascist and communist dictatorships, they should not be taken as evidence of congressional ability to exercise any significant measure of power in the process of government. Most of the legislators are likely to be the president's men—and he uses them, or ignores them, largely as suits his purposes.

The Legislature in the Emergent States. The modern legislative assembly is one of the more recent western governmental institutions, and one most difficult to operate effectively under the best of circumstances. To no one's surprise, the legislative institution has been the least successful of the organs of government introduced by the states of the "third world." In their constitutions these new states commonly have adopted the formal structure of Western parliamentary bodies, but have discovered that something more is required to breathe life into them and to develop a parliamentary *esprit de corps.* The result has been legislatures in the main weak, unrepresentative, executive-dominated, and redundant.

A principal reason is the absence of any parliamentary traditions, previous governments having usually been colonial or monarchical, bureaucratic, and even quasi-dictatorial. And without well-organized popular parties and associational interest groups, these parliamentary bodies represent only a small portion of the population. Also, in a legislature either dominated by a single-national party or divided and immobilized by a multiparty system, the opposition is ineffective and offers no alternative government. Thus, such legislatures tend to act as rubber stamps for the executive, rather than as deliberative bodies independently weighing the special interests against the general welfare.

In many respects, the new regimes tend to resemble those in central and eastern Europe following World War I. Here such states as Germany, Poland, Austria, Hungary, and Yugoslavia—lacking significant parliamentary traditions—were unable to develop legislative institutions capable of coping with the stresses of the times and succumbed to dictatorship. It seems clear that tradition and training are vital. Where legislative bodies in the newer states have demonstrated some measure of success and ability, they are also drawing on earlier experience. For example, members were first elected to the Philippine Legislature in 1907; to the Indian Legislative Council in 1909; and to the Kenyan Legislative Council in 1919. These states were thus able to build on their own legislative traditions and experience when they achieved independence after World War II.

National Legislatures in the Dictatorships. Despite the fact that dictatorship constitutes the very negation of representative government, modern dictators, even totalitarian ones, have managed to find at least a formal place in their system for the legislative institution. This is the best evidence, perhaps, that the legislature has come to be universally viewed as essential to popular government and the promotion of mass interests. Though the method of selecting its members and the practical limitation of its powers will assure that it exercises no real political authority, the dictator has some very good reasons for paying tribute to the outward forms of democracy.

First of all, the presence of the legislature, in form if not in substance, helps to conceal—both at home and abroad—the naked concentration of authority. Modern dictators, like medieval autocrats, find some reassurance in the appearance, albeit manufactured, of popular support and approval. The election of its members, even though they are carefully chosen by the single-party monopoly, provides an opportunity for placing the stamp of pseudolegality on the ruler's acts —conducting propaganda, disseminating information, and arousing enthusiasm. The meetings of the legislature in a dictatorship also offer occasions for the party leaders to instruct the masses in official political doctrines. At the very least, finally, the legislature can be used to provide additional titles, jobs, and emoluments with which to reward the politically faithful. We may see these factors demonstrated in the case of Nazi Germany and Soviet Russia.

Nazi Germany. Under the Weimar Republic (1919–33), the *Reichstag*, the main legislative organ, was chosen by popular election; the *Reichsrat*, which shared the legislative process, was a council of the seventeen German states, and its sixty-six members appointed by them. Following Hitler's designation as Chancellor in January, 1933, the existing *Reichstag* was dissolved and new elections called. Even in the face of Nazi pressure, propaganda, and violence, the German voters elected only 288 Nazi deputies out of the total *Reichstag* membership of 647—less than half. But by winning support from a small group of Nationalist members, Hitler was able to command a bare majority; and by excluding the Communists, he then pressed through an enabling act authorizing legislation by executive decree. This attack on the *Reichstag* opened the way for Hitler to dissolve all non-Nazi parties and complete his absolute dictatorship. The *Reichsrat* was abolished outright in 1934 when the federal system was suppressed; meanwhile, the *Reichstag* was converted into an exclusively Nazi preserve. It degenerated rapidly as an organ of government; for the remainder of its existence it held only twenty sittings and approved seven laws. Though *Reichstag* elections continued to be held, the body performed no real function other than to provide an audience and cheers for an occasional speech by Hitler.

The Soviet Union. The Supreme Soviet of the U.S.S.R. is neither the

vestigial remainder of a previous regime of representative government, as was the case of the Nazi chamber, nor is it a real parliamentary body, comparable to the national legislatures of Great Britain
and the United States. No parliamentary tradition ever developed in
Russia. Following revolutionary uprisings in the country, the Czar
was obliged in 1906 to set up a two-chamber body, composed of a
Duma, or popular assembly chosen by a restricted system of election,
and balanced by a Council of State, which could be controlled by the
autocratic ruler. Four elections to the *Duma* were held between 1906
and 1917, and though this body made continuing attempts to break
down the despotism of the Czar, it failed. Elected by an increasingly
restricted suffrage, limited in power to legislate, unable to enforce
any ministerial responsibility, and with its membership continually
manipulated toward still more conservatism, it was largely ignored
after the outbreak of World War I in 1914, and was finally swept
away by the Bolshevik coup d'état in 1917. Consequently, after this
most modest experience with parliamentary bodies, the Russian people would thereafter know only the soviets, or councils, managed by
the Communist dictatorship.

The Soviet Constitution of 1936 provides for a Supreme Soviet,
composed of a Soviet of the Union, now containing 767 members chosen on the basis of one deputy for each 300,000 people, and a Soviet
of Nationalities of 750 members chosen from the various constituent
republics, regions, and other political subdivisions. If one were to examine the constitutional provisions relating to the Supreme Soviet, he
might well conclude that the Soviet legislature differs little from those
of the western democracies. The Constitution states that the Supreme
Soviet is "the highest organ of state power in the U.S.S.R.," and that it
exercises "exclusively" the legislative power. Elaborate provisions also
govern the nomination and election of deputies, and describe immunities, procedures, functions, and powers of the two bodies. However,
the difference between constitutional provision and actual practice is
vast.

First, the nomination of candidates for membership is controlled
entirely by the Communist party, which approves a single candidate
for each electoral district (although not all those nominated are members of the Communist party); no other candidates are allowed to
compete. After an elaborate electoral campaign, the expenses of
which are borne by the state, the voters on election day must either

vote for the official candidates, or deface the ballot. Negative votes are discouraged in a variety of ways, and as a consequence, somewhat more than 99 percent of the voters cast affirmative ballots in this one-sided contest. Second, the Supreme Soviet is given very little to do. It meets once or twice a year, for a week, listens to speeches from party and government leaders, and occasionally is invited to approve a law or a resolution. In these carefully staged proceedings there is a complete absence of any really critical debate, questioning, or examination of budget matters and, of course, no opposition. Indeed, these two like-minded houses have never in their history refused a request, nor have they adopted any measure other than unanimously. Clearly, though the Supreme Soviet superficially resembles a legislature, its legislative functions are purely fictitious.

III. Problems of Representation

Within democratic systems of government, legislatures have certain features broadly in common, though they vary in details of organization and procedure. What factors account principally for these features? First of all, England, the "Mother of Parliaments," from its long and successful parliamentary history has influenced the character and procedures of all legislative bodies to some extent, and those of the Commonwealth and the United States quite considerably. Further, because the institution of democratic government is closely associated with the idea of universal suffrage, its achievement requires that one parliamentary chamber be organized as a "popular" house. Also, during the century or more in which the modern legislature has prevailed, most countries have had one or more occasions to reorganize their legislative institution. In such event, within particular national traditions, there were usually efforts to make the legislature more representative, more responsible, or more efficient. In sum, all national legislatures have been influenced in part by their English prototype, by universal ideals of representative government, and by their own national experience.

The Number of Houses. For long, most parliamentary bodies were composed of two houses. There is, of course, nothing sacred about bicameralism, and medieval assemblies originally had from one to four houses. Nevertheless, the centuries-old English model of a two-house parliament was most influential and most generally imitated for several major motives. First, it permits a dual basis of representation. A second chamber may represent different areas, various institutions, subordinate levels of government, or particular classes within a nation—in addition to the representation of the population on a direct basis by the lower house. A particularly important justification for bicameralism is found in federal states—as in the United States, Canada, Australia, India, Switzerland, and Germany—where previously independent areas are joined in a single political union and given special representation. Other bases for the second chamber may be provided by an hereditary aristocracy, as in the British House of Lords; by vocational groups and educational and cultural bodies, as in the Irish Senate; or by ethnic elements, as in the Burmese Chamber of Nationalities (dissolved in 1962).

Second, bicameralism avoids concentrating the legislative power and reduces the possibility of its despotic exercise. This was an argument that appealed strongly to the framers of the American Constitution, who were convinced of the desirability of incorporating checks and balances into the political system. In Great Britain, as well, there has been apprehension at the thought of the great parliamentary powers concentrated in a single body of men, subject to no documentary constitutional or judicial restraints. The members of a second chamber will not as a rule possess equality of powers with the first chamber, but they may commonly be given certain special functions.

Third, two houses can obtain fuller deliberation. In the nature of things, the action of a legislative chamber can be hasty, inadequately considered, ill-advised, or based on insufficient information. A second chamber therefore may act as an examining and revising body, drawing on the special knowledge and experience of its membership, to review the work of the popular house. Thus, the members of the German *Bundesrat* are state government officials; the French Senate is composed in large proportion of persons who are former members of the National Assembly or who are experienced as local government officials; the House of Lords contains many peers with years of experience in public and political life.

Finally, bicameralism may impose a conservative restraint upon a popular, directly elected body. At first glance this may seem undemocratic; but democracy is not merely a matter of effecting the will of the majority—it requires some protection of the interests of minorities as well. And although it is not popular to speak of the excesses of democracy, many examples may be found. An upper house need not be conservative in a partisan sense, but may be so constituted as to be resistant to extremist tendencies, from whatever direction, as well as to emphasize continuity and stability in policies. To be sure, a second chamber is commonly given only delaying influence and not power to impose an absolute veto; however, it may oblige the popular chamber to reexamine its action, thus allowing time for public opinion to form and assert itself before a final decision is reached. Examples of bodies intended to perform this conservative function include the Canadian Senate, whose members serve until seventy-five; the Italian Senate, whose members are elected from regional areas (by voters at least twenty-five years of age); and the British House of Lords.

Yet organization of the legislature into two houses does not automatically produce these results, nor is the arrangement necessarily relevant to every national situation. In some states there may be but one significant basis upon which representation rests. And bicameralism as such has not always been a bar to despotism and dictatorship, as the Italian, German, and Russian experiences attest. Also, it does not even guarantee greater deliberation. The chambers of bicameral bodies not uncommonly act in haste and assume that the other house will be more deliberate; when both houses make that assumption over the same measure, the result can be most unfortunate. Finally, the opportunity for conservative delay is no assurance of parliamentary wisdom; the British House of Lords was shorn of much of its power early in this century as a result of its failure to keep up with changing times and political opinion.

Bicameralism is no longer the most common legislative arrangement. Unicameral national assemblies now outnumber bicameral by a ratio of about three to two. There is no particular explanation for this development other than the preference of the many new and small states for the simpler assembly. The emphasis on egalitarian democracy is a factor, especially in small homogeneous states such as Denmark, Finland, and New Zealand. Another is the absence of any significant basis for a dual system of representation, as in Costa Rica, Honduras, Panama, and El Salvador. Many states whose representative systems are of recent creation—Israel, Lebanon, Malta, Senegal, and Sierra Leone—and most of the communist states as well, require only simple systems.

It may also be noted, incidentally, that the unicameral form is found in many subordinate legislative bodies, even in states which have bicameral national parliaments. Among these legislative bodies are the *Landtage* (Diets) of the German Federal Republic's *Länder* (except Bavaria), the legislatures of the Canadian provinces (except Quebec), and the legislature of Nebraska.

Unicameralism is supported by several arguments. Because authority is concentrated in a single house, the electorate knows where responsibility rests for any legislative action. A single house also avoids duplication of effort, additional expense, and the tendency of separate bodies to disagree for the sake of asserting their independence. Further, procedure through a single house may allow greater speed in the legislative process—a significant consideration in modern times when action rather than delay is a significant consideration. Finally, it is asserted that unicameralism is more democratic because it avoids the possible obstruction of the popular will by an unrepresentative upper house. Nevertheless, none of these propositions is easily demonstrable in practice, nor have they been largely persuasive, it would seem, in determining the incidence of unicameralism. Unicameralism is not a Scandinavian fixture, for Sweden long had a bicameral parliament. Ireland and Austria, also with bicameral parliaments, are at the same time both small and homogeneous countries, and are not likely to be more heedless of expense or legislative delay than New Zealand or Israel. Certainly the unicameral legislatures of the Central American states reflect no significant democratic aspirations. Indeed, unicameral national assemblies are also found in the communist-dominated states of Bulgaria, East Germany, Hungary, Poland, and Romania; in the Chinese People's Republic; and in Spain under the Franco dictatorship. In these countries, where the legislature has little or no authority, it obviously makes no difference whether there is one house or two. It appears, then, that the presence of unicameralism must be explained by individual national circumstance. It seems likely, too, that the general preference for bicameralism in most of the older and larger states will continue, given the useful functions a well-constructed second chamber can perform. There is rarely much opportunity left, moreover, for that chamber to obstruct democratic demands; such conflicts have largely been resolved by reducing its powers or making it as popularly elective as the lower chamber.

The Size and Terms of the Houses. Legislatures may be large or small, What factors, then, properly determine their dimensions? Ideally, a parliamentary body should be large enough to represent the varying interests of all sections and classes of a nation's population effectively, and small enough to be able to deliberate efficiently. The translation of these propositions into parliamentary arithmetic, however, is not a matter of any particular agreement, though a few generalizations may be drawn from an examination of existing bodies. Lower houses tend to fall into one of three categories: first, those with less than one hundred members, such as Barbados, Jamaica, and most of the small states of Latin America; second, those which range between one and two hundred members, including such states as Australia, Chile, Ireland, the Netherlands, the Philippines, and Switzerland; third, the most populous countries, in the range from four hundred to upward of six hundred members, such as France, the German Federal Republic, Great Britain, India, Italy, Japan, and the United States.

The size of upper chambers tends to be more limited, with most of them between twenty-five and one hundred members. Several states exceed this, of course; the Italian Senate has 321 members, the French Senate, 283, and the Belgian Senate, 178. Generally speaking, unicameral legislatures compare more closely in size with upper rather than lower chambers; the New Zealand Parliament has 80 members, and the Israeli *Knesset,* 120. Yet the single house may be a large one even in small states: the Parliament of Denmark numbers 179, and that of Finland numbers 200.

In determining parliamentary dimensions, pressure for wide representation weighs more heavily than the need for efficient deliberation. A body of a hundred or so can debate and deliberate with effectiveness, permit the presentation of a wide variety of views, and still achieve a degree of consensus upon relatively complex matters that may appropriately be described as "the sense of the house." When legislative chambers contain four or five hundred members or more, however, the process becomes increasingly difficult: only a small proportion of members can be heard on any particular subject; their views are thus less likely to be representative of the whole; and any specific agreements they accept will probably have been reached by their parliamentary leaders and committees. The United States Senate of one hundred members, for example, takes pride in its tradition of allowing full and unlimited debate.

By the time the United States House of Representatives reached a membership exceeding four hundred, however, there was already feeling that it had grown too large; it inevitably has very restrictive rules governing debates and length of speeches, and the Speaker is authorized large discretion in directing proceedings. In the British House of Commons, a substantially larger body, similar circumstances prevail, and it is also assumed that extensive absenteeism will keep to manageable proportions those members participating in any one debate. Nevertheless, backbenchers express continual dissatisfaction over the monopolization of debate time by ministers and opposition front-bench speakers. The House of Lords, with an even greater membership, manages to operate because rarely are more than two hundred members present at any particular sitting. Yet there is little inclination toward a reduction in size of the large—and inevitably unwieldy—national legislatures of the major states. By their nature, their populations tend to great heterogeneity; they have social, economic, and external problems of great complexity; and each of their multitude of interests and urban localities demands a special delegate. Indeed, such states also invariably have a huge governmental apparatus, and only through the intermediary of what they feel is their own local representative can the administered masses believe their voice will be heard at all.

There is also little in the way of principle governing the subject of legislative terms. Ideally, the office term of the member of a popular chamber ought to be sufficiently long to permit him to gain a useful familiarity with his duties, and short enough to keep him responsible to his constituency. The first of these propositions is reinforced by the fact that the continuity of membership in most such bodies is not high; a turnover in 25 to 50 percent of the seats at each election is common. Also, too-frequent elections oblige the legislator to devote excessive time and attention to his reelection; they bore the voters and encourage apathy among them. Very short terms also detract from continuity in legislative policy and reduce the opportunity for an assembly to complete a comprehensive legislative program. To be sure, the legislator needs to account to his constituency at regular intervals; but the most accurate measure of public opinion on his representativeness can be taken at election time.

It should be obvious, once more, that these considerations cannot be translated into mathematical formulas. Probably most voters, and certainly most legislative representatives, would consider a one-year term—and thus annual elections—a downright harassment. Further, many members of the United States House of Representatives, as well as a number of students of the problem, believe that their two-year term is too short for maximum effectiveness. On the other hand, a lower-house term as long as six years, which is to be found in a few Latin-American states, certainly does little to enhance the representative character of government. And given the rapid pace of events in modern public life, a popular chamber close to the end of even a five-year term not uncommonly appears tired, indecisive, and uncertain how to apply such mandate as it may have received at the time of its election. As a result, the most general practice is to give the popular house a four-year term. However, a five-year term applies in Canada, Great Britain, France, India, Ireland, Italy, and South Africa; Australia and New Zealand set the limit at three years. Even so, all such terms of office in parliamentary systems of government are maximum, and will be shorter if parliament is dissolved earlier. This is in contrast to systems where terms are rigidly fixed, as in Switzerland and the United States.

An upper chamber, as we have noted, is commonly constituted on a basis of representation separate from that of the popular house and is intended to be a more independent body. There are three principal forms of organization, which may also be used in combination. In a few cases members may have life terms, as in the British House of Lords or the Canadian Senate. Or, the chamber may be a continuing body, with a portion of its members chosen at fixed intervals; one-third of the United States Senate is chosen every two years, and one-half of the Australian Senate is chosen every three years. Finally, members of the upper house may simply be given longer terms than the lower, as in Italy, Mexico, and Japan. All of these devices give the second chamber, in varying degree, some independence of the electorate and some continuity in membership. Whether they produce a greater wisdom, a more mature opinion, and a keener awareness of the national interest is debatable.

Systems of Representation. We come now to the problems of selecting members of legislative chambers. Historically, the oldest form of parliamentary representation is by estates—that is, the representation of a political or social group or class sharing recognizable interests, rights, and status. In medieval Europe, the clergy constituted one estate, the nobility another, the commoners a third, and in some countries, the rural freemen a fourth. However, these were in time generally drawn into two houses, providing the basis for bicameralism. But representation by estates has long been abandoned; the British House of Lords represents a vestigial—and the sole—survival of the system. At present there is little either in principle or practice to recommend it. In the complex societies of the modern world there simply are no longer a few clearly distinguishable groups with identical and identifiable interests into which people can be separated, and any attempts to do so would produce the most artificial results.

Modern representation has long been based, therefore, on territory or geography. The result is a simple and, at first glance at least, a logical system. Representatives are chosen from districts—either those already existent or those which can be created, large or small, many or few, as may be needed, by drawing on a map. These representatives then undertake to represent all the people in the given territory. The system has the advantage that the representative can easily recognize his constituents, and vice versa; he can visit with or live among them, identify their general and special interests, and note improvement (or decline) in their situation. Obvious examples of such territorial units of representation are the American congressional district, the British parliamentary borough, or the Norwegian *fylke* (county).

Despite its simplicity and utility, territorial representation is not a system of perfection. Its validity rests substantially upon the proposition that all of the people living in a given area are much alike and as a result have common interests. Obviously, this is not and cannot be so in many respects: geographical propinquity does not automatically produce homogeneity. Hence, the organization of voters into geographical areas produces a certain amount of dissatisfaction. In an age, therefore, where universal suffrage in the selection of the popular legislative chamber is so general, the question is no longer who should choose the representatives, but how should they be chosen? In consequence, a system of "functional" representation of the electorate has sometimes been proposed. But advocates of such systems are few, and hardly in agreement over their specific arrangements. Presumably, representatives would be chosen by voters grouped according to their function in society—their occupation, economic activity, or vocational interests. But any such scheme confronts serious practical and theoretical obstacles. Any one person has a great diversity of interests; he may at the same time be manager and employee, property owner and debtor, producer and consumer, taxpayer and government pensioner, and so on. It would be difficult to determine the category which would represent each person, and the sort of legislative institution which would be the product of such representation. Surely, the functional cure would appear to be worse than the territorial complaint.

Electoral Systems. We have observed that the territorial basis of representation is almost universally employed for the selection of representatives. Within it, however, considerable variations are possible in constituting the electoral system, though these generally reflect one of two forms. The first, the single-member district system, involves choosing each representative from a single electoral district. In its simplest form, this may be observed in an American congressional district, from which one Representative is chosen, or in a British parliamentary constituency, which selects one Member of Parliament. Election in each case is by plurality vote—that is, there may be any number of candidates, and the one with the largest number of votes wins. The deputies of the National Assembly in the French Fifth Republic are also elected one from each constituency, but here they must receive a number of votes equal to a majority of those cast and to at least a quarter of the total number of voters registered. If no candidate receives this many, in order to encourage a greater degree of electoral consensus, a second balloting or runoff election is held. This time a plurality suffices for election.

The single-member district system is best suited to countries with a stable biparty system. It is simple to count the votes, and the electorate easily understands the results. It emphasizes the direct relationship between the representative and his district, for his success in election depends in part on his association with it. The system also encourages the maintenance of the two-party system and obliges candidates to make broad, rather than narrow, appeals to the electorate. This tends in turn, however artificially, to produce a majority for one party in the legislative assembly.

The system is criticized, however, upon two principal grounds. First, it may exaggerate or even distort popular majorities when translated into legislative seats. In 1945, for example, the British Labour party with 48 percent of the popular votes gained 61.4 percent of the seats in the House of Commons. In 1951, however, the Conservative party got 48 percent of the votes compared to Labour's 48.8 percent, but won 51.3 percent of the seats in Commons. Second, it tends to discriminate against the representation of minor parties, especially those whose support is not concentrated in single constituencies. In another example, the Liberal party in the British election of 1970, with 7.4 percent of the popular votes, won less than 1 percent of the seats. The exaggerations of the single-member district system may also be seen in an extreme form in the French election of 1968, where the second balloting permitted candidates and voters to make political realignments to the disadvantage of small or extremist parties. On the first ballot, the Communist party won 20 percent of the votes, and on the second, 18.6 percent; the (De Gaullist) Union of Democrats for the Republic won 46 percent and 50.8 percent on the same ballots, respectively. As a result of the second ballot, however, the Communists received only 34 seats, less than 7 percent of the total in the National Assembly; the U.D.R. took 292 seats, or 59 percent of the total. Obviously, on the second ballot many voters concentrated on the moderate non-Communist candidates.

For more than a hundred years, therefore, there have been various proposals for a second type of electoral system, based on the principle of proportional representation. Of course, all systems may produce proportionate results to a degree, unless the voter must take all legislators from one single national list or another. The essence of proportional representation systems, however, is that the allotment of seats in the legislature is directly proportionate to the distribution of votes cast. Though a very considerable number of schemes to this end have been applied, at various times, in such countries as Belgium, France, Germany, Ireland, Israel, the Netherlands, and the Scandinavian countries, for example, the fundamental variations are two. The first, known as the single transferable vote system, was developed by Thomas Hare in mid-nineteenth-century England. Briefly, the voter is allowed to express a series of preferences for candidates whose names are arranged alphabetically on the ballot; on the basis of the total number of ballots cast, a quota for election is established to permit the choosing of as many candidates as will fill the prescribed number of seats; and the ballots are so distributed that some candidate may receive usable support from each voter.

The other major form of proportional representation is known as the list system. Here, each party offers a list of candidates to the number of the legislative seats to be filled, arranged in an order it determines. The voter casts his vote for one of the party lists, and the seats are distributed from the top down in each party list according to its share of the total votes cast. In this manner, a party receiving, say, 25 percent of the votes will secure the election of the top fourth of its list.

Several advantages are claimed for systems of proportional representation. There is less distortion of popular preferences in constituting the legislature, and a party with the fewer votes cannot obtain the most seats. Minor political parties of any significant dimensions secure representation which reflects the extent of their popular support. It is thus easier for new parties to win a place in the legislature, and for small ones to perpetuate themselves. It is also asserted that the mathematical consistency of proportional representation renders it more democratic. Despite the zeal with which proportional representation is supported by some of its advocates, its opponents insist that such systems have serious defects. The most obvious, of course, is that the average voter does not find it easy to comprehend the mechanics of such systems, particularly the Hare system. The voter also feels no particular sense of association with the candidates chosen, who in turn cannot easily recognize their supporters. Opponents also contend that such systems unnecessarily encourage small minor parties and do nothing to discourage, at least, a multiparty system, which they fear may prove to be dangerous to stable democratic government.

To assert any distinct superiority between the single-member district system and proportional representation is scarcely possible, if only because one must weigh what are certain practical advantages against certain theoretical preferences. If one sees the prime purpose of the legislature as that of creating large stable majorities to sustain a government and enact its legislative program, the single-member district system is preferable. Minority groups are not thereby repressed or destroyed; rather, they generally must resort to other means than direct legislative representation for the expression of their interests and the influencing of government policy. If, as well, a people are habitually willing and able to make rough-and-ready compromises in the conduct of politics, and are devoted to a biparty system, they will undoubtedly have little enthusiasm for elaborately technical election arrangements. The experience of the English-speaking peoples has generally run along these lines, and they seem to be reasonably well satisfied with the single-member district system.

On the other hand, if the primary purpose of the legislature is seen as the provision of a wide and varied range of all possible political opinions, then a proportional representation system is preferable. This is likely when a multiparty system exists, and each organized political group has as its first concern the ability to exercise a veto over any legislative or administrative action—a feeling that may well reflect past experience of political repression or fear of it in the future. Thus, the choice of electoral system in a particular country seems to reflect, rather than primarily to determine, the kind of party system it has. The evidence really does not support the conclusion that the electoral arrangements create the party system. In Canada and Australia the single-member district system has not preserved a biparty system; in the Scandinavian countries proportional representation has not precluded the creation of stable government majorities. The German Federal Republic elects one-half of the members of the *Bundestag* by each method, to maintain the relationship between constituent and representative, and at the same time give fairer representation to minority groups. The best electoral system for a particular state will be one which will provide a legislative institution that, to the satisfaction of the electorate generally, is capable of performing the major legislative functions. To do so effectively, however, it is unnecessary either to make arbitrary exclusions of minor parties or to ensure that they present a mirrorlike reflection of every single political interest.

The Character of Legislative Membership. Legislative representatives—whose role is one of standing for, or in the place of, other persons—have the greatest influence on the character and quality of the legislature. And probably no other officials of government are regarded with so much cynicism, are so quickly criticized, and so often maligned. Why is this so? First of all, legislators of the present are commonly and invidiously compared with those of some golden age in the past. "There were giants in those days," it is asserted. Yet to the extent that such feeling is not the result of illusion, or downright bad memory, it constitutes an unfair comparison. A century ago, legislators were much more likely to be drawn from the relatively smaller educated, propertied, and privileged classes—though to that extent they were far less popularly representative. Moreover, they were called upon to deal with public issues certainly fewer in number and of far less complexity than those of today—issues about which the average voter might have a relevant or interested opinion. The voter might then see his representative as a better informed and more fluent advocate of interests than the voter could be himself. Today, however, legislation calls for little oratory; instead, the representative is likely to be a hard-working servant of his constituency, dividing his time between sessions of the legislature and numerous visits to his electoral district, where he must be available for meetings, conferences, and innumerable services to his constituents.

In the second place, legislative representatives are often unfavorably compared with the executive. The executive may well be a politician, but he can also be something of an expert; he draws on official sources of information; he may act and be judged by his actions. The legislator is also a politician, but he must be essentially a generalist; he reflects the layman's opinion; he must talk and vote—functions less impressive than taking action; and if he is not a member of the majority, he must continually oppose—a practice which casts him into an apparently unconstructive and negative role. The executive is commonly obliged to take the large view; the legislator may be induced to take the small one. In a legislature where party discipline is strict, the legislator's vote may be controlled by his party; and where it is not, it is controllable largely by local considerations prevailing in his constituency. He may advocate a policy, but knows the frustration that by his own efforts he cannot put it into effect. He makes speeches, persuades, obstructs, maneuvers, trades votes, and compromises. To be most effective in his various roles as politician, broker, critic, investigator, and lawmaker, he must often abandon the ideal dignity of the statesman. Rarely can he appear to be heroic.

The legislature's membership is obviously affected by the sources from which it is drawn. Significant legal qualifications are rare—and usually only those of a voter are essential—though in upper chambers, particularly, some additional maturity of age may be required. Women are almost everywhere equally eligible with men, yet their numbers in the legislature are always disproportionately small. Legislators tend to be drawn from much narrower occupational groups than those prevailing in the nation as a whole. Some approximation of this situation may be demonstrated in the accompanying table which compares four national legislatures of recent years. It should be noted, incidentally, that the percentages indicated suggest only tendencies; they were collected at different times under varying schemes of classification, and thus are not precisely comparable.

OCCUPATIONAL BACKGROUNDS OF LEGISLATORS

	A BRITISH HOUSE OF COMMONS	A FRENCH NATIONAL ASSEMBLY	A GERMAN FEDERAL BUNDESTAG	A UNITED STATES HOUSE OF REPRESENTATIVES
Business	18%	20%	18%	18%
Law	20	15	8	54
Agriculture	5	12	12	8
Workers	18	10	21	—
Public Employees	7	10	23	—
Miscellaneous				
(mainly professional)	32	33	18	20

A comparison of the proportions illustrates some features of public life in the several countries. The proportion of representatives with a business background is much the same in each country, and nowhere are they the dominant element. Lawyers in each case are present in much greater numbers than the proportion their profession bears to the total of occupations, and they compose more than half of the membership of the American Congress. Primarily this prominence of lawyers reflects their customary employment as agents of interest groups, it would seem, rather than an overrepresentation of the legal profession. Representatives with an agricultural background display the relative economic importance of this enterprise in each country, though it may be expected that most such representatives will be substantial landowners rather than "dirt farmers." Again, the representatives of workers' groups tend to be trade union officials, and indicate the presence of Socialist (and in the case of France, Communist) parties, which draw much of their leadership from these elements in European countries. Public employment is not incompatible with legislative membership in Europe as it is in the United States, and hence the varying distributions in the table. The elements of the miscellaneous category are widely assorted, but in the European parliamentary bodies constitute mainly journalists, teachers, doctors, clergymen, engineers, and those from the professions other than law, none of which is found in comparable numbers, however, in the legislative bodies of the United States.

Finally, the quality of legislative representatives, though not always as distinguished as might be hoped, is much higher than popular esteem ordinarily accords it. Whether compared in terms of age, amount of formal education, professional position, military service, political and public office experience, or economic status, all studies suggest the legislator achieves a considerably higher average than that of the constituents whom he represents.

IV. Legislative Functions

The modern legislature's functions reflect the essential purposes for which it was called into existence, or which it was subsequently obliged to assume during development to its present form. Thus the original representation of interests, the counseling of the ruler, the supply of revenue, the supervision of the administration, and the presenting of grievances—all are clearly reflected in the functions of contemporary legislative institutions. We may now examine the five major functions these bodies perform today.

The Representation of Opinion and Interests. In the most general sense, the legislature is a great national forum in which representatives, through their debates and votes (and, not unimportantly, through private discussions in the lobbies and other gatherings), inform those exercising political authority of what the people think, want, and need; the representatives then inform the people of what their government is doing. The provision for this informing function is the justification for making assemblies multimember bodies—often constituted into two houses with one of them at least containing representatives who are popularly elected at frequent intervals. The legislature is thus that organ of government intended most immediately to be the voice of the people. Yet we cannot discuss this function without confronting an ineluctable problem: whom does the legislator represent? Does he speak for all the people of the nation, for all of those in his constituency, for only some of them, or merely for himself? Is he, indeed, a *representative*, present in the place of his constituents and acting as a free agent on their behalf; or is he a *delegate*, pressing demands and carrying out instructions furnished him?

These questions have never been satisfactorily answered. The classic
response was provided—and deserves quotation—by Edmund Burke
in his address to the electors of Bristol in 1774. Speaking of the relationship between a representative and his constituents, he said in
part:

Certainly, gentlemen, it ought to be the happiness and glory of a representative to live in the strictest union, the closest correspondence, and the
most unreserved communication with his constituents. Their wishes ought
to have great weight with him; their opinion high respect; their business
unremitted attention. It is his duty to sacrifice his response, his pleasure, his
satisfactions, to theirs—and above all, ever, and in all cases, to prefer their
interest to his own.

But his unbiased opinion, his mature judgment, his enlightened conscience, he ought not to sacrifice to you, to any man, or to any set of men
living. These he does not derive from your pleasure—no, nor from the law
and the constitution. They are a trust from Providence, for the abuse of
which he is deeply answerable. Your representative owes you, not his industry only, but his judgment; and he betrays, instead of serving you, if he
sacrifices it to your opinion.

My worthy colleague says his will ought to be subservient to yours. If
that be all the thing is innocent. If government were a matter of will upon
any side, yours, without question, ought to be superior. But government
and legislation are matters of reason and judgment, and not of inclination;
and what sort of reason is that, in which the determination precedes the
discussion; in which one set of men deliberate, and another decide; and
where those who form the conclusion are perhaps three hundred miles distant from those who hear the arguments?

To deliver an opinion is the right of all men; that of constituents is a
weighty and respectable opinion, which a representative ought always to
rejoice to hear; and which he ought always most seriously to consider. But
authoritative instructions, *mandates* issued, which the member is bound
blindly and implicitly to obey, to vote and to argue for, though contrary to
the clearest conviction of his judgment and conscience—these are things utterly unknown to the laws of this land, and which arise from a fundamental
mistake of the whole order and tenor of our constitution.

Parliament is not a *congress* of ambassadors from different and hostile interests which interests each must maintain, as an agent, and advocate,
against other agents and advocates; but Parliament is a *deliberative* assembly of *one* nation, with *one* interest, that of the whole—where not local purposes, not local prejudices, ought to guide, but the general good, resulting
from the general reason of the whole. You choose a member indeed; but
when you have chosen him, he is not a member of Bristol, but he is a
Member of *Parliament*. If the local constituent should have an interest or
should form a hasty opinion, evidently opposite to the real good of the rest

of the community, the member for that place ought to be as far as any other from any endeavour to give it effect.

Although Burke provided a counsel of excellence, and an ideal to which many legislators do perhaps aspire, it is not simple to apply in practice. Most persons may not find it difficult to assert that "what is good for my nation is good for my community and me, and vice versa." But the determination of what truly are the national and local interests, and whether they are identical or opposed, is the very essence of politics. This is not a matter that constitutions can solve. The British Parliament recognizes a right of petition, but also draws a line —not always easy to determine—between legitimate political activity and illegitimate pressures on members, so that any attempt by improper means to influence parliamentary conduct is a punishable "breach of privilege." The United States Constitution guarantees the right of the people "to petition the government for a redress of grievances"; it provides also that "for any speech or debate in either house [the members of Congress] shall not be questioned in any other place." The Basic Law of the German Federal Republic (1949) stipulates that members of the *Bundestag* "are representatives of the whole people, not bound by orders and instructions, and subject only to their conscience." The French Constitution of 1958 states that "All binding instructions [upon members of Parliament] shall be null and void. The right to vote of the members of Parliament shall be personal."

Still and all, legislators have to answer to more than their conscience. They are party members; they owe their party organization some debt for their election and hope for its assistance in reelection. They must in the nature of things share a point of view with their party leaders and fellow members, and see certain matters in the light of partisan policy. Legislators are also influenced in varying degree by the pleas, and sometimes pressures, of interest groups. They hear constantly from their constituents, both individual and organized, and many of their demands are not lightly disregarded. From what we have said about the occupational background of legislators, it should not prove surprising to find that some, at least, have their own axes to grind. Thus, the voice of the people may sound from many directions; and the best of legislators must either largely relinquish any unshakable convictions of his own, or cultivate a rather extreme adroitness, if he is to continue to be returned to office.

The Formulation of Policy. As a result of these varied influences, the individual legislator determines his position and takes his stand on the issues. In the chamber of which he is a member, it is necessary that the total of these issues be reconciled—at least into some kind of majority compromise—so that broad national policies can be achieved. National policies, in the simplest terms, relate to what the government will do and how it will go about it. Their formulation is an incredibly complex and frequently difficult task, and legislators are by no means left to their own resources in the process. Other influences of significance will likely be brought to bear directly on the legislature in the making of policy: the proposals of the chief executive and his cabinet, the needs of administrative officials, the programs of political parties, the force of national traditions, the influence of various interest groups and perhaps foreign governments, the views expressed in the press and other communication media, the testimony of scientists and experts, and public opinion generally.

General lawmaking and financial legislation are, of course, an aspect of policy determination; but the latter function is considerably more extensive—for laws and appropriations are normally the consequence of major policy decisions. Thus, a legislature may choose a national policy in the face of depression conditions to revive the economy by large infusions of government spending, construction of extensive public works, and substantial public support of unemployed persons. Or, it may approach the problem by adopting a policy to nationalize under state ownership substantial proportions of the factors in economic production. Legislative policy, then, may be expressed by resolutions, the authorization of treaties and other international agreements, the elaboration of administrative agencies, and the approval of appointments to office. Thus, even if the legislature does not always make national policy, it has the important function of legitimizing political decisions.

In this process of formulating policy the legislature must be provided leadership, though we should note the differing means employed to accomplish this in parliamentary and presidential systems of government. In the parliamentary system, as illustrated by Great Britain, legislative leadership is provided by the Prime Minister and his Cabinet, who are members of Parliament. The standing-committee system is not highly elaborated in the House of Commons; the committees control neither the content nor the destiny of legislative measures. The Speaker of the House of Commons is an impartial moderator and has no part in expressing partisan views or applying party discipline. As we noted in the preceding chapter, the British Cabinet is well situated to exert a very positive leadership of Parliament; it monopolizes the framing and introduction of all important legislation, controls the allocation of parliamentary time, decides on adjournments and dissolutions, and has an assured majority to back its decisions.

In the presidential system, as it prevails in the United States, the provision of legislative leadership is more complicated. The President and his Cabinet are not present in Congress; to exercise leadership of that body the President must be unusually ingenious. The Constitution gives him only indirect powers; he may deliver messages to Congress and has been given a reversible veto of bills it may pass. Beyond these, he must depend largely upon the exertion of personal or party influence, the judicious distribution of such patronage as is available, and appeals made directly to the people. Not surprisingly, in the absence of any executive leadership inside Congress, both the House of Representatives and the Senate organize their own. The House, therefore, has a set of powerful standing committees, each controlled by members of the majority party. The Speaker functions as the parliamentary moderator, a responsibility which he administers with impartiality; but he also acts as majority party leader and is expected to assist, in any appropriate manner, the enactment of his party's legislative program. He is aided by the floor leader and the chairman of the Rules Committee, who are also majority party members. The situation in the Senate is similar. Thus, leadership in the two houses is provided by both external and internal means.

In both systems, the complexity of the governmental process renders the legislature increasingly dependent upon the executive for the initiation of major policy proposals. The nature of the parliamentary system obliges the legislature to assume what is essentially a reviewing role: to examine and criticize such proposals, and modify, adopt, or in extreme cases reject them. The American Congress has found itself increasingly cast in a similar role; but here the tradition of the separation of powers, along with the capacity of the houses to provide something of an internal leadership of their own, makes this passive position more difficult for congressmen to accept.

The Control of Finance. The power to control the purse strings is one of the oldest functions of the legislature. The levy of taxes and the appropriation of funds are not only an aspect of policy formulation—for all significant policy decisions have financial consequences—but are also important devices for control of the executive and supervision of the administration. In addition, control of the purse has come to be a central activity in the operation of government because of the major influence that public finance exerts on the state of the national economy. Through the use of the tax power, the legislature can influence the general standard of living as well; this can be accomplished by directing, limiting, or even virtually prohibiting, various kinds of consumption. The initial obligation for the preparation and presentation of a comprehensive government budget— proposing the monetary needs of the various departments and services, and balancing those needs with the expected or required revenues—is generally regarded as an executive responsibility. But it is also the hallmark of representative government that the legislature retains the final right to authorize taxes and grant appropriations. The principal ways in which legislatures exercise this control, whether as an immediate or as an ultimate power, may be demonstrated in the contrasting American and British arrangements.

Under the Constitution of the United States, Congress is given the power "to lay and collect taxes, duties, imposts, and excises, to pay the debts and provide for the common defense and general welfare. . . ." Bills for raising revenue must originate in the House of Representatives, though the Senate may amend them. The Constitution further stipulates that "no money shall be drawn from the treasury, but in consequence of appropriations made by law. . . ." The Budget and Accounting Act (1921) established a budget bureau—headed by a director under the authority of the President—which prepares the annual financial program to be presented to Congress. Once this has been done, Congress is free to do what it wishes with the President's proposals, and the procedures it employs in enacting the budget display a distressing lack of integration. The supply portion of the budget is considered by the separate Appropriations Committees in the House and Senate; revenue measures are considered first by the House Committee on Ways and Means, and subsequently by the Senate Finance Committee. Further, individual members of Congress, without any responsibility to secure compensating revenue, are entirely free to introduce bills involving the expenditure of funds for in-

dividual projects and to trade votes with other congressmen to effect
their mutual adoption. As a result, the President's budget is only a
starting point for financial legislation; Congress independently exercises its power to reduce or increase the proposals made. The President may veto whole financial bills, of course, but not individual
items in them, so that his authority is only a rough instrument for effecting economy. In truth, then, the budget's enactment requires a long
series of involved skirmishes, and some outright battles, between the
President and Congress.

In Great Britain, the principle that the Crown may tax only with
the consent of Parliament goes back to the Magna Carta (1215), and
the right of the Crown to spend only with the same consent is prescribed in the Bill of Rights (1689). Since 1911, this parliamentary authority has rested entirely with the House of Commons. It is also a
constitutional rule that only ministers may propose a tax or an expenditure. The House could vote to refuse or reduce an appropriation, legally speaking, but any such action would constitute the withdrawal
of its confidence in the government. The preparation of the budget is
a responsibility of the Treasury, headed by the Chancellor of the Exchequer, who also presents it annually to the Commons. Supply, and
ways and means, are considered separately by the House while sitting as a committee of the whole; standing committees have no power
over financial measures. At no time, therefore, do the ministers relinquish control of the budget proposals. They may agree to accept certain amendments; but for the most part they do not, and need only
crack the whip of party discipline to produce the required majority
support for their demands. Consequently, since members of the House
may not by their own orders increase the financial estimates and cannot for political reasons expect to reduce them, the several weeks of
debates allotted to the budget are devoted to a discussion not of public expenditure at all but of public policy. Thus the House of Commons has only an ultimate control over finance; it can alter the budget contrary to the government's wishes only by the extreme step of
driving the latter from office.

The highly integrated system of budgeting is widely admired and
in its general features is the one most usually employed; it is, however, somewhat less ideal than many of its advocates claim. For one
thing, it does not produce the same results in all parliamentary systems. In France, for example, before the establishment of the Fifth

Republic, ministers were frequently overthrown by legislative rebellion against their budgetary proposals; in Great Britain none ever is. The British arrangements do have the great merit of centering responsibility for the budget in the executive, who prepares it with the assurance that it will be enacted and with the obligation to see that expenditures and revenues are brought into balance. Members of Parliament are relieved of any pressure by interest groups seeking to raid the Treasury and denied any opportunity to refuse to support government programs or to organize pork barrel schemes of their own. But there are disadvantages. The Cabinet is not necessarily more economy minded than Parliament; indeed, the pressures of interest groups seeking government expenditures are not eliminated but are merely transferred to the executive. In any event, British expenditure has risen every bit as steadily as that in other comparable countries. Members of Parliament, having no opportunity to participate actively in the preparation of or hearings upon financial measures, acquire little expertness on the subject; in practical effect, then, the power of the purse is in the hands of the Treasury.

The criticisms of the American system center on its diffusion of responsibility and on the opportunity it affords for legislative extravagance. The first is probably an inevitable result of the separation of powers and the essentially equal authority conferred on the houses of a bicameral Congress. It is not likely that either of these fixtures of the American system would be relinquished and replaced by the parliamentary system. Instead, the solution for these deficiencies seems to lie in the direction of integrating the congressional financial committees, consolidating appropriation measures, and authorizing a single-item veto power to the President. One might also conclude, on reflection, that a legislative judgment respecting the national fiscal interests is not always and inevitably inferior to one made by the executive; and unmitigated cabinet dictatorship in the field of finance comes close to turning legislative control of finance into a fiction.

It may be noted in conclusion that control of allocation is, to be sure, always prospective. For that reason, legislative bodies take a large interest in seeing how allocated funds have actually been spent. New appropriations are inevitably made with an eye to how effectively money has already been applied in public programs—hence, the various national systems of post-auditing executive accounts by the legislature. At their best, however, such systems have only a limited utility, illustrating a proverbial locking the barn door after the horse has been stolen.

The Supervision of the Executive. The function of the representative legislature which has been steadily growing in importance is the supervision and control of the executive. It receives the greatest emphasis in parliamentary systems, whose principal feature is the enforcement of executive or ministerial responsibility to the parliament; and it has also gained continually in importance in the presidential system, where the control of the great and ever-enlarging powers of the president is a major problem. The operation of parliamentary controls follows various patterns, reflecting the relationships between ministers of a government and their parliamentary bodies. There are, first, those states where ministers may not be members of either house, as in France, the Netherlands, Norway, and the United States; second, those where ministers must be members, as in Australia and Ireland (this is also the usual practice in Great Britain and Canada); and third, those where ministers may but need not be members, as in Belgium, Denmark, Finland, Italy, Luxembourg, and Sweden. We noted in the preceding chapter the apparently inevitable tendency toward the expansion of executive authority; yet if the principle of limited and responsible government is to be maintained, the executive must be held to a continuous accountability for the exercise of his powers.

There are several methods whereby the legislature supervises the executive. The first is the legislative control of executive appointments and certain official acts. In the parliamentary system this power amounts to full legislative control only of the selection of the prime minister and his ministry. Where a biparty system is in operation, as in Great Britain for example, the majority party naturally will accept only the leader of their party for appointment as prime minister; he, in turn, makes his own choice of ministers. However, the ministry as a whole must have the support of a majority or it will not be able to govern. Where a parliament is in the hands of a number of parties, its control over the personnel of the ministry is even greater; each party joining to form the majority coalition will bargain for ministerial posts. In the United States, though Congress does not choose the President, the Senate must approve all of his appointments to the higher offices of the national government. These civilian officers include the members of his cabinet, other heads of establishments, ambassadors, consuls, federal judges, and others—to a total of more than 5,000 appointments. Certain other executive acts are, in various countries, made subject to legislative approval; these include ratification of treaties, issuance of decrees having the force of law, and declarations of emergency.

A second, and extremely important means of controlling executive officers in all systems is the requirement that they furnish information to the legislature. Essentially, if the legislature is to hold the executive accountable, it must know what he is doing. In consequence, all departments and agencies of government are obliged to issue a great volume of reports, regular and special, accounting for their activities. A most efficacious device for day-to-day surveillance of the executive is the parliamentary question period, employed in Great Britain and the Commonwealth countries, in which members require ministers to answer specific questions relating to matters within their jurisdiction. Another device, the interpellation, is employed in Belgium, Switzerland, Italy, the Netherlands, formerly in France, and in other parliamentary systems. This procedure involves an even more thorough inquiry into a minister's actions and policies, followed by a formal vote reflecting favorably or unfavorably upon him. These techniques are not available in the United States, for cabinet members may not appear on the floors of Congress. Something of a counterpart may be found, however, during hearings on legislative and financial proposals, when congressional committees take the opportunity to question thoroughly cabinet members and other administrative officers. Ministers and other officials may also be invited to give statements to and discuss policies with committees or informal groups of congressmen; their desire to stand in well with the legislators is ordinarily sufficient inducement to accept such invitations.

Parliamentary bodies also have power to establish select or special committees to conduct investigations of executive actions or the results of administering certain legislation. Exercising its authority to obtain essential information upon which legislation may be based, the United States Congress has through its history investigated subjects ranging from American Indians to "un-American activities." These have commonly proved a useful device through which to supervise administration in some respects. Certain efforts of recent years, however, where some congressional committees have turned essentially from examining the administrative process to inquiring into the beliefs of private citizens have produced widespread feeling that individual congressmen in these circumstances have abused their authority. In the case of *Watkins* v. *United States* (1957), Chief Justice Warren agreed that congressional investigatory power is "inherent in the legislative process" but cautioned that "there is no congressional power to expose for the sake of exposure."

A third legislative control is found in the practice of discussing and criticizing executive action by formal debates on motions of confidence and censure, or by indirect means on other subjects. Arising from information obtained in ways just described, the legislature has the signal responsibility to review executive policies and actions; to publicize those which are inefficient, ineffectual, or extravagant; to champion the cause of persons treated unjustly or arbitrarily; and to place the findings before the forum of public opinion. Here, then, the legislature acts as the "grand inquest of the nation." As Sir William Anson described the attributes of members of Parliament in his *Law and Custom of the Constitution*, they may "discuss all matters of national or imperial concern, and criticize the conduct of ministers; either House collectively may address the Crown on matters of general policy, may institute inquiries, in the public interest, into the conduct of persons or public bodies; while in the last resort, Parliament may bring to justice a great political offender." Indeed, Woodrow Wilson, in his *Congressional Government*, concluded that: "The informing function of Congress should be preferred even to its legislative function. The argument is not only that discussed and interrogated administration is the only pure and efficient administration, but, more than that, that the only really self-governing people is that people which discusses and interrogates its administration."

Finally, as a fourth control, there is the legislative power to drive the executive from office. In terms this narrow, this is a function of the legislature only in the parliamentary system, where ministers are collectively and individually responsible to the popular chamber; it is not, however, entirely without counterpart in the presidential type of government. Even among the former types of government this authority is not identically employed, but it is in all of them "the shotgun behind the door" to be used as a weapon against an entirely impossible executive. As we noted in the previous chapter, a British ministry is virtually irremovable unless an election alters the party balance in the Commons. Restraint is also imposed in this function upon the

German *Bundestag,* which can vote a ministry out of office only by agreeing on its successor. In the Third and Fourth French Republics, however, Parliament exercised its power to drive ministries from office so zealously and frequently as to destroy all governmental stability. In the American presidential system, Congress does have the power to remove the President, the Vice-President, and all civil officers of the United States from office "on impeachment for, and conviction of, treason, bribery, or other high crimes and misdemeanors." Such procedure is not intended, of course, to resolve merely political differences between the two. However, excepting the President, all offices and agencies of the national government are created by act of Congress, as well as being equipped with authority, staff, and funds. Not surprisingly, if Congress does not obtain a considerable measure of cooperation from the President, it may choose to restrict the resources with which he acts.

The Enactment of Law. We are discussing this function of the legislature last, not because it is the least important, but because it is the most obvious and the one to which parliamentary bodies devote the largest amount of their time. This lawmaking function includes not only the enactment of ordinary statutes and resolutions, but usually the very basic power to initiate, and perhaps even adopt, constitutional amendments. We may note at the outset that it is customary to separate legislative proposals into one of two groups—public bills, those of general application, or private bills, which apply only to individual persons or localities—and to subject them to somewhat different procedures. Bills originate from different sources; the largest proportion in most assemblies come from the executive, are known as government bills or administration measures, and are initiated or introduced by a minister. All others are "private members' bills" (to use the British phrase that sharply distinguishes them), which may be of either public or private application. In the United States, it may be noted, where Congress is rather uniquely organized to originate legislation on its own, private bills constitute a very large proportion of legislative measures.

To carry out its duties, a legislative assembly undertakes its formal organization at the beginning of each session. It chooses a presiding officer, variously titled Speaker, President, or Chairman; one or more deputy officers to serve in his absence; a clerk; and certain other officials as are necessary. The function of the presiding officer is, of course, to maintain order, to recognize members wishing to speak, to ensure that they do so more or less relevantly, to rule on matters of procedure, to put questions, to announce the result of votes, and to sign bills and resolutions. The moderator usually also has power to repress disorder, if necessary, by suspending proceedings. He is everywhere an official of authority and dignity, though none exceeds in impressiveness the Speaker of the British House of Commons, splendid in wig and gown.

The legislative process in all chambers divides consideration of measures between the house as a whole and its committees. Every assembly organizes a set of standing or permanent committees; and each committee is provided as a rule with competence over a specific area of governmental activity and receives all bills upon that subject. Parties are represented on these committees in proportion to their strength in the house. Committee consideration may come either before or after first consideration of a bill by the whole assembly, depending upon the particular parliamentary procedure; in either case, its function is to act as the "house in miniature" and to subject the bill to such revision and amendment as will commend it to the membership generally. A bill is normally considered by the entire house at least twice, so that both its general principles and its details may be examined. The United States, Great Britain, and the Commonwealth countries also make use of a committee of the whole house— essentially a means of proceeding under less formal rules which permits wide participation in debate. Parliamentary bodies create other kinds of committees, of course, for special purposes.

The parliamentary procedure of a legislative chamber is ordinarily governed in part by constitutional provisions and statutes. In addition, an assembly adopts a set of standing rules; and a body of precedents—derived from rulings of the moderator, and supplemented by orders of the day and special rules—grows up around these rules. The elaborate and formal rules of a parliamentary body have several purposes: to ensure that party leadership can make itself felt and that the more important measures will receive priority of consideration; to let members know at any one time precisely what action may be taken respecting a measure; to allow the minority to be heard, to oppose, and to offer alternative measures; and to expedite procedure so that the majority may work its will.

Debate proceeds either from specific motions, as in English-speak-

ing countries, or on more general subjects, as is the European practice. The presiding officer usually has some discretion in recognizing
members, though in his selection of those who may speak, he is sometimes assisted with lists provided by the party leaders; where ministers may be present in a house, they ordinarily enjoy preferment, as
do also committee chairmen. It is common to set advance limits to
the length of a given debate, and nearly everywhere the majority can
adopt a closure motion so that action may be taken. Voting practices
vary, of course, though several methods are widely used. These include the viva voce vote, in which members call out in turn the ayes
and noes; voting by sitting and standing, which has much the same
effect; by division, which involves a physical separation of the ayes
and noes, and their count by tellers; balloting, either open or secret;
and roll call, by which members' votes are recorded as their names
are read. Only a few parliaments—among them those of France, Sweden, and Finland—have adopted electric voting machines.

Where the legislature is bicameral, there must be some procedure to
deal with the important matter of reconciling differences between the
two houses over the terms of a bill. As we have previously noted,
upper chambers in most instances do not enjoy an equality of power
with the lower; consequently, in such countries as Australia, France,
the German Federal Republic, Great Britain, and Ireland, there are
procedures permitting the popular chamber to override the second
house. In other countries, such as Belgium and Italy, a bill is passed
back and forth between the chambers until agreement is reached, or
it is obvious that none can be. A third arrangement, employed in
Switzerland and the United States, is to draw a joint conference committee from the two houses to reconcile their disagreements. The final
step in the process of legislative enactment involves executive approval of the bill. In parliamentary systems, the titular head of state
normally must approve or promulgate a bill for it to become effective
as a legislative act. Since he is guided by the advice of ministers, the
exercise of the veto, if there is one, actually rests with them; and only
under rather unusual circumstances are they likely to reject bills they
have themselves originated and guided to passage. In the United
States, the step has some real importance, however; the President
may veto a bill passed by Congress, which can in turn repass it
against his objections by a vote of two-thirds of each house. To be
sure, this power fails to provide the President with legislation he may

want, but it is commonly effective in dealing with legislation he does not.

V. The Decline of the Legislature

The legislature, we have noted, has been considered the indispensable organ of modern democratic government. The emergence of legislative authority was directly related to the extension of modern democracy, reflecting the principle of government by the consent of the governed. Yet the conception of the legislature as a central institution conducting all affairs of state, formulating policies and laws, and overseeing their administration, is no longer valid. Parliamentary bodies have lost much of the power they held in the eighteenth and nineteenth centuries; unlike the executive, they have made few adjustments to the changed circumstances of the twentieth century. Several decades ago, the distinguished authority on legislatures, Robert Luce, warned that "the old methods of representative government are nowhere equal to the problems springing from the complexities of modern life."

That the legislature has substantially lost place to the executive is by now a well-confirmed phenomenon. British parliamentary government has evolved into cabinet government. American congressional government has become presidential government. The German Federal Republic has been facetiously described as the "Chancellor Republic", while the traditional assembly government of France has been replaced, under the Fifth Republic, by presidential government, and converted, in one view, into "a technocracy managed by bureaucrats." But parliamentary bodies have suffered subordination to more than just the executive. As Professor Peter Campbell has observed: "National policy is made by the governing party's leaders, subject to the influence of their back-benchers and their supporters outside parliament, the civil service, and the various sectional interests and opinion groups; the fate of governments is decided mainly by the voters at general elections. The government, the majority party, the civil service, the pressure groups and the electorate at large—it is from their discussions that decisions emerge; only a small part of these discussions take place in the two chambers and their lobbies." In short, more and more power passes from elected persons to selected persons. Inevitably, then, the legislature's role becomes somewhat subsidiary. We may now briefly examine the twofold basis upon which much of the disparagement of the contemporary legislature rests.

The Problem of Legislative Power. First of all, the subordination of legislative power is an inevitable reflection of the aggrandizement of the executive. The idea of parliamentary supremacy was originally concomitant with the object of replacing absolutist by popular authority. But, as we have seen, the expansion of governmental activity has produced an inevitable extension of executive powers; and the need for strong leadership and vigorous action respecting the problems of defense, foreign relations, and domestic economy of the modern nation has obliged the executive to accept the central role in the political process. Even states with the strongest parliamentary traditions, emphatically committed to the maintenance of executive responsibility, have witnessed this phenomenon.

Second, the role of the legislature is reduced by the difficulty within the modern state of effecting consensus upon national goals and policies. More and more nations are finding it almost impossible to resolve satisfactorily various constitutional, political, economic, or diplomatic crises confronting their society. For all states, whether among the most or the least powerful, circumstance and not choice dictates their degree of involvement and position in the international community, and their relative success in reconciling the various domestic conflicts of interest. As parliamentary bodies frequently mirror society's opposing and hostile interests, and find themselves unable to resolve the controversies raised by them, they further accentuate irreconcilable conflicts within the fabric of the nation itself and themselves cease to be functioning and coherent institutions.

Third, the weakness of parliamentary traditions and spirit frequently renders the legislative institution impotent. The periods following both World Wars I and II witnessed the difficulties of a number of new states suddenly confronted with the problem of self-government, either because their heretofore autocratic system was overthrown or their colonial status of dependency was terminated. Obliged for the first time to undertake the responsibility of operating complex parliamentary institutions, they have faced formidably difficult tasks. In these new governmental systems, the distractions of personal jealousies, partisan rivalries, nationalistic sensitivity, and economic complications do not make the going easier. Such states as Burma, Ceylon, Indonesia, the Korean Republic, Pakistan, and Thailand, to name only a few, have all had experience with these problems.

The Problem of Legislative Efficiency. Even in states with long traditions of effective representative government, legislatures display various institutional shortcomings. One of these inevitably arises from the problem of leadership. Though leadership cannot dispense with the personal element, if it is to be truly effective and continuous it must be institutionalized through the mechanism of party. Where party leaders are able to apply a strict parliamentary discipline, however, as in Great Britain and the German Federal Republic, a common complaint is that members of parliament are the servants of the party machines—frustrated, denied the exercise of initiative or discretion, and dragooned through divisions. Where parliamentary party discipline is weak, on the other hand, as in France and the United States, the criticism is that the party is unable to carry out its election promises or accomplish its mandate, and that the individual legislator is inordinately sensitive to and preoccupied with the demands of local or special interests. Thus, few legislatures have satisfactorily achieved an ideal middle ground where party leadership is neither too strong nor too weak.

Critics of the legislature today also remark upon the inability of such bodies to cope with the volume and complexity of legislation before them. Legislative procedures are commonly described as slow, cumbersome, and anachronistic; and under them legislators are called upon to make decisions involving matters of the utmost technicality and complexity. There is always pressure upon parliamentary time; yet legislators commonly appear not to make effective use of what time they have—often occupying themselves at length with trivial affairs, then rushing through with indecent haste legislation of the highest importance. In the United States Congress, for example, far too much time is devoted to private bills dealing with matters that might more properly be delegated to administrative authority. In an age when few subjects of legislation can be simple, the legislature appears most inadequately equipped with expert staff and advisory assistance.

Still further, parliamentary bodies are widely criticized as having inadequate means of supervising executive authority. The traditional methods for holding the executive accountable appear definitely insufficient in the face of the expanding powers and activities of modern government. Assemblies continually struggle unsuccessfully to obtain sufficient information about what the executive is doing, and yet without this information effective criticism of the administration is impossible. An inattentive and ineffective opposition may prefer to air spectacular but petty grievances rather than perform the hard work of systematically surveying a government's policies and proposing reasonable alternatives to them. Where party discipline is strong, governments are virtually irremovable, except by the electorate; where party discipline is weak, and responsibility is diffused among many small parties, the power to overturn governments can be easily abused. Even in Great Britain, despite the finesse with which legislative-executive relationships were shaped, it is frequently asserted that the executive has long since upset the balance and that cabinet dictatorship of Parliament is the result. Such entirely legitimate devices of control as the investigating committee can be abused when conducted in a hostile partisan manner; in America, the spectacle of congressional bloodhounds baying loudly at every suspicious scent is not always a reassuring one.

Finally, it is clear enough that legislatures have suffered a serious decline in prestige, reflecting an adverse popular view not only of the legislature's membership but also of its organization and operation. It is a commonplace in Great Britain today that truly independent-minded men no longer will offer themselves as candidates for House of Commons seats. The German *Bundestag* is contemptuously spoken of as *Die Schwatzbude* ("the gossip shack"); and during serious political crises, Frenchmen have been known to post signs on their automobiles stating: *"Je ne suis pas député"* ("I am not a Deputy"). Italy too has the shout: *"Abbasso i deputati!"* ("Down with the Deputies!"). As Walter Lippmann observed a few years ago, "it is one of the great facts of our public life that the Congress of the United States is today short of men of ability and high purpose and much too long on blatherskites." These views, if not universally held, do not reflect mere momentary irritations. They are, rather, commentaries on a variety of unsatisfactory aspects of the legislative institution: its frequently unrepresentative character, its dilatory procedures, its solicitude for narrow and selfish interests, and its unseemly propensity for maneuvering and bickering over trifles of partisan advantage.

The Improvement of the Legislative Institution. After examining such a list of criticisms, some have been led to conclude that the legislature ought to be abolished. Yet the democratic state cannot dispense with the legislature; its essential functions cannot be performed by any other agency of government. The task of democracy, then, is to find ways to restore the legislature to a position in which it can effect its fundamental purposes. To examine the welter of proposed solutions for such a restoration, in even modest detail, would take us far beyond the allowable dimensions of our present discussion. Yet we must ponder the problem, which can probably be resolved as much by changes in public opinion and parliamentary spirit as by alterations in laws and forms. Certainly there is room for improvement in several principal directions: among them, raising the representative character of parliamentary bodies; streamlining and modernizing their procedures; forging more effective devices for their supervision of the executive; and improving the quality of the legislators. In this latter regard, though a minimum age for legislators is constitutionally required to assure appropriate maturity, now far more needed are retirement ages. The matter deserves attention; given the need of these bodies for members with stamina and mental vigor, it seems highly desirable that they not become refuges for the senile and superannuated.

Legislative bodies need also to reexamine their role in the governmental process. They have not yet adapted to current times and grown in stature as has the executive. Slow to concede sensibly the paramount need for the executive to act and govern, too often they have either displayed subservience to executive power, sought to obstruct it, or ineffectually contested for a share of it. The legislative institution can enhance its status by providing a major forum for the debate of grand policy—international as well as national—and of the onerous problems which face all national societies. At the same time it must also develop better means to protect worthy individual and local interests which can be too easily overlooked in the executive's need for general solutions to importunate problems.

These are matters of the highest concern today, not simply because popular disillusionment with legislative bodies should be dispelled but because the fate of representative government is everywhere at stake. It may be true that we expect more of parliamentary bodies than they are able to give, and that we set our expectations at unattainable levels of perfection. Nonetheless, the enhancement of the reliability and efficacy of our representative legislatures must be a continuing process if we are to sustain the popular foundation upon which our entire democratic edifice rests. Parliamentary bodies are everywhere today confronted with weighty and vital tasks; and the wisdom needed to resolve them is not theirs for the asking. "To govern is to choose, no matter how difficult the choices become," Pierre Mendès-France has observed. To choose rightly, and to support political authority that can, is the challenge the legislature faces.

9

The Judiciary

THE cry for "equal justice under law" rings through the centuries. Although justice may be separated from law and even from equality, the linking of these three terms has supported the development of the third great institution of government, the judiciary, as an independent system of courts and judges. But sometimes the pursuit of justice—or some more mundane objective—can lead to a judiciary more like an arm of government than an independent branch of it. Such differences in the organization and activity of the judicial power make it extremely difficult even for judges to say precisely what the judicial process is. Nonetheless, we can indicate its general distinguishing characteristics.

In any society disputes are likely to arise among private parties, and between public officials and private persons, concerning their respective rights, powers, and responsibilities within the framework of law. The judicial process resolves such disputes; it hears and decides causes. In doing this the judicial power completes and coordinates the other two processes of government; naturally, its own organization and procedures, as well as its degree of independence, will depend to some extent on how and to what end the executive and legislative functions are exercised.

Like the legislative, the judicial organ marks a branching off from an original concentration of authority in a single ruler. Whereas the legislature is a relatively modern development in its present form, the judicial institution is much older. Indeed, in very ancient times, kings appointed judges to administer justice in their behalf. Courts have, therefore, a very long history; and of all the parts of government, they have changed the least in form and function. The reason for this is probably inherent in the nature of their work and their role in society.

Characteristics of the Judicial Process. Three characteristics have always marked the judicial process. The first has to do with the object of judicial proceedings: to administer justice. The search for the meaning of the powerful abstraction "justice" has continued for centuries in legal and philosophical thinking, and many different conclusions have resulted. We will not pretend, then, that we can simply define it here. Doing justice, in a primarily legal sense, was defined by Ulpian as rendering to every man his due. Others have defined it differently. Even so, some essential qualities of justice are well known; we associate what is just with what is rightful, equitable, virtuous, reasonable, and lawful. To assure justice to individuals in their various affairs is clearly one of the oldest service functions of government. As Augustine observed: "Set justice aside, then, and what are kingdoms but great robberies?"

A second characteristic relates to method: the provision by the state of an impartial judge to decide a cause. A man is not justly to be condemned or his rights prejudiced without being heard. In the process, impartiality is the judge's first duty; and to ensure this he must be entirely without personal interest in the proceedings before him, and free from all interference in his performance. We insist on judicial integrity of a very high order; irregularities in character or behavior displayed in the executive or legislative branches are considered intolerable in a judge. As Lord Hewart observed: "Justice should not only be done, it should also be seen to be done." Thus, the judiciary plays a unique role. The legislature, on the other hand, must enact general rules and cannot apply them to individual cases; and for the executive to have final authority to settle disputed cases would often make it judge in its own cause.

The third characteristic of the judicial process is its conduct by determinate standards: that causes be resolved according to law. This feature gives the qualities of order and predictability to the disposition of individual interests. Despite the difficulties in attaining it, judicial administration clings to the ideal of certainty. There must be a sense of substantial continuity in the character of prevailing rules or the judicial process will not serve its essential social purpose.

I. Law and Legal Systems

"Law" is another great abstraction which is used in a number of senses. Men speak of *divine* law—as composed of commandments and precepts they believe have been ordained by God, and contained in such works as the Bible, the Koran, or the Torah; of *moral* law—as rules of ideal human conduct based upon personal conscience and community opinion; and of *natural* law—as rules inherent in nature or the universe. The term *scientific* law is used to describe the sequence of cause and effect in natural phenomena, which operates entirely without reference to man's will. Obviously, these various laws differ greatly as to their source and their sanction—that is, the means which induce obedience to their rules. None of them, however, constitutes the kind of law we are primarily concerned with in the conduct of government.

The Nature of Law

Positive Law. Ordinarily, we speak of *jural* or *positive* law, which is man-made law; it may be broadly defined as the rules of conduct that are enforced by public officials. The purpose of law is to order and stabilize human relations in society; yet it is not the only means which is employed to this end or which determines how men behave. Society prescribes conduct in several different ways. As Professor Munroe Smith has observed: "To knock a man down, for example, or to wrest from him portable valuables is, in most instances, at once unmannerly, immoral and illegal." The observance of manners is enforced by the desire to avoid ridicule and to achieve social ease; and of morals, by the desire to avoid shame and social ostracism, and to achieve honor and good conscience. The rules of law, however, are distinguishable from other social controls in that they are expressed through the organs of government and will be enforced by them, if necessary, with physical force. Moral and legal rules are further distinguishable in that the latter can be formulated in terms of rights, and hence are capable of judicial application. In sum, then, positive law is laid down through the machinery of the state and is discernible particularly as those rules that the courts will enforce.

In primitive societies, men tended to make little distinction between morals, customs, religious beliefs, natural phenomena, and positive law. They saw all rules of behavior—for things animate and inanimate—as prescribed by their environment, immutable, and implicitly to be obeyed. They assumed, in other words, that the same controlling forces determined all rules, whether prescribing the movement of the tides, the forms of politeness to one's mother-in-law, or the exercise of rights over personal property. Thus what we call "positive law" was originally considered to be something fixed and static; laws were not deliberately made but discovered. Through most of the history of law the attitude prevailed: law was what had ever been; it was found, and then declared. Not until well toward the end of the middle ages was the idea fully accepted that laws might be made.

The Sources of Law. Rules of law are drawn and developed from several starting points. A first source of positive law has been the moral and ethical principles which have always provided important guides to human action. It is obvious that these principles will be given jural sanctions in many instances—murder is a crime as well as a sin. To be sure, some positive law rules are based upon little more than convenience or expediency, but the larger body of law may be seen as reflecting man's fundamental moral sense. The idea of natural law, for example—a concept known to men from the ancient Greeks to the American founding fathers as an ideal law which positive law should approximate—exerted an influence throughout the entire formative period of western institutions. Men have disagreed, of course, over what constitutes the law of nature. To some it has been established by God; to others, it is dictated by and discoverable in reason, or in man's ability to distinguish right from wrong. In any case its rules are considered by many to have a reality and force apart from any positive action or consent by individual men or states. As Alexander Hamilton wrote: "The sacred rights of mankind are not to be rummaged for among old parchments or musty records. They are written, as with a sunbeam, in the whole volume of human nature, by the hand of the divinity itself, and can never be erased or obscured by mortal power."

A second source of positive law has been custom. In the life of a community certain practices acquire the support of tradition and common usage. When such practices come to be enforced through government, we may say that they have become part of the positive law. Such provisions, often called "customary law," are an important part of all bodies of law; and even in modern times customary practices continue to be turned into customary law through the process of public, or judicial, recognition. The assertion that custom is a source of law, however, is ambiguous. Adherents of the historical school of jurisprudence hold that custom—representing a long and uniform development of a rule together with a conviction of its rightness—is an instance of society, not government, creating law. More usually today, however, it is held that only public officials can create law as such, although it is admitted that customary practices may in fact dictate the content of the legal norms they create. But in either case, it is difficult to determine just when and to what extent a custom becomes a legal rule, for customary law is necessarily unwritten law. The advantage of customary law is that it may be expected to enjoy popular support and to reflect common sense and experience; but it tends to be slow-developing and conservative. For this reason it is not so significant in contemporary judicial processes as it was in those of less revolutionary periods.

A third source of law is adjudication. Presumably, the rules of law are developed in this manner by a judge called upon to decide controversies between individuals: the local customs or customary laws are declared; the judge chooses among these and other available rules; and judicial rulings assimilate the chosen rules to the total body of law. The classic example of judge-made law is found in the English system. In its development the judges were not, technically speaking, considered to be the source of the law; rather, they were the means by which its existence was declared. The fiction was that the royal justices merely applied "the custom of the realm." Actually, however, this development of a body of precedents by professional lawyers and judges constituted the making of law. English law thus became a case law rather than a customary law system; once the rolls of the courts began to be kept, the law was unwritten only in the sense of being uncodified.

Finally, a source of law is legislation. In the broadest sense, legislation is enacted law, whether comprising constitutions, constitutional laws, treaties, statutes, or decrees. As we have seen, the legislative power may be exercised by the people in constitution-making, by the legislature in adopting a statute, or by the executive in issuing a decree. Only the judiciary may not enact law, though as we have suggested, they may well make it. Legislation is considered superior to judge-made rules; it is a more democratic form of lawmaking, and provides the means whereby old rules may be modernized and new rules given immediate effect. A significant aspect of legislation is that it clearly displays the element of command by the sovereign. This is most important in the view of the analytical school of jurisprudence; its adherents consider law as the command of a superior to an inferior, supported by a monopoly of force—and these elements as essential to its validity.

The views of the historical and the analytical schools of jurists cannot be reconciled, but their conflicting perspectives do help to emphasize important characteristics of law. Law must be enforced by the machinery of state, or we have not distinguished it from other means of social control; but no state, however despotic, can successfully command obedience to that which is utterly repugnant to the community. An effective body of law, enjoying stability and continuity, must reflect a general conviction as to its rightness and appropriateness; it is a part of human culture and civilization.

Legal Systems

Historically speaking, the law of the western world has been drawn from numerous elements. The oldest of the ancient systems known to us is found in the Code of Hammurabi, published by the king of Babylon about 2000 B.C., which drew mainly upon old Sumerian law. The Code reflects a society well advanced from barbarism, and probably had considerable influence in other areas of the Mediterranean. Relatively little is known of other ancient systems. Despite its great achievements in intellectual speculation in other areas, Greece made no significant contributions to jurisprudence. It was left to Rome and Norman England to originate the two great legal systems of the world.

The Civil-Law System. The civil law system developed in continental Europe, taking its name as well as its contents from the *jus civile* of Rome. Rome's first great law code, drawing together the early customary law and dating from about 450 B.C., was the famous Twelve Tables; it constituted the foundation upon which Rome's monumental legal edifice was constructed. The Romans, thereafter, developed two bodies of law—a *jus civile* for Roman citizens, and a *jus gentium* for the subjects of their empire, which in time largely superseded the former. After its civilization and empire were well in decline, however, Rome produced a crowning effort to the work of ten centuries of jurists: the celebrated Code of Justinian, dating from approximately A.D. 533. This restatement of Roman law constituted a legacy which enriched the legal systems of Europe and much of the world.

Justinian's Code was soon superseded, however, as the collapse of Rome opened the way for other bodies of law to prevail in Europe. A German system of law, originating in tribal rules extensively intermingled with those from Roman law, provided the rude society of the times with a limited scheme of tort and criminal proceedings. It was much more primitive than the Roman system, but became of increasing importance as the royal authority of the Teuton kings was consolidated. Later, compilations of feudal law were made; an important example, the *Libri Feudorum* from Lombardy, reflected the way in which the similar conditions of land tenure of the times produced substantially uniform rules. In addition, a body of canon law—the law of the Church, but a law based extensively on Roman legal ideas —evolved as the Church itself became a great estate in medieval Europe. From its concern with morality in general and jurisdiction over the clergy in particular, the Church developed rules of law and a court system to govern such varied matters as marriage, wills, usury, oaths, contracts, and a considerable list of crimes. Canon law became particularly influential as it was compiled and codified after the twelfth century. Finally, the growth of cities, their development as mercantile communities, and the extension of foreign commerce gave rise to bodies of commercial and maritime law—the law merchant.

During the twelfth century, interest in Roman law revived, and study was renewed in the universities of southern France and northern Italy. The rediscovered Roman law now proved particularly valuable: to the doctors of law, for offering solutions to the new social and economic problems confronting Europe; to the kings, for suggesting means to strengthen royal absolutism; and, generally, for supplementing and refining local customary law. Roman law naturally exerted its greatest immediate influence within those areas which had been most intensely subjected to Latin civilization. But it ultimately exerted influence well beyond these—in England, Scotland, Scandinavia, and the Slavic countries.

Through the next several centuries, the various legal rules commingled; but Roman law, at first secondary to local customary law, increased in influence through the writings of jurists and the teachers of law in the universities. Obviously, the extent to which the several bodies of rules—Roman, feudal, customary, canon, and commercial —would prevail in a particular country varied considerably; the inclinations of the ruler, the depth of the roots of the local law, the effectiveness of the court system, and the complexity of the contemporary society were all factors which influenced their adoption. Yet the tendency everywhere was to reduce the rules to writing. Though this restricted an extensive development of the law by judicial decision, it gave impetus to its codification.

France produced the first great contribution to the modern civil-law system in 1804 with the French Civil Code, prepared for the Emperor Napoleon; this was followed by four other major codes. The French Civil Code was widely imitated or adopted; those of Belgium, Italy, the Netherlands, Portugal, Spain, and the Latin American countries were all based upon it. French influence also carried to the German-speaking countries. After the unification of the German Empire, a German Civil Code was completed in 1896. A third major system, the Swiss Civil Code, emerged in 1907–12. As non-European states— such as Japan and Turkey—sought to modernize and Europeanize their institutions, they too drew from the civil-law system. Indeed, all civil-law countries owe something to the French, German, or Swiss codes.

The Common-Law System. The common-law system prevails in most English-speaking countries, and takes its name from the medieval English practice of describing the rules administered by the king's courts as that law common to the whole realm. It, too, can be explained only in terms of its historical development.

For more than three centuries, England was a province of the Roman empire and governed by Roman law. In the fifth century the Roman soldiery were withdrawn, and thereafter England was invaded by the Anglo-Saxon tribes. Making England their homeland, they seem to have obliterated all but some physical traces of Roman civilization—replacing it with Germanic customs, institutions, and law. In the ninth century the invading Danes, and in the eleventh century the conquering Normans, further reinforced the Teutonic influences. Although William of Normandy created no new legal system, he and his successors established a system of government and judicial administration that did.

In the two centuries following the conquest, the Norman rulers began an unprecedented centralization of power—which their successors extended. During this time, a multiplicity of local Anglo-Saxon rules and customs was largely reduced to a single body of law. Though continuing the old communal courts of the hundred and the shire, the Normans established powerful and superior royal courts at Westminster. The king's judges were also sent on circuit to administer justice in his name among the localities. The new doctrine of the king's peace broadened royal authority to punish offenses; the king's inquest, as a method of finding facts, became the basis for the jury system; and the king's writs were used to enlarge the scope of judicial remedies. If Germanic custom and doctrine provided the raw material for the earliest common-law rules, still other influences made their mark upon English law. These were, indeed, essentially the same elements that went into the making of the civil-law system. As on the continent, the revived Code of Justinian was studied at the English universities and attracted the interest of men of learning. English feudalism also developed its rules, among them the most advanced system of land tenure in Europe. In this formative period most of the king's judges were also clergymen, trained in the canon law; inevitably its principles were absorbed, especially after the jurisdiction of the ecclesiastical courts was restricted. England also knew the commercial and maritime law of Europe. Important, too, in shaping the common-law system were the contributions of legal scholars —such as Glanvil and Bracton in the thirteenth century—and the guilds of lawyers gathered at the Inns of Court, which were organized soon thereafter. Though the works of jurists did not have an importance here comparable to those of the civil law countries, Coke's *Institutes* and Blackstone's *Commentaries* on the English law of the seventeenth and eighteenth centuries, respectively, and Kent's *Commentaries on American Law* (1826–30), are outstanding contributions to its literature.

Especially significant from the beginning in the formulation of English law was the practice of following precedent. Over a number of centuries, this convenient practice hardened into binding principle— hence the singular technique of the common-law system: *Stare decisis et non quieta movere* ("To adhere to precedents, and not unsettle things established"). When deciding a case, a judge normally referred to prior decisions rendered in similar circumstances. Case by case, over many years the judges selected, reinforced, and shaped their legal principles, weaving together the great fabric of judge-made law.

Thus, although the common law derives its name from its origins in customary or conventional law it was the custom of precedent in judicial decision—and not of popular usage—that determined its specific quality.

Even so, the common-law system does not comprise a body of judge-made rules alone. Alongside of these grew the rules of equity. Originally, the rules of equity were special dispensations made by the king as "the fountain of justice." Then this function was handed over to the king's chancellor, acting as "keeper of the king's conscience," to supplement the common-law rules where they failed to be equitable and to ensure substance as well as form in the administration of justice. In time a separate court of chancery, or equity, was provided; it developed a further body of rules to be merged into the English system. Finally, in the thirteenth century, legislation by Parliament began to acquire significance—though for some time to come, Parliament's role was more nearly that of declaring or clarifying the law than of enacting it. Not until the nineteenth century did Parliament undertake an extensive recasting of the common law, modifying and modernizing its rules to meet the needs of an industrial and urbanized society. Thus the modern English common-law system was integrated from three strands: law, equity, and statute.

The common-law system was also brought to prevail in Ireland, and among the Commonwealth states—Canada (except Quebec), Australia, and New Zealand; it has further influenced the legal systems of India, Pakistan, Israel, and to some degree the Scandinavian states. It was early carried to the American colonies by British settlers; and though the colonists at first had no need of such an advanced system of law, its reception later came to be extensive. In 1774 the Continental Congress claimed that the "colonies are entitled to the common law of England," and some states subsequently stipulated its adoption formally, either by constitutional or statutory provision. Its spirit and doctrines provide the basis for American jurisprudence, and most of the rules applicable to American situations have been absorbed either by judicial decision or statute. American law has been extensively developed and codified by statute—and each state has its own system—but all, except that of Louisiana, derive from the common law.

The Common- and Civil-Law Systems Compared. It should be emphasized at the outset that in distinguishing these two major systems we are speaking actually of two broad patterns of legal origin and development. All states now have much that is indigenous in their particular national system of law. The American system, for example, not only differs in many respects from the English—reflecting its own local circumstances—but actually includes fifty different state systems. Again, though France, Germany, and Switzerland are all civil-law jurisdictions, their respective national systems are not at all the same as the classical Roman type and differ much from each other as well. We have observed that the civil and the common law have, indeed, drawn from much the same historic sources; they are distinguished, then, primarily in the way in which these elements have been proportioned and developed. In sum, the civil law is a complete code of rules promulgated by a central authority; the common law is a system of reported precedents developed by judicial reasoning.

Developed by precedent through the continuing process of judicial resolution of actual legal controversies, the rules of common law must be searched out of decided cases. Hence they are capable of endless extension by judicial reasoning and improvisation; as Coke said, "the common law is nothing else but reason." Yet rules developed by argument over precedents and adherence to *stare decisis* may produce some conflicting results; the common law may be reasonable, but it is not always logical. "The life of the law," said Justice Holmes, "has not been logic; it has been experience." Statutes and codes are only a part of the system, no matter how completely they may be developed; for even when they replace common-law rules, the latter still serve to provide definition and interpretation. We may note, lastly, that in part because of its origin in custom, and in part because of the role played by courts in the Anglo-American countries, the common law has been particularly solicitous of the individual's rights as against the government. Its doctrine of "the rule of law"—that all public officials as well as private persons are equally subject to the same law in the ordinary courts of justice—is one of its proudest features.

The civil-law system is characterized by its adherence to code, which is the sole authoritative exposition of the law. It has always been amenable to restatement by codification; as Sir Henry Maine observed of the Roman system, it "begins, as it ends, with a code." The preparation of the great national codes has been the work of jurists and scholars; it is scarcely an exaggeration to say that law here has been developed, not by courts, but by universities. It is the legislator, then, and not the judge who may give approval to new rules. The civil law also has given high place to reason and logic; hence, it displays in great measure symmetry, consistency, balance, and polish. A general grasp of the rules of civil law can more readily be obtained by the individual citizen; he is less indebted for explanation by a lawyer than is his counterpart in common-law countries.

In the administration of the civil law, reference is always to the letter of the code and not to judicial decision or precedent. The civilian does not follow the principle of *stare decisis*. Nonetheless, it should not be thought that in civil-law systems there are no judicial precedents or that judges can apply the codes mechanically. Lower courts follow the decisions of higher courts, important commentaries supplement the codes, and interpretations of the codes do accumulate. Although judicial decisions are delivered in such brief form in France, for example, that the development of anything like case law is virtually impossible, in German-speaking countries rather full decisions are delivered and reported—especially by appellate courts. Also, the Swiss Civil Code goes so far as to authorize the judge—when the Code furnishes no applicable provision—to decide according to customary law, or lacking that, according to the rule he would establish as a legislator. Finally, it may be observed that, reflecting its origin, the civil law as the conscious creation of a central authority tends to assert the interests of the state before those of the individual. Perhaps this is inevitable. The civil law reflects more rapidly the collectivist and centralizing tendencies of the modern state. Moreover, its judges, as we shall see, do not occupy a position that permits them to act primarily as the defenders of individualism, as has been their role in English-speaking nations.

Islamic Law. Of course, systems other than the civil and the common law widely prevail. The Islamic system applies today, in part at least, to the some four hundred million Moslems in Africa and Asia. Undertaking to regulate the entire area of human conduct, it is both legal and moral law. As a religious law, it is considered immutable and divine, resting upon the will of Allah, the Supreme Being. Though based upon the principles of the Koran, it is not, contrary to general impression, drawn from that source. Its actual derivation is from the *Sunna*—or practices of Mohammed, as elaborated in the several centuries after his time by the *imams* (priests)—and it rests on the elements of Arabic customary law. The Islamic system thus

covers subjects ranging from fasting and pilgrimage, contracts and inheritance, to dietary and criminal laws.

As the various Moslem areas extended their contacts with the western world and developed their commerce, the monolithic law of Islam
proved inadequate to achieve the social progress and modernization
desired in many of these countries. During the nineteenth century,
therefore, civil codes from Europe were adopted to supplement Islamic law in Egypt and Turkey, among others; Turkey later officially
adopted civil law entirely. Most of the other states have retained, in
combination with the civil law, part of their traditional law—
especially in such matters as personal status and family relations;
these states include Iraq, Lebanon, Morocco, and Tunisia. A few,
such as Pakistan and Saudi Arabia, however, have attempted to retain their Islamic inheritance unimpaired.

Soviet Law. In distinct contrast to a system based upon long tradition is Soviet law. In one respect only, in the view of Soviet jurists, is
their system like others. Marxists see the state as an exploitive organization which promotes and defends the interests of the dominant
class, and the law merely as the will of that class. Soviet law, therefore, acknowledgedly gives expression to the will and interests of the
Soviet state, and thus by definition affords class justice to the proletariat. In the official view, its uniqueness stems from the fact that, unlike western systems, it is the first law which does not exploit; it promotes only the interests of the classless (workers') society; it is based
on the existence of socialist public property; and it is guided by "the
dictatorship of the proletariat."

To develop an exclusive philosophy of communist law, however,
has been a difficult problem for Soviet theoreticians. In the first place,
Marxist doctrine regarded law as only another capitalistic institution
for the promotion of "bourgeois" interests. With the establishment of
a classless society, the state would ultimately wither away and, so
Marx and his adherents believed, most of its compulsory machinery
would no longer be necessary. However, the Russian communist leaders have not found it possible to dispense with an elaborate set of
laws. Secondly, though claiming that they have adopted a wholly
new socialist form of law, the Soviet leaders have not been able to
detach their legal organization completely from the past. Because so
much property is state property, and so many aspects of individual
activity are subjected to state regulation, there is an enormous preoc-

cupation with offenses against the state, which are viewed as considerably more serious and punished with greater severity than those against an individual. By the same token, a distinct category of private law is not recognized; there can be no private rights exercisable against the state. Nevertheless, Soviet law codes cover much the same ground as do those of other continental systems, drawing partly upon Russian traditions and partly from the European civil codes, as well as upon communist ideology.

In the third place, Soviet law is viewed officially, in its essence, as an instrument of the class struggle—that is, as comprising whatever rules will perpetuate and promote the Soviet regime. It can have no objectivity; it cannot serve to limit the exercise of government authority, either by substantive or procedural restrictions. Its rules are frequently vague, often purposely so, and sometimes not even published. The difficulty here, of course, is that by its very nature law embodies the ideas of stability, continuity, and certainty. None of these are qualities Soviet law may acquire so long as it is purely an instrument of policy in the hands of the Soviet rulers. One can only conclude that in such totalitarian systems of government there cannot exist a system of law in the usual sense of the term; there can be only administrative orders and ordinances.

The Divisions of Law

Legal Classification. The rules of law have been developed to regulate a considerable variety of relationships between individuals and institutions. As a result, there are a number of ways in which legal rules may be classified to distinguish the category of persons to which they apply, the kind of activities they control, or the functions which they perform. A first broad division distinguishes *international* law, the rules observed by states in the international community as legally binding in their relationships (discussed in Chapter 11); and *municipal* law, the rules regulating all internal or domestic affairs of the state. Municipal law, in turn, may be divided into the categories of *public* law, which governs the organization of the state and its relations to the individual; and *private* law (or *civil* law), which regulates the relations of individuals with each other.

Public Law. Public law is subdivided into three broad divisions: constitutional, administrative, and criminal. *Constitutional* law (discussed in Chapter 4) is defined as the rules relating to the scope and nature of the powers exercised by government. It may be studied in historic charters and constitutional documents, in fundamental statutes of constitutional importance, and in the decisions of the highest national courts. *Administrative* law (discussed in Chapter 10) consists of the rules specifying the competence and procedures of government agencies. Its rules are to be found in statutes, executive orders, and in the rulings of administrative agencies and courts. *Criminal* law is concerned, of course, with crimes and their punishment. Crimes may be offenses against the state or public authority, in the oldest historic sense—as treason, rebellion, or regicide; or offenses injurious to the public—as arson, burglary, murder, rape, or robbery. In either case, they are acts injurious to the peace and security of the community which the state will take cognizance of and punish. Although originally recognized by customary and common law, crimes are everywhere today also meticulously defined in statutory codes. It may be noted, too, that the law of both civil and criminal procedure is a part of public law.

Private Law. Private law is concerned with the rights and duties of individuals to each other. In general, the state does not intervene in the face of many invasions of the individual's rights in private law. It merely provides judicial machinery and rules with which the wronged individual may undertake the enforcement of his rights. Private law has a number of subject subdivisions. These include, employing common-law terminology, *contracts:* agreements creating an obligation and enforceable at law; *domestic relations:* marriage, divorce, parent and child, guardian and ward; *personal property:* movable things, goods and chattels; *real property:* lands, tenements, and hereditaments (in the classic phrase); and *torts:* civil wrongs which are not breaches of contract, such as assault and battery, deceit, defamation, negligence, and trespass. A particular act may constitute a tort and, under certain circumstances, a crime as well.

The common- and civil-law systems do not classify laws in identical fashion. In France, for example, as in other civil law countries, there are a number of subject matter codes: the Civil Code, Code of Civil Procedure, Commercial Code, Code of Criminal Procedure, Penal Code, and others. It may be properly emphasized, too, that there are not only variations in the rules of the two systems, but that many identical legal terms, as used in the various national systems, vary in meaning.

Other Classifications. From the standpoint of function, law may be distinguished as *substantive* and *procedural*. Substantive law defines primary rights; procedural or adjective law defines the remedies by which infringements of substantive rights may be redressed. There are also some special divisions of municipal law. *Military* law is the body of rules governing the members of the armed services and is enforced by courts-martial. *Martial* law (or "state of siege" to use the comparable civil-law term) may be proclaimed for the civilian inhabitants of an area in emergencies when civil administration is replaced by military authority; it is a state of affairs—a martial rule—rather than a body of rules. Military government is further distinguished from the preceding terms as a system of military administration for a hostilely occupied or conquered enemy territory. We may note, lastly, the existence of the body of *maritime* law, the rules relating to navigation, ships and crews, marine contracts, cargoes, and marine commerce generally.

II. Judicial Organization

The history of the law is accompanied by a history of judicial development. The administration of justice is also a means of creating and developing law; hence, as our knowledge of ancient history confirms, the judicial function must be as old as the law. Precisely how the earliest judges began to function, whether they were arbitrators or adjudicators primarily, is debatable. It seems clear, however, that the judicial function was only one of a number of prerogatives exercised by the ruler; and the earliest judges probably had a variety of duties of general administrative or supervisory character.

The Development of the Judicial Institution. The office of judge, authorized in the ruler's name to resolve disputes and apply the law, was known in Babylonia, Egypt, Assyria, and elsewhere in the ancient world. Again, the Greeks took the next step forward: to distinguish judicial institutions from other governing agencies in the community. As Athens evolved through monarchy, aristocracy, and democracy, the judicial power was transferred from the *Areopagus* (the old council) to the *archons* (magistrates), and then to the *Heliaea* (the judicial assembly).

The Roman courts evolved from primitive forms to a most highly elaborated system, and ultimately produced what had not existed before—a body of professional jurists. Judicial power passed from king to consul when Rome became a republic. Then, in the fourth century B.C. judicial administration was entrusted to the *praetor,* an elected magistrate. Under the empire, the magistrates were appointed by the emperor and required to be learned in the law. A supreme court was also established, to which appeals could be taken. And in addition to professional judges, a class of practicing lawyers emerged.

The Germanic peoples in western Europe originally administered justice through a tribal assembly, or *Thing.* When all warriors of the tribe convened, the king presided; a lesser assembly of the hundred was held under a prince or count. Proceedings were crude, but formal, conducted largely by the recitation of precise formulas: the contenders made their pleas; the wisemen proposed the judgment or the "word"; and the assembly pronounced the "full-word," or assent. Courts such as these, for the shire and the hundred, prevailed in England until after the Norman conquest.

Throughout the medieval period, European feudal lords maintained the hundred courts to deal locally with crimes and controversies—the latter mainly taking place over land tenure. Significant innovations during this period were the royal employment of *missi*—judges sent on circuit to administer the king's justice—and the development of the inquest. In the Germanic courts, the methods of proof had been limited to oath and ordeal; the inquest, used initially as a royal measure to obtain evidence from reputable persons in a locality, gave rise to the jury system.

Full success in supplementing local judicial power by royal judicial authority came first in England, as we have seen; the process was slower and more difficult on the continent. The personal authority of the king in the governmental process was also first greatly restricted in England. The defeat of the Stuart claims to absolutism in the seventeenth century resulted in enhancing the power of both Parliament and the English courts; indeed, their enforcement of the supremacy of law against the king's will gave them an unrivaled and assured position of independence. On the continent, however, the royal courts continued to be employed to reinforce the position of the monarch. Both practice and civil law doctrine, as well, combined to retain the courts as a part of the general system of royal administrative machinery. Inevitably then, even after the popular revolutions of the nineteenth and twentieth centuries, national court systems continued as auxiliary to the executive, or as essential elements in the bureaucratic system, rather than achieving the status of independent branches of the government.

The Hierarchy of Courts. The organization of a judicial system is hierarchical—that is, the courts are ranked in a graded order, with a base of ordinary courts at the foundation; an intermediate level ranged above; and still higher, a final supreme court. Broadly speaking, then, judicial tribunals fall into one of two categories: courts of original jurisdiction and courts of appeal. Courts are thus always accorded a specific jurisdiction: the precise authority to hear and determine particular causes.

The standard court of first instance, or original jurisdiction, is a trial court with general jurisdiction to hear original actions and prosecutions in civil and criminal proceedings, respectively. Usually with a single judge on the bench, it must consider the facts and apply the law; it proceeds by the taking of evidence and the argument of attorneys. If a jury is employed, which is usual in criminal prosecutions and available in some civil actions, it will be at this level in the court hierarchy. The jury reaches a verdict, or formal finding; the judge delivers the official decision of the court in the form of a judgment. In civil proceedings the judgment is enforced by a writ of execution or similar measure; in criminal cases, if the jury finds a verdict of guilty, the judge imposes a sentence. Among courts of first instance—or ranged below them to hear minor cases under limited or special jurisdiction—are the justice of the peace, police, traffic, juvenile, and probate courts.

A smaller number of courts are appellate, or courts of appeal; they review the work of those below them to correct judicial errors and to ensure the uniform interpretation of the law. In certain instances an appeal from the decision of a lower court is available as a matter of right; generally, however, permission to appeal must be granted either by the trial court or the appellate court. Only a small proportion of all cases is appealed. As the function of the appellate court differs from that of the original court, it employs a different procedure. It reviews questions of substantive law and the procedures by which the facts were determined; but it does not collect additional evidence and has no need of a jury. Instead, the procedure is by submission of a certified record of the lower court's proceedings, a statement of the points in controversy, and printed briefs or arguments of the attorneys, which may be supplemented by their oral arguments if the court wishes them. Depending upon its findings, the court of appeal may reaffirm or reverse the judgment of the lower court, or return the case for retrial because of errors in procedure. An appellate court is composed of a collegial or multimember bench; it reaches its decision by majority vote—and if a common law court, delivers a majority opinion; however, individual judges may write dissenting opinions. English judges, it may be noted, deliver their opinions seriatim; in civil-law courts dissenting opinions as such are not feasible, though individual judges may show their disagreement with a majority decision. The highest court in any jurisdiction—usually designated the supreme court—is the tribunal of last resort, beyond which there is no further appeal. We may now undertake a brief examination of several national court systems to observe specifically how judicial institutions may be organized.

The United States Court System. One significant feature of American judicial organization—the dual system of federal and state courts —is a product of the federal division of powers; another—establishing the judiciary as a separate branch of government—results from the application of the separation-of-powers principle. The jurisdiction of the state courts extends broadly over the general body of civil and criminal law as defined by the state constitutions and statutes. The fifty American state systems do not provide a carefully unified body of courts. The minor courts of the states exist in considerable variety, with numerous municipal and other limited-jurisdiction courts dealing with petty cases and special subjects. Each state has courts of first instance, including those with general civil and criminal jurisdiction over cases of importance—variously styled county, circuit, district, or superior courts. A number of states have one or more intermediate courts of appeal, whose decision in many cases is final. All of the states have a supreme court—though it goes under a different title in some of them—which is final on those legal questions solely within the state's jurisdiction. Where rights under the federal Constitution, federal law, or treaties are involved, however, there may be further appeal to the Supreme Court of the United States.

The federal judicial system has a much more limited jurisdiction. Without entering into technicalities, we may say that its jurisdiction is determined by the Constitution upon a twofold basis: according to the character of the controversies—principally those involving the

Constitution, the laws, treaties of the United States and cases of admiralty and maritime jurisdiction; and according to the character of the parties to the case—including those cases to which the United States is a party, to which foreign ambassadors and consuls are a party, those between two or more states, between citizens of different states, and certain others. Federal jurisdiction, where applicable, is usually but not always exclusive. The United States district courts, approximately ninety of them, are the courts of original jurisdiction, hearing both civil and criminal cases. The eleven circuit courts of appeals have from three to thirteen judges each, with two constituting a quorum; they hear only appeals from the district courts and from some of the federal regulatory agencies. The United States Supreme Court is composed of the Chief Justice of the United States and eight associate justices. This highest federal court has original jurisdiction in two types of controversies: those affecting foreign diplomatic and consular representatives, and those to which a state is a party. Otherwise, it hears cases only on appeal. Congress has also provided courts for the District of Columbia, and some others to hear special controversies over patents, customs, and claims.

The English Court System. The English court system (which applies also in Wales and with modifications in Northern Ireland, but not in Scotland), though reflecting its long historical development, is integrated and entirely independent. While all courts derive their authority from the Crown, they are not subject to control by the Queen or the Prime Minister, and are equally free of interference by Parliament. The English courts are broadly distinguishable as civil and criminal, but not precisely so in every case. Ordinary civil cases are heard in the county courts—of which there are over four hundred, presided over by single judges. At London is the Supreme Court of Judicature, composed of the High Court of Justice and the Court of Appeal. The High Court sits in three divisions: Queen's Bench, which hears the most important civil cases; Chancery, which hears proceedings derived from the equity system and certain other cases; and Probate, Divorce, and Admiralty, which covers an assortment of cases as its name would imply. Appeals are taken to a Court of Appeal, and by leave may even go finally to the House of Lords—which is the highest court in the United Kingdom, as well as the second house of Parliament. Its judicial function is not performed by the peers generally, but by the Lord Chancellor and the law lords.

There are several courts with criminal jurisdiction. The courts of summary jurisdiction—which try minor offenses without a jury—are known as magistrates' courts. In London and some of the largest cities, these are maintained on a full-time basis by a stipendiary (paid) magistrate; elsewhere the magistrates are justices of the peace—persons of some distinction in the community who are unpaid, and need not be lawyers. More serious criminal offenses are tried with a jury in the courts of quarter sessions; these are presided over by a chairman sitting with a number of magistrates—except in some cities where the recorder, a barrister, presides and serves as sole judge. The most serious offenses are tried before the courts of assize, held throughout the country three times a year, and conducted by a Queen's Bench judge—or appointed commissioner, traveling on circuit. Assize courts use juries in criminal proceedings, and they may also hear some civil cases. London, Liverpool, and Manchester have their own permanent courts of assize; that of London is known as the Central Criminal Court. Appeals from the magistrates' courts go to quarter sessions, and on points of law to the High Court; those involving serious offenses go to the Court of Criminal Appeal and, in rare instances, beyond that to the House of Lords.

The French Court System. The most striking feature of French judicial organization is the array of courts to be found in the two separate systems of ordinary and administrative courts. As in England, civil and criminal courts are distinguished. At the lowest level some 455 courts of first instance hear minor civil cases. Above them are the courts of grand instance, with unlimited civil jurisdiction, and the courts of appeals. Lesser criminal cases are heard by police and correctional courts; appeals go to assize courts—which also have jurisdiction over the most serious criminal offenses, when they will employ a jury. The highest of the ordinary courts, the Court of Cassation, hears appeals in its civil and criminal sections; if it quashes the decision of a lower court, the case must be retried by another tribunal at the same lower level. There are certain other courts with special jurisdiction—such as labor, commercial, and juvenile courts. It may be noted that most French courts have a collegial bench of three, five, or more judges, depending on their rank.

France provides the classic example of a system of administrative courts applying a distinct body of law. Its structure comprises the twenty-four administrative tribunals at the regional level, and the

Council of State at Paris. The regional tribunals hear the lesser cases; the Council of State—which has administrative as well as judicial duties—exercises jurisdiction at the highest levels. In either case, they hear complaints against government officials and employees for wrongful, negligent, or illegal administrative acts; they may annul the act by reestablishing any rights denied, and even assess damages to be paid by the government to the complainant. There are also other bodies with special administrative jurisdiction over matters of military service, public instruction, and pensions. To resolve any controversy over whether a case belongs to the ordinary or the administrative courts, there is a Court of Conflicts.

Because Anglo-American legal doctrine has always emphasized the amenability of all public officials, high and low, to the ordinary courts, the idea of a special system of administrative tribunals has tended to be viewed by common-law lawyers as providing public authorities an undue privilege. According to the French doctrine of the separation of powers, however, the ordinary judiciary should not be allowed to interfere with the executive or the legislature. Hence, administrative courts are provided to control the administrative machinery of the government. They are designed, then, not to defend the executive generally, but rather to hold public officials to their legal authority and thus protect individuals and the public interest against the excesses of bureaucracy. To the extent that administrative courts provide the citizen with speedy and inexpensive redress for such wrongs, there is much to be said for them.

The Soviet System of Courts. It should be emphasized at the outset that the judiciary of the Soviet Union is an instrument of state power. Like Soviet law, it functions to promote the interests of the regime; it is not, therefore, in any way independent, but a part of the administrative apparatus. Because the Soviet Union nominally has a federal system, there are technically separate union and constituent republic courts; actually, however, they are ranged in a single system.

At the lowest level is the people's court—composed of one judge and two people's assessors (lay judges)—which has minor civil and criminal jurisdiction. Next are the regional courts, which may operate at several levels in the larger republics: these have civil jurisdiction over litigation between public enterprises and the state, criminal jurisdiction over offenses against the state and socialist property, and appellate jurisdiction over the courts below. The highest judicial organ of a republic, the supreme court, has primarily appellate jurisdiction—though it may hear cases of the greatest importance in original jurisdiction. Finally, there is the Supreme Court of the U.S.S.R.—composed of a chairman, two vice-chairmen, nine judges, and a number of people's assessors, all chosen by the Supreme Soviet. Organized into three divisions—civil, criminal, and military—it hears appeals in these classes respectively, with the latter type coming from the high military tribunals. The Supreme Court may also have original jurisdiction.

The people's assessors, sitting at each judicial level with the regular judge when cases are heard in original jurisdiction, are presumably a means of introducing popular participation in the judicial process; for there are no juries in the Soviet Union. The assessors are elected from factories, places of residence, and such—along with the judges—in groups attached to each court and serve a few days a year. They are allowed a vote to decide questions of law and fact equally with the judge; however, they are drawn from all walks of life, and without legal training, they rarely disagree with the judge.

One aspect of Soviet judicial organization is most important: the role of the procuracy. The procurator-general has supreme supervisory power to ensure observance of the law. Chosen by the Supreme Soviet for a seven-year term, he appoints all procurators at each court level below. The procuracy has broad authority on behalf of the Communist leadership to intervene in all phases of judicial and state administration. It not only conducts political investigations and prosecutes criminal cases, but determines that "socialist legality" is maintained; it may remove cases from any court, challenge decisions, or appeal them. The procuracy has equally broad authority over administrative agencies. Thus it guides, supervises, and centralizes the enforcement and administration of Soviet law. The Ministry of Justice also has some control over the judicial process and law enforcement.

Court Systems in Other States. The court systems of other states display one or more of the characteristic features of the national systems we have just briefly described. A few federal countries, such as Brazil and Mexico, follow the American practice of organizing a dual system of courts, state and national. Most federal states, however— including Australia, Canada, the German Federal Republic, India, and Switzerland—have no separate federal courts except for a supreme national tribunal to review the work of the courts below. Some states observe the British practice of maintaining a system of ordinary courts only—these include Denmark, Norway, Israel, and the Commonwealth countries generally, where common-law ideas have affected judicial arrangements. Most of the continental European countries—such as the German Federal Republic, Italy, Spain, and Sweden—have systems of administrative courts in addition to the ordinary institutions, though they are not all of equal importance to those in France. Also, as might be expected, the people's republics of eastern Europe have judicial systems resembling that of the Soviet Union in function and organization—including the people's courts, assessors, a supreme court chosen by the national assembly, and a powerful procuracy. Lastly, among the developing states, the organization and administration of the courts have frequently tended to be among the most westernized of their institutions, where traditionalist or tribal procedures are being replaced. This not only reflects a widespread ambition to modernize, but also the fact that judges and lawyers are commonly European-trained and thus have well-established professional standards to observe as well as a stake in maintaining them.

The Judicial Office: Selection and Tenure. The method of recruiting and appointing judges has an influence on the character of the judiciary. Broadly speaking, judges are drawn to office in one of two ways. In the civil-law countries, generally, judicial service rests as a rule upon a career basis. All judges are members of the magistracy, which they enter by obtaining an appropriate law diploma and passing competitive government examinations on the completion of their formal legal education. They begin service as court attachés or judges at the lowest level; vacancies in the various ranks are filled by promotion. In the common-law countries, on the other hand, judges are drawn from the membership of the bar, after some years of experience in practice before the courts and the attainment of some distinction in the profession. There is as a rule little in the way of promotion of such judges from court to court.

Which method of recruitment is to be preferred is certainly debatable. The career system insures a high degree of professionalism, for the examinations are rigorous and the magistracy is especially trained for its function. Nonetheless, such judges early identify themselves as government functionaries, acquire certain bureaucratic tendencies, and become immediately dependent upon the preferment of government superiors for advancement. Judges chosen from the bar, however, while not specially trained to preside, have had more practical experience and are more likely to have independent inclinations. The quality of their professional attainment is measured in their maturity; and this permits evaluation of their suitability for the highest judicial office. Of course, such a method of selection may afford somewhat greater opportunity for the exercise of partisan influence, though this is not automatically eliminated in the career system.

There are essentially four different ways in which judicial appointment is made. The first, popular election, is not widely used, and in the view of most observers is not to be recommended. Its principal employment is in the state courts of the United States, where it was stipulated by the democratic zeal prevailing during the middle of the nineteenth century. For rather different reasons, the judges of the people's courts in the Soviet Union are also popularly elected, though the party leadership here always offers only one official candidate in such election. The principal objections to popular election are that the voters simply are not qualified to make an informed and intelligent choice of a judge, considering that his qualifications are professional and not representative; that to oblige a judge to seek votes in an election is incompatible with the dignity and obligation of the office; and that an elected judge may be made intolerably dependent upon popularity, publicity, or partisan support. Obviously, some good judges are obtained by election, but this must be largely despite the system rather than because of it.

A second method is election by the legislature. This is not much of an improvement on popular election if judges are selected for fixed terms, because it opens the way to immediate partisan interference with the courts. In the Soviet Union, judges above the lowest courts are elected by the Soviets for five-year terms; thus their political reliability will be frequently reexamined. In addition to the Communist states, some of the Central American states also employ the legislature to elect judges—mainly as a means to free them from executive control. The members of the Swiss Federal (Supreme) Court are elected by the Federal Assembly for six-year terms. These judges are usually reelected; and here, perhaps, legislative election can be justified as a means of assuring an appropriate distribution of German-, French-, and Italian-speaking members of that bench.

In a few countries, as a third means, provision is made for judicial selection of judges. In some of the Latin-American countries—among them Bolivia, Honduras, Nicaragua, El Salvador, and Uruguay—the Supreme Court appoints the members of the inferior courts. The Supreme Court of Finland also chooses the lower court judges. Judicial selection has the merit of ensuring that those appointed to judicial office are likely to be professionally qualified; it tends to make the judiciary a self-perpetuating body, however, and somewhat limits independence—not of the judiciary, but of the individual judge.

A fourth method, appointment by the executive—with or without exclusive discretion—is the most widely employed. In the United States all federal judges are appointed by the President with the consent of the Senate. The British judiciary is entirely appointed by the Crown; the choice of judges for the House of Lords and the Supreme Court of Judicature is made by the Prime Minister—usually in consultation with the Lord Chancellor, who selects the lesser judges. Executive appointment is also the practice in such countries as Canada, New Zealand, Denmark, Norway, and Sweden. In the German Federal Republic, federal and state judges are chosen by the ministers of justice in consultation with committees of their respective legislatures. A modified system of executive appointment is found in France and Italy, where judges are chosen by a superior council of the judiciary —composed of the President of the Republic, and representatives of the Parliament and the judiciary. The weight of practice and opinion in the preferment of executive selection of judges is substantial; it concentrates responsibility, permits flexibility, and affords opportunity, at least, for well-informed choices to be made.

Judicial tenure may range from a fixed period of years, during good behavior, until a fixed retirement age, or for life. Fixed terms generally accompany popular or legislative election, and may extend from two or three years to as many as twenty. In the career systems judges usually hold office until a determined retirement age is reached. British judges originally served at the pleasure of the Crown, but they now—like American federal judges, and those in some of the states —serve "during good behavior"; in any case this amounts to life tenure if they choose not to retire. Provision is usually made for the removal from office of judges who misbehave or become incompetent or incapacitated. The judges of the Soviet people's courts and those in some of the American states may be removed by recall through popular vote. Federal judges of the United States may be removed only by impeachment and conviction; this method is available in the fifty states as well. Great Britain and the Commonwealth states generally, as well as a number of others, authorize the removal of judges on an address presented by the parliament to the executive. A considerable number of countries allow removal only by a superior court. In still a few others—such as France and Italy—judges may be disciplined, but are irremovable from office.

Judicial Independence. We have emphasized previously the great importance of judicial impartiality. If a judge is to be impartial, he must be independent—that is to say, free from control or interference by anyone wishing to influence the administration of justice. Here we can see again the objection to the popular election of judges, for one who must answer to the electorate at relatively short intervals may need partisan political support. Even elections which are officially nonpartisan do not always exclude party influence; and where judges must be party men, and the party is machine-controlled, the result has been in some states to corrupt the administration of justice. In the career system, though judges may be secure in their tenure, they can still be made dependent for promotion upon the favor of a political minister of justice—which introduces another kind of partisan influence; and though immune from popular pressure, such judges may be overly susceptible at least to an official point of view.

Judicial compensation can also affect judicial independence. If tenure is to mean anything, compensation must be not only adequate but secure. Judicial salaries must compete with the rewards available to practicing attorneys; and though they cannot equal those of the most successful, they ought to be sufficient to attract men of superior talent. Where salaries are abnormally low, they have inevitably reflected on the prestige of the judiciary and, in some countries, even opened the way to bribery. Where it is the intention to secure judges against financial reprisals, it is the usual practice—as in the American Constitution, and those of most of the states—to stipulate that judges' compensation "shall not be diminished during their continuance in office."

The Legal Profession. The legal profession is closely associated with the system of judicial administration, for any but the most primitive system requires a body of trained professional lawyers. Their professional status is therefore recognized in their acceptance as officers of the courts and authorization to receive fees for giving legal advice and prosecuting or defending causes. In Great Britain the legal profession is divided into two categories. The larger is composed of solicitors, who provide legal advice, draft legal instruments, and conduct litigation. They may appear only before the lowest courts; if a client requires higher court counsel, the solicitor retains on his behalf the services of a barrister. Barristers, being much more specialized in their function, are a small group numbering barely two thousand; they are limited to appearing in the higher courts. Professional judges are drawn solely from their ranks.

The legal profession in the United States and in most of the Commonwealth countries has not retained this division. Attorneys-at-law perform as both adviser and counselor. This is also the case in the German-speaking countries, where the *Rechtsanwalt* performs a dual function. In France, on the other hand, there is a still larger professional division of labor than in Great Britain. Here the *avocat* corresponds roughly to the barrister, and the *avoué* to the solicitor, while the *notaire* prepares deeds and acts as their custodian. Soviet lawyers, though not officials of the government, are organized under governing bodies regulated by the ministries of justice, the courts, and local authorities. Like Soviet judges, they may not disinterestedly pursue the ends of justice—nor even the interests of their client—for the interests of the state take precedence over all. The position of the Soviet attorney is thus ambiguous, and may become rather awkward when he undertakes to defend a client accused of a serious political offense.

III. Judicial Functions

The nature of the judicial process inevitably limits the extent of judicial functions—as compared with those of the executive and the legislature—though in no sense reduces their importance. We have already seen that in many countries, the judiciary does not constitute a separate branch of government. And even where it does, we may note, it is definitely the weakest branch. The courts are, after all, dependent upon the executive to provide the ultimate enforcement of their orders, and upon the legislature for their organization and financial support. Their very role is essentially a passive one; courts are said "to sit," which means that, like legislatures, they conduct their transactions in a particular place. But unlike legislatures, they do not initiate; judicial institutions examine only such controversies as are brought to them, whether in civil or criminal cases, by private persons or public officials. To hear and decide cases actually requires the performance of several different functions, which we may now examine.

The Establishment of Facts. Most legal controversies involve a dispute as to facts, and their precise determination is commonly more difficult than establishing what is the law. Courts are particularly qualified to perform this function both because of the impartiality of the judges and because of the elaborate procedural rules employed in receiving evidence—that is, the means by which any matter or fact is proved. Evidence may consist, among other things, of public records, documents, articles, or the oral testimony of witnesses. In many proceedings the judge alone may determine the facts. Where the case is of substantial importance, however, or the establishment of a particular fact has most critical consequences—as in a criminal trial—a jury may be used to decide what facts the evidence tends to prove.

The procedures employed by common-law and civil-law system courts diverge in certain ways. The common-law courts generally treat hearsay evidence as inadmissible; and the determination of matters in dispute in a civil controversy is effected mainly by the pleadings of the opposing attorneys. The civil-law courts take a much wider view respecting the admission of relevant evidence; their judges, too, have an influential role in selecting the issue in a case upon which a decision will be based. There are also procedural distinctions in criminal trials. The common-law courts follow a procedure characterized as "accusatorial." A person may be tried for an offense only after a preliminary determination that there appears to be sufficient evidence to warrant a charge being made. The trial begins, nevertheless, with a presumption of innocence of the accused, who may choose not to testify with respect to the charge and cannot be obliged to incriminate himself. The prosecutor must make out the case against him by evidence he has collected, or obtained in conjunction with police authorities, and introduced according to strict rules which give the benefit of the doubt to the accused. The judge presides as an umpire between the prosecution and defense, and instructs the jury as to the significance of the facts and the law; on the charges brought, the prosecution must prove the defendant's guilt to be "beyond reasonable doubt." Civil-law system courts, by contrast, employ what is described as an "inquisitorial" procedure. A professional judge makes a thorough pretrial investigation of a crime, examining both witnesses and suspects; and if he believes a trial is justified, he delivers an official accusation. The accused then stands trial. Though it would be going too far to say that in the civil-law system one is considered guilty unless he proves himself innocent, there is a substantial presumption against him at this stage. The judges, as well as the prosecution, interrogate the defendant in order to get at the truth of things; and it remains only to prove or disprove the pretrial findings. Of course, the differences between the two systems can be exaggerated, and both have their respective merits.

The Finding and Interpretation of Law. Essential to the judicial process is the function of deciding what rules of law are applicable to a given set of facts. Sometimes this is immediately apparent, and with the facts resolved, the appropriate rules of law fall into place. But often it is not at all clear what law is relevant. In common-law countries, it may be necessary to choose from among Constitution, statute, and common-law rule; in the latter instance, the parties to a controversy may offer conflicting citations of precedent and a choice must be made between them. There may be contradictory clauses in a single statute, or ones enacted at different times may be in conflict. While this is less of a problem under the civil-law systems, it is not unknown; and even there the judge must decide, perhaps, by which part of a code a controversy is to be governed, or whether by ordinary or administrative law.

But in any case, bodies of law are not self-interpreting. By their very nature they are general commands and prohibitions; their rules must be applied to an endless variety of acts and circumstances. As Justice Cardozo has observed, "No doubt the ideal system, if it were attainable, would be a code at once so flexible and so minute, as to supply in advance for every conceivable situation the just and fitting rule." Yet there is no such system. Statutes are ambiguous, if only because they are composed of words. The judge must take cognizance of many things: the intent of the legislator, the reasonable meaning of words, judicial precedents, and the practical consequences which will follow various constructions of a particular legal principle. Penal statutes are generally construed strictly, those conferring substantive rights liberally, and so on. Hence, the judge always has a sifting and elaborating function in deciding what the law is and what its rules require. As Justice Holmes said in a classic remark, "General propositions do not decide concrete cases."

Judicial Lawmaking. We have observed that there is a judicial function of lawmaking. To find and interpret the law is to participate in its creation. The English common-law system was indeed developed by generations of judges. In the national common-law systems today the contributions of the judiciary to this process continue, even though somewhat diminished, and are more extensive than is commonly realized. To be sure, judges are always reluctant to acknowledge that they make law, if only because this would suggest that its rules lack predictability and constancy; nor do they wish to be accused of usurping the province of the legislator. Hence, adherence to the principle of *stare decisis* helps to maintain a general consistency between the decision in one like case and another. Yet every decision leaves its residue; and as each judge contributes his own small embellishments, the law is "broadened down from precedent to precedent." Of course, such judicial contributions are more modest in the civil-law systems, but they do not thus avoid accumulating interpretations and a judicial shaping of the law.

Probably the most obvious demonstration of judicial lawmaking occurs in connection with the exercise of judicial review—that is, the power of a court to determine the constitutionality of a legislative act and to decline to enforce it if found in conflict with the superior law of the constitution. The exercise of this power has been raised to its highest degree in the United States, where any court may examine the constitutionality of an act when it is immediately necessary to dispose of a case before it. Because the United States Supreme Court is the court of last resort for the judicial interpretation of constitutional questions, its decisions in this respect are of great importance. It may not only determine what the clauses of the Constitution mean, but may set aside acts of Congress and of the states—or parts of them—as contrary to the supreme law.

When, as a significant example, the Supreme Court ruled in *Brown* v. *Board of Education of Topeka* (1954) that "in the field of public education the doctrine of separate but equal has no place. . . . Segregation is a denial of the equal protection of the laws," it was clearly deciding what the law is. The Constitution did not specifically confer the power of judicial review upon the courts, but they have considered it a necessary incident to the judicial power under the American system of government. "It is emphatically the province and duty of the judicial department to say what the law is," said Chief Justice Marshall for the Supreme Court in *Marbury* v. *Madison* (1803).

"Those who apply the rule to particular cases, must of necessity expound and interpret that rule. . . ."

The power of judicial review exists in more limited form elsewhere. The High Court of Australia and the Supreme Court of Canada may review the constitutionality of the acts of their respective states and provinces. The postwar Constitutions of Austria, the German Federal Republic, and Italy all provide for special Constitutional Courts with review power over the legislation of the national governments and their subdivisions. France of the Fifth Republic has also undertaken the creation of a Constitutional Council to review the constitutionality of laws. In Great Britain, by contrast, acts of Parliament are not subject to judicial review, though of course the courts are obliged to construe them. Judicial review may have political significance, as well; political disputes, in some cases, may be argued in legal rather than political terms.

The Enforcement of Authority and Remedies. Judicial institutions are considered to possess a right of self-preservation, with inherent powers to maintain their dignity and to enforce order in their proceedings. They may punish persons for contempt in consequence of disturbing their proceedings or for disobeying or resisting their orders. Contempts committed in the presence of the court may be punished summarily by the presiding judge.

To oblige compulsory attendance at court proceedings the common-law system developed a variety of writs. A writ is an order issued by a court, directed to an officer, and authorizing him to execute it. A *warrant* authorizes the arrest of a person charged with an offense and his detention in court custody; or it permits the search of a house or other place for stolen goods, unlawful articles, and such things. A *summons* is a notice to a person calling for his appearance in court to answer a civil complaint. A *subpoena* commands a person to appear in court to testify as a witness, or to produce there papers or other items relevant to a proceeding.

The common-law system also provides numerous other writs which permit the courts to enforce their judgments, such as a writ of *execution, mandamus,* or *prohibition.* Most famous of all is the writ of *habeas corpus,* which directs a person detaining another to produce him in court and thus permit the judge to determine if he is being legally confined. If the detention is unlawful, the judge sets the person free. This writ has long been cherished in the common-law countries as a means of removing arbitrary or illegal restraint of personal liberty.

There are, finally, certain preventive actions which courts employ to avoid injury to an individual's rights or the performance of certain unlawful acts. Among these equitable remedies, two are best known. The writ of *injunction* is an order of a court commanding a person to do, or not to do, some particular act. A decree of *specific performance* is a court order directing a party to a contract to the performance of his obligations. In a civil-law country, most such interferences with executive actions will be undertaken only by administrative courts.

Administrative Responsibilities. Finally, it has become common practice to assign various administrative responsibilities to the courts. These miscellaneous functions do not involve controversial matters in every instance; judicial performance is desired because of its impartiality and independence. In other instances, elements of controversy are present; and here the courts are preferred, of course, because of their experience as arbiter of differences. There has been a particular inclination in the United States to devolve various administrative duties upon individual courts. Here they may have such tasks as probating wills and the management of estates of persons deceased, granting and revoking licenses, granting admission to the bar and disbarment, administering bankruptcy proceedings, performing marriages and granting divorces, and administering the naturalization of aliens. British courts have somewhat similar duties, with the important exception of naturalization; and disputed parliamentary elections, if involving corrupt and illegal practices, are decided by two judges of the Queen's Bench. Here, however, as in most states, the conferment of citizenship by naturalization is an administrative act. In the civil law countries, the courts have fewer duties of an administrative character, though they commonly exercise jurisdiction over probate, divorce, bankruptcy and, in some instances, elections.

IV. An Evaluation of the Judicial Process

We have surveyed the development and characteristics of legal systems, and the organization and functions of courts. We may now undertake some evaluation of the judicial process related to the ends it serves. We shall not give further consideration here to such administration in the totalitarian states; as we have already observed, both their law and their courts are the instruments of their rulers—devoted to enforcing the policy of the regime as their major purpose, and being denied impartiality or objectivity. The judicial process is characterized essentially as the just resolution of causes by an impartial judge according to determinate standards. We are concerned here with judicial administration only where the ideal, at least, is a government of laws, not men. Of course, this is nowhere perfectly achieved, because laws are man-made, and judges, lawyers, and those who appear in court are human.

Criticisms of Judicial Administration. In what ways, where the traditional ideals of justice prevail, does the judicial institution fall short? Complaints over the administration of justice reveal several dissatisfactions. A basic one arises from the inability of any legal system to assure the certainty of law. The state does not dispense justice automatically; civil disputes arise under the body of private law, and invasions of one's rights in property generally require him to take the initiative and seek redress by litigation. Though both litigants in a controversy presumably appeal to the same law, one must ordinarily be disappointed. To many a layman, the intricacy of legal rules, the complexity of legal terms, and the processes of the courts themselves are mysterious, if not suspect; they appear to threaten means of taking from him as much as ways of giving him his due. It is this feeling, probably, which gives rise to a popular belief that lawyers would not consider it in their interest to simplify these mysteries, even if they could. There are, in addition, some very real concerns.

In the next place, the costs of litigation are high. Though justice may not be bought—to contest for it can be an expensive enterprise when court costs, fees, travel to the place of the court, and attorney's retainers are considered. Persons without means to afford these or who cannot attract some supporters with such means, may thus be deprived of the opportunity to enforce or defend their rights. There may also be differences in the administration of criminal justice for the rich and the poor. Although it is the usual practice to furnish legal counsel to an accused person who cannot provide it for himself, such assistance is not likely to be the equal of expensive legal talent others may be able to command. The price of taking an appeal is also great; in addition to further costs and fees, the appellate briefs and other materials must usually be printed, and this can be a substantial expense. Thus, a litigant or defendant who can afford the costs of appeals and their delay is distinctly at an advantage. Even after a litigant secures judgment in his favor, he may have won a hollow victory if its execution goes unsatisfied. As Voltaire said, "I was never ruined but twice—once when I won a law suit, and once when I lost one." There appear to be no easy solutions to these problems. It would scarcely be practicable for the state to assume all the costs of resort to the courts; provision of legal-aid bureaus, public defenders, and voluntary help by members of the bar seem to be all that is obtainable under the circumstances.

There is a further problem of congestion in the courts. The dockets of the courts are usually long, and those seeking a judicial resolution of their legal differences may be obliged to await many months their day in court. The "law's delay" is a centuries-old complaint, yet the delay of justice can well be a denial of justice. Through various maneuvers and appeals, one litigant can avoid a final judgment sometimes for years; while to remain in the contest, the other litigant may be required to exhaust not merely his patience but his funds. Moreover, defects in legal procedure attract much criticism. In the attempt to enhance certainty and restrict judicial discretion in the matter of procedure, simple rules are turned into complex ones, and over the years become encrusted with a myriad of technicalities. The rules of evidence alone have become so complicated that today few judges or lawyers can hope to master them. No more are there simple solutions to the problem. Courts are, after all, obliged in reality to construe and apply rules; they have no Olympian license to distribute justice freely and easily as a kind of largess. Implicit in the judicial process is a much greater inflexibility than in other ways of transacting man's affairs.

We should know that there are substantial strictures raised everywhere against the administration of criminal justice—in some cases because of its harsh treatment of the accused, and in others because of its leniency. The efficiency of criminal proceedings in British courts is often much admired, and those charged with crimes rarely seem to escape their just deserts. Yet most persons sentenced there have been convicted in summary jurisdiction by professionally untrained justices sitting without a jury. The speed with which those accused of the most serious crimes in Great Britain have been charged, tried, convicted, given an appeal, and hanged is also considered impressive. But again, it might further be remarked that until the death penalty was abolished there, Britons discovered occasionally that their courts irretrievably had hanged the wrong man!

By contrast, American criminal procedure frequently appears overly generous to the accused. Leaving aside the many criminals who are not apprehended—and all of those who are, but avoid prosecution—the courts of many states seem barely equal to the task of convicting any but the most stupid, impoverished, or confessed criminals. In many American jurisdictions judges are simply not allowed to be the masters of their courtroom. Trials become battles of wits and wrangles between opposing attorneys; judges' rulings are subjected to inordinate exceptions and appeals; witnesses are intimidated; and juries are allowed to reach irrelevant verdicts in matters beyond their competence. Technicalities of the law often seem to be used not to achieve justice but to evade it. It scarcely need be added that when, in addition, newspapers are permitted to exploit cases *sub judice* and turn sensational trials into public orgies, the dignity and impartiality of the courts are gravely impaired.

The administration of justice has nowhere been perfected in this age, but where it has not been perverted to the service of dictatorial government, it widely produces practical results in general accord with the public ideal of it. Perhaps of greatest significance is that appropriate courts are open to the public; that they can provide a juristic, as opposed to a personal or administrative, resolution of disputes; and that peaceable means are available to bring conflicts and disputes to an end. To executive and legislative participation in the pursuit of justice through democratic government, the judiciary adds the sense that justice is being done in each individual case—an element essential to confidence in the legitimacy and reasonableness of political power.

10

The Administration

"FOR forms of government let fools contest; whate'er is best administer'd is best." These lines from Alexander Pope's *Essay on Man*
(1733) draw a very naive—or cynical—distinction and represent the
thought of an age that made limited demands on political leadership
and imagination. The efficient conduct of obvious governmental business was Pope's dominant concern and, in the corrupt English conditions of that time, this was in fact a worthy aspiration. Public policy
still expresses the objectives a political community sets for itself, however; and the public administration is one of the principal means
through which such objectives are clarified and promoted.

The extent, organization, and procedures of public administration
itself are closely influenced by the objectives being pursued and the
social conditions prevailing. Since these are not constant, neither are
the forms of administration. In the ancient Greek democracies, for example, ordinary citizens took their turns in administrative as well as
deliberative and judicial offices; this was desirable, given the political
ideals they held, as well as practicable, because of the small size of
their communities. The Roman empire, on the other hand, developed
expert administrators and an organized service, which continued into
the Byzantine and Turkish empires. In feudal Europe of the middle
ages, however, only minor and occasional exceptions are to be found
to the disappearance of a specialized administration. Apart from the
Roman Catholic Church, which built up an impressive and influential
administrative system, all political responsibilities were undifferentiated and highly decentralized functions of land ownership.

With the collapse of the medieval order systematic administration
flourished for some time as an offspring of mercantilism, in which ab-

335

solute monarchies endeavored to organize their realms effectively to expand their power. Such regimes were most developed in England, Prussia, Austria, and France. As the middle classes came to power and democracy emerged, however, interest in administration flagged. Representation of the people became the central political demand, and the political process was seen most often as one of deliberation, issuing in legislation that defined the rights and duties of citizens. Law so created was expected to require little more than judicial processes to enforce it. Except for an occasional criminal prosecution, private citizens would initiate the legal actions necessary to protect their rights. Few public officials—as distinct from judges and political representatives—were required for such a government, nor was it assumed that their responsibilities were particularly exacting. Loyalty to their political superiors was generally taken to be the principal desideratum in public officials. The consequence, frequently, was inefficiency and corruption.

Against this development a reaction set in during the last half of the nineteenth century, resulting in both a renewed study of public administration and significant changes in the organization and procedures of administration in government. The aim was to secure integrity, political accountability, and efficiency in the public service. At the same time, it became increasingly apparent that legislative enactments and constitutional provisions were not self-sufficient vehicles for public policy, and that policemen and judges were not the only instruments of government needed in the modern community. The reaction was in part a protest against corruption, but even more a response to the expansion of public functions in modern life.

I. Public Policy in the Modern State

What we call "public policy"—a phrase denoting the purposes and programs governments pursue—has not always been democratic; but it always reflects the values of those most influential politically, together with their judgments of how in prevailing conditions those values may be promoted. The last few centuries—and particularly the last few decades—have witnessed most remarkable changes in the distribution of political influence, in the nature of the values most highly held, and in the character of the conditions within which men must act. Public policy has been radically affected.

Traditional Public Policy. Governments have always engaged in what we call today "public works" or "public services." Ancient empires of the Middle East constructed and maintained irrigation systems, public buildings, and highways. Nonetheless, the basic and indispensable end served by all governments has been the maintenance of order. Government must preserve the peace among its own people and protect them against attack from abroad. Failure to do this precludes success in any other endeavor.

Throughout much of the world until very recently governments have been primarily engaged in the preservation of an existing and quite stable order, and particularly with maintaining the customary privileges of a traditional aristocracy. Among the more progressive communities of western Europe in the eighteenth century, however, arose the idea of a dynamic society based on equal rights and freedom, in which the role of government was important but limited. The watchword was *laissez faire, laissez aller* (literally, let things alone, let them go of themselves), in the phrase of the French physiocrats, an idea which Adam Smith's influential *The Wealth of Nations* (1776) generally supported in England. Government was not to interfere with citizens taking care of their own legitimate business, on the assumption that they could do so best—to their own advantage and to that of the whole community—guided by an "invisible hand" through free competition.

Laissez faire, with its bias against positive government action in any realm which could possibly be managed privately, persisted in more advanced countries in the nineteenth century. Yet the "negative state" had a brief and imperfect reign, even in the United States, where commitment to it was greatest. Ideas of desirable economic and social development, coupled with private desires for special favors which government could bestow, led inevitably to public support of particular interests through protective tariffs, land grants, and other assistance. Furthermore, critics soon denounced the negative state, which was accompanied in fact by many special privileges inadequately controlled in the public interest, as neither efficient nor humane in its consequences. When such countries as Germany and Japan began to develop modern economies at the end of the last century, laissez faire was ignored; and in Britain, France, and the United States, its dominance gradually declined. By the mid-twentieth century, following the impact of depressions, great international conflicts and tensions, and the necessity of economic and social transformation in formerly colonial and backward areas, the negative state had almost completely been replaced by the positive state.

The advent of highly organized industrial society, with its complex patterns of interdependence and its great promise, has produced a tremendous expansion of public policy aimed at remedying its evils, coordinating the fantastically diverse activities of its members, and promoting progressive development according to some idea of a general welfare. At the same time, however, given the nature of the contemporary community and its international environment, even the traditional functions of government have become enormously more demanding of imagination, skill, energy, and organization than in days gone by.

The Regulatory State. The rise of industrial economies and the weakening of earlier ethical limitations on economic activity and social relationships led very quickly to miserable and dangerous working conditions, long working hours, low incomes, and great insecurity for large numbers of people. The result, first appearing in Britain in 1819, was legislation to control these evils, regulating working conditions and hours, requiring compensation to employees injured at work, and providing assistance to the unemployed. At the same time, it was observed that the collection of industrial workers within towns created problems of public health and of care for the aged and incapacitated which had been largely unknown to agricultural communities. Governments were early compelled to undertake "welfare" services in these fields, services which have grown into far-reaching responsibilities. To meet these needs, furthermore, governments had to increase greatly their financial resources and broaden their powers of inspection, regulation, and condemnation of dangerous conditions.

The Promotional State. Such regulatory activities were the dominant aspects of the positive state until the 1930's, although the small Scandinavian countries undertook extensive welfare activities much earlier. Since that time, however, among the highly industrialized states public policy has extended increasingly beyond attempting to prevent this evil or that, to actively pursuing the welfare and expansion of the economy. The Soviet Union's program of total social and economic reconstruction, begun in the 1920's, is an extreme example —doctrinaire and undemocratic in its means and ends—but highly influential nonetheless. In ways more pragmatic and more compatible with liberal values, the Rooseveltian New Deal in the United States experimented with a new and more positive political economy; and after World War II Britain and France followed suit, and even undertook substantial economic operations by the state. As new states were formed in the postwar period, those with sufficient unity and drive—such as India and Israel, for example—joined those employing an extensive array of governmental powers for social and economic development.

These powers are quite diverse. In the first place, public expenditures for traditional as well as new purposes have become immense; government has become the largest single employer and purchaser of supplies in all countries. Variations in how, when, and where public funds will be spent have great effect upon economic activity. Second, many of the public regulatory functions, although initially aspects of the "police power"—to provide for the health, safety, and welfare of the population—may equally be used to control the character of and to encourage economic development. Government action in the realm of flood control, slum clearance, payments to the unemployed and disabled, and minimum wage levels may or may not be designed primarily for their effect upon the economy in general, but they do have an effect. Third, all governments may affect substantially the extent and nature of investment and purchasing power through adjustments in the amount and incidence of taxation, and through the control they now possess over their money and banking systems.

Fourth, most governments protect industries through tariffs, price controls, and other forms of aid—agriculture in both the United States and France is a prime example—and thus influence the production of those industries directly, and of others indirectly. In times of shortages and when production cannot immediately expand to meet demand, governments have also established maximum price levels and introduced rationing. Fifth, and finally, public works and services, generally undertaken previously for quite limited purposes, have become both more numerous and of very broad impact in the life of the modern community. In many respects they amount to a clear subsidization of some private entrepreneurs who use their services, while at the same time competing with others; at their best, however, such public enterprises also make possible improvements in both quality and efficiency of production. Typical of such activities are agricultural and other scientific research, together with programs to encourage use of its results; construction and operation of public transportation and communication facilities; great programs of river development, such as that of the Tennessee Valley Authority, and of rural electrification; and operation of coal mines in Britain, and automobile factories and coal mines in France. Public housing developments have also become quite general, usually for low income groups, with special credit facilities available to assist others.

Planning and Public Policy. This brief sketch can give only the most rudimentary idea of the tremendous range of contemporary governmental activities and their impact on the whole of social life. Yet it should indicate clearly the desirability of their coordination if coherent purposes are to be achieved. Thus, the crowning public policy should be—logically—a social and economic plan. Planning is simply an integrated choice of programs realistically appropriate to the ends sought and the conditions prevailing. It is an activity whose value no rational person can deny; however, it is also an ideal very difficult to implement in a complex and economically advanced community.

In communist economies, such as those of Russia and China— industrially primitive at their inception—public policy has been integrated by the dogmatic objectives of rapid industrialization and political unity under communist leadership. Most of the new states of the last few decades have much in common with the needs these objectives reflect; and even if noncommunist in ideological conviction, they are often drawn to the Soviet Union as a model rather than to the western democracies. On the other hand, immediately after World War II the West Germans, the Dutch, the British, and the French also adopted quite extensive planning, but which was still far short of the total economic controls of the communists. Yet their considerable success should not lead one to overlook that in these cases the problem was one of reconstruction after decades of economic stagnation and war. As their immediate objectives were realized and priorities became more disputable, the early dominance of integrated economic plans declined.

Public planning is now a much more flexible activity than the term seems to imply. While no government today can abdicate responsibility for the general well-being and strength of its community, and thus for the effects of its far-flung activities at home and abroad, planning tends to be manifested more often in pragmatic coordination of diversified programs than in the imposition of a unified policy. Overall planning agencies are rare, and those with any significant authority are nonexistent in democratic countries with developed economies. The emerging international organizations—such as the European Economic Community, Latin American Free Trade Association, Nordic Council, and the Organization for Economic Cooperation and Development—manifest a similarly limited tendency, even in the realm of broader and more extensive action. This characteristic of public policy in economic and other matters makes the relationship between politics and administration a special problem.

II. Politics, Law, and Administration

The great expansion of governmental activities in recent years has entailed a concomitant expansion of the civil administrative staff of government. Civil employees of government have increased far more rapidly than the population in all modern communities, and even in noncommunist regimes comprise from 10 to 20 percent of the total working force. This development raises problems. One concerns how large numbers of people may be organized, recruited, disciplined, and motivated for the effective performance of their tasks; and also what means of action their tasks today require—topics to be given attention in the later sections of this chapter. Another, which will be treated briefly here, concerns the political and legal context of administrative action. Since successful government depends not only upon the efficiency but also upon the responsibility of public officials, the problem is obviously an important one.

"Responsibility" is a rather ambiguous word. When we say that a person is responsible we may mean that he is trustworthy or that he is technically competent. We may also mean that he is answerable to someone else. As a practical matter, however, in the development of political and administrative institutions and procedures, a considerable range of methods has emerged through which the responsibility of public officials can be maintained.

Legal Responsibility. Once government and its activities had expanded to the point where personal loyalty to a king was no longer a sufficient guarantee of responsible service—and especially after representative assemblies had come to share the basic political responsibility—an accountability of public officials in courts of law for the legality of their acts became quite firmly established. A continuing ideal of constitutional government in the western tradition has been that public officials must have legal authority for all their acts. The ultimate determination of whether such an authority was present in any particular case has generally been held to be properly judicial, for the function of judges is to define rights according to the provisions of existing law.

Yet two quite different interpretations of the legal responsibility of officials emerged in the western world. The Anglo-American approach has been to hold officials accountable in the ordinary courts of law, and according to the same standards which apply to private citizens in their controversies with one another. The approach of continental European countries, with French practice particularly outstanding, has been to insist that public officials are not ordinary citizens; but that in the execution of public purposes they must have both exceptional powers and be subject to exceptional restrictions. Consequently, these countries developed a special administrative law and, usually, special administrative courts to develop and apply it.

Both patterns were designed to ensure the responsible performance of administrative functions; but the Anglo-American approach reflects the ideal of limited government, while the French system reflects a concern with the effectiveness of public service. The relative merits of the two systems were hotly debated some decades ago. More recently, however, the Anglo-American world has accepted an increasing amount of special administrative law, developed through legislation, decisions of ordinary courts, and administrative practices. Experience has shown that administrative law and special courts are not necessarily destructive of the rights of private citizens who claim to be injured by administrative action. Actually, the problem today is not a choice between defense of private rights and effective administration, but the reconciliation of these. In this, France has done at least as well as Britain and the United States.

A rather different approach to the control of continually enlarging administrative authority is manifested in the Swedish *Ombudsman,* or parliamentary commissioner, originating by royal appointment in 1713 but with the present system established in the constitutional settlement of 1809. More recently, Denmark, Finland, Norway, and New Zealand, among other countries, have created comparable offices, some even at subordinate levels of government. The growing interest in the ombudsman reflects increased concern for fair treatment of the citizens in administrative decisions and actions, and an awareness that this may not adequately be ensured by traditional judicial protection. In Sweden, for example, the ombudsman is elected by, but is not a member of, parliament. Acting on its behalf, he has sweeping powers to investigate citizens' (and civil servants') complaints of administrative arbitrariness, negligence, or discrimination. Thus, through inspection, recommendation, mediation, publicity, and even occasional prosecutions—the procedures and scope of authority varying among the countries—the ombudsman acts to keep administrative officials functioning according to their legal responsibilities and in the public interest.

Political Responsibility. The ideal of the rule of law suffers important limitations. On the one hand, we now recognize that men make and interpret the law; on the other, that the laws directing administrative action these days inevitably leave room for considerable discretion. To prevent administrative irresponsibility, administrators must be accountable to political leadership, and in democracy this means primarily to elected officials. Such political responsibility, however, is not automatic; plentiful experience indicates that civil servants, long in office and secure, are likely to reflect particularly the ideas of those who originally appointed them, the dominant opinions among their fellow officials, or narrow professional interests and ideas —and these may be quite at odds with the programs and ideas of their political superiors.

Two extreme reactions to the resulting problem may be noted here. The radical democracy of Jacksonian America inaugurated a spoils system, in which the victorious party in an election appointed its friends to as many posts, high and low, as it wished and for whatever reason. Unfortunately this led in practice even more to corruption than to political responsibility; and the method, never adopted by any other stable government, was soon progressively limited in the United States. On the other hand, the totalitarian regimes of this century have attempted to ensure political responsibility—to the dictator, of course—by placing highly disciplined party members in crucial positions and by organizing party cells throughout the administrative structure. Conformity to party policies is enforced through direct hierarchical control, through intensive indoctrination, and through punishment for deviations from the party line or failure to fulfill expectations. Fortunately, no democracy has such techniques available.

The methods used to promote political responsibility in modern regimes other than totalitarian dictatorships are more limited, but are also quite varied, for they unavoidably reflect the general constitutional character of the regimes. Well-established governments depend heavily upon a tradition of administrative neutrality, according to which administrative officials take their lead from duly constituted political officials, and within the law faithfully serve whatever leadership electoral or other fortunes place above them. In Britain, such neutral permanent civil servants comprise the entire staff of all executive departments except for the political minister and a very few aides. In Sweden they comprise the totality of administrative departments, which are independent of the political ministries although subject to rules they set forth. In all stable governments, permanent civil servants—politically neutral in presumption if not always in fact—constitute the bulk of the administrative staff.

Given the size and complexity of contemporary government, however, and the fact that many politically important decisions must be made below the level of the minister or department head, a limited version of the patronage system is often employed. Especially in the United States, persons sympathetic to the policies of the chief executive and the department head are placed in numerous policy-making positions in each agency, presumably ensuring that political responsibility is more effectively maintained throughout the entire administrative structure, but without interfering with the efficient performance of technical and routine operations. Still, the political life of a modern nation is not neatly summed up in the policies of its chief executive, or even in the laws passed by a parliamentary majority. Political responsibility is also maintained through channels other than the normal executive hierarchy, although it becomes rather diffuse in the process.

Professional Responsibility. The public administration of today is a professional bureaucracy. The term "bureaucracy" is often used derogatorily, but properly denotes only a large-scale organization of appointed officials, systematically interrelated in the realization of complex purposes. Bureaucracy is unavoidable in modern life, and is found not only in government but also in business, labor, and religious organizations. It does, of course, have its disadvantages, tending toward impersonality, conservatism, inflexibility, and slowness in action. These are in good part, however, merely the obverse of its virtues, which include deliberateness, predictability, specialization of function, and a formal and open organization of cooperation. Any machinery has its costs of operation; only idealistic utopias promise benefits without them.

Administrative personnel is drawn in large measure from the politically dominant classes of the population, and is therefore at least indirectly representative of them. In democracies, that personnel is drawn widely from the people, and is to a degree a cross section of them. Over the last century, civil service recruitment has slowly become increasingly democratic as popular government has become established. Popular representativeness of the bureaucracy is far from perfect, though, and an important reason for this is that the modern bureaucracy is also a professional one. That is to say, it must comprise persons of special abilities, intelligence, and training in its more crucial positions.

Thus, professional skills—whether of surveyors, educators, or organizers—do in themselves provide their own particular responsibility and representativeness. Communities do not manifest themselves only in the momentary whims and fancies which so often elect politicians, but also in the way those politicians sometimes transcend popularity contests to deliberate on public issues. Similarly, communities express themselves significantly in the professional standards to which administrative officials at their best hold themselves responsible. The informed criteria for judging what to do and how to do it—criteria with which a professional bureaucracy is imbued—are particularly important when public policy thrusts upon them heavy responsibilities but limited guidance from either judges or political leaders. Because this is precisely the case in most nations today, professional responsibility in the public service must be granted its place alongside the traditional legal and political forms of responsibility in government.

III. Administrative Organization

To organize administration is to give some ordered structure to the means of enforcing public policy. The subject has been given significant attention only in the last hundred years. Prior to this time there was little need to do so. As we have seen, the number of government functions was limited and the level of government services low. The articulation of government offices, too, was relatively simple; law enforcement was a matter largely for police and courts, and fiscal management and record-keeping were the principal tasks of administration.

The emergence of the modern regulatory and promotional state, however, produced big government in the present century, and along with it large new problems in contemporary public management. It is easy enough to say that the ideal of administrative organization is to arrange government structures to be responsible and responsive, efficient and economical, integrated and flexible. Yet there are no simple answers to how this may be done. We shall only suggest, for the present, some of the principal features of administrative organization as it has developed.

General Features of Administrative Organization. While there are no universal rules of administration, there are certain principal features of any particular administrative system. First of all, we find everywhere means of exercising control throughout the structure by a series of superior-subordinate relationships. A long line stretches from the head of a government to the postmen, customs officers, tax clerks, and others carrying out their duties in direct contact with the public; there must be many intermediate units of administration between them. In order to enable a large organization to act as a single cohesive body, it is commonly given a hierarchical structure. Thus administrative organization—like that in all military, many industrial, and certain ecclesiastical systems—follows some kind of pyramidal pattern, with lines of authority running down and lines of responsibility running up, linking together the lower, intermediate, and higher units of administration.

There are numerous variations in the ways a pyramiding hierarchy may be constructed. A highly integrated hierarchy with a direct chain of command is clearly displayed by military organization in the relations of the squad, platoon, company, battalion, regiment, and so on upward. In civil administration rarely is authority of each higher level so complete and hierarchy so tightly knit; however, well-integrated administrative structures approximate such a pattern. In contrast, some administrative systems are decentralized to the point that agencies or departments may have areas of independence from control by the chief executive. In American state government, commonly, the several administrative departments are headed by independently elected officials. There may be some benefit, of course, in having a nonhierarchical chain of command to handle functions that do not readily fit into the existing organization. For example, in the United States the Central Intelligence Agency, rather than being embedded within the hierarchy of the Department of Defense, reports through the National Security Council directly to the President. A high degree of integration may be ideally preferred in terms of administrative considerations; authority and responsibility reconcentrated at each succeeding level produces a distinct unity of command. But practical political considerations often call for a measure of disintegration and dispersion of authority to permit various kinds of legislative or popular control.

A second feature of administrative organization is that its structure must reflect some form of division of labor. Traditionally, the criteria for administrative organization are considered to be four: purpose, process, clientele, and area. The meaning of "purpose" is self-evident; "process" refers to specialized forms of action and skills involved; "clientele" refers to persons being served while "area," of course, refers to geographic territory. The distinctions are ultimately arbitrary, since such a purpose as public health clearly involves a process appropriate to it, deals with some portions of the population more than others, and even determines its own appropriate area—an epidemic is not likely to respect boundaries drawn for political and administrative purposes. Thus, patterns of organization vary so far as these criteria are concerned according to convenience and historical accident more than from the objective validity of one criterion or another. Yet, to be manageable, administrative organization must be broken down into interrelated divisions of labor; and these terms indicate roughly how this usually has been done.

These divisions of labor may be simply illustrated. It is clearly a purpose of government to protect life and property; to do so it organizes police, safety inspection, fire, and coastguard services. The police themselves may be employed for considerably different services, however, dealing with separate kinds of persons or problems, such as juveniles and narcotics, or using different skills or techniques, as in traffic or detective work; hence, administrative structure within a police force may appropriately be based on separate services meeting these particular needs. Finally, police may also be separately required for different areas and their respective law enforcement programs: national, state, district, or local.

Another division of labor within administrative organization follows the distinction between line, staff, and auxiliary services. The line departments and agencies conduct the major substantive programs of government and directly serve the public. A department of agriculture, a ministry of pensions, a post office, and a highway department are all line agencies. A staff advises officials or agencies; it has no operational responsibilities and is not formally in the line of command. It plans, studies, conducts research, and advises the executive. The American Bureau of the Budget and the French Council of State, with respect at least to part of their functions, are staff agencies. An auxiliary service provides technical, secondary, or "housekeeping" assistance of various kinds to the line agencies; these may be personnel recruitment, supply and purchasing, legislative drafting, and so on. Both staff and auxiliary services exist to aid the effectiveness of the line agencies and have no justification apart from the needs of the latter—neither planning, nor economy, nor purchasing being ends in themselves.

A third important feature of administrative organization is displayed in the extent and character of its centralization. From one perspective this is a political question: a decision by constitution or statute at what levels below the central one there are to be vertical subdivisions for administration—regional, provincial, local, and the like; and how many there should be. The other perspective is administrative: how to divide responsibility between central and field offices. A highly centralized system maximizes the concentration of authority and discretion at the higher levels and heavily circumscribes it at the lower; a highly decentralized system does, of course, the contrary.

As the problems of government become increasingly complex and of greater national concern, and as communication and travel have become so rapid, there has been a distinct tendency toward centralization in administration. This is usually desirable to produce integrated policy and uniform administrative procedures. But central authority is often remote and unresponsive, and excessive centralization weakens initiative and flexibility in the field. Among the three major features of administrative organization we have mentioned, this is probably the most crucial; failure to achieve some appropriate balance between centralization and decentralization produces bureaucratic administration in its most negative sense.

National Systems of Administration. Every country has its own particular administrative structures, arrangements, and techniques. Nevertheless, within the western world two main patterns may be observed: a continental European type, developed largely by France and influential within the Roman law countries; and an Anglo-American type, the product of British and American experience, and extended also to the Commonwealth countries. These two types are in the main the result of three differences: those in attitudes over the centralization of state power; those between the two legal systems; and those in their nineteenth-century experiences.

The continental pattern generally has continued the traditions of concentrated monarchical ruling power and the control of government from its center. Though the French revolution destroyed the authoritarian *ancien régime*, Napoleon restored central control of the administrative hierarchy and created the office of prefect to give him direct authority in local areas. The growth of government in the nineteenth century thereafter tended to be an elaboration of this well-entrenched central authority. Here, therefore, local levels of government are viewed primarily as administrative conveniences, to be dominated by the center, rather than as autonomous units for self-government. The public service is professionalized and relies particularly on the expert. As an accompaniment to the civil-law system, there is commonly a separate body of administrative law and courts.

The Anglo-American pattern of administrative arrangement is the product of a greater dispersion of authority traditional in these countries. Their earlier development of and experience with representative government encouraged more popular—and certainly, more legislative—control of administrative authorities and administration. The tradition of local self-government has also been strong. In both countries, too, the large growth of government in the nineteenth century was mainly at the local level; only in the twentieth has higher authority loomed large in local affairs. Finally, under the common-law system, officials are responsible to the ordinary courts, which have also applied more in the way of ordinary legal controls to integrate the administrative process.

We have been speaking, of course, of highly generalized patterns. Important variations are introduced from state to state both by national traditions and, for example, where a federal as opposed to a unitary form of government exists. In France's unitary system, for example, the central government's ministries apply to subordinate levels a *tutelle administrative* (tutelage), through their own inspectors, the prefects in the *départements,* and the mayors of the communes, that directly reaches local government. The result, as a President of France once observed, "is a republic at the top but an empire at the base." In Germany, on the other hand, there has been some tradition of local self-government, but it has been considerably stifled by tendencies to authoritarianism at the top. The present German Federal Republic, though reflecting much of the continental pattern of administration, continues the German tradition of leaving to the *Länder* (states) the bulk of administrative organization, including the enforcement of much federal law and the administering of many federal services. The federal ministries are thus relatively small, since they administer directly only the postal service, customs, finance, and railroads, as well as defense and foreign affairs. Local government is created and regulated by *Land* law and, in turn, performs many functions for the *Länder*.

Within the Anglo-American pattern, there are also obvious differences. Great Britain, with a unitary system of government operating within a relatively small area, has only two main governmental levels, central and local. There are no intermediate levels of state or provincial government as in the United States and Germany; neither are there prefects, as in France, representing central authority at the local level. Only a few of the British ministries maintain sizable regional or local services of their own; much of their administration is effected through local governments, over which they exercise a variety of controls; though these are not centralized in a single ministry, they nonetheless achieve a very close supervision of local authorities. The American administrative system reflects its English origins in many ways, but owing to the American federal system and an even greater commitment to home rule, it is much less centralized. The federal government has maintained its own administrative field service, relying on direct state and local conduct of its programs only in limited instances. And under the federal system, of course, control of local government is a function of the states.

Administrative Agencies. The principal administrative agency is the department or ministry. There is no standard terminology. British usage speaks of "the governmental departments," but many are designated "office" or "ministry." France also uses the term *ministère;* a *département*, it should be noted, in French usage describes an administrative area. These primary administrative entities are devoted to some broad and substantive purpose—such as domestic order, foreign affairs, government finance, commerce, or health. The number varies from country to country. The United States has eleven; Norway, fourteen; France, India, and Australia, often two dozen; in many states the number changes from time to time as political or administrative convenience requires. The principal subdivisions of departments or ministries have more narrowly defined functions, and again no uniformity in their terminology—which makes their comparative discussion difficult. The Hoover Commission in 1949 proposed that the American usage—in descending order—be department or agency, bureau, division, branch, section, and unit. In Britain, however, the principal subdivisions of ministries are called "departments" or "divisions"; they are *directions* ("directorates") in France, and "services" in Canada.

By no means are all administrative agencies contained within and under the control of the departmental hierarchy. Indeed, it is a phenomenon of modern government that an increasing number of independent entities have everywhere been established and set apart, to some degree, from superior administrative authority. There are various motives for doing so; but they have resulted primarily from the desire to achieve a measure of regulation, adjudication, or management independently of the chain of command in the regular administrative hierarchy. Some of these agencies are headed by one man; others are controlled by multimember boards or commissions. In the United States, a number of important independent agencies have been created by Congress; these include the independent regulatory commissions, of five or more members, appointed by the President for fixed terms, but not removable by him or subject to his direction. Among the important ones are the Interstate Commerce Commission, regulating the railroads and other carriers; the Federal Communications Commission, regulating telephone, telegraph, radio, and television; the Securities and Exchange Commission; and the Civil Aeronautics Board. Other forms of this device may be seen in such bodies as the British Independent Television Authority, the Danish Monopoly Control Authority, and the Japanese Board of Audit.

As the business of government has expanded, increasing the number and variety of private claims and official decisions affecting private persons, the conduct of public affairs has come to require greater speed, simpler procedures, and more specialized knowledge than the ordinary courts can usually provide. Special administrative tribunals, as a second kind of agency, have consequently been established in most modern states to consider claims and to review on appeal many official decisions protested by those affected. Such, for example, are the Unemployment Compensation Boards in the states, and the Court of Claims in the United States federal government. The independent regulatory commissions just mentioned also have authority to conduct administrative adjudication, thus joining quasi-judicial functions to their quasi-legislative powers of making—within the limits of their enabling legislation—rules and regulations having the force of law. In Great Britain a vast number of administrative tribunals are arrayed throughout the government's structure, reviewing cases and controversies in such matters as pensions, claims, transport, town planning, public housing, and so on. Their decisions can usually be appealed to the ordinary courts; where they exist, as in France, appeal is to administrative courts.

A third kind of independent agency commonly employed is the public corporation. To be sure, examples abound of direct ministerial operation of governmental commercial undertakings: the postal and telecommunications system in France, railroads in the Scandinavian countries, public forests in New Zealand, and the like. A frequently preferred device for operating a nationalized industry, however, is its separate control through an independent public corporation, which is created analogously to a private corporation and provided with somewhat similar powers. This may be done where highly specialized management is required, to allow application of commercial techniques and profit-making, or to give an enterprise freedom from normal budgetary or other political influences or controls. The use of the corporate form of organization is displayed in the United States Postal Service and St. Lawrence Seaway Development Corporation; British Overseas Airways Corporation and National Coal Board; in Electricité de France and Gaz de France; and in the Norwegian State Liquor Monopoly.

IV. The Civil Service

As important as the form of administrative institutions and their relationships are the people who comprise them. Every government today, and its citizenry generally, must be concerned with what has come to be called "public personnel administration"—the recruitment, training, organization, and management of civil servants. This process acquired its special significance as government reached its modern dimensions.

The Development of the Modern Civil Service. The civil service had its beginnings with the emergence of the modern nation-state, as monarchs organized royal services to centralize and extend their power and employed bureaucracies as instruments of government. Appointments to the service were largely a matter of monarchical patronage; prevailing qualifications were those that met internal requirements of effectiveness. On the European continent, these were essentially centralization, discipline, and efficiency. In their higher reaches, the services became the preserve of the aristocracy; state service was thus an exclusive occupation, and royal prestige enhanced the civil servant's status at all levels. After absolute monarchy was generally ended in the nineteenth century, the traditions of a professionalized service, aristocratic in tone, still prevailed—largely continuing with the qualities which have characterized the continental pattern of administration.

In England, however, the establishment of parliamentary supremacy over the monarchy in the seventeenth century prevented the creation of a comparably centralized royal service. Under parliamentary control, the English civil service became instead a source of patronage for parliamentary politicians, filled with their relatives and partisans to an extent that—during the eighteenth and much of the nineteenth centuries—it was looked upon as a system of "outdoor relief" for the aristocracy. The result was administration sometimes corrupt and often inefficient; its ineffectiveness was shockingly revealed in the Crimean War. The sweep of the nineteenth-century reform movement touched this, as it did other realms; some tests for "merit" were first applied for appointments to the service in India, and subsequently to the home service. In 1870, appointment by competitive examination was made obligatory throughout the service, and recruitment through a merit system continued thereafter. Similar systems have been carried to the Commonwealth countries, though Canada's civil service reflects more typically American characteristics.

The United States inherited the eighteenth-century English tradition of a patronage-based system. Yet in the post-revolutionary period some attempts were made to displace it by providing extensively for elected and rotated offices in state and local government. In the earlier decades of federal administration, too, a reaction to excessive democracy prevailed; President Washington's precedent was for some time continued in requiring a recognizable competence for appointment to the limited number of federal offices. But the spoils system of the 1830's—created by the spirit of frontier equalitarianism and Jacksonian democracy, and bolstered by the emergence of popular political parties—soon was deeply entrenched at every level of government service. All too easily the democratic dogmas of the day, insisting on the equal ability of all citizens to discharge the functions of public office or employment, and the need of a multiplicity of elected officials to have rewards for loyal supporters, succeeded in placing the public service of the United States in the hands of party politicians. This array of officeholders—or would-be officeholders— joined the ranks of "political machines" and made "political bosses" of those with access to substantial patronage and privilege. Once introduced, they were self-perpetuating, and nearly impossible to dislodge. Ultimately, demands for reform followed those in Britain—if approximately a generation behind—and in 1883 the Pendleton Act introduced the merit system in the federal service. State and local governments much more belatedly began to institute the practice. With increments over the years, the merit system extends almost throughout the federal service; at the lesser levels of government, however, it has made slow and limited progress.

The Levels of Public Administration. From top to bottom in the administrative structure three principal levels operate in the executive branch: top leadership, middle management, and rank-and-file. The top leadership embraces those persons close to the chief executive and involved in policy making—the department heads or ministers; their undersecretaries; in some cases bureau, service, or division chiefs; and others at this level—who are concerned with the department and its program as a whole. Because of their primary concern with policy, these officials are usually appointed directly by the chief executive or the department head out of political considerations, though in some cases, as in Britain, the three or four highest permanent civil servants—the permanent secretary and his deputies—are included in this group. This is obviously a small and narrow category. As a rule these officials are politically answerable to the legislative institution; they are spokesmen for their department before the public as well; and they ordinarily lose office with changes of government. They function in a "civil" capacity, of course; and yet they are not, except in the instance mentioned, a part of the civil service.

The rank-and-file, on the other hand, make up the largest category of civil servants. The "production personnel," as they have been called, includes the army of clerks, draftsmen, inspectors, accountants, postal workers, guards, foresters, and so on, who perform the routine—but indispensable—tasks in public service. A major part of the employees of government, it should be noted parenthetically, are to be found in arsenals, docks, nationalized industries, public corporations, and in the schools and utility services of local government. Though technically within the civil service, most such employees are recruited as are their counterparts in private business and industry and have similar status. The popular imagination commonly overlooks this fact, and often prefers to conjure up, from the total number of government employees, the image of a monstrous empire of superfluous clerks and petty bureaucrats. Yet most of these people are not engaged in "government," "politics," or even "administration," in the ordinary senses of those terms; rather, they do work that would need to be done regardless of the form of government or whatever the division between the public and private sectors of enterprise.

It is the middle-management group in the public service that is most concerned with administration in the strict sense. In this category are some of the bureau and division chiefs, other primary supervisors, officers of the departmental auxiliary agencies, and directors of field offices and institutions. Their duties are those of management, direction, and supervision; they constitute the repository of departmental knowledge and accumulated experience. Transmitting orders and decisions downward and information upward, they are at the center of the organizational communications system. They create and conduct programs appropriate to departmental policy, and they see, in short, that the work is done. Upon the professional skill, energy, and efficiency of the middle managers rests to a very large degree the success of administrative operations.

The Service Classes and Their Recruitment. The ways in which governments classify and recruit the career members of their civil service vary considerably, and reflect differing national traditions. The British long followed broadly the distinctions in service levels outlined above, tying them as well to its educational and social class system. There were three major classes: first, a small administrative class of a few thousand, recruited by highly competitive examinations from among recent university graduates with arts or science degrees, to plan and direct policy and advise the ministers; second, an executive class, drawn from those having an academic secondary education, to act as the managerial force in directing and supervising work programs; and third, a clerical class—the largest—to perform the routine tasks of clerking, accounting, and recording, recruited at the age of sixteen or seventeen from those with some secondary education. In 1971, however, this three-way division was abolished and replaced with a single grading structure for the nonindustrial service.

The American federal service has had no counterpart to the administrative class of the British service, with its exclusive and aristocratic traditions. Many appointments at the highest administrative levels are filled, as we observed, by political appointees who are not civil servants. Instead, the federal service has a General Schedule, with eighteen grades, ranging over clerical, protective, and custodial positions at the bottom to professional and scientific positions at the top. College graduates are recruited beginning at Grade GS-5, through competitive examinations based on a variety of college "majors," and can aim, at least, at achieving by promotion the higher ranks that range up to GS-18. Appointments at the higher grades are based not on competitive examinations but upon the evaluation of evidences of academic training and professional experience.

In France, West Germany, and European countries generally, the service classes are organized and recruited much alike and follow the principal levels of educational attainment. The highest category in France—that of *administrateur civil*—is chosen by extremely rigorous examinations open to university graduates in political science, history, or law and to civil servants already members of the executive class. These are then given several years of additional training in the

Ecole Nationale d'Administration, combining academic and "on the job" work, which must be successfully completed. In Germany, the higher service (*der höhere Dienst*) comparably seeks those of distinctive academic attainment. It is accessible only to university graduates, generally in law; candidates must pass a very difficult competitive examination, following which they serve three years of preparatory training in various offices, and then must pass a second examination.

An Evaluation of the Civil Service. In evaluating the problems of obtaining an effective civil service, it will be useful again to distinguish between the upper and lower ranks of personnel. To acquire an effective rank-and-file, all services require a wide variety of persons with particular skills, most of which have similar or fairly close counterparts in private enterprise. The need here is to recruit persons by essentially practical tests who already have such skills or who are sufficiently educable that they can become qualified in them by a reasonable period of in-service training. A merit appointment system, then, is properly based not on some negative idea of "keeping the rascals out" but on positive assurance of competence at entry. If appointments are not to be partisan spoils, civil servants must also be given some kind of tenure system, which protects them against political dismissals, though by no means making them irremovable under any circumstances.

A job classification system is essential to ensure equal pay for equal work, compensation appropriate to duties, and some avenue for advancement by promotion or increased pay. In the public interest, too, some decision must be made as to which categories of employees cannot be allowed to strike, and how to provide alternative methods for them to present grievances and have them settled. There must be a determination of "sensitive" areas in government employment, what characteristics should disqualify particular employees from serving in them, and sensible means of ensuring loyalty and security. To make continued careers in the service attractive to the able, frequently at lower pay than in comparable nongovernmental work, requires a retirement and pension system, and attention to other similar morale-building factors.

At this level of specific job performance in public administration, the undesirable features of bureaucracy are likely to be felt most immediately by the general public. There is no sovereign remedy for them, but a recruitment system that sets standards of competence for appointment and advancement is probably the best. Most of the vices of bureaucracy reflect shortcomings in organization and management of service at this level. Officiousness is not infrequently the product of incompetence; apathy, of poor morale; delay, of understaffing; red tape, of excessively enforced routine; unimaginativeness, of rigid supervision; graft and corruption, of a spoils system of appointment and inadequate pay. And all are remediable if the public so demands and refuses to pay what are the real, if hidden, costs in incompetent and irresponsible administration.

The problems of staffing the higher service, while including many of these points, are much more complex. The European approach has been to create a separate administrative class to head the bureaucracy. This is truly an elite corps, recruited from young university graduates. Whether stressing traditional general education as in Britain, intellectual sophistication as in France, or legal training as in Germany, in each case emphasis is placed on securing persons who give early promise of a high order of attainment. The result is to offer attractive careers in state service to the most talented and to produce a politically impartial class of experts devoted to the interests of the state and possessed of high morale and prestige. These are not inconsiderable accomplishments, yet they have certain drawbacks. Men who go from university to service career leave one rarefied atmosphere for another; often they have little experience with the practical side of the world and its affairs. The products of a relatively exclusive higher education (as is the case in Europe) tend to be drawn from the upper classes, and in the superior grade of service perpetuate a sense of caste status. Such administrative classes—expert, professional, and entrenched at the highest levels—are also a powerful influence in policy making, and sometimes resist complete political control.

As we have observed, the United States has no such administrative class. The American tradition has been that the public business is the public's business and not service in the glory of the state. Although the federal government has placed substantial emphasis in recent years on attracting young college graduates to administrative positions, they enter them in the considerably less exalted levels of lower middle management. The recruitment system also continues to emphasize the selection of professional technicians rather than the best broadly educated students the universities produce. Admission to the service commonly stresses equality of opportunity, without low age limits for entry, with the result that persons may find haven in it after being sifted out of other employment. The highest administrative positions are also frequently filled by political selection, intermingling partisan and career appointees. The resulting interchange between the worlds of government, business, politics, and education has some advantage; but it produces a service uneven in quality and experience, and a turnover rate that is unsettling. Anything in the nature of caste spirit—even of the intellect—is also avoided, satisfying popular American prejudices, if not necessarily needs. Thus, the higher American service tends to be political-minded, practical, and democratic in its outlook, and technically proficient for the most part. Its principal shortcomings, as distinguished from national differences—when compared with its European counterparts—are perhaps its failure to incorporate a sufficient number of persons with the breadth of outlook, and with the capacity for effective communication across departmental and functional lines, that are necessary to meet the demanding responsibilities of administering late twentieth-century public policy.

In the underdeveloped states, European influence and example have shaped efforts to organize effective civil services. A major obstacle to such accomplishment has been the insufficient supply of trained administrators for the middle-management level. A relatively small top leadership can be commonly drawn from among the western-educated; a widespread ambition to be on a government payroll brings many applicants—frequently an overstaffing—for jobs with the rank-and-file, who can be minimally qualified by brief on-the-job training. But all such countries lack professionally trained and practically experienced technical personnel, who are the heart and brains of an effective bureaucracy. As most of these regimes seek advancement to their ambitious goals through highly centralized systems of administration, they impose severe burdens on its upper levels. Not uncommonly, the functioning of these new services is impaired by the presence of buck-passing and inertia, nepotism and corruption, the grip of custom and excessive legalism—as well as by the absence of traditions of personal initiative, sufficient resources, popular habits of cooperation, and above all, competent personnel. Egypt's President Nasser once summed up this great need of the emergent states: "I can import machinery," he said. "I cannot import Egyptians."

V. The Methods of Administration

To treat the methods of administration in any detail would take us well beyond the space available. But it will be useful if we make a brief excursion into the procedures of handling the public business. Public administration, though it may often resemble its counterpart in private enterprise in certain ways, differs significantly from it too. The public business is essential, not optional; it has an urgent and frequently monopolistic character, unlike private pursuits. Legal rules alone govern and direct its conduct and determine the funds available to it, and its continuance is dependent upon neither success nor profit. It serves equally all persons with claims to service, and does so under public scrutiny. We shall examine it from two principal perspectives: first from that of administrative management, which concerns its internal operations; and second, from that of administrative action, which involves its external procedures.

Administrative Management

Organizing the Work of Administration. A fundamental step in the organization of administrative activity is program-planning—the formulation of plans and policies to reach a chosen objective. A program may have the most ambitious aims or purposes, but it still must be conducted by limited means. An administrative agency is assigned a particular program by the legislature, through statute, or by superior executive authority, through administrative order. In either case the agency head necessarily must decide what shall be done and how to go about it in terms of the finances and manpower available to him. From his general instructions he evolves more particular ones, and issues them in the form of policy directives; these in turn produce additional specific orders as they move down the line. In today's complex administrative system, the administrator can no longer rely on simple common sense alone as the basis for planning and policy making. He must depend upon his staff and auxiliary services to provide advice and information, to conduct research, make surveys, and consult with other agencies.

Program-planning is followed by management-planning—the formulation of schemes for the conduct of a particular activity. Perhaps the existing administrative structure can absorb the new program, or it may be necessary to design additional administrative entities. Personnel required by the program must then be recruited, assigned, and organized into the chosen number of operating units; and these must be related to staff and auxiliary services. A system of office management must also be established; equipment installed; and secretarial, filing, communications, custodial, and other services provided. Finally, a method of work distribution must be instituted so that production or operations may get under way.

Controlling the Work of Administration. The work of an administrative agency is internally controlled in a number of ways, of which budgeting is a highly important one. We have seen that the preparation and proposal of the government budget is an executive function, and its adoption, a prerogative of the legislature. The annual executive budget is organized from the requests made by each department and agency head, based upon their estimates of needs and responsibilities. These are examined by the central budget office, along with the justifications accompanying them, forecasting programs to be performed, staff additions and salary increases, capital equipment and expendable supply needs, and so on. Under the direction of the head of the government, the central budget office determines the actual figures to be presented to the legislature; after the budget's adoption—and quite possibly revision—by that body, an allocation of funds is made to the operating agencies. So that an agency will live within its means, it must divide its funds into allotments to cover the budget period, relating them to commitments already assumed and contingencies which may arise.

Effective management of funds further requires that expenditures be made only for purposes legally authorized. This is accomplished by a system of accounting, recording, and review—both to control funds available for disbursement and to account for expenditures already made. Attention must also be given to supply and purchasing. Procurement of supplies is commonly performed by a central auxiliary agency, which sets standards and specifications for matériel; contracts for the supplies on the basis of competitive bidding; and inspects, stores, and issues the goods it receives. Finally, it may be noted, an administrative agency must give attention to reporting and public relations. Government agencies are avid record-keepers—not only because this may be one of their substantive functions, as in the case of a census bureau or a pensions office, but because they must account for their transactions and funds through reports to and audits by superior executive authority and the legislature. But official accounting alone never entirely suffices in democratic societies, where public opinion is important; an administrative agency must also look to its public relations to inform the citizenry of its performance and progress.

Administrative Action

We turn now to the process of administration in its external aspects —administrative action affecting the public. The procedures available here are considerable in number and constitute those activities most peculiar to public administration. Without attempting to examine them all, we may give attention to four principal categories of action.

Publicity and Education. We have emphasized before that governments do not rely exclusively upon coercion to achieve their objectives. The devices of publicity and education are important means, therefore, to persuade people to act in particular ways consonant with the aims of some public program. Publicity is quite likely to be used where a government desires, but has no authority to require, a particular action—as when the head of a government may make public appeal in time of rapid inflation for people to buy less and save more, or in the face of business recession, to buy more and save less! Educational programs are also commonly employed to support and supplement coercion in realms where the public generally is concerned or involved. Programs of education in traffic safety, fire prevention, the conservation of natural resources, and the prevention of environmental pollution, are continuous. We are also all familiar with government efforts to educate regarding such matters as public health, infant care, income tax returns, and social security benefits.

Inspection and Licensing. Inspection involves official examination to insure that certain standards are met. It is a coercive device, yet it emphasizes preventive rather than punitive action and seeks to avoid harm or loss before they occur. By inspection, government oversees such things as the purity of water, medicines and cosmetics, the wholesomeness of foods, the safety of aircraft and factory machines, and the seaworthiness of ships and life preservers. Licensing consists in granting an official permit to perform a particular service or to exercise a certain privilege. It may be employed as a regulatory device to control the practice of highly skilled professions—such as medicine, law, engineering, or teaching; or to limit and supervise in the public interest the conduct of particular enterprises—such as theaters, bars, dance halls, private detective agencies, small loan offices, and the like. In all such instances, administrative authority to suspend or revoke such licenses, or institute judicial proceedings to such ends, carries highly important supervisory power. In many cases, however, the issuance of licenses is not intended as a restrictive or selective process, but rather for the purpose of collecting revenue, as for automobiles, hunting, and fishing.

Regulation. The essence of regulation is rule-making, which is one form of the lawmaking process. We have seen that authority to make laws is one of the oldest functions of government. Originally it was a generalized power of the monarch, but in time specialized legislative and judicial institutions came to exercise a measure of it; constitutional doctrine of the eighteenth century, indeed, established the representative legislature as the primary lawmaking body. Yet the executive function of administering the law never excluded it from a share in lawmaking, if only to provide by the issuance of subordinate rules for more effective application of statutes. With the growth in complexity of modern societies and in the technical nature of matters requiring regulation, administrative rule-making has become commonplace in the twentieth century. Legislatures simply cannot anticipate every possible situation or provide for every circumstance. Statutory legislation is now commonly adopted, therefore, in general terms; and administrative agencies are authorized in many cases to supplement it with necessary rules and regulations. As we have seen, too, it is now common practice to create special regulatory agencies in certain realms and endow them with power to issue orders of individual as well as of general application and to conduct adjudication respecting their enforcement. Nevertheless, administrative rule-making is always viewed with some degree of misgiving. It is often seen as a partial surrender of power by the legislature, allowing anonymous administrators to create legal rules inadequately criticized or publicized in their formulation and application, and encouraging executive arbitrariness. Yet rule-making has clear advantages in introducing flexibility to administration, capitalizing on the administrator's expert knowledge and avoiding undesirable delay. It is a practice that requires proper safeguards, but it has become unavoidably an essential form of administrative action today.

Enforcement and Prosecution. At some stage in the administrative process it may become necessary to enforce authority by distinctly coercive action. Common among these procedures are withdrawal of benefits, such as exclusion from farm benefit payments for failure to restrict production; revocation of license, in refusing to allow a radio or television station to continue broadcasting; the destruction of unlawful goods, as narcotics or gambling machines; the deportation of aliens, for illegal entry or habitual criminality; the attachment and sale of property, for nonpayment of taxes; and so on. Prosecution, of course, normally is available as a final coercive device to deal with those who wilfully resist authority or violate the law. Criminal prosecution requires resort to the courts and involves, on conviction, punishment by fine, imprisonment, or both. But as we suggested earlier, coercive measures in the administration of government are the exception rather than the rule. This is partly because such measures are always present in the background; but it is also because the citizenry generally accept the moral and social advantages of cooperation with administrative authority.

VI. Local Government and Administration

In many countries, local government historically antedates that of the central authorities. It performs a number of functions that touch very closely the everyday life of the people. Most significant is the fact that city government is local government—and today's cities are the centers of our civilization. We shall not be able to do justice to the subject of local government and its administration, but we may at least draw attention to its importance.

The Functions of Local Government. The functions of local government, most obviously, consist to a large degree in providing a great array of services—with the extent and nature of these varying as a rule in fairly close proportion to the concentration of people within the particular area. Thus, rural local governments, with sparse populations, may be confined to a few limited services such as police protection, roadbuilding, and elementary education. The government of a large metropolitan community, by contrast, may well undertake more distinctive activities than we could possibly enumerate on this page. Other factors also control the matter. There may be local choice; activities are mandatory in some cases and discretionary in others. While some functions involve purely local concerns, others constitute the carrying out of duties for superior levels of administration. There are differences in local financial resources, too; some functions depend upon locally collected revenues, while others are supported, in whole or part, by senior levels of government.

Although there is no precise way in which to classify local government functions, they fall generally into six principal categories. First are the physical services: these include provision of streets and sidewalks, parks, public buildings, and sewerage. Second, there are the proprietary services: many local governments operate one or more public utilities, furnishing water, electric power, gas and transportation—bus lines, subways, tramways, and ferries. Third, there are the protective services: these include police, fire, and public health services, waste and refuse collection, and street-cleaning. In a fourth category are various welfare services. Here we have local provision of schools, libraries, hospitals and clinics, swimming pools and public baths; assistance to the aged, infirm, and dependent children; and even the construction of housing. Fifth, there are the regulatory services: planning and zoning; many kinds of licensing and inspection; the regulation of building construction, markets, restaurants, and other places of public resort; and the abatement of nuisances. Finally, there are the many administrative services which local government units may perform on behalf of higher authority. These may involve such matters as general law enforcement; conduct of elections; registration of vital statistics; judicial administration; military recruitment; and road, bridge and highway construction.

Local Government Systems. It is impossible to fit the variety of local government systems into any significant scheme of classification. Particular national systems are a product of their own philosophy of government, their historic needs and experiences, and their style of administration. To some degree, local government by its nature must always be subordinate government under the control of a higher level. Yet there is considerable variation in the extent to which local inhabitants influence the conduct of their government; there may be substantial or little self-government. Another significant feature of the pattern of local government results from the number of tiers into which the local body politic is organized. There may be a single local level of government—an all-purpose local authority that performs all functions; or, more commonly, there may exist several different levels, ranged one above another to form successive layers of authority. In some countries local authorities are treated permissively and exercise broad grants of power and discretion, but in others their operations are narrowly defined in detail.

Further, there are major differences in the extent to which local government is supervised. The matter of supervision may be left largely to the legislature and courts, and thus to general legal controls; or the central government may apply a close administrative tutelage. There is also considerable disparity in the extent of uniformity among local government entities and their structure. In some countries all are poured from the same mold; in others, particularly if their organization rests with the individual provinces or states of a federal system, they are likely to take a number of different forms. Finally, there are many different ways of constructing the governing body of a local authority. There may be a council or committee, or several of them, producing a type of government in which responsibility is highly diffuse; there may be local counterparts to the three main branches of central government—executive, legislative, and judicial; or the governing authority may be primarily executive.

A brief examination of some national systems of local government will suggest how these several features may be combined in practice. In the American federal system, the organization and control of local government is left to the fifty states. The traditions of self-government and home rule are strong; and administrative supervision by the state has been limited, but is increasing because of local dependence on state financial aid. There is, therefore, uniformity neither of unit, structure, nor function. Local government is basically two-tiered, with the states divided into some three thousand counties altogether, and the counties subdivided in turn—though with very little regulatory power over the subordinate units—into cities, for urban government; or towns, townships, and the like, for village and rural government. A feature of American local government is the extensive use of special single-purpose districts created to maintain schools, build roads, or provide parks, and the like; these exist in considerable number separate from the basic units of local government, often overlapping them and each other.

Canada, a federal state leaving local government control in the hands of the provinces, has a system uniform in neither structure nor terminology. Generally, local government is one-tiered, with rural municipalities established for rural areas and urban municipalities—village, town, or city, depending on size—governing in the more populated areas. There are exceptions to this pattern: Ontario and Quebec, for example, have two-tiered government with county municipalities superior to, and containing, the local municipalities. Also, the sparsely settled areas of the north are largely administered directly by provincial departments of municipal affairs. Provincial supervision of local government has increased considerably in recent decades, particularly in the realm of finance and accounting; there has also been a tendency toward provincial assumption of the administration of some services in health, education, and welfare.

British local government displays a still higher degree of subordination and supervision. Britain, too, shares the tradition of local self-government, but the integrating tendencies of its unitary form and the density of its population have come to produce an ever-increasing supervision of the work of local authorities by central government departments—though still short, to be sure, of the degree of control customary on the European continent. British local government is one-tiered in the largest population centers, which are organized into county boroughs; there are over eighty of these, resembling what would be called "county-city" consolidations in the United States. Otherwise, local government is essentially two-tiered, with the rest of the country divided into administrative counties, and these subdivided into municipal boroughs, urban districts, or rural districts according to the degree of population concentration. The system in Scotland differs in minor ways.

Our fourth example of local government systems is the French. It has been said that France has no local government but only local administration—an exaggeration which emphasizes the high degree of subordination, supervision, financial control, and uniformity of structure imposed by central authority. Local government is formally four-tiered: the country is divided into ninety-five *départements;* these are subdivided into *arrondissements;* these, in turn, into cantons; and the latter, into communes. Only the *départements,* as the principal areas for central government administration, and the communes, which are units of local administration, both urban and rural, are of real importance. Both have elected councils, though of distinctly limited powers. The departmental prefects, appointed by and answerable to the Ministry of the Interior, are the key figures in local administration. The communal mayors are locally selected, but act as agents of the central authorities and are removable by the prefect. With individual variations, the commune or *Gemeinde* (in the German term) is the common unit of local government on the continent.

Urban Government. The subject of urban government deserves some special attention; though cities are legally subordinate as units of local government, they are not at all politically unimportant. Some great cities of Europe—London, Paris, Madrid, Rome, and Vienna— had their beginnings as centers of government and trade. With the development of the industrial revolution still other urban centers came into existence—such as Birmingham, Liverpool, Hamburg, Marseilles, New York, and Chicago—as centers of industry, commerce, and transportation. Urbanization, the concentration of large populations within a limited land area, has become one of the most important features of contemporary life. In Great Britain, France, Germany, Sweden, Belgium, Denmark, New Zealand, Canada, and the United States, among others, more than half of the population lives in urban areas; and in some cases, even in metropolitan areas. For the western world, wealth, power, education, and culture have concentrated with the masses of people in the large cities. Yet these concentrations of population are not always admired. Thomas Jefferson said: "I view great cities as pestilential to the morals, the health, and the liberties of man."

Urbanism, particularly metropolitanism, does produce a distinct way of life, in which the individual becomes relatively mobile and largely anonymous. City life requires a high division of labor and a wage economy; it produces splendor and slums; it concentrates yet segregates; it spreads culture but also disease; it increases crime and decreases the birth rate. It tends to alter familial, religious, and other traditional attitudes and to disorganize personal and social behavior. The result is an atmosphere of impersonality, tension, and strain. Important political consequences ensue from all this: the need for new forms of social control replacing those which have broken down, and for substantial physical, protective, and welfare services. The supply of these requires more government—and one vastly more elaborate, complex, and expensive than for simpler communities.

Though facing quite similar problems, city governments vary considerably from country to country. The great cities of Britain are organized into county boroughs, as we noted, and are governed by a council, composed of popularly elected councillors and a small number of aldermen co-opted by them. Annually, the council selects one of its number to serve as mayor. There is no single municipal government for the great urban complex of London, there being really several Londons. The mile-square City of London at its heart has its own Lord Mayor and Council. Greater London, containing the Counties of London and Middlesex, and parts of other adjoining counties, is governed by the Greater London Council and organized into thirty-two metropolitan boroughs for administrative purposes. London's Metropolitan Police District provides a single force under the direct control of the Home Office for a wide area beyond Greater London.

In France, municipal government, whether small or large, is conducted by the commune; but the standard pattern is altered for Paris. National governments traditionally have been reluctant to allow Paris any real measure of political independence and have kept it under the close control of central authority. Paris has several meanings. The historic city of medieval times was walled into an area of 675 acres. The modern city of Paris, with a population of three million, has a council, a prefect of Paris, and a prefect of police; it is divided into twenty *arrondissements,* each with a government-appointed mayor. The Paris Regional District was created in 1964 to provide some common planning and services for the larger metropolitan area of 8.5 million people; the Region includes seven *départements* in addition to the city of Paris. German cities are not so uniformly constituted as the French; however, they are generally organized as *Gemeinden* (municipalities), with an elected council and a *Bürgermeister*—in some cases chosen by the council, and in others by the voters.

The forms of city government in the United States are anything but standardized; nevertheless, they involve variations upon three principal patterns. The mayor-council type operates in about half of the American cities, and particularly in the largest. It reflects adherence to the separation-of-powers principle, with legislative authority exercised by the council and executive power by the mayor. In some cities, however, executive authority is so divided between the mayor and other elected officials that the arrangement is characterized as the "weak-mayor" system. The commission type of municipal government places authority in an elected commission, usually a nonpartisan body of five members, who collectively exercise legislative authority and individually head one of the city's administrative departments. One commissioner serves as mayor. The council-manager type is composed of an elected nonpartisan council which forms policy; it appoints for an indefinite term a professional city manager who is responsible to it for the administration of the municipality's affairs. He is expected to recruit and manage the personnel of the municipal departments on a merit basis. The commission form has declined steadily in incidence since World War I, while the council-manager type has spread widely, especially among medium-sized cities. Mayor-council government may be seen in New York and Chicago; commission government in Salt Lake City and Portland, Oregon; and council-manager in Cincinnati and Albuquerque.

An Appraisal of Urban Government. The great cities have their individual problems, of course, but they share several in common. The city is the child of the state, it has been said; but it is often treated as the legendary "stepchild." Professor Luther H. Gulick has observed, "The major institutions of our free society were not evolved by or for metropolitan communities." As a result city government is far too commonly a ramshackle affair, burdened with a collection of unsatisfactory compromises and belated afterthoughts. A general disinclination to make the city into a strong and effective unit of government has widely prevailed, with unfortunate consequences often for the majority of the population. There are, for example, more people in London than in both Scotland and Wales; there are five American cities each more populous than any one of sixteen American states. Yet cities are commonly equipped with inferior governing power and facilities. Not surprisingly, then, a report of the World Health Organization has declared: "After the question of keeping world peace, metropolitan planning is probably the most serious single problem faced by man in the second half of the 20th century."

The reasons for civic inadequacies are not hard to find. During the past century, cities have simply outgrown the forms of government provided them; yet there is still reluctance to afford them adequate modernization and sufficient jurisdiction. Their difficulties accumulate because they "just grew"—inadequately planned or arranged for the tasks confronting them. Today it is a rare city that does not have substantial blight areas; excessive noise, air pollution, and overcrowding;

strangling traffic and insufficient open space; and inadequate housing and transportation. The remedy for such ills calls, among other things, for larger, one-tiered, all-purpose units of urban government; a better balance between central control and self-government; a sounder basis for municipal financing; and far-sighted programs of planning and modernization. It ought to be clear that city government of the future is going to have an increasing variety of functions and will become substantially more expensive.

The problems of city government in the United States have been intensified by several circumstances. The growth of cities has been more than ordinarily haphazard—rapidly assembling, but not always assimilating, their populations from rural and immigrant elements. They have been regulated most commonly by rural-minded and even urban-hostile state legislatures with results—to take only the inadequacy of their tax and spending powers, for instance—that are often grotesque. They have been obliged to contend with dispersed and overlapping multi-tiered units of local government dating from another age, and staffed by amateur and partisan-selected personnel. And, not least important, they have been afflicted with graft and corruption, in part because there have been both popular attempts to make illegal such things as liquor, gambling, prostitution, and narcotics—and at the same time popular demands for them.

Fortunately, there is some evidence that a new day in urban government is to dawn; many cities have begun to bestir themselves with efforts at confronting the significant problems of urban and metropolitan life. Most such efforts aim at eliminating the jurisdictional conflicts, overlapping of territory, and duplication of functions—as well as their attendant excessive cost and inefficiency—by the consolidation or federation of county, city, suburban, and special district units into a single local government for the entire metropolitan area. The creation of the Municipality of Metropolitan Toronto offers a progressive model of what may be done by federation. Here Toronto and a dozen suburban areas were merged; a metropolitan council and mayor administer water supply, highways, parks, sewerage, housing, and planning for the entire area; local municipalities provide police, fire, most public health services, and building regulation. Complete city-county consolidation has been attempted in some instances, though it has usually failed for constitutional, political, or practical reasons; Baton Rouge and Nashville are among the few exceptions.

Separation of a city from the county, and consolidation of city-county functions in the one remaining level of government, may be seen in Baltimore, Denver, St. Louis, and San Francisco with generally beneficial results. Boston, Miami, Los Angeles, and Seattle have also attracted attention to their efforts at achieving integration of their metropolitan areas for special functions. The city has been expected to serve as the school of the citizen; if we allow it to break down from the unbearable weight of its burdens, we have undermined all our democratic foundations. Yet even a mayor of New York City, John Lindsay, has dared express optimism: "The cities can be governed. They can be livable. And if the world can save its cities, it can save itself."

11

The Modern State in
International Law

"THERE will not be one law for Rome and another law for Athens, nor one law today and another tomorrow, but among all peoples and for all time one and the same law will apply." When Cicero delivered these lines he was looking to a future unity of law—an ideal still unattained. But though there is no world law, there is a body of international law and, in part, the relations of states in the international community do take place according to certain rules. Even where no rules exist, the actions of states are influenced both by the qualities inherent in their statehood and by the dictates of community life. To understand the character of interstate relations, then, we must see how the international community originated, the qualities of its members, and the nature of their legal relations.

I. The Development of International Relations

The modern western or nation-state system has a long history. Though it is very largely a product of the last five centuries, it has its roots in antiquity. Our knowledge of the ancient world is taken from the beginning of written history in the fifth millennium B.C.; by this time man had already evolved relatively elaborate forms of political organization.

Contributions of Antiquity. The earliest state system of principal significance to the west originated in the Middle East. For the ancient empires of Egypt, Assyria, Babylonia, and Persia, however, there was little in the way of regularized international relations. War was their normal form of intercourse; yet some treaties of peace, alliance, and arbitration date from as early as 3100 B.C. Diplomatic emissaries were also occasionally employed, though negotiation was as likely to be undertaken to aid the promotion of war as to substitute for it.

The development of the great Greek civilization after the second millennium B.C. produced the characteristic city-community. The existence of numerous independent, relatively equal, and small entities encouraged the establishment of relations among them; and ancient Greece became a world community in miniature. In their mutual relations, at least, the Greeks considered peace to be the normal condition. They exchanged diplomatic representatives and entered into treaties, coalitions, and alliances. A rudimentary body of practices— "the customs of the Hellenes"—regulated the exchange of envoys, the right of asylum, truces, and the status of aliens. The conduct of war was considered subject to some rules, except in the case of hostilities with barbarians, who were viewed as natural enemies having no right. The Greeks also employed arbitration to resolve disputes involving territorial boundaries and commerce.

Rome made further contributions to the development of international relations. In its earlier history it entered into treaties with its neighbors, though it was unwilling at later periods to deal with non-Roman countries on a basis of equality. Rome nonetheless continued to emphasize the observance of formalities in interstate relations—the sanctity of ambassadors, the practice of extradition, and the special status of aliens. It also acknowledged certain rules for the conduct of hostilities as binding on all belligerents, and distinguished between "just" and "unjust" wars.

Two branches of Roman jurisprudence distinctly influenced subsequent international law. One body of rules, the *jus fetiale*, governed the declaration of war and the ratification of peace treaties. Another, the *jus gentium*, was concerned with judicial principles common to all the nations under the administration of Roman magistrates. Although the latter body of rules dealt primarily with commercial matters, it was most influential in the law of the middle ages. Rome made other practical contributions; its rules on the subject of jurisdiction were later drawn upon when the European states began to concern themselves with precise boundary demarcation.

The Middle Ages. Following the collapse of the Roman empire, the Frankish kingdom in the sixth century united a large portion of western Europe. This accomplishment was celebrated in A.D. 800, when the Pope crowned Charlemagne emperor at Rome. But despite this proclamation of universal authority for the Holy Roman Empire, European society was actually splintered into many small units, both joined and separated by the arrangements of the feudal system. War was common and waged often for casual reasons. Fortunately, the Church was able to mitigate some of the barbarism of the times. Through the "peace of God" and the "truce of God" the Church placed an interdiction on warfare levied against noncombatants and during specified periods of the year. Popes and bishops extended the range of canon law and often undertook to arbitrate political disputes.

Definitely more influential upon later international relations were other practices instituted during the middle ages. The growth of commerce brought about the development of a body of maritime law and, beginning in Italy, the institution of the first consulates and embassies. By the year 1200, the office of consul, exercising jurisdiction over foreign merchants in major trading cities, was well established. The system of foreign representation and the development of diplomacy as an art were particularly advanced by Venetian practice during the thirteenth century, and thereafter widely imitated in Europe. Also significant was the establishment of the principle, arising out of the feudal system of land tenure, that the exercise of political authority is coincident with the possession of territory.

The Age of the Nation-States. The process by which the nation-state emerged in western Europe was gradual and uneven. Prior to 1500, England, France, Spain, and Portugal were clearly recognizable as national entities. Thereafter Sweden, Poland, Prussia, Switzerland, and the Netherlands, among others, appeared; and the Italian city-states won a precarious independence of papal and imperial control.

If there is any landmark for the establishment of the new order, it is the treaties comprising the Peace of Westphalia, 1648. This was produced by Europe's first international conference of states, and created the constitutional foundations for the modern community of independent nation-states. Although the Holy Roman Empire nominally continued, it was now confined to the Germanies; and the sovereign power of each German prince was acknowledged. All other states of western Europe, moreover, were released from political allegiance to the Emperor or to the Roman Church. Thus, states could now exist independently in "an exact and reciprocal equality"—whether Catholic or Protestant, monarchical or republican—and without acknowledging any legal superior.

By the sixteenth century, the practice became general of exchanging resident diplomatic emissaries, personally representing the monarch. The conduct of diplomacy developed increasingly into a profession—albeit one of dubious honesty. In Sir Henry Wotton's often quoted double-entendre of the seventeenth century, "An ambassador is an honest man sent to lie abroad for the commonwealth." Large impetus was given to the formalization of diplomatic practice after 1648, with the formal categories of diplomatic agents as they exist today being laid down by the Congress of Vienna in 1815.

The international community was originally composed exclusively of European Christian states, associated by many common bonds and a similarity of interest. In time, however, this western state system began to accept additions to the community and to extend itself to non-European and non-Christian areas. Successful colonial revolutions in the Americas created a number of new republics. The opening of the east to contacts with the western world brought the admission of such states as Turkey, Persia, China, and Japan. Finally, the political turmoil surrounding World Wars I and II, the decline or collapse of the great colonial powers, and the even freer application of the principle of national self-determination, have greatly increased the number of states composing the international community.

II. The Concept of State in International Law

The world today has come to be organized into distinctive units known as "states." The concept of "state" is a complicated one and may be approached from a variety of standpoints. Our concern here, however, is with the state as the international person, an entity having a status in international law.

The State

The Definition of State in International Law. As a subject of international law, the term "state" cannot be defined with precision; yet it has commonly accepted essentials. The first article of the Montevideo

Convention (1933) among the American republics, for example, provides that the state as a person of international law should possess the following qualifications: a permanent population, a defined territory, a government, and a capacity to enter into relations with other states.

It is impossible, of course, to conceive of a state without people; though international law does not require any minimum size for its population. The people who compose a state commonly constitute a nation. The terms "nation" and "state" are often used interchangeably in designating the members of international society, but strictly speaking they are not synonymous. A nation is a body of people who feel they are united by several factors such as common ethnic origin, historical association, culture, language, religion, and customs. Most nations are so united, though the people of some display considerable diversity in their religions, as in the United States and Great Britain; they may speak more than one language, as in Switzerland and Canada; and they may contain a number of ethnically distinguishable groups, as in India and Brazil. The ties of nationhood are essentially social and cultural, and such a group inevitably aspires to statehood as the means to preserve the unity and advance the objectives of the nation. Thus, most nations comprise a state; but there are also multi-national states, as Yugoslavia and the Soviet Union.

A state must have a defined territory, both to provide an area where its population may exist and over which its jurisdiction may be exercised. A people who are scattered about the world, however united otherwise, could not constitute a state. Essential also is an organized government: the state must contain some constituted authority which commands reasonably habitual obedience from its inhabitants, maintains order, and assumes responsibility for the discharge of its obligations to other states. International law is not concerned with the form or character of the government. A violent or revolutionary change of government does not affect the state's existence; indeed, during wartime a government may even be driven into exile without the state's ceasing to exist.

These three elements may, of course, also be components of other organizations—such as universities, colonial settlements, and municipalities—that are not states. A state must also have a degree of independence providing a capacity to enter into relations with other states.

Independence and Sovereignty. The term "independence" is employed to describe the capacity of a state to be free of the legal authority of other states. Independence is not absolute, of course, and no state has unlimited freedom of action. The fact that a state is a member of the international community is taken to mean that it has implicitly assented to the rules of international law, which place some limits on the state's freedom of conduct. States further find it necessary to enter into a considerable number of treaties and other international agreements. Finally, states are obligated to undertake many kinds of international cooperation if they are adequately to protect their national interests.

The singular attribute which has been historically claimed for the state to justify this independence, and which sets it apart from all other social organizations, is its sovereignty. The United Nations Charter, for example, speaks of the "sovereign equality" of all its members as one of the basic principles of the organization. The word "sovereignty" is a highly abstruse one to which are given many confused, and sometimes intentionally confusing, meanings.

"Sovereignty" was introduced into political terminology in 1576 by a French lawyer, Jean Bodin, who defined it as the "supreme power of the state over citizens and subjects, unrestrained by law." Bodin was concerned with formulating a legal justification for the exercise by the monarch of supreme and undivided power as a means of consolidating the authority of the central government within the state. He sought a legal rationalization of the authority of the monarchical sovereign or the powers of the crown to oppose the disruptive and decentralizing tendencies of feudalism, and to justify centering in the monarch the responsibility for the conduct of foreign affairs.

Although absolute monarchs no longer reign, the concept of the sovereign state endures. And today, the state may claim itself sovereign in the sense that it alone, through the agencies provided by its fundamental law, has exclusive power to legislate for its citizens. As one authority put it in a famous arbitral award, "Sovereignty in the relations between states signifies independence. Independence in regard to a portion of the globe is the right to exercise therein, to the exclusion of any other state, the functions of a state." This legal conception of sovereignty, if carried no further, would create no significant international problems.

But some have sought to interpret the doctrine in an external sense to mean that there can be no earthly authority above or beyond the state that may impose law or restraint upon it. The maintenance of this view places great difficulties in the way of organizing international law; treaties have no legal effect, but become mere promises; member states of international organizations cannot be obligated to any commitment or responsibility whatever. To view sovereignty as conferring upon the state the exercise of unrestrained political power is to allow the concept to become a justification for the conduct of international relations on the basis of power alone. This can only produce—as indeed it often has in the past—international anarchy and chaos.

It is acceptable to designate the state as "sovereign," when the term is intended to connote the state's power to make law within its own territory, its position of independence and of separateness from other states, and its capacity to enjoy full membership in the international community. Nevertheless, many scholars have insisted that the term "sovereignty" should be discarded from the terminology of international relations as both practically and theoretically meaningless. The simpler term, "independence," they assert, could be more aptly and usefully employed.

Other Persons in International Law

There are a number of political entities in the international community which—because their exercise of independence and full state powers is impaired, or because they are not states at all but do exercise some kinds of governmental powers—have some status in and are recognized by international law. They are easier to describe individually than to classify generally; however, a few main types may be noted.

States under Special Limitations. One type of state lacking full legal freedom of action in international relations, though enjoying control over its internal affairs, is the perpetually neutral or *neutralized state,* which has accepted a guarantee of its territorial integrity by other states and in return has renounced an intention to participate in war. This position was arranged for Switzerland by a treaty of 1815; for Belgium from 1831 to 1919; for Luxembourg from 1867 to 1948; and for Austria in 1955. Such states may have normal diplomatic relations with other states and may be armed; but they agree to abstain from alliances and to take up arms only to defend themselves.

Another instance of restricted status was the case of Cuba, between

1901 and 1934, when it was obligated to the United States not to alienate any of its territory, under certain circumstances to permit American intervention therein, and to accept other restrictions on its freedom of action. After World War I, the succession states of eastern Europe were obliged to afford by treaty certain guarantees to the minority populations within their territories. After World War II for some years, both Germany and Japan were forbidden by the Allies to possess armaments.

Dependent States. Another group of political entities includes those whose international personality is obscure or seriously limited. A protected state, or *protectorate,* is placed under the protection of another state, in return for which it relinquishes control over its foreign affairs. Monaco was placed under the protection of Sardinia in 1815, and subsequently under that of France in 1918; San Marino agreed to a treaty of protection with Italy in 1862; Japan obtained a protectorate over Korea by treaty in 1905, and then annexed it outright in 1910. Brunei is a protectorate of Great Britain; Sikkim stands in this relationship to India. Protectorates are denied the right to engage in any relations with third states except through the intermediary protecting state, though they normally retain control of the powers of internal government.

A *vassal state,* or a state under suzerainty, was a type well known as recently as the nineteenth century. It was one ordinarily in the process of becoming independent, so that it enjoyed the grant of a considerable measure of autonomy from the parent state; however, the latter still retained control of its foreign affairs. Russia and China recognized Outer Mongolia as under Chinese suzerainty by declaration in 1913; its independence was recognized in 1945. As other examples, Egypt was considered a vassal of Turkey until 1914; the tiny republic of Andorra has been under the co-suzerainty of France and the Spanish Bishop of Urgel since 1278. Andorra appears to be the last remainder of this feudal status.

In the turbulent years prior to and following World War II, still another type of dependent state appeared, the *satellite.* To be sure, this is a political, rather than a legal term, applied to states allowed to keep many outward manifestations of control of their domestic affairs and external relations, yet dominated through ideological, political, economic, and military means of various kinds by the paramount state. Japan's creation and control of Manchukuo, and Germany's of

Croatia and Slovakia are examples. Contemporary satellite relationships are demonstrated in Communist China's influence over Albania and North Vietnam, and in the Soviet Union's paramountcy in Outer Mongolia, Bulgaria, and other east European states. Given the ideological ferment at work within the communist bloc, however, these relationships seem subject to change without notice.

Members of Unions and Federal States. Certain political associations possess common organization or ties of various sorts which condition their international personality. The members thereof may enjoy essentially unimpaired international status or may be denied it entirely. The members of the British Commonwealth of Nations, for example, defined their status at the Imperial Conference of 1926 as "autonomous communities within the British Empire, equal in status, in no way subordinate one to another in any aspect of their domestic or external affairs, though united by a common allegiance to the Crown. . . ." Today, even Crown allegiance is not essential, since several of the members are republics and recognize the Queen as Head of the Commonwealth. Consequently, the *Commonwealth countries*, the United Kingdom, Canada, Australia, New Zealand, India, Pakistan, Ghana, Nigeria, and roughly two-dozen other former portions of the British Empire exercise all of the rights of fully independent states. The association is neither an alliance nor a federation; as a British Commonwealth Secretary, Duncan Sandys, observed: "To us, the Commonwealth is, above all, a collective relationship in which we consult together, think together and, as far as possible, work together for the advancement of broad, common objectives."

The Constitution of the U.S.S.R., as amended in 1944, authorizes its fifteen Union Republics "the right to enter into direct relations with foreign states, to conclude agreements with them, and exchange diplomatic and consular representatives with them," and to maintain their "own military formations." It is not clear what, if any, international status the Soviet Constitution intended to confer upon the constituent republics by this authorization. Two of them, the Byelorussian and Ukrainian Republics, have been given separate memberships in the United Nations; but this action was taken in recognition of the Soviet Union's political importance and not of the constitutional provisions mentioned.

A *confederation* usually is composed of a number of independent states bound together by a compact and with certain common organs of government. The confederation is not recognized as a state in international law because its members retain their international personality. A *federal state*, on the other hand, is a single entity; and the members of its federal union, as in the case of the United States, are denied any international status. According to the United States Constitution, the individual states may not "enter into any treaty, alliance, or confederation," nor, without the consent of Congress, "enter into any agreement or compact with another state, or with a foreign power, or engage in war. . . ." The states of the American Union are thus not states at all in the sense we have been using the term, and they are not sovereign.

Dependencies, Mandates, and Trust Territories. A *dependency* is a territory distinct from the metropolitan area of the state that holds title to it and exercises legal control over it. The term *colony* is sometimes used synonymously—though strictly speaking a colony has been settled by the citizens of its controlling state, who remain subject to it. At the end of World War I Germany and Turkey were obliged by the peace treaties to relinquish their dependent and colonial possessions. By Article 22 of the League of Nations Covenant, these were placed as *mandated territories* under the control of various mandatory powers who were given their administration in behalf of the League of Nations. Most of the fifteen mandated territories have now become independent states. The mandate system was replaced at the end of World War II by an international trusteeship system of the United Nations, whereunder, by agreement, remaining mandated territories and certain others have been constituted as *trust territories*. Dependencies and colonies have no international personality recognized by third states; but mandated and trust territories have some limited international status, because the arrangements for their control are the product of international agreement.

International Entities. Increasingly in recent years various bodies and organizations, which are not states but associations of them, have acquired such important governmental functions as to give them some degree of international personality. These *international entities*, created by treaty or convention, include the general international organizations, as we may describe the League of Nations and the United Nations; the regional organizations, such as the Council of Europe and the European Coal and Steel Community; and various specialized and functional organizations, such as the International Labor Organization and the Universal Postal Union.

In a decision handed down in 1949, the International Court of Justice stated that the United Nations "was intended to exercise and enjoy, and is in fact exercising and enjoying, functions and rights which can only be explained on the basis of the possession of a large measure of international personality. . . . It is a subject of international law and capable of possessing international rights and duties. . . ." The United Nations Charter (Article 105) stipulates that "The organization shall enjoy in the territory of each of its Members such privileges and immunities as are necessary for the fulfillment of its purposes. Representatives of the Members of the United Nations and officials of the Organization shall similarly enjoy such privileges and immunities. . . ."

The European Economic Community (Common Market) formed by the Treaty of Rome (1958)—originally joining France, West Germany, Italy, and the Benelux countries—again is a body, along with now more than a hundred other such organizations, that must be recognized as clearly possessing a degree of international personality.

Manifestly, such entities as these are not sovereign states, but they have a capacity to enter into relations with states. They may administer territory and property, confer a degree of diplomatic immunity on their officials, be parties to suits before courts, impose fines, and so on. To the present, their status rests largely on treaty; before a clearer definition of their international status can be made, the present rules of international law will have to be considerably extended.

III. The International Community

The aggregation of states in the world was described as recently as the nineteenth century as the "family of nations." Obviously, this has ceased to be an appropriate term, when association is no longer limited primarily to the sovereign princes of Europe; and as we have seen, it is not "nations," strictly speaking, which enter into association, but "states." Let us examine, then, what is better described as the "community of states."

The Community of States. The term "community" is variously employed to describe a body politic, or a body of persons having common interests; it indicates the presence of a group who share, or have an identity or likeness of, interests. There can be no doubt that the some four billion people who live in the world today, and are divided among some one hundred and fifty independent political entities, constitute a community. These states do share at least existence on the same globe, and therefore must coexist to some degree.

Yet it is a community not made up of uniform or homogeneous units. Some of the states existed with a high degree of integration before the concept of statehood originated; others are creations of the last few years. They display extreme differences in area, population, geographic character, military power, wealth, degree of civilization, and form of government. Nevertheless, there is present something of a legal basis of association for the states of the world. By general acceptance and definition, the international community is composed of all states which accept the rules of international law. Limited in character in so many ways as this legal system is—a subject we shall discuss later in this chapter—the community has achieved something more than the anarchy of the jungle, or the vigilante-maintained order of the frontier. But many vestiges of these conditions still remain.

The Creation and Recognition of New States. A few states were original members of the international community; most, however, have achieved membership by admission, granted by the other members through the process of recognition. Recognition is the act by which one or more states indicate that they are willing to have full diplomatic relations with the new state, and that they acknowledge this state as independent and capable of acting responsibly for the people and territory it controls. In the process it is tacitly assumed that the relationships between these states will be governed by the accepted rules of international law. Usually, the major powers take the lead, and when they have granted recognition the smaller states follow. Though recognition is occasionally granted collectively, it is ordinarily an individual action. An occasion for recognition also arises when the government of a state is overthrown and replaced by violent means. Then all other states must decide whether they are willing to acknowledge the legitimacy of the new political regime and to undertake normal diplomatic relations with it.

In each case, a state is free to grant or withhold recognition to a new state or government, and there is no right to demand it. Because the granting of recognition is often based upon political rather than legal considerations, states may withhold it as a matter of national policy, as when most states refused to concede the existence of an independent state of Manchukuo in territory wrested from China by Japan in 1931. Further, they may even use the act of recognition on occasion to help ensure the achievement of the independence supposedly being recognized, as in the case of the precipitous American recognition of Panama in 1903. The occasion for the recognition of new governments arises even more frequently, and in granting it, states are especially prone to pass a self-interested judgment on the new regime. Most states, for example, were in no haste to recognize the Bolshevik government of Soviet Russia after 1917, and many have been even more reluctant to do so in the case of the Communist government of China.

The creation of new states may take place under several circumstances. The most common is when a dependent territory capable of undertaking its own government and maintaining its independence is separated from the state which has been in control of it. This may come after a successful colonial revolution, as in the case of the American colonies, or by peaceful agreement, as in the case of the Philippine Republic, India, Pakistan, and Ceylon. Occasionally, an existing state has been dissolved, as when in 1905 Sweden and Norway voluntarily separated as independent states, or when the Austro-Hungarian Empire was divided into a number of new states by the peace treaties in 1919. A new state may also be created by joining together several existing ones, as was the case with Italy in 1860, and with Germany in 1871. The contemporary era has been prodigious in the birth of new states; their number has more than doubled since World War II.

The Diversity of States in the Community. The members of the international community display the widest kind of diversity. They range in number of people from China with an estimated 800,000,000 population and India with over 560,000,000 to Iceland with 200,000 and the Sheikhdom of Bahrain with 220,000. There are equally great variations in area. The Soviet Union covers a territory some 8,600,000 square miles in extent, and Canada 3,800,000; on the other hand, Israel possesses less than 8,000 square miles, and Lebanon, barely 4,-000. The populations of the United States and the United Kingdom are more than 95 percent literate, while those of Haiti and Saudi Arabia are more than 90 percent illiterate. States may be composed of island chains, as are Japan, the Philippine Republic, and Indonesia, or they may be entirely landlocked, as are Austria, Switzerland, and Bolivia. The United States and western Europe account for nearly two-thirds of the world's total production; national per capita average income ranges from over $3,500 annually in the United States to $75 in some underdeveloped countries.

Consequences of Membership in the International Community. The legal position of the state in the international community can be generally described, but not very accurately defined. The classic treatises on international law discuss in some detail the "rights" of members of the community, though they give much less attention to the "duties." As a means of assuring some minimal order in the community and recognizing the personality of the state, attempts are still being made to get agreement upon what these should be.

Two efforts in this direction have been the Inter-American Convention on the Rights and Duties of States, signed by the twenty-one American republics in 1933 and later included in the Charter of the Organization of American States; and the Draft Declaration on Rights and Duties of States, prepared by the United Nations International Law Commission and submitted to United Nations members for consideration. The two documents stipulate that the rights of states include independence, self-defense, choice of governmental form, legal equality, and the exercise of jurisdiction over their own territory. Duties involve such obligations as not to intervene in the affairs of other states, not to recognize territorial acquisitions obtained by force, and to settle disputes by peaceful means.

That the terms "rights" and "duties" in this context are not entirely satisfactory must be acknowledged. It is a legal axiom that for every right there must be a remedy; yet the international community has as yet created no court before which a state may be assured even the fundamental right to exist. The establishment of such a system is still an aspiration, and the rights and duties described in the two documents above are really only principles of desirable and responsible conduct for states. This is not to say that propositions such as these have no significance; they are statements of what states do expect in their relations with each other. The widely adverse reactions to interventions of recent years in Hungary, Cuba, and Czechoslovakia, for example, lend testimony to the general resentment of states to such acts of intervention.

Indeed, we should observe that international relations are conducted practically as if such rights and duties do exist. Each state does expect equally, for example, to be entitled to grant or withhold assent to any new rule of international law, to be capable of becoming a party to a treaty, and to have one vote—in the absence of agreeing otherwise—in any international conference or organization. Certainly no state will concede that it may not be its own judge of what measures it may take in the interests of its self-defense and security. It expects to send and receive diplomatic representatives; and much diplomatic protocol is devoted to the preservation of the illusion, at least, of state equality. Each state determines the laws which will apply to the persons and things within its territory, as well as the conditions under which those who are alien may enter it. It undertakes to assume the protection of its citizens abroad, and holds accountable any government which fails to exercise due diligence in protecting the safety of its nationals. The history of diplomatic practice is replete with instances wherein one government has paid substantial damages to another for its negligence in such matters.

Independence and Interdependence. It is ironic that, as more and more states achieve independence in the international community, they also become more and more interdependent. A century ago, when Europe was mainly composed of large states such as France, Germany, Austria-Hungary, and Russia, the states of Europe could be much more independent of each other than they can today, when the continent is divided among more than two dozen. A state's real independence, in the sense of its freedom of action, is considerably dependent upon the amount of power and influence it can exercise, and what other and stronger states are willing to concede to it. The many newly created small states, therefore, do not necessarily enjoy a large measure of assertable independence.

One cannot observe the history of international relations since World War II without seeing how great is the fiction of state independence and how extensively most states are dependent upon others. In recent years, the United States has been providing financial aid by grants or loans and technical or military assistance to at least a hundred countries. And several dozen other states, on both sides of the Iron Curtain, have undertaken foreign assistance programs of some sort. Also, the postwar tendency of states to organize for economic purposes, as in the European Economic Community and the European Coal and Steel Community, and to associate as international pressure groups, as in the case of the Arab League, the communist bloc, the Latin American bloc, and so on, constitute further evidence of the inability of single states to promote their interests successfully by reliance solely upon their own efforts. The tendency of states as well to organize international alliances for their collective self-defense offers additional evidence of the lack of ability to ensure their security solely with their own resources.

We should also keep in mind that though states are the persons of the international community, it is people who have international relationships. Official relationships are conducted by government officers and diplomatic representatives; otherwise, the people who cross international boundaries are tourists, businessmen, students, soldiers and sailors, and so on. Millions of people would not live well, nor some perhaps live at all, if goods and funds could not exchange internationally: the position of the populations of Great Britain, Switzerland, and Israel, for example, obviously bears testimony to this fact. As self-sufficient a country as the United States depends heavily, or exclusively in some cases, on foreign supplies of oil, rubber, nickel, chromium, newsprint, coffee, bananas, and many other items. Many of the world's leading corporations—such as British Petroleum, Royal Dutch Shell, Standard Oil of New Jersey, International Harvester, Union Carbide, and International Telephone and Telegraph—are examples of business enterprises international in character and operations. Most persons engaged in the scholarly and scientific professions, in art, music, and religion, inevitably have interests, and frequently associations, which transcend their national community.

We have indicated some of the paradoxical and anachronistic features of the modern international community. A discussion of the problems and possibilities of providing it with international organization requires first some examination of the legal basis of the international community, to which we now turn, and of the dynamic forces at work in the community of states, which will be undertaken in the next chapter.

IV. International Law

Definition. "International law" is the body of rules and principles commonly observed by states as legally binding in their relationships. It undertakes to perform for the international community—though far more imperfectly—functions somewhat similar to those performed by the body of municipal law within the domestic community; that is, it is used as a regularizing force upon the actions of its subjects, independent states. It originated because necessity and convenience induced states to conduct their relations with some degree of uniformity and order. While it assumes the basic independence of states, it arose as a product of community life as states realized that international anarchy is impossible. Its concepts have sometimes been criticized as unreal and utopian, and some writers have sought to argue that there really is no such thing as "international" law; at the other extreme, its most ambitious exponents have claimed far more for it than at present seems at all realizable. Before we examine some of the features of international law, we should be clear as to what it is not.

International Law Distinguished from International Practices. Some of the misunderstandings about the nature of international law may be avoided if we make certain distinctions at the outset. First, international law should be distinguished from international ethics. There is, of course, no lack of views as to how states ought to act in their relations with others. To the extent that there is consensus upon the principles of justice to which state conduct should ideally conform—and of the moral duty for states to observe them—we have a body of international ethics, inadequately developed as it may be. But these are not rules of law which states are obliged to observe.

We should not confuse international law with international comity. The latter consists of practices which are observed as a matter of courtesy and convenience between states, but which, again, involve no obligation. Canada and the United States, for example, allow each other's citizens to enter their territory for short visits without passports, but they need not do so and do not extend this privilege to other foreign travelers. Still further, international law is not the same thing as foreign policy. A state's foreign policy lies in the more or less consistent attitudes and courses of action it adopts in its relations with other states and areas. The Monroe Doctrine, a long-standing principle of American foreign policy, has sought to bar the intervention of non-American states in the affairs of the western hemisphere. Yet the policy cannot legally forbid other states to undertake such intervention; and the Doctrine has been effective not as a rule of law, but because of the power of the United States.

We are concerned here only with public international law. Private international law deals primarily with the position of individuals who, because of diversity of nationality or national jurisdictions, are subjected to two or more sets of national law and thus require some reconciliation of their status. This body of law is also known as the "conflict of laws"—which more aptly indicates its nature. Similar to this in certain ways are the rules of admiralty and maritime law, which comprise the usages and principles accepted by commercial nations in regulating maritime commerce. Both of these branches of law are applied in the main by national courts.

International law is to be distinguished, finally, from those obligations imposed by treaties, which are written agreements between two or more states. Generally speaking, treaties are not international law, but are analogous in the relations between states to contracts between persons of municipal law. Although their obligations are expected to be observed in good faith, as indicated by the ancient doctrine of *pacta sunt servanda* (agreements must be observed), their terms are subject to change at the agreement of the parties. The great many simple bipartite treaties cover matters that are of concern only to the immediate parties, dealing with such subjects as commercial relations, immigration, boundaries, and extradition. On the other hand, treaties may be employed specifically to create rules of international law. Such "lawmaking" treaties are multipartite in character, and to be effective generally they must be ratified throughout the international community. The terms "treaty" and "convention" are commonly used synonymously—though, strictly speaking, a convention is an international agreement of a technical character, and one of less permanent importance.

The Development of International Law

The Origins of International Law. The Peace of Westphalia (1648) constitutes the first formal recognition of the modern nation-state system; it also marks the origin of the modern system of international law. As we have noted, states began to regularize some of their relations in earlier times: the ancient maritime law, the customs of the Hellenes, the *jus gentium* of Rome, the laws of the Hanseatic League and other medieval trading cities all evidence this. The substantial development of a "law of nations," however, was dependent upon the existence of an international community of states, which emerged in the seventeenth century.

The existence of a new state system inevitably stimulated the interests of jurists and scholars in its resulting legal problems. Although several writers of the sixteenth century—notably Vitoria, Ayala, and Gentilis—produced commentaries on the international practices of the times, the title "father of international law" is generally conceded to Hugo Grotius, a Dutch scholar and diplomat. Appalled by the international lawlessness of his day, Grotius searched for the existence of some law higher than that of individual monarchs which could restrain the anarchic tendency of interstate relations. His major work, *De jure belli ac pacis* ("On the Law of War and Peace"), published in 1625, exerted an immediate influence in Europe. Concerned more with the laws of war than of peace, it was the first systematic treatment of the whole subject and was mainly responsible for the introduction of the study of international law in the universities of seventeenth-century Europe. It served as an inspiration for numerous other studies of the subject to follow; and its authority is still appealed to by writers and publicists today.

The international law developed thereafter did not become a tidy and easily ascertained body of rules. During its formative period in the seventeenth century, states drew first on fundamental precepts of justice and right which were sought in the principles of natural law —that law inherent in the universe and existing independently of any promulgation by man. Grotius employed its tenets to provide a rational basis for his system of international law, and in this practice he was subsequently supported by other writers of the seventeenth and eighteenth centuries. Thus, in the earlier stages, the principles of natural justice, reason, and equity provided a source of international law; and its rules gained much in ethical content thereby.

Once the concept of an existing body of international law became widespread, it was substantially expanded by a second source—that of rules based upon consent and actually observed—positive law. Positive law as distinguished from natural law is established by some human authority. Positive international law, then, rested upon state consent to its rules, which might be expressed either in custom or agreement. Custom is, of course, the oldest source of law generally, and inevitably made a large contribution to the original rules of international law. Expressed in practice, usage, habit, and sentiment, customary law enjoys a most powerful sanction; states are led to observe its rules because they are accustomed to do so. Agreement, on the other hand, involves explicit consent, most commonly obtained by adopting treaties or conventions in which states consciously acknowledge their acceptance of a particular rule.

For some time, there was argument over whether the foundations of the system of international law should be theoretical or practical. Disputes of schools of jurists were overtaken by facts, however; the eighteenth century saw international law expanded increasingly on the exclusive basis of consent, and its progress since has rested more on development by general agreement to specific rules of conduct than upon appeals to abstract principles of justice. As a source of international law, then, positive law has emphasized practicality: rules are accepted as binding when states acknowledge them as law and fail when they do not.

The Nature of International Law

The Evidences of International Law. The term "evidences" of international law is used to designate the various documents and acts that are adduced to prove the existence of a rule of international law. In some cases it is possible to find adequate evidence from a single international act. More often, however, the proof of a specific rule is very difficult, particularly because a large portion of international law rests upon customary development. At what point, therefore, does a particular international practice acquire the necessary general acceptance to be regarded as a binding legal rule? To answer this question is often as puzzling as to determine at what precise moment, say, a set of wagon tracks becomes a road. Generally speaking, when evidence exists that all or nearly all states have given express or tacit recognition to the obligatory character of a principle, it becomes an effective rule of international law. It is not enough to show that states commonly act in a certain way, for such usage may be indicative of no more than international comity, state policy, or convenience; what is required is that the evidence demonstrates that states do believe the rule to be a binding one. There are fewer absolute rules than is commonly imagined, for such general agreement among states is extremely difficult to attain.

The Statute of the International Court of Justice (1945) provides that in the general order of their obligation, the principal evidences of international law are the following: (1) Treaties, conventions, and other international agreements by which states avowedly declare their acceptance of international rules. By no means do all treaties have this purpose; most, indeed, as we have pointed out, look only to the establishment of contractual agreements between states relative to matters of immediate and mutual interest. The number of treaties that are intentionally "lawmaking" ones, however, has tremendously increased in recent years; and it seems likely that international law will continue to have its greatest development through this means. (2) Customary rules, which have originated in the practice of states and have come to be so widely accepted as to create obligation, represent definite state consent. The evidences of customary law may be found in many places: historical documents recording international practice, state papers, the records of foreign offices, the practices of international organizations, and even state laws. (3) General principles of law recognized by civilized states. Here many rules derive authority, not because they are a part of the legal system of particular states, but because they reflect substantial principles of justice to which virtually universal adherence can be found. Particularly influential in developing rules on this basis have been arbitral tribunals, prize and admiralty courts, the international courts, and the highest national courts, such as the United States Supreme Court. (4) Decisions and writings of jurists, publicists, and other authorities on international law who are qualified to express opinions on the basis of their learning and experience. Such works, a justice of the United States Supreme Court stated on one occasion, "are resorted to by judicial tribunals, not for the speculation of their authors concerning what the law ought to be, but for trustworthy evidence of what the law really is." One wishing to acquaint himself with the extent of the cosmopolitan resources available to demonstrate the rules of international law should examine a standard casebook on the subject.

The Enforcement of International Law. Another unusual characteristic of international law is found in the arrangements—and lack of them—for its enforcement. The doctrines of international law were developed concurrently with those of state sovereignty, with a resulting international legal system in which the enforcement of rules against states was left to the states themselves. This has not meant that international law has gone unenforced, but that compliance with it must be essentially voluntary.

The fact that the rules are based upon consent and agreement makes it a matter of simple convenience for states commonly to observe them. The very nature of international law produces a close coincidence between its rules and the standards of conduct which states are ordinarily willing to observe; they have never accepted rules which substantially limited their freedom of action in matters of vital importance. There is also a distinct advantage for states in their reciprocal relations to observe rules with which they expect others to comply. Further, states may obey the rules out of long-standing habit, because of the influence of world opinion, and in a desire to be of good conscience and reputation. These forces are not insignificant; habit, convenience, and self-interest foster the usual observance of international law as they do, ultimately, of all law.

But observance is not the same thing as enforcement. When a state commits an intentional and flagrant violation of the law, who is to assume responsibility to see that the breach of law is redressed and justice done? According to international law, only the state or states injured as a result are normally expected to take notice of the matter and bring the offending state to terms. The devices available for this purpose have included retaliation and reprisals, blockades and economic pressures, forceful intervention, and war. In effect, enforcement rests upon the offended state's ability to use its national power, or self-help. And if the injured state is the weaker of the two—unwilling or unable to apply measures of force, fearful of risking a war, unable to obtain any assistance, or for any other reason takes no action—the violation will likely go unpunished. On the other hand, if the injured state is the more powerful, it may be quick in retaliating on the slightest provocation, may apply force far beyond what is required to redress the injury, or depending on the international balance of power, may even find its superior power disadvantageous.

Under these circumstances, each state acts as its own attorney, judge, and executioner; there is no compulsory machinery for enforcement by and in the interests of the entire international community. And though the frequency of clear violations of international law is not great, the inadequacy of the system of enforcement is a substantial obstacle to the development of rules that can regulate much more than the procedural aspect of international relations. In the present century, through the League of Nations and the United Nations, the international community has provided procedures for the application of international sanctions. These will be discussed in a later chapter. It must be noted, however, that they were intended mainly to deal with breaches of the peace, and not with the ordinary rules of international law.

The Scope and Content of International Law. The rules of public international law apply almost entirely to states, who are thus the persons or subjects of its rules. Ordinarily, individuals are subjected to regulation by it only indirectly through their own governments. Thus, the Constitution of the United States, for example, gives Congress the power to "define and punish . . . offenses against the law of nations," and a decision of the Supreme Court has stated that "international law is a part of our law and must be ascertained and administered by the courts of justice of appropriate jurisdiction, as often as questions of right depending upon it are duly presented for their determination." The rules of international law do operate, however, to give a partial status to some entities which do not qualify as states. Thus, international organizations and entities, belligerents, insurgents, prisoners of war, pirates, and individuals in certain circumstances and certain areas may be subject to some of its rules.

Traditionally, the subject matter of international law has been grouped under three headings: the laws of peace, war, and neutrality. The laws of war have been developed primarily on a conventional basis, and are concerned with such matters as the rights and duties of combatants, rules for the conduct of hostilities, treatment of enemy property and nationals, prisoners of war, and occupation of conquered territory. This portion of the rules has tended to shrink in the present century, if only because the character of modern warfare since 1914 has produced weapons and techniques that scarcely lend themselves to the humanization of hostilities. It is important to note that, contrary to popular belief, the rules of international law do not prohibit war in every circumstance; they not only acknowledge its existence but recognize the results of conquest arising out of it. To be sure, its rules do seek to regularize hostilities, holding them to some civilized standards. But war itself has not thereby been made illegal; rather, it has only been regularized as a necessary, if unpleasant, evil.

The laws of neutrality, developed largely in the nineteenth century, govern the position of states and their nationals who are not parties to a war, their rights and duties as regards the belligerents, and such subjects as blockade and prize law. But again, the wars fought in the twentieth century have made many of the traditional rules respecting neutral status anachronistic. It is possible to argue that with the emergence of schemes of collective security, neutrality is an untenable position in the face of worldwide total war, and that if hostilities are to occur primarily when force is being applied by the majority of states in the community to an international malefactor, no such status can be allowed.

The laws of peace, so-called, cover the principal topics of international law—among them, persons of international law, rights and duties of states, state succession, jurisdiction, boundaries and territorial waters, nationality, aliens, asylum, treaties, and diplomatic and consular status and immunities. Space does not permit a discussion of these rules. We can do little more than to suggest that, under such a rubric as jurisdiction, for example, exist rules which determine to what extent and over what persons and things a state may enforce its law. These include laws governing the acquisition of territory, fixing of national boundaries, status of vessels and persons on the high seas, control of airspace, exemptions from jurisdiction, questions of national conflict of jurisdiction, and such matters.

The Legal Character of International Law. One following the discussion so far may well ask: is international law really law? The answer to this question turns essentially, of course, on how the term "law" is defined—and there are few terms more diversely employed. The positive school of jurisprudence accepts the definition of law enunciated by an English jurist, John Austin, as "a rule laid down for the guidance of an intelligent being by an intelligent being having power over him." This definition emphasizes law as an emanation from superior state authority enforced against political inferiors, violations of which can be penalized by the superior. Necessarily, this definition will not include international law within its specifications. Arguing from this point of view, then, a negative answer to the question might be this: since the sovereign state recognizes no political superior, the rules of international law cannot be the commands of such a superior; a state may thus reject the obligation of any particular rule; there are no sanctions or external forces to compel obedience; the very idea of rules binding a state is incompatible with state sovereignty, or unlimited power; and, therefore, the rules may be violated with impunity. Thus international law is relegated to being essentially a body of moral obligations, but one of no compelling legal effect.

However, another definition, accepted by the historical jurists, identifies law with custom; that is to say, law is what has been sanctioned by immemorial usage, and the test of law is in its observance and not in its source of authority. This definition rejects the Austinian view as more nearly explaining legislation than law, and as being narrowly restrictive. By the test of the historical school of jurists, then, international law may qualify as true law. In this view—that law may be derived from sources other than the command of the sovereign—an affirmative case is presented. It is argued that historically law arose out of custom and was not originally considered to be man-made; that consent is as important as authority in obtaining obedience, and states do consent to be bound by the rules of international law; that sanctions are available for its enforcement, ranging from the influence of public opinion to outright war; that the sovereignty of the state must necessarily be subject to limitation externally; and that all laws are violated on occasion, but consent largely determines whether particular rules are or are not regularly observed.

How is a choice to be made between these opposing arguments? What is evident, of course, is that neither the sources nor the sanctions of international law are identical with those of domestic law. But regardless of the theoretical line of reasoning pursued to define the concept of "true" law, any resulting conclusions which exclude international law still face a barrier of hard facts. As we have observed, abundant evidence is available to show that states consider themselves and other states legally bound by its rules; they enter into solemn engagements defining these rules; their national legislatures, courts, and sometimes their constitutions, acknowledge the rules; and they join in the creation of international tribunals empowered to decide disputes according to international law. All over the world, litigants win and lose cases in national courts on the basis of rules of international law. The rules of international law do, perhaps, lie at the extreme frontier of law, and are in a less advanced and more imperfect state than those of municipal law; but no great harm is done to the concept of law by including them.

An Evaluation of International Law

The Contributions of International Law. In formulating a balance sheet for the effectiveness of international law, we can show that as a force in the international community it has made important and useful contributions. Too much should not be claimed for it, assuredly, and we must not deny its imperfections; however, we need not be disdainful of its accomplishments. International law is of some significance if only for the fact that it has been brought into existence at all. Its very concept posits the existence of some sort of community of states—if indeed a rather primitive one—and a body of rules defining it. Lacking this concept of a community, we could make no progress toward its ordering at all. International law provides evidence of the willingness of states to make some concessions in their freedom of action to the need for organizing an international community. It also has had the effect of regularizing to some extent the conduct of warfare, particularly to the end of mitigating its more barbaric features and minimizing, where possible, its consequences for combatants and noncombatants. As defined by the Geneva Convention for the Amelioration of the Condition of the Wounded and Sick in Armed Forces in the Field (1949), for example, "wilful killing, torture or inhuman treatment, including biological experiments, wilfully causing great suffering or serious injury to body or health, and extensive destruction and appropriation of property, not justified by military necessity and carried out unlawfully and wantonly" are "grave breaches" of the agreement. Even so, shocking lapses from these standards are still encountered today.

The body of international law further provides an extensive collection of rules regulating the conduct of international relations on a peaceful basis. The broad scope of its subject matter has already been indicated; but attention might be drawn here to the single topic of state jurisdiction, which has been defined in considerable detail and has largely eliminated the endless misunderstandings that might result between states if there were no accepted rules on the topic. International law has been in a constant, if not always even, process of growth; and one cannot turn to any half-century period since 1648 without remarking important additions to its rules and its obligations. In spite of admitted setbacks within periods of international conflict, and recurring attacks on international order made by totalitarian dictatorships, the obligations of international law have reduced some areas of state irresponsibility.

International law has led, finally, to the elaboration of the machinery of international government. Increasingly, the need for the extension and refinement of its rules has brought the adoption of new multipartite lawmaking treaties and conventions, the calling of international conferences upon legal subjects, and the creation of an increasing number of international administrative and judicial bodies. The broad experience of mankind suggests that the development of law, historically, has been antecedent to the organization of elaborate governmental machinery; and for the international community, this principle is probably not an exception. Much of the present international organization could, indeed, come into existence only after some sort of body of international law existed. Certainly, the task of organizing the United Nations would have been immeasurably more difficult in the absence of any such rules. If international law has not played the fully effective role that might be hoped for it in the international community, its contributions are not at all negligible.

The Deficiencies of International Law. The contributions of international law to the problem of world order, however, cannot obscure its deficiencies. Its shortcomings are easy to discover and, to one not acquainted with the slow and painful process by which its rules have been brought to their present development, might be considered so serious as to damage its whole structure. At best, international law stands as a motley and haphazard collection of rules, having grown slowly within a limited range. It fails to provide any rules at many of the points where international friction is most intense. In those areas where states have been unwilling to see their freedom of action limited, as in the practice of imperialism or the promotion of military security, the community of states has failed to agree upon any rules. International law also places excessive emphasis on state sovereignty, requiring the individual consent of every state to each new rule. Thus each state is encouraged to oppose any rule which might prove to be especially inconvenient to it. The result is that *inter*national law is a law *between* states, but not a *supra*national law *above* states.

International law is seriously deficient in legislative bodies which might actively participate in the process of developing new rules and reinterpreting older ones, as well as inadequately equipped with international tribunals to administer these rules. So long as the development of new rules is left to the slow-moving process of custom, or to the calling of infrequent international conferences for the adoption of lawmaking treaties, the rules will continue to lag behind the needs. International law further lacks adequate agencies for its enforcement. In our domestic communities, we have long abandoned the idea that rules will enforce themselves, or that an individual may take the law into his own hands; and yet that is essentially the case internationally. Finally, international law has not prohibited resort to war or the use of force as an ultimate means of settling disputes between states. Indeed, the existence of the rules of war as part of international law has had the effect of legalizing the employment of war and force, so long as they are confined to certain prescribed practices. Whatever else a community may hope for from the existence of law, the most important expectations include at least a demand for the maintenance of peace and order, and the exercise of force only by constituted and controlled authority. By this test, international law is woefully inadequate.

The Future of International Law. The more serious deficiencies of international law have brought a number of proposals concerning what remedial steps the international community could take if such law were to be brought to its full effectiveness in contributing to international order and peace. Some of the more important proposals are the following: (1) to formulate rules extending to those areas of state action as yet unregulated, and to codify existing rules which now rest largely on a customary basis; (2) to establish appropriate machinery of a lawmaking and law-interpreting character to keep pace with the needs of a dynamic international community; (3) to create adequate agencies for the enforcement of international law to control the powerful forces that are unleashed in the community, and to prevent the irresponsible use of force by its individual members; (4) to bring states to recognize a legal duty to settle their disputes by pacific means conformable to previously established principles; (5) to extend the rules, finally, to apply directly to individual human beings as its subjects, both in order to hold to legal accountability persons guilty of waging aggressive warfare and committing crimes against international society, but also to provide a measure of protection to the inhabitants of each state against inhumane treatment by their own governments.

These suggested essentials for an adequate body of international law, it ought to be clear, will not soon be achieved in the present world atmosphere. We have undoubtedly lost ground in these directions during the present century. The waging of two total world wars and widespread guerrilla wars, with consequent periods of international instability and tension, have strained many of the well-established rules of international law to the breaking point. By the end of World War II, new weapons—such as submarines, airplanes, rockets, and atomic bombs—had led to the complete disregard of traditional rules seeking to distinguish combatants and noncombatants, and to prevent the conduct of hostilities against the latter. Neutral rights counted for less and less, and became increasingly incapable of winning respect when virtually all of the world's military power was drawn into the struggle.

Another fragmenting effect on international law results from the attitudes of the communist states, which tend to pick and choose among rules and their interpretation according to their usefulness to the communist cause, and from the attitudes of the vast number of newly independent nonwestern states, which incline to see some traditional rules as framed only to the advantage of the advanced western states, and therefore no longer appropriate and binding upon them. With the world thus divided into three mutually suspicious and dissentient camps, the prospect dims for a rapid development of universal law.

Even where opportunity is offered, states appear to be reluctant to move forward vigorously. The preamble of the United Nations Charter announces a determination "to establish conditions under which justice and respect for the obligations arising from treaties and other sources of international law can be maintained." Article 13 charges the General Assembly to "initiate studies and make recommendations for the purpose of . . . encouraging the progressive development of international law and its codification." In pursuance of this Charter provision, the General Assembly created an International Law Commission, which has been at work since 1947. Some important lawmaking treaties have resulted from various international efforts—including the Convention on the Prevention of Genocide (1948), the Convention on the Territorial Sea and Contiguous Zone (1958), and the Convention on Diplomatic Relations (1961)—but achievements in this realm still remain limited.

At the same time, a host of international problems continues to call for regulation: control of the ocean floor and its resources, pollution of international waters, access to international canals, jurisdiction over outer space, the dimension of territorial waters, and so on. Disturbing also are the frequent outbursts of anarchy in the world. The widespread resort to various kinds of urban guerrilla warfare through assassinations, hijacking planes, bombing buildings, kidnapping officials, and other terroristic behavior suggests that disorder—if perhaps not always gaining its ends—is gaining ground. And rather than uniting against such acts of subversion, certain governments give aid, reward, and sanctuary to their perpetrators, affording political support to militant anarchy.

What of the future of international law? Clearly, the body of international law developed to the present is weak law—a system of customary rules largely refined and augmented by treaty-made law. Such an incomplete system of law can serve the needs of only the most primitive sort of community. Further, it cannot bring order to an international society which has as yet only partially, and for limited periods of time, restrained its anarchistic impulses. The solution to the problem of international order, we believe, is not to be found through adopting more or new rules of international law, but through the effective organization of the entire international community. Truly, the system of law for the international community can be no stronger than the community itself.

12

The Elements of
International Politics

TO PORTRAY objectively the realm of international politics is difficult, for, as Shakespeare asks, "Who can be wise, amazed, temperate
and furious, loyal and neutral, in a moment?" Here we examine the
political relationships of nation-states in their contest for power and
influence. This process is often described as the conduct of "power
politics," though that term is essentially redundant, for the conduct of
any politics always involves some element of power. In international
affairs, however, the role of power is more constant and its measure
more obvious than in other politics.

International politics involves a searching examination of the forces
that direct the relations of nation-states in the international community. As we undertake an introduction to the subject we wish to enter
two cautions. First, our treatment must be brief, and an examination
of the array of facts and theories of international life within limited
dimensions will not provide any mastery of the subject. Second, we
must simplify, even though Professor Alfred Zimmern has pointed
out, ". . . the greatest danger which confronts our subject is to regard
it as a subject for beginners. . . . Our subject is not easy; it is difficult. International relations are not simple; they are complex. To simplify them is to destroy their essence, to eliminate the whole substance of their problem." What follows therefore is, in modest
compass, a survey of the principal elements of national power, of the
nature of foreign policy, and of the means employed by states to promote their interests internationally.

I. National Power

We have observed that a feature of the international community is the great variation in the power possessed by the many countries it comprises. So important is power status, indeed, that states have been referred to, in diplomatic terminology, as "powers"—great, middle, or minor, as the case may be; thus, even the very smallest think, and are thought of it, in power terms. The purpose of this part of our discussion, then, is to examine the nature of power, its instruments, and manifestations.

Power. In international politics, "power" describes the capacity of the state to exert strength, authority, or influence. Possession of power allows a state to exercise command, control, or coercion in international affairs; it makes possible the achievement of certain ends against the will of others. There is sometimes argument over whether states contest for power or for ends that power can produce. Both reasons are true; power is prized for itself as well as for what it can achieve. States like to enjoy reputation for power, which confers prestige, enhancing national status and influence. Of course, national prestige is acquired by means other than the possession of sheer power alone. A reputation for dignity, restraint, responsibility, acceptance of and faithfulness to obligations may accord a state prestige. Canada and Switzerland, for example, enjoy such a cachet. And one may ponder the fact that the United States formerly enjoyed a greater international prestige in certain respects when it possessed much less power than it does today.

The state's search for a minimum of power is at least as much a matter of need as choice; a powerless state cannot protect its rights, redress offenses, or defend its existence. States which cannot defend themselves in the long run, or find others to do so, cease to exist. A state's will to live thus requires a willingness to utilize the instruments of power. Power is, however, always a relative and changing quality; it does not exist in a vacuum. A state's power must always be weighed with reference to other states and their position. The power of a state is affected by a considerable number of factors: for any state these may alter in the course of time; the power position of other states may change; and new instruments of power may come into existence.

Power in itself is neither good nor evil. It has been glorified in some states, not infrequently with disastrous results, and deprecated in others, usually from a misunderstanding of its nature. There has been an American tendency to consider power as immoral—as one may say, to prefer right to might—largely because of the United States' long isolation from the centers of power in Europe, where its use has produced recurring warfare. Only in recent decades have the American people become conscious of their own power and of their responsibility to employ it for the defense of other countries. But whatever one's preferences, it remains that power is a fact and it exists; it will be used, and its use may produce triumph or disaster.

The Factor of Nationalism. Any analysis of state power must place nationalism as easily the most powerful and dynamic force in world politics. We introduced the concept of "nation" in earlier chapters as representing a body of people who feel they are united by such characteristics as ethnic origin, historical association, culture, language, religion, and customs. Yet it is by no means necessary that all such characteristics be identical; for the same nation may well include persons of differing race, religion, or language, for example, and their sense of historical association may be as old as England's or as new as Nigeria's. "What constitutes a nation," said Ernest Renan in his classic essay, "is not speaking the same tongue or belonging to the same ethnic group, but having accomplished great things in common in the past and the wish to accomplish them in the future."

Nationalism, the sense of loyalty and attachment to the nation, began to emerge as a significant sentiment in the eighteenth century following the creation of the important modern nation-states in Europe. It became the dominant political emotion of the masses in nineteenth-century Europe, and has spread to all corners of the world in the twentieth. As the feeling of separate national identity is aroused within a people, they seek its full gratification in the possession of separate statehood. This claim to national self-determination—to organize the nation as an independent state—came to be spoken of as a basic political right in the nineteenth century, and has helped to unleash wars and upheavals continually since that time.

Nationhood inevitably has statehood in prospect; and in the case of dismembered and captive stateless nations, in retrospect as well. Thus nationalism may operate within a state both as a centrifugal and as a centripetal force. Nationalism tends to pull a multinational state apart, as each nation seeks to go its own way. Where a portion of one nation is contained within the state territory of another, such a "national minority" will also tend to seek political association with those of the same nationality on the other side of the frontier. The demands for such concessions to national self-determination have added greatly to the international tensions and frictions of the past century, and many European frontiers especially have smoldered as a result. The Soviet Union is the most important multinational state existing today, and it is held together largely by force; indeed, at least part of the repressive character of its government can be attributed to efforts at holding political control of many national groups against their will.

As a unifying force, nationalism acts to induce men to give their highest loyalty to the nation-state, to submerge their personal interests into those of the nation, and to make the ultimate sacrifice of their lives in its behalf. As a state of mind, nationalism evokes emotional ties to the group of a strength and depth that could not be engendered through mere appeals to a legal duty owed the state. "Put only Americans on guard tonight!" "England expects every man to do his duty." "France—and France alone!" All such rallying cries reflect the same theme. In modern times men have generally proved likely to respond to the cause of nationalism as superior to any other appeal, whether to personal conscience, religious conviction, Marxist-Leninist or communist class loyalty, or to the brotherhood of mankind. In an extreme form, it has been characterized as "integral nationalism"— the exclusive and absolute devotion to national power.

National solidarity thus becomes an important source of power in itself. This circumstance permits evaluation of power in terms of national character, energy, and morale: the ways in which a people— especially as a nation in arms—will behave, work, persevere, and fight in behalf of the nation's perpetuation and defense. To develop these qualities, and to achieve the strength which they supply, the peoples of Asia and Africa during recent decades have enthusiastically embraced the cult of nationalism at the very time when many peoples of the older western states have begun to react against its excesses. It seems likely, then, that the dynamics of nationalism will continue to exert a profound influence on world affairs, disrupting political associations which repress national interests, and promoting or supporting widespread international quarrels and clashes.

The Geographic Factor. It is obvious that the geography of a state affects its power, but what precise conclusions follow from that proposition are debatable. Geographic factors determine the physical dimensions of a state, its setting, and its immediate material supply. But size, shape, topography, climate, location, and resources are in no case conclusive determinants of strength; they produce in conjunction and interaction with each other a varying human ecology for the population of every state. Though some writers see the geographic factor as the most permanent element of power, it is actually largely contingent. That is to say, geographic features generally remain constant, but their significance may well vary in time and place.

For example, great area may permit the presence of large populations, as in China and India, but does not assure them—most of the comparably extensive territories of the Soviet Union, Australia, and Canada, for example, are uninhabited. The relative immensity of the United States and the U.S.S.R. adds to their superpower status by giving them military advantage; both are difficult to invade, destroy by aerial attack, or occupy. On the other hand, small island states such as Great Britain and Japan have been great powers in modern times; today, however, their vulnerability to air attack makes them difficult if not impossible to defend. Some states are the rather obvious creation of their topography—such as Spain, Switzerland, or Turkey—with natural features historically improving their defensibility; others, like Belgium and Poland, have seen their territory used again and again as highway and battlefield by more powerful neighbors. A state's terrain may promote or hamper its national unity. Natural frontiers, however—such as mountains, forests, and oceans—have in recent times steadily declined in strategic value.

Climate is influenced both by topography and location; it has much to do with the support of human life and the expenditure of human energy. The great industrial centers of the world are all located within the temperate zone; however, industrialization is not inherently excluded from other areas by climatic circumstances alone. Location determines such matters, for instance, as whether a state may possess a navy and achieve sea power, or whether it is to be landlocked and practically excluded from using the maritime highways of the world. The advantage of access to the north Atlantic or to the center of Europe, and their important trade routes, has long been obvious. Location may repeatedly embroil a state in the military struggles of its neighbors, as in the case of Korea, or largely remove it from the scene of significant controversy as in the case of Liberia.

A concomitant of the geographical factor of power is the availability of natural resources and raw materials. A state must possess or have access to these, in substantial measure, to be powerful. First in importance, of course, is food. Most major powers are essentially self-sufficient in basic foodstuffs, though Great Britain has been a well-known exception, obliged to import half or more of its supply, and obviously dependent upon a continuing ability to do so for national survival. Next come fossil fuels, such as coal and petroleum products (for which hydroelectric power or atomic energy can be a partial substitute), and the basic raw materials of the industrial process, such as iron, bauxite, timber, lead, tin, copper, and nickel. Of ever-growing importance are certain critical materials essential to the complex technology of modern industrial and military production, such as chromium, cobalt, manganese, tungsten, uranium, and vanadium. Finally, states with aspiration to power require substantial supplies of such agricultural commodities as cotton, wool, and rubber—or appropriate substitutes; it is also rather obvious that the maintenance of national morale in many western states requires ample quantities of beef, cacao, coffee, tea, sugar, and tobacco.

Clearly, only a highly industrialized state can be powerful, but no industrialized state can any longer be self-sufficient in raw materials. Inevitably, states have been led to seek ample supplies of the commodities their industry requires, preferably by immediate expansion of their own territory, as both the United States and the U.S.S.R. have done extensively; or by the development of overseas colonial empires, as did Great Britain, France, and Italy. States, or their private enterprisers, may also develop the resources of others outside their territories, or buy needed commodities as they are offered on the world market. Ideally, the latter practice should serve as the best means to give the people of all states access to the world's resources; but states much prefer to control resources, if at all possible, at their source. Otherwise, supplies may be insufficient, overpriced, or withheld as a result of war or for various political reasons—and at a time when need can be most critical. Hence, states are driven to acquire controllable sources of supply for the materials they require—a situation bound to provoke rivalry and conflict in international relations.

The Factor of Population. The very term "manpower" suggests that population size constitutes a measure of national strength. Yet once again we must emphasize the relativity of population as a power factor. If a state is to command substantial power, it must have a large population—not only to equal the numbers of those great powers which do, but to supply the masses of soldiers and workers essential to military strength. The most modern weapons for air, sea, and land use can, of course, vastly augment the firepower and destructiveness of the individual soldier; but to the extent that they permit any reduction in the number of men needed at the front, they substantially increase those required for service and supply in the rear echelons. There is yet no reason to believe that the day of mass armies has passed or that the infantryman (even though motorized or airborne) is obsolete. World War II saw all belligerents pressed for manpower before its conclusion and, even then, large forces were required to occupy the defeated states.

A huge population may, nonetheless, be a liability where the national economy is unable even in peacetime to support it at or above a subsistence level. During war, such a population continues to consume and can thus be an even greater burden. Overpopulation is not a new phenomenon historically, but its growing accentuation in certain areas of the world is creating serious problems. For centuries, the world's population grew slowly, kept in check by famine, disease, and war. From an estimated one-half billion in the seventeenth century, it is now approaching four billions. In the western world generally, though the average life span has been substantially extended, population growth has been moderate; birth limitation, urbanization, and industrialization have, indeed, permitted a general rise in living standards where the population increase has been orderly.

Asia, on the other hand, is having a real population "explosion." In five Asian countries alone—China, India, Indonesia, Japan, and Pakistan—live approximately one-half of the world's population, and on less than 10 percent of the world's land area. Only Japan, among these states, has been able—through its industrialization and by recently halving its birth rate—to support its growing population. For the others, their slow and modest increases in industrial production and food supplies barely keep alive their increasing numbers. It is not at all clear, however, how long they can keep ahead of starvation for many; in recent years, the increase in world food production has ominously lagged behind that in population. If existing trends continue, the world's population will reach six billions in the course of the present century. Whether we call this "overpopulation" or "under-development" makes little difference; the miseries of overcrowding, starvation, and degradation of our environment that must result are bound to provide a serious cause for international tensions in the decades to come.

The Economic Factor. The economic measure of power is determined by the interaction of the basic elements of production: land (with its resources), man's efforts, and capital. A territory that is rich in resources and contains a population able to provide a large labor force is not enough. There must be a supply of highly skilled managers, scientists, technologists, and workers, supported by abundant capital (that is, accumulated wealth capable of producing more wealth) for the state to have a high degree of industrialization—and economic power. Thus stated, it may seem simple, but it is not. Today's high level of industrialization in some countries is the result of the commercial, industrial, and technological revolutions of the past four centuries; even so, it has been reached in only limited portions of the world.

To achieve this high level of industrialization, only a small portion of the state's population must be devoted to food and agricultural production. By the mechanization of agricultural methods—including the use of fertilizers, insecticides, and selected seeds—and by controlled methods of breeding, maintaining, and feeding livestock, abundant food supplies can be produced for a population while leaving the largest part of its labor force available for industrial work. The industrial plant, in turn, must be large enough to permit mass production of all significant goods under the direction of managers and technologists, and by workers possessing the knowledge and skills to operate at highly efficient levels of productivity. To permit the population to consume the foodstuffs and goods so produced, there is required further an effective system for their distribution and marketing; and this in turn depends on well-developed systems of transportation and communication, and substantial provision of service trades. Not least essential to a high level of industrialization is surplus capital, which must be saved or accumulated—whether by private or public means, voluntarily or under duress—to provide the wealth to build and expand industry, replace obsolete facilities, support research, provide the machines which build machines, hazard the risks of economic venture and so on.

Advanced industrialization not only affects a state's power, among other things, but supports the forward impetus of further industrialization. The resulting increments to the gross national product of a state (unless drawn off by a totalitarian government for the direct increase of its power) permit a steadily rising standard of living for the population. Better quality or greater variety in consumer goods; higher standards of education, nutrition, and medical care; adequate housing and other amenities; and improved opportunity for recreation and entertainment are among the earmarks of the national condition. Important, too, is the ability of an industrialized society to defer the entrance of a large portion of the younger population into the labor market, and to support it through a longer period of formal education, thus extending the scientific and technical knowledge essential to military and technological efficiency. More and more educated people and educational facilities are needed to keep complex modern societies running. National power is further enhanced by the fact that the industrialized state is a substantial consumer of goods produced abroad, as well as a supplier of them and of surplus capital. Finally, such a state is able to afford and to produce the military establishments and armaments which are themselves a further measure of power.

It is in the economic context that the contrast between the highly industrialized and the underdeveloped countries is sharpest. The characteristics of the underdeveloped state are, indeed, the very opposite of those we have been discussing and tend, moreover, to perpetuate its reduced circumstances in a vicious circle. Most of its population is devoted to subsistence farming—with resulting substandard living conditions, inadequate nutrition, enervating disease, and illiteracy. Its economic resources available for sale abroad are limited to one or a few primary products for which world demand is not elastic; it is thus vulnerable to world competition in its exports and lacks sufficient foreign exchange to purchase goods abroad. It has an inadequate educational system and is unable to train the administrative, scientific, and technical personnel and skilled workers essential to efficient industry; generally, modern industrial and business practices are not known. Primitive tax systems are commonly regressive and barely touch the rich; or, in some cases, they largely discourage economic enterprise. Thus large-scale industry is lacking; this is also because the demand for capital exceeds the supply. Capital must be saved, either at home or abroad, but the absence of industrialization makes this difficult on any large scale at home. The efficiency of government in an underdeveloped country is not likely to be high; the many grievances and dissatisfactions of the population offer fertile ground for exploitation by political extremists. In the face of resulting political instability, even small domestic accumulations of capital may well be sent to safer repositories in Great Britain, Switzerland, or the United States. Foreign suppliers of capital are not attracted to a situation unpromising for the protection either of their investment or the income from it. The frustrations of such underdeveloped states have become a particularly disturbing factor in international relations in recent years, since they seek to lay blame for their lot at the door of a powerful neighboring state, of the colonial powers, or of the rich capitalist states.

The Ideological Factor. Ideas have always been powerful; men and nations are not only what they know, but also what they feel and believe. Politics at the international level then, as at all others, is significantly influenced by the patterns of ideas we call "ideologies." By "ideology," we mean generally a body of doctrines, beliefs, and symbols. Ideologies may undertake to interpret reality or to conceal it in elaborate disguise—to explain the world or remake it. They may rest upon generally accepted truths, but are as likely to contain substantial myth. Because ideologies are accepted primarily on faith, they may indeed be compounded of completely synthetic dogma.

One should not underestimate the importance of the role that ideologies serve, for they fulfill some very basic human yearnings. Men not only live by them but die for them. To the great questions and problems about the ends and aims of human existence, for example, they may offer answers that are not found by ordinary methods of ascertaining the truth. They give men a sense of certainty and security, of purpose and self-justification; they supply the reassurance of absolutes that otherwise tend to be lacking. Ideological doctrines may well be too complicated to be fully understood by the masses of people, but their slogans and symbols can be widely disseminated and grasped. Considering that such doctrines are often embraced by relatively sophisticated people, their impact upon masses of illiterates or semi-illiterates can be enormous.

Historically speaking, the first ideologies with important political significance were religious. Such controversy inspired in part the

Christian-Moslem and Catholic-Protestant wars of the later middle ages. Substantial secular ideologies produced the English, American, and French revolutions in the seventeenth and eighteenth centuries; thereafter they emerged in considerable profusion, and can be seen in a wide range from the racialist creeds of Pan Slavism in imperial Russia and the *apartheid* of South Africa to the politico-religious doctrines of Shintoist-emperor worship of Japan and the *Satyagraha* of Gandhi's India, among many examples. Ideologies commonly interact with national character and culture. Indeed, the most ubiquitous ideology in the contemporary world is nationalism and—in combination with liberalism, socialism, militarism, imperialism, or tribalism in different countries—it may provide a variety of particular and most exclusive ideological systems.

Ideologies are a source of national strength, and may become a cause of international conflict. The present century has seen the emergence of totalitarian political ideologies, such as communism and fascism, claiming from their followers allegiance in all things and setting exclusive value standards. German Nazism was too peculiarly Teutonic to have more than minor appeal beyond Germany. The communist leaders, however, have fashioned a dynamic, expansionist, and militant creed, which serves not only to maintain the oligarchic control of their own countries but also to augment the international power of the communist states. Intensive conspiratorial efforts to introduce and impose such militant ideologies throughout the world by creating or exploiting political and social disruption in other states inevitably provoke international friction and controversy.

The Military Factor. Military strength is such an obvious element of state power that it tends to be viewed as its prime indicator. It also appears amenable to measurement; for some of its components—such as infantry divisions, aircraft carriers, missiles, and megatonnage— can be counted. But such evaluations rest largely on weighing the nature and quantity of a state's military hardware, and the number of its men in military service, and measuring these against the general results produced in a previous war when men used similar weapons. Actually, however, military strength can never be gauged with any accuracy until it is applied in war or confrontations in conjunction with all other elements of national power, with which it is inextricably involved, and the final verdict of victory or defeat is pronounced. Guerrilla forces, used in the right circumstances, may be far more effective than conventional armies. The measure of military power is thus complicated for many reasons.

For centuries military strength consisted essentially in formations of armed men, afoot or mounted, equipped with weapons that were only variants of the spear, the sling, and the sword. Even the invention of gunpowder, and the development of a variety of small arms, did not alter the relatively equal effectiveness of individual soldiers similarly equipped. Approximately a century ago, however, a revolution began in the character of weapons. The result has been the development of armored ships, long-range heavy artillery, machine guns, submarines, tanks, poison gases, heavy bombers, and nuclear weapons, among others, reflecting the technological advances of the contemporary era, and permitting new destructiveness. In consequence, the arsenals of modern military establishments are so complex in their equipment that it is impossible to be dogmatic today about the results to be achieved by any particular national system of armaments.

Military strength depends upon men, and the human element inevitably adds another unknown quantity. All else being equal, military units commanded by professional soldiers trained in the science of strategy and tactics should enjoy an advantage over those which are not. Men of intelligence—with high morale, sound physique, and mechanical aptitude—should prevail over those without. The volunteer ought to be superior to the conscript, the offensive-minded to the defensive-minded, the better equipped to the poorer, and so on. But things never are equal, as the outcome of battles and wars has often surprisingly demonstrated. Leadership and valor, as the long history of warfare attests, are qualities required for martial achievement from the commander-in-chief to the last man in the ranks; and displayed at the right time, they may well be the determinant in victory.

Finally, we may observe that military strength depends upon the other factors of power. Modern land, sea, and air forces require large space for training and deployment. They are voracious consumers of raw materials and resources—foodstuffs, wool, nitrates, steel, copper, lead, and oil. They need communications systems, transport, docks, and arsenals. Manpower is necessary not only to fill their ranks but to provide the work force essential to their support. Scientific laboratories, universities, factories, and industrial plants must develop and produce their matériel. They must be inspired with a sense of mission and a will to fight. The extent to which these and other elements of power are possessed by a state affects not only the degree of military preparedness which it can achieve at any time but, equally important, its military potential for the long run. Thus, the factor of military strength is also a relative and continually changing element of national power.

As we enter the age of astronautics, the defensive posture of the most heavily armed state becomes even more uncertain. In a time of chemical and bacteriological weapons, of intercontinental ballistic missiles and electronic computers, of death-rays and brainwashing, of reconnaissance satellites, moon landings and space stations, the efforts of states merely to ensure their security and defense—not to mention the attempts of those ambitious for overwhelming military superiority—seem often to increase, rather than reduce, the danger of the disturbing international crises of these times.

II. National Policy

A substantial proportion of the study of international politics is devoted to the subject of foreign policy. We cannot undertake an analysis of various national policies; but we may offer a brief account of the principles underlying them, how and why certain ones are chosen, and by what agencies they are administered. The interests of any state ought ideally to be those of all men. Hence, it might appear that there would be common national goals and that international collaboration would best enhance each nation's interests. Unfortunately, international behavior is at sharp variance with such an ideal.

Foreign Policy: Nature and Objectives

The Nature of Foreign Policy. The term "foreign policy" describes the attitudes, courses of action, and objectives that a state's government adopts in its relations toward other states and areas abroad. It may be consciously and carefully chosen; or it may reflect only a fairly consistent behavior, influencing situations abroad without any precisely selected aims. Foreign policy reflects what a state does as well as what it seeks to do. Foreign policy is not something applied only abroad, existing in a compartment distinct from domestic policy; they are inevitably both aspects of a state's total national policy. Thus, national policies are foreign policies to any extent that they affect or influence other states. The character of state policies varies considerably. Toward certain countries a state may have very specific objectives and may seek to apply carefully delineated courses of action; toward others it may have no more than indefinite aims, perhaps of maintaining peace or commerce. The foreign policy of a state can hardly be thought of as a blueprint, exact in its measures and specifications. Relations with other states are too unpredictable for that to be possible. Like any national policies, those which are foreign are a mixture of elements—reactions to the past and present and plans for the future.

The Determinants of Foreign Policy. The basic determinant of a state's foreign policy is commonly found in the objective "to promote the national interest." National interest, however, is a vague concept; it is generally considered to embrace the state's security and welfare. But what specific goals will best achieve the safety and well-being of a state are rarely matters of agreement and often subjects of serious disagreement. Security may be sought in terms of a superiority of armaments to repel or deter attack from any other state; yet this very superiority may appear menacing to other states, constituting aggressive behavior in their eyes, and may induce them to take reciprocal action. The nation's welfare is after all bound to be differently interpreted by various economic groups within the state—by farmers and manufacturers, exporters and importers, workers and employers. It has been suggested that national interest is equivalent to national security, which in turn is essentially equivalent to national power. But even if they are close to being identical, the circular character of such an equation is not very helpful in defining the national interest.

A second determinant of foreign policy objectives is the state's capabilities. In the preceding section of this chapter we examined the major factors which allow the state to act and exert power and influence in the international community. These characteristics, both tangible and intangible, clearly condition—though without necessarily determining directly—what a state may undertake in its relations with others. Its capabilities may well deny it particular courses of action, but beyond that a variety of choices can ordinarily be made. To take a hypothetical example, Mexico would lack the capability to force the United States to cede it California; it might, however, be able to induce Great Britain to undertake a boundary rectification at the expense of British Honduras; it undoubtedly could oblige Guatemala to relinquish territory in its behalf.

A third determinant of foreign policy is provided by prevailing international circumstances. No matter how carefully a state chooses its policies, and however accurately they reflect its capabilities, its courses of action must be accommodated to the existence of other states, the policies they are pursuing, and the climate of international relations which results. It is probably not sufficiently appreciated how much the making of any one government's foreign policy is frequently little more than a reaction to those of other states. State policies inevitably interact, and the extent to which other states cooperate or compete is of large consequence. For example, in the early post-World War I period Poland behaved as the *enfant terrible* of eastern Europe, effecting many of its objectives by force; in the 1930's, caught between a rearmed Germany and Russia, its freedom to act became much more circumscribed; in 1939, when the latter two powers joined in its dismemberment, Poland as a state ceased to exist. Again, Italy was able to take advantage of the prevailing international situation —the mutual preoccupation of the principal major powers—to seize Tripoli in 1911, conquer Ethiopia in 1936, and annex Albania in 1939. But as an Axis partner in World War II, it was quickly eliminated from the lists in 1943 when confronted with the military power of Great Britain and the United States.

The Objectives of Foreign Policy. We have seen that the foreign policy of a state is determined by its interpretation of its national interest, its capabilities, and the international atmosphere. Taking these three determinants into consideration, the state may then attempt to achieve various goals; broadly speaking, these aim at producing certain external and internal effects. From an external point of view, a state may seek to increase its power; this requires, of course, a change in the overall distribution of power, and it distinctly affects other states. Such a policy may incline the state toward imperialism, gaining dominance of strategic areas or critical resources, or aggressive warfare and the conquest of territory. This is a policy of expanding state power. Or a state may seek a more modest goal, with its external objectives aimed at preserving the "status quo," that is, the existing situation, especially so far as its own power position is concerned. Although this is a more conservative response to one or more states seeking a change in the power distribution, it can also be intentionally chosen by a state satisfied in its power aspirations. Though such a policy may lead the state to various kinds of passive reactions— such as undertaking defensive alliances, appeasement, or offering to bargain and make concessions—it may also lead to the employment of the same devices as those used by an aggressive state in the belief that the best defense is a good offense. This is a policy of maintaining power. A third alternative is a policy of neutralism, whereby a state withdraws entirely from the power contest and refrains from involvement in power controversies or with states which do enter them. This is no less a self-interested policy than the others, of course, chosen as a rule by states unable to exercise significant power in international politics and based on the assumption that such abnegation will be respected by all other states. However, few major states have been able successfully to follow this policy—the renunciation of power—for any length of time.

Innumerable examples of these various policies may be found. Germany and Russia, for instance, pursued expansionist goals before both World Wars I and II. Great Britain and France were expansionist in the nineteenth century, but adopted status quo policies after World War I. Switzerland and Sweden have traditionally pursued a neutralist course effectively through more than a century; Austria and Finland have attempted to do the same since World War II. A state may at the same time follow different policies in different areas. It may be said—though without absolute consistency—that the United States in the latter part of the nineteenth century observed a policy of neutralism toward Europe, one of the status quo toward Latin America, and one of expansion toward the Pacific area.

From an internal point of view, the objectives of foreign policy are to preserve or attain certain conditions within the state. Obviously a state hopes to achieve security; for contained under this rubric are its self-preservation, protection against attack, and freedom from foreign intervention and interference. As we have also noted, the maintenance of national welfare leads the state to seek wealth and goods, enrich the national life, extend production, improve living standards, support a larger population, and generally enhance its power. Beyond these basic goals, a state's foreign policy may seek a variety of internal consequences. It may pursue an expansionist policy partly from fear of an aggressive rival, as did Japan toward Russia at the turn of this century. Or quite perversely, a state may press an expansionist policy partly to engender counterpressure and tension, which it can then capitalize upon in promoting harsh domestic policies, as have contemporary Communist China and Soviet Russia. A state following a status quo policy may be seeking to enhance its role as an international middleman, broker, and trader; it avoids pronouncing moral judgments, giving offense, and is generally willing to do business with anyone—as in the case of contemporary Britain. Where states pursue an external policy of neutralism, they may be attempting to effect a kind of national isolation, as in the case of the United States through much of its history. Such a choice of policy is based on the conclusion that the national security and welfare can best be promoted by contracting out of the power struggle.

Foreign Policy: Formulation

It is difficult to imagine a much more complex process than that by which the foreign policy of a major power is determined. In the space available here we can do no more than sketch the main outlines. Certainly, for example, vastly more has gone into the making of United States policy toward Latin America than the insertion of a few paragraphs into President Monroe's message to Congress in 1823, and much more into India's policy of neutralism than some quiet meditation by the Prime Minister. Contributions to the formulation of foreign policy are made by a number of agencies of government and in this task they are subjected to influences by a great variety of groups and institutions.

Government Organs. The central role in the formulation of foreign policy is assigned everywhere, as we have noted earlier, to the executive. This is, indeed, one of the major executive functions; and the president, prime minister, or premier holds his office in part because of certain expectations concerning his approach to foreign affairs held by those who voted for or supported him. He must, in short, have made some fundamental interpretations of his country's national interest and chosen certain means to achieve them. It is the executive who has the authority to commit the nation to a course of action and to speak for it within the community of states. In performing his responsibilities the executive is assisted by a minister of foreign affairs, who is often chosen because of his special knowledge and experience in this realm, and who has the function of conveying the views of the head of the government to the foreign ministry, and of providing for his chief and his fellow cabinet members the results of studies and staff work undertaken in the foreign ministry, as well as information and views furnished by foreign service officials abroad.

Concern with and advice upon foreign policy is not a monopoly of the foreign affairs department, however. One of the difficult problems such ministries face these days is that foreign-policy making cannot be confined to this ministry alone. The nature, cost, and complexity of modern weaponry and warfare require that the military establishments be included in the policy-making process. Yet how and at what point is a matter of considerable controversy. Any particular national policy requires certain military postures and may well involve certain military risks; such a policy can scarcely be chosen if military leaders are unwilling to answer for its consequences. A serious difficulty arises here, however, because it is not a great step further to allow purely military considerations to determine policy; but if there is military dictation of foreign policy, the result is a military-civil authority relationship incompatible with constitutional government. To have learned this one lesson alone might well have saved Germany disaster twice in the first half of this century.

The treasury secretary is bound to reflect concern with the taxing and spending consequences of foreign policy. Intelligence agencies, information services, and government departments involved with trade, commerce, labor, law enforcement, agriculture, and fisheries, for example, will inevitably contribute. It is the task of the chief executive to weigh these various considerations affecting policy and to unify them into some degree of consistency.

Though the executive is given the exclusive right to speak, listen, and act for the state in foreign relations, this does not exclude the legislature from a share in foreign-policy formulation. Legislative influence may be exerted directly by such means as the granting or withholding of consent to make certain appointments, to ratify a treaty, to annex or relinquish territory, to join an international organization, to contract an alliance, or to declare war. Even where such actions are discretionary with the executive, a parliamentary body may withdraw support from a government whose policies it does not approve. The legislature may apply further influence indirectly through its control of financial and lawmaking power generally, through interrogations and investigations of executive officials, by participation of legislators in international conferences and as diplomatic negotiators, through debates, and generally by all the usual means available for supervising the executive.

Some measure of legislative supervision of foreign policy is intended to reflect popular sentiments and attitudes over matters which deeply affect, even if they do not actively concern, the mass of the people. To the extent that parliamentary bodies effectively perform this representative role and ameliorate certain bureaucratic propensities which the professional formulation of foreign policy may produce, their value can be recognized. Nonetheless, legislative participation in this area has not been without unfortunate consequences on some occasions, and does not always prevent unwise executive action. Legislators may be inadequately informed, narrow in their interests and outlook, and inordinately influenced by partisan or local demands. As we have suggested before, a parliamentary body is not capable itself of formulating and administering foreign policy; but it can, by a sufficient degree of irresponsibility, make it extremely difficult for the executive to do so.

Public Influences. Foreign policy in a democratic system of government, then, to a large degree must be made in public. That is to say, major policy proposals must be placed before parliamentary bodies, and thus the general public; they will be discussed and debated, and exposed to popular demands. At the same time the proposed policies, their motives, and objectives, necessarily become equally known to all foreign governments, friendly and unfriendly, concerned and unconcerned alike. Yet policy makers find such procedures and their attendant revelations—given the necessary characteristics of effective policy, which may well require secrecy, decisiveness, and flexibility—always difficult and sometimes nearly impossible. Theoretically, the foreign policy of a state rests upon a base of prevailing public opinion, and is guided and sustained by it. But public opinion is a nebulous concept that by no means always provides the kind of solid and stable footing that adequate policies require.

Additional influences on policy making are exerted by political parties, both to the extent that they shape public opinion and that their leaders hold executive or legislative office. As a rule, political parties represent their differences on foreign policy to be greater than they actually are, for the basic determinants in national policy are likely to offer far narrower alternatives than the parties are willing to admit.

Interest groups and minorities of various kinds may also have an effect on policy making, whether their influence is exerted through the legislature or directly on the executive. Differing economic interests inevitably lead business, agricultural, and labor groups to take different stands respecting foreign trade, tariffs, immigration, public expenditure, and related subjects. Veterans' associations usually express strong views about foreign policy; religious organizations may exert influence in behalf of their coreligionists abroad; minority ethnic and nationality groups may have particular attachments to or interests in various areas abroad.

Obviously, then, the formulation of foreign policy in a democracy is a difficult task. The general public is slow to accept new policies; much of it does not want to be obliged to ponder the subject; and often most of it is not sufficiently informed to have truly relevant opinions. Also, the average person tends to view foreign nations in terms of stereotypes, and thus does not appreciate the complex and dynamic nature of international politics. Popular communications media largely ignore foreign affairs, or distort the information they do provide. Political parties often avoid discussion of the real problems or alternatives of foreign policy for fear of losing popular support. Organized groups frequently promote narrow or self-interested objectives. In consequence, only leadership of a very high order can hold the democratic state to the sustained pursuit of a successful and practicable foreign policy.

Foreign Policy in the Dictatorships. The formulation of foreign policy in the totalitarian dictatorships contrasts with democratic procedures. Obviously, policy making occurs at a highly elevated and centralized level in a dictatorship; it can thus be made with greater speed and less controversy than by democratic methods. This is not to say that there may be no high-level differences over policy; often great controversy, not always entirely concealed, may take place among the top leadership until a course of action is selected. Foreign policy can be closely coordinated with other national objectives and programs, however, heightening the overall appearance of consistency and unity. Within a dictatorship, policy is made secretly and may then be applied with considerable surprise to seize the initiative. The dictator is not obliged to consult or reckon with legislative, popular, or interest group influences or interferences. Instead, the party machine, the press, and all other media of communication are employed to shape popular opinion—while censorship helps blind it to any conflicting views—for the support of the centrally chosen policies. Finally, the dictatorship is free to reverse its foreign policies.

These circumstances give certain considerable advantages to the dictatorial regime. Yet one should not fail to observe that the means do condition the ends—that they have important consequences upon policies, not all to the interest of the dictatorship in the long run. Foreign policies generally reflect the regime's striving for power, its aggressiveness, and its need continually to stimulate international tension, even if by artificial measures. The opportunism present in dictatorial policy is rarely successfully disguised, at least abroad, and works to reduce the dictatorship's dignity and to deny its disinterest. Though generally well repressed, popular dissatisfaction may nevertheless be present, weakening the apparent monolithic unity of the state and people. Moreover, with the elimination of any adequate correctives, such as popular debates and criticism, policy may well reflect the worst features of bureaucratic formulation, as well as possible psychopathic tendencies of the dictator. Still worse, the ideological prepossessions of the dictatorial leaders often limit their ability to interpret objectively the affairs of the external world, and thus may color their decisions and constrict their choice of policy alternatives. In sum, although the dictatorship may at times produce a strikingly successful turn of policy, it is inevitably prone to catastrophic errors of judgment, as the histories of many such regimes, now defunct, will readily attest.

Foreign Policy: Administration

The Executive. The administration of foreign policy, especially at its higher levels, is only partially separable from its formulation. Nevertheless the two processes are sufficiently distinct in important ways to justify separate consideration. Foreign-policy administration begins, of course, with the executive, who everywhere possesses the authority to direct the conduct of foreign relations and their related activities. The role of the formal chief of state in such matters is normally limited to ceremonial and social occasions. The functions of the head of a government, however, as a political executive, are considerable. He has certain regular responsibilities of appointing diplomatic envoys, receiving those from other states, ordering negotiations with and representations to foreign governments, and so on; and he enjoys considerable discretion over the extent to which he will devote his immediate personal attention to such activities.

The executive may choose to send special agents to represent him on particular missions abroad. He may also undertake personal diplomacy by means of direct correspondence, telephone conversations, good-will visits abroad, and meetings with the heads of other governments. In the years before World War II high-level personal diplomacy acquired a special vogue which lasted through the next two decades. Such practice can undoubtedly be useful and expeditious when employed by two or more heads of friendly governments for the purpose of exchanging views, consultations, and the alignment of policies to be pursued jointly. The use of such procedures, however, in an attempt to negotiate a settlement of serious international disputes and differences between states has much less to recommend it. There were widespread criticisms of the results of the Munich Conference (1938), the Yalta Conference (1945), and the Geneva Conference (1955), among others. The collapse of the much-publicized Paris summit conference in 1960, however, seems to have discouraged subsequent high-level meetings and encouraged a return to more traditional channels and procedures of international contacts. The simple good-will visit exchanges between government leaders do continue.

The advantages claimed for summit diplomacy are that heads of government, who are the chief policy makers, can speak with the highest authority; that they may gain a direct appreciation of the views of their opposite numbers; that top-level meetings focus public attention on the issues being discussed; and that national leaders are able to break through the complex bureaucratic process of policy making and other possible impasses to achieve needed agreements. The procedure carries with it nonetheless some serious disadvantages. In the first place, such meetings must be hurried. Government heads are ordinarily not professional diplomats and may well lack skill in conducting negotiations; since they are themselves the source of authority, their maneuvers may lack flexibility and range; they may dangerously overcommit themselves through ill-considered compromises; and such conferences may degenerate into contests of propaganda. And the attention attracted to such meetings may unreasonably raise popular expectations; if no substantial agreements are reached, their failure is glaringly emphasized and magnified. Not surprisingly, many experienced diplomats view such occasions with strong misgivings.

The Ministry of Foreign Affairs. Governments have one ministry or department principally responsible for the administration of foreign policy. Its head—with such various titles as Secretary of State for Foreign Affairs in Great Britain, Secretary of State in the United States, Minister of Foreign Affairs in France, Secretary of State for External Affairs in Canada—is the regular intermediary between his government and those of foreign states, sending and receiving communications, overseeing the negotiation and execution of treaties, and many other similar functions. He is responsible for supervising the foreign ministry and directing the work of the foreign service. His importance is marked by first place in precedence among government ministers; in the parliamentary type of executive, the prime minister on occasion even assumes the office of foreign minister himself, thus lending it further prestige. In addition to his policy-making and advisory functions earlier mentioned, and the administrative duties respecting his ministry, the foreign minister has the further important task of assisting the chief executive in explaining the government's foreign policy to the legislature and to the electorate. Finally, the foreign minister has come to be the principal diplomatic negotiator for his government; to an even greater degree than the chief executive in recent years, he has tended to engage in personal diplomacy with other foreign ministers, bypassing the conventional channels. Both advantages and disadvantages result from this kind of summitry—generally similar to those arising from negotiations by heads of governments.

In the performance of his many duties the minister is aided by several deputy and assistant ministers, who may have special responsibilities, and a number of undersecretaries, who administer the various divisions of the foreign office. Obviously each foreign ministry follows its own practices and needs in organization, but they are all similar. Some of the divisions will be organized to deal with staff functions, such as legal affairs, press and information, archives, personnel, finance, passports and visas, security, research and intelligence, and protocol. Additional divisions may be geographic in character, supervising the work of embassies, legations, and consulates by particular areas, such as western Europe, eastern Europe, the Middle

East, Latin America, and Africa. Still others, finally, may be devoted to particular subjects, such as economic affairs, international conferences, the United Nations, and like matters. The foreign ministry is thus the administrative center at which, on various levels, decisions over policy application are made, information collected, research conducted, messages received, instructions distributed, and programs reviewed.

The Diplomatic Service. The diplomatic service is distributed abroad in missions established at the seat of government of each state with which diplomatic relations are maintained. The head of a mission holds one of three ranks: ambassador, which is the highest; minister, usually exchanged with small states; or chargé d'affaires, a member of the mission temporarily substituting for the regular envoy. The diplomatic agent has several functions; as Walter Bagehot contended, "an ambassador is not simply an agent; he is also a spectacle." He formally represents his government both as a symbol and spokesman in residence and as a participant in ceremonial and social occasions. He observes and reports home upon all significant developments of a political, economic, and international character. He conducts negotiations, ranging from formal conferences producing treaties and other international instruments, to informal conversations and exchanges of views leading to mutual understandings. Finally, he is responsible for protecting and promoting the interests of his government and his fellow countrymen in the state to which he is accredited.

A considerable staff assists the envoy in the performance of his duties. These other members of the mission are designated counselors, secretaries, attachés, and officers of various grades. The foreign service usually is constituted on a career basis—though some states use some political appointees as heads of missions—with a highly selective system of entry; its members ordinarily may be interchanged in either diplomatic or consular posts, or assigned to work within the foreign office. In order that they may perform their duties effectively and without interference, and to avoid affronts to national dignity that might otherwise occur, members of the diplomatic corps are granted certain privileges and immunities. These include their full immunity from criminal or civil action, from the local law, and the inviolability of their official premises and residence, when on duty abroad.

The Consular Service. The foreign service also includes consular officials stationed abroad in important cities to promote various interests of their government and to provide assistance to their fellow nationals. It is important to note that consular officers do not act as official spokesmen to the government of the state in which they are authorized to perform their duties—a function limited to the head of the diplomatic mission. Their relations are instead with local officials. Consular duties embrace a wide range of activities, which include the collecting of information, particularly on commercial matters; ensuring observance of their immigration, navigation, and tariff laws; and performing general administrative tasks related to the visa of passports, attesting of legal documents, registering marriages, births, and deaths of their own nationals, and jurisdiction over merchant ships and seamen of their country when in local ports. On behalf of their fellow nationals they perform certain services, including provision of information about local economic and trade conditions, aid to those in legal difficulties, and assistance in international emergencies. Consular officers enjoy a partial immunity from local jurisdiction in the performance of their official duties, and some exemptions may be granted to them by treaty or as a matter of local courtesy.

Other Agencies. In the broadest sense, the administration of foreign policy is no longer limited to members of the foreign service alone. The increasing complexity of foreign relations and the broadening of its dimensions throughout the world have vastly extended the instrumentalities through which the international objectives of states, particularly the major powers, may be effected. Governments now commonly employ information services and shortwave radio stations to explain their views. Trade, scientific, technical, and agricultural missions are sent abroad to assist and advise other governments. The military establishments have become increasingly important; several of the major powers station large bodies of troops abroad and commonly send military missions to the aid of lesser states in which they have a particular interest. Cultural and educational programs, involving orchestral tours, ballets, art exhibits, teacher and student exchanges, supplies of books and periodicals, are also devices for exerting influence abroad. Even private citizens, entirely outside of any official direction or program, are considered to play a part in international relations. Every student, soldier, businessman, professor, or tourist makes some kind of an impact on foreign public opinion when

he goes abroad, and to some degree—not always a limited one—
helps to create in foreign eyes an image of his country, its character,
and its objectives.

III. The Promotion of National Interests

States have five major means for the promotion of their national interests abroad: diplomacy, imperialism, war, political warfare, and international organization. What choice they make is dependent, first, on
the measures of national power they possess, and second, on the foreign-policy objectives they adopt. The first three means are the traditional devices for achieving national goals in the international realm;
the last two are, to an important extent, much more recent in their
development. A third factor also conditions the choice of means. The
reduced effectiveness of diplomacy, the retreat from western imperialism, and the now most obvious hazards accompanying resort to war
have drawn states to other measures for promoting their national interests. The totalitarian states have elected political warfare for the
most direct achievement of their strategic objectives short of actual
war—a choice unquestionably influenced by the distinct advantage
they derive from the employment of such weapons. The democracies
are at a considerable disadvantage in employing political warfare
as a weapon; and they have failed to use effectively their best
counterweapon—a high degree of international organization and cooperation among themselves.

Diplomacy. The term "diplomacy" has been used in several confusingly different ways; it is employed by some as a synonym for foreign
policy—much too general a sense—and by others as signifying the
professional skill of the diplomat—an overly limited usage. Essentially, diplomacy means the conduct of negotiations between governments. As we have seen, these are undertaken by heads of government on occasion, nowadays frequently by foreign ministers, but most
commonly by diplomatic agents. The key to the concept of diplomacy
is negotiation; forensic duels, the exchange of vituperation, public
haggling, and the threat or use of force, whatever other place they
may have in international relations, are not negotiation. The process
of diplomacy has several essential characteristics. It requires a modicum of shared confidence between governments intending to treat

with each other, a recognition of their mutual needs, and a reciprocal belief that each is acting in good faith; it proceeds by persuasion, the pressing of advantage, and the offering of concessions; it produces compromise and agreement in which there is mutual benefit.

Diplomacy has a twofold utility: first, it has been the normal and traditional method of states to promote their interests, and it is certainly the most inexpensive. States use diplomacy to promote cooperation with other governments and to effect collaboration to some purpose; to obtain political or economic concessions or the recognition of other special interests; and to contract alliances or create international associations of various kinds. Second, diplomacy is a method for the peaceful settlement of disputes. Negotiation is thus the simplest procedure for resolving a controversy and terminating a dispute. It is an alternative to the use of forceful means and war. To be sure, diplomats may press any advantage their state possesses, including a superiority of power, but an ultimatum accepted in the face of *force majeure* is not truly within the transactions of diplomacy.

In view of what we have already said about the administration of foreign policy, we can be brief in our conclusions. It should be noted, however, that there is definite disagreement about the importance of diplomacy as an instrument for the alteration of relations between states. On the one hand, some assert that the promotion of national interests is best entrusted to professional diplomats; men of similar training, background, experience, and ideals—given reasonably generous room in which to maneuver—are then able patiently and quietly to conduct continuous and confidential negotiations, employing their special skills, knowledge, and finesse. Such procedures achieve bargains of mutual advantage and the maintenance of peace. On the other hand, some deflate the importance of traditional diplomacy. They insist that it was only truly effective in the once-narrow circle of European states, when societies were largely united in values even if rivals in aspirations, and insist that the emergence of communist governments, rejecting any standards, has put an end to this situation. Diplomatic agents as individuals are said to count for very much less today: diplomatic success is not dependent upon the personal charm, the social grace, or professional skill of the envoy, but upon the policies of his government, backed by will, resourcefulness, and power. It is argued finally that traditional diplomacy has been considerably supplanted by modern means of communication, the availability of other sources for foreign information, and the personal diplomacy of national leaders.

The actual utility of diplomacy seems to lie between these two extreme positions. It has its greatest effectiveness, particularly in the representational and reporting functions, between states that are basically friendly and share some common interests and objectives. As a continuous process it can usefully strengthen the cooperation of states in association or alliance, and it offers a technique for the solution of minor disputes between them. Its ineffectiveness—and here is the nexus of the problem today—lies in the fundamental fact that all differences between states cannot be solved by negotiation. States do not invariably misunderstand each other's motives and policies; sometimes they understand them only too well. When, as in the present century, the major powers include rigid dictatorial regimes, dedicated by ideologies and political structures to altering the prevailing international order, conflicts of national interest become too great to be adjusted by accommodation. With differences so extreme, between states unable to relinquish their objectives without accepting disastrous defeat, there is little about which to bargain. Diplomacy, then, cannot resolve the irreconcilable, for the basic decision to negotiate always precedes, rather than follows, the practice of diplomacy. In this situation, diplomacy will undoubtedly continue to decline.

Imperialism. To provide an effective definition of the term "imperialism" is no easy task. At the very least it almost always carries some subjective coloration, and it is often used for propaganda purposes as an emotion-laden epithet to cover sins real and imagined. Many Britons have believed, with Lord Rosebery, that imperialism meant "a greater pride in Empire, a larger patriotism," while communists accept Lenin's definition of imperialism to mean "decaying capitalism." Scholars are no more in agreement. Some define imperialism in terms of national policy, as any expansion of a state's powers beyond its frontiers; others view it in terms of national goals, often stressing the economic ones. There is no possibility of reconciling such indiscriminate usage. The term has significance, therefore, only in some precise and limited meaning; we shall use it here to describe the forceful exercise by a state of continued control over an alien people and the denial of their right to self-government.

Empire-building at the expense of foreigners is a very old institution. Ancient and medieval periods of history witnessed the imperialism, among others, of the Persians, Saracens, Romans, Mongols, Turks, and Muscovites, who sought land, loot, and slave labor. From the early sixteenth to near the end of the eighteenth century, the more powerful states of western Europe pursued overseas imperialist ventures, combining colonization and mercantilism mainly in the western hemisphere, while those of eastern Europe conquered vast contiguous land domains. The empire of the Russians was ultimately to extend from the Baltic across Asia to the Bering Sea. In the latter part of the nineteenth century a new imperialistic surge resumed—led by Britain and France and directed mainly at Africa and Asia—in which non-European powers, the United States and Japan, partly joined. Finally, as a result of the alteration in major-power status after World War II, when most of the imperial powers moved into retreat, the Soviet Union and Communist China pressed new imperialist courses.

The essence of imperialism is the adverse political domination of a foreign people. It involves an exercise of state power for the purpose of extending authority and prestige by establishing control over a people, their territory and resources. Imperialism constitutes a superior-inferior relationship, the action of the strong against the weak, as well as the imposition or perpetuation of some sort of authoritarian rule, whether including or excluding part of the local inhabitants, on behalf of the imperialist power. There are several methods for exercising authority over an alien people. These include annexation and full or partial absorption; colonization; the establishment of various kinds of dependencies, such as protectorates, leaseholds, and mandates; and the creation of puppet regimes and satellite states. Some of these arrangements are, indeed, intentional disguises for imperialism, though they vary rather more in name than in substance when the intent to imperialize is present. Thus, the domination of Great Britain in British Honduras, of Communist China in Tibet, of the United States in Samoa, of the Soviet Union in Czechoslovakia, and of France in New Caledonia—despite the great variety of means by which they established themselves and the motives for which they remain—are all acts of imperialism. In the years after World War II, however, the old Colonial empires were liquidated, partly by necessity and partly by design. The Soviet Union, which after 1939 forced within its domain some twenty-four million people and under communist domination another hundred million, is today the leading imperialist power.

We should be clear about what imperialism is not. It is not a product of capitalism, for empire-building was practiced centuries before the system of economic arrangements bearing that label came into existence; it is actively being practiced by states that are avowedly anti- and noncapitalistic; and, indeed, only a relatively few states have empires, colonies, or satellites, whatever their economic arrangements. Further, every form of political or military interference within a foreign territory does not constitute imperialism; interventions for a particular occasion, such as for the protection of nationals or property, the contraction of alliances and the stationing of military forces abroad in a common defense program, or the military occupation of territory at the end of war—all have other purposes. Such acts are intended to effect a particular result and ordinarily are not continued, unless they are a prelude to, or concomitant of, actual political domination. Finally, the exercise of every kind of economic role or cultural influence abroad is not imperialism, though these might accompany political domination. The investment of American capital in Canada, the teaching of English literature in India, or the performance of Russian ballet companies in the United States may variously redound to the profit and prestige of the countries in which they originate; but they are not imperialism.

Even though newer techniques of enforcing political domination by the powerful over the weak may be expected—and some of the peoples most recently released from imperialist domination have already set about applying it to others—imperialism is in decline. The large colonial empires of the West have been dissolved, and future conquests by the communist powers will not be attained with the ease of some of their earlier expansion.

War. Within the community of states, war is international conflict waged by armed force. (We may distinguish a "state of war," which is a legal condition in the relationship between states who are formal belligerents, from the conduct of hostilities themselves.) War has always had an important part in the advancement of national interest —in the classic dictum of Clausewitz, it "is nothing else than the continuation of state policy by other means." It is also the most universally condemned method of promoting national goals, attracting such adjectives as "hateful," "wasteful," "inhuman," "destructive," "wanton," and "barbaric"—sentiments epitomized by General Sherman's "War is hell."

It would be easy with a subject so great and the literature upon it so vast to become lost in its reaches; we are concerned here only in dealing with war briefly as another instrument of national policy. War involves the direct application of the state's military power to some end, supported by other forms of national strength. Differences in the extent of such commitment are among the distinctions between two basic types of war. Through most of the history of the nation-state system, wars could be characterized as "limited." A limited war is one waged for specific objectives, and with a restricted range of weapons, involving and affecting only a small portion of a nation's population, and terminated when its objectives are achieved or become demonstrably unachievable. A classic example of such a conflict is the Austro-Prussian war, 1866. More recently, American wars in Korea and Vietnam held to these essentials, as did the Arab-Israeli war of 1967; but they have also left behind them deep dissatisfactions and frustrations. In "total" war, on the other hand, essentially all of the resources of the nation, human and material, are put behind the war effort; weapons of mass destruction are employed against combatant and noncombatant alike; and the aim is nothing less than forcing the enemy to unconditional surrender—hence, the attainment of total victory. These features characterized World Wars I and II, prolonging their length and enlarging their cost and destructiveness, leaving totalitarianism and international instability in their wake.

War has come to be seen inevitably as the major political problem of our time; no other kind of activity conducted by government is near to being so costly as wars—past, present, and future. Endless studies have searched for the causes of war. They have produced a great complex of answers—in terms of causes underlying and immediate, primary and secondary, just and unjust, psychological and material, and with many of them conflicting. Explanations have ranged over many disparate factors, from trade restrictions to a decline in religion. Yet the matter need not be overly complicated. It is clear that states may go to war over any question of national interest; given the existing international community, war always presents itself as an alternative means of state action. The fundamental question, of course, is why states choose war at some point in preference to other means of promoting national interest. Recalling our earlier observation that there may be substantial disagreement over what is in the national interest, we can only say that somehow a calculation is reached that war is advantageous—that it is, under given circumstances, preferable to other alternatives—for any purpose from national enrichment to national survival. The solution to the problem of war, however, will not be found by categorizing its causes, but through fundamental alterations in the character of the international community—and this is a topic we shall treat in the next chapter.

Yet something needs to be said here about the current reevaluation of the role of war. Traditionally, war involved a partial employment of national power to a particular end—an end which might be bad or good—and manifestly much good resulted from some wars. It was, it has been said, the paramount method of "changing the other fellow's mind." But the two great total wars of this century involved costs entirely out of proportion to any objectives sought by the belligerents at their outset. And as hostilities continued, they grew in bitterness, and the warring nations' aims were translated into moralistic and ideological principles—rather than specific ends—which were by their nature entirely unattainable. Not least important, their total quality and the total defeats suffered by the vanquished produced international chaos and convulsion following their end. Such total wars obviously carry a price which no state can afford to pay. They therefore cease to be a controllable instrument of national policy.

The world is now obliged also to confront military weapons having a capacity for total destruction. The advent of thermonuclear weapons, revolutionizing warfare, has produced a situation unprecedented in human history: a national power able to destroy humanity and all human values. Of course, such extreme weapons need be aimed only at enemies who possess them, and who are by that fact capable of retaliating in kind. Because such weapons offer an enormous advantage to the aggressor, states who are members of the nuclear club must also be prepared to respond instantaneously. Thus atomic war has become a potential instrument of mutual suicide; as General Douglas MacArthur declared in his address to Congress in 1951: "The utter destructiveness of war now blocks out this alternative. We have had our last chance." If a decline in war will be effected only when there is a clear decline in its utility, one might think that would end the matter, but regrettably, it does not. For one thing, not all states are equally reluctant to use force. And there is a basic streak of irrationality as well as intelligence in the makeup of *Homo sapiens*. Those who are reassured by the thought that only a madman would start World War III can only have forgotten that it was a madman who started World War II.

Political Warfare. The term "political warfare" can be used to describe generally the promotion of national interest by belligerent means short of declared or full-scale hostilities. It is a condition neither of war nor peace between states. It involves relations virtually the obverse of the Clausewitz formula—the continuation of war by other means. Though often reflecting very old ideas and practices, the fundamental weapons of political warfare were developed by the major totalitarian dictatorships after 1917. They have thus been significantly shaped by communist, fascist, and Nazi ideologies, and reflect techniques developed by revolutionary political groups to gain power within a state, then applied in the international community with the full power of a heavily armed police state behind them. The dictatorial states find a number of advantages in political warfare, beginning with the fact that they are themselves less vulnerable to it. It is less expensive than actual hostilities, and offers greater room for maneuver and the practice of opportunism. It further gives an advantage to the aggressor in that it can be broken off largely at will, and occasions relatively low risks.

Political warfare is warfare and not peaceful relations, it must be emphasized; and those engaged in it really seek to win victory over their chosen enemy. The citizens of a state at whom it is aimed may properly find it distasteful, like all war, and may be disinclined to use it themselves because they are not accustomed to similar political techniques at home. But moral indignation is no defense, and a rather pointless response; as in all war, the ends chosen are thought to justify the extremity of means, and telling lies to people, confusing or frightening them, is, if anything, less reprehensible than killing them. So long as political warfare, like any kind of war, offers an alternative means of self-interested state action within the prevailing international community, we cannot pretend surprise or dismay that some states will choose to wage it. Indeed, given the sharp differences that have emerged between the world's opposing political coalitions, as well as the danger from nuclear weapons, it seems likely that the most powerful states will be obliged to promote their interests more often by stealth than by naked confrontations, and to channel their power increasingly into insurgency and counterinsurgency operations.

We have an instructive example of the formidable and effective weapons of political warfare in the cold war (or policy of "competitive coexistence" as the communists have preferred to call it) conducted for many years between East and West, and more recently between Communist China and Soviet Russia. The objectives of the communist offensives in the cold war are to win an acknowledgment of their superiority of power and a surrender to their terms in all international relationships. To this end they seek to create fear and to provoke hysteria. They attempt to induce cautiousness in western policy, a withdrawal from forward positions, and a general weakening of democratic government and its procedures. They also aim at attacking their opponents' reputation and prestige, to unsettle and divide allies, and to win over uncommitted states to "positive neutralism" or outright alliance. Finally, they seek to undermine traditional institutions that contribute to order and stability in the international community: the practice of diplomacy, the observance of international law, and the utilization of international organization.

The arsenal of weapons employed in the political warfare offensive —which we can only partially list here—testifies to the ingenuity and relentlessness of its practitioners. From the communist base of operations, for example, propaganda is conducted through an array of channels, interpersed with insults and name-calling. Falsehoods are routine; issues are regularly confused; and siren calls alternate with fearsome threats. Censorship restricts outgoing and incoming news and information, increasing uncertainty and confusion. The perversion of diplomacy turns negotiations into endurance contests of bazaar haggling. The harassment of foreign diplomats and nationals, the forgery of documents, the use of *agents provocateurs*, and the show trials of "spies" manifest contempt and arrogance toward rivals. Border incidents make displays of combat readiness and are supposed to demonstrate the aggressiveness of the enemy.

Still other measures are used or applied abroad. Subversion—by infiltration, sabotage, and conspiracy—and the disaffection of police and military forces, seek to weaken or overthrow government authority; and "wars of liberation" are encouraged. Communist political parties and their adherents at different times have organized peace demonstrations, political strikes, and prolonged riots, and have stimulated guerrilla and civil warfare, which they hope can be escalated into wars of liberation. The nuisance value of small or underdeveloped states is exploited; in return for promises of economic aid and military support they are induced to confiscate foreign property, harass aliens, crusade against imperialism, and emulate communist policies generally. Intervention is threatened in order to force expensive military mobilizations, engender repression, enfeeble authority, and thus foment political and economic crisis. Economic pressures are applied wherever opportunities are exposed. These various techniques are alternated, and often regularly intermixed, with apparently peaceful and friendly overtures, to put the victims off guard and render them increasingly vulnerable to shock tactics.

There are no certain defenses in political warfare, and countermeasures are often awkward and difficult. A high degree of military preparedness, forward bases, counterespionage, and general deterrence all help to maintain security, to provide a position of strength from which to resist, and to contain intervention or expansion—though these are extremely expensive and are of limited use against nonmilitary attacks. Information programs, especially where they publicize the truth, are of some help in combating propaganda; yet some slander always sticks, perhaps, and its honest refutation never fully restores reputation. The "big lie" technique in the hands of any government, it has been demonstrated many times, can be extraordinarily difficult to controvert. Alliances are a means of strengthening the will of other states to resist political warfare, especially when helping to repair military or economic deficiencies. Economic aid and technical assistance, though particularly helpful to underdeveloped countries, are no sovereign remedy against their subversion.

"Brinkmanship" has also been employed as a counterweapon, a practice which John Foster Dulles was quoted defining as "The ability to get to the verge without getting into the war. . . ." Perhaps necessary on occasion, it is obviously a risky weapon if its practice becomes mutual and "hot war" is unleashed. Finally, of course, counterweapons include the identical political warfare weapons of the aggressor.

We must point out that to reply in kind is the least attractive solution. To employ an arsenal of lies, deceit, ruthlessness, and treachery is to embrace all that democracy supposedly opposes. Democracy by its very nature is not a militant creed, to be preached by zealots, nor is it a kind of consumer goods, to be merchandised like soap. Nor is it a packaged and exportable system of political and economic arrangements that a government can impose. There are dangers in conducting foreign policy by slogan: a substantial one is coming to believe one's own propaganda. There are no means of subverting a political system to democracy; the values of freedom and individualism must be chosen and practiced by a people.

Democracies may be properly concerned that they do not lose the vital contests of political warfare, but they should also not deceive themselves about the fact that many of their policies and countermeasures in the eyes of others are also as provocative, suspect in motive, and lacking in virtue as those of the communists. Propaganda has undoubtedly already been overdone in the contemporary world. In the long run, people are most impressed by what governments do, and not by what they say. The democracies do continue, indeed, to allow nationalist emotions to obstruct the kind of effective collaboration among themselves by which they could, if truly united, contribute both to world order and their own preservation and prosperity.

13

International Organization and the Problem of Peace

THE minimal objectives of government—whether local, national, or international—do not differ fundamentally: to maintain peace and order and advance common human interests. The larger the area, the wider the peace, security, and interests that the government must protect. Small wonder, therefore, that the concentration of political authority produced by the Roman empire—which extended to most of Europe—and its resulting Pax Romana, were long considered in the western world as one of mankind's greatest achievements. By contrast, the fragmented political authority of the middle ages seemed scarcely effective in performing the most elementary responsibilities of government. And for those who sought peace instead of unremitting war, the emergence of the nation-state system was only a little less frustrating. Indeed, it has become increasingly clear that under such a system no state is capable of accomplishing—except partially and sporadically—the principal objectives of government.

I. The Development of International Organization

The Desire for Peace. As is so often the case with major political innovation, some centuries of utopian thought preceded practical attempts to deal with the problem of international organization. One of the earliest of these pleas to organize against disorder was made by Dante Alighieri. In his *De monarchia*, written in the fourteenth century, Dante argued that "the human race is at its best state when it is ruled by a single prince and one law. So it is evidently necessary for the welfare of the world that there should be a single monarchy or princedom, which men call the Empire."

A contemporary of Dante's, the French lawyer Pierre Dubois, proposed creation of a league of independent European princes—with a consultative council, an arbitral court, and collective action when necessary to restore peace. The "Grand Design" of Henry IV, possibly originated by the Duc de Sully, proposed the organization of Europe into a federation of fifteen units, governed by a general council which would pacify quarrels and command an international army to enforce its decisions. Other projects, most of them virtually unnoticed by the people or their rulers in this period, were propounded by the monk Emeric Crucé, the Quaker colonizer William Penn, and the French diplomat the Abbé de Saint-Pierre. When the latter sent copies of his *Project to Bring Perpetual Peace in Europe* to contemporary monarchs, Frederick the Great is supposed to have remarked, "The thing is exceedingly practical, nor is anything wanting for its accomplishment—except the consent of all Europe and some other such trifles." Nevertheless, neither the rebuffs of rulers nor the continuation of wars of ever-increasing extent and destructiveness deterred other political thinkers from searching for ways of uniting the independent nation-states. Later in the century, Rousseau, Bentham, and Kant all elaborated similar themes on ways to perpetual peace.

Plans for international organization multiplied after 1800, and the peace movement was extended as numerous private national and international peace societies generally attempted to promote pacifism, convened peace conferences, and otherwise sought to eliminate war. The wealth of philanthropists provided the Nobel peace prize, the Carnegie Endowment for International Peace, the World Peace Foundation, and similar institutions. The popular strength of the peace movement was nowhere better demonstrated, indeed, than in the espousal of pacifism by nearly all of the European political parties characterized as socialist or proletarian, which received the support of large sections of the working-class population.

By the beginning of the twentieth century, when it was recognized that large-scale war would be of unprecedented cost and destructiveness, many began to insist that international organization for peace was no longer merely desirable, but had become imperative. The great Hague Peace Conferences of 1899 and 1907—unlike most peace conferences in that they were convened not for the termination of a war but to mitigate or avoid warfare between states—were, therefore, the outgrowth of a century's efforts and almost universally expressed desires. But even at this relatively late date, the accomplishments of these two conferences were extremely modest, and the prospects for promoting peace in the twentieth century little more likely of realization than six centuries earlier. When the second Hague Conference convened, there had already occurred the first of the major diplomatic crises which would lead to world war in 1914.

The Necessity for Cooperation. Not only did the peace movement grow steadily throughout the nineteenth century, but this period produced profound changes in the character of international relations. The "age of discovery" of the fifteenth and sixteenth centuries enormously increased Europe's contacts with the rest of the world and opened an era of great expansion in the number of units composing the international community.

Such an enlargement of the geographically known and accessible world further expanded the range of international intercourse and set in motion the powerful forces of economic change known as the "commercial" and "industrial" revolutions. These developments in turn gave rise to a worldwide network of transportation and communication facilities. Modern technology produced a host of new instrumentalities—the telegraph, telephone, and radio, and the railroad, steamship, and automobile—whose efficient use was partly dependent on some degree of cooperation and regulation.

At the very time, then, when the world was being rapidly divided into a large number of politically independent units, it was also slowly being drawn together by their cultural and economic interdependence. As no state could live in self-sufficient isolation, states would somehow have to live together. So, without conceding any diminution of their formal independence, states were inexorably led, all during the nineteenth century, to make considerable concessions to expediency, and to employ increasingly measures of international cooperation.

The Growth of International Organization. The evolution of the body of *international law,* as we have seen, brought about the legal definition and organization of the community of states. On the foundation of this law—and in the absence of any central political authority within the world—the European powers, with the increasing participation of non-European states, began to create a number of instrumentalities of international organization, based upon cooperative effort and interstate agreement. Even today, these still provide the institutional framework of international government.

Following the Napoleonic Wars, the European powers had frequent resort to the *international conference,* which is an assembly of governmental representatives—heads of states, diplomats, or technical experts—for the purpose of simultaneously exchanging views and reaching agreement on some given subject. Earlier international conferences, such as those of Westphalia (1648), Utrecht (1713), and Vienna (1814–15), had been employed to achieve peace settlements ending major wars. But now representatives of states began to meet frequently in international conferences to secure common action on international problems as the normal means of advancing state interests generally. Between 1826 and 1907, more than three hundred conferences were held, dealing with such matters as Belgium's neutralization, independence for Greece, establishment of the International Red Cross, conditions for the acquisition of African colonial territory, treatment of social questions, and so on.

Another device employed to achieve uniformity of action is the multilateral *international convention,* a document in which a number of states register their formal agreement on a matter of international policy and define their reciprocal obligations thereunder. The multilateral convention is an extremely simple form of international collaboration, since the responsibility for carrying out the agreement is left entirely to the governments that are parties to it. Usually framed at an international conference, the convention became an important instrumentality of nineteenth-century state relations. Major conventions were adopted on such subjects as the navigation of the Elbe River (1821), creation of the Cape Spartel international lighthouse (1865), protection of North Sea fisheries (1881), protection of submarine cables (1884), suppression of the African slave traffic (1890), and control of pelagic sealing in the north Pacific (1911).

This same period marked the creation of a rudimentary international administration, dictated by the increasing complexity of economic interests, the growth of communications, and the recognition of social problems. The *public international union* was organized to deal with the common interests of a number of states by the establishment of a permanent administrative office or bureau. The international union was created by an international convention framed at an international conference, which could be reconvened from time to time for revising or supervisory functions; the bureau acted as a permanent secretariat to collect and distribute information, enforce rights and duties, supervise the regulated subject, and to perform other similar administrative activities. Some twenty such organizations were created prior to World War I, including the Universal Postal Union, Rhine and Danube River Commissions, International Telegraphic Union, Pan-American Union, International Office of Public Health, and International Opium Commission.

Still further, the international community had available by 1914 a variety of procedures for the pacific settlement of international disputes. The most commonly employed method of settlement was *diplomatic negotiation.* Ordinary disagreements could usually be settled through the adjustments of diplomacy if states acted in good faith to reach an understanding over their differences. If states did not reach settlements by negotiation, a third state might intervene to the extent of bringing the parties at issue to a renewal of negotiation, which constituted the exercise of *good offices;* or a third state might go a step further, offering a solution to the dispute, which constituted *mediation.* Where international differences resulted from disagreements on points of fact, the parties could agree to the creation of a *commission of inquiry,* which—undertaking an impartial investigation to elucidate the facts—might provide a virtually automatic solution of the difference. Where parties to a dispute referred it to a commission or third state to conduct a hearing and recommend a basis for settlement, they employed the procedure of *conciliation.* Finally, the device of *arbitration,* which was as close as states had come by 1914 to anything resembling an international judicial procedure, involved the settlement of a controversy between states by its submission to a tribunal whose award after a hearing, it was agreed, would be recognized as binding upon them. Arbitration was long conducted by arbitrators especially selected by the disputants; but the Hague Conference of 1899 was able to create a Permanent Court of Arbitration with national panels of judges designated as available to act as arbitrators, though still to be selected for each occasion.

Summing up the nature of the system of international organization developed by 1914, then, we find within the international community: first, a body of international law which only moderately restricted a very broad freedom for state policy and was not concerned, in the main, with issues of peace and war. Second, a system of international conferences, convened primarily on an *ad hoc* basis—that is, held only for a particular occasion, initiated and organized by an interested state, and providing no continuity or regularity in approach. Third, a collection of multilateral international conventions, whereby states effected a degree of uniformity in some of their national policies, and were able to develop some new regulatory standards or rules of international law. Fourth, a group of public international unions, confined largely to the administration of the technical aspects of international relations, but easing the way for international cooperation where power considerations were not present. And, fifth, a variety of methods for the settlement of international disputes on a peaceful basis as an alternative to settlement by force or war.

Thus, the world organization developed to this point was haphazard, piecemeal, and uncoordinated. It could often deal effectively with practical and unspectacular matters, but it had little to do with the great political issues that divided the major powers and perpetuated the insecurity of all states. Governments did cooperate for the solution of specific and routine problems on a basis of consent and where their self-interest was rather immediately served. But they had not agreed to the creation of any general or universal international organization. In 1914, there was still no conviction that such organization was necessary to the international community.

II. Experiments with International Organization

The nineteenth century is often thought of as a century of peace. Though it began with the Napoleonic Wars—which raged over the continent from Spain to Russia and were the greatest military conflict Europe had theretofore known—and no decade afterward escaped additional hostilities between two or more European states, it was nevertheless an age of relatively small-scale wars, short in duration, and fought by professional soldiers for limited objectives. At least, for a hundred years, no general war upset the substantial order and equilibrium established by the Congress of Vienna or seriously alarmed civilians by its destructiveness.

The Concert of Europe. Throughout this period, the intermittent consultations and conferences of the major European powers, known as the Concert of Europe, were a leading factor in maintaining the general peace. None of its members—Great Britain, France, Prussia, Austria, or Russia—enjoyed anything like enough power alone to flout successfully the wishes of the others for any length of time. Then, too, with large areas of southeast Europe, the Middle East, Africa, and Asia yet available for division into spheres of interest, there was quite as much to be gained by the powers in concert as in conflict. Still an era of little popular interest in or control over the conduct of foreign relations, it was the golden age of the professional diplomat, who could devote himself to the achievement of skillful and secret compromises. When the powers acted in unison, therefore, they were able to arrange and enforce agreements for their own benefit, and if necessary coerce the smaller states.

It must be emphasized that the Concert of Europe rested on nothing more than an informal consensus; it had no treaty basis, no organization, no regular meetings. It functioned rather effectively in the earlier part of the century when the powers were disposed to meet, consult, and act together. It faltered after 1879, when the alliance system began the division of Europe into two heavily armed camps and whose every difference produced a diplomatic crisis and a new test of strength. It failed entirely when the conflicting forces of European nationalism, imperialism, and militarism produced the final crisis of 1914—and "peace hung upon the mercy of an accident." Though many invitations were issued to have the Austro-Serbian controversy submitted to an international conference, the leading antagonists on both sides, Germany and Russia, each feared that their acceptance would be interpreted as signs of weakness and irresolution. Thus, the European powers were rapidly propelled into World War I.

World War I. Although both sides had chosen to submit their differences to the arbitrament of force, neither governments nor their peoples were prepared for the holocaust that was to follow. Military leaders on both sides had planned short campaigns to produce early and decisive victories, but the conflict degenerated into one of attrition and virtual stalemate until the United States joined the Allies in 1917 and finally tipped the scales in their favor. In a war lasting over four years, involving much of the world, and nearly total in character, the costs in human life and wealth were staggering. Some sixty-five million troops were mobilized for military service; nine million were killed, and another twenty-two million were wounded. The conduct of hostilities produced even more civilian deaths, and some ten million refugees. The material costs of munitions, supplies, property losses, and diverted production were estimated for all belligerents to reach over $300,000,000,000—some ten times the total national income of the United States in 1914. Still further, lasting wounds— psychological as well as physical—that could not be counted nor valued monetarily were left on the European continent.

Long before the war came to a conclusion, therefore, demands were widespread in the Allied countries for the creation of some kind of permanent international organization that could make a recurrence of such a conflict impossible. Indeed, it seemed to many that only such an achievement could possibly justify the four years' drain on blood and treasure; thus the Allied governments called forth the final efforts of their citizens with an appeal that they could now win "the war to end war."

The League of Nations Covenant. The Paris Peace Conference of 1919 had the twofold task of arranging peace terms for the defeated Central Powers and preparing the Covenant, or constitution, of the League of Nations. Though many diplomatic figures participated in the conference, the creation of the League was mainly the work of Anglo-American political leaders; and of these Woodrow Wilson exerted the greatest influence. He had advocated the idea of a league in his Fourteen Points in 1918 and insisted on making the Covenant a part of the peace treaties ending the war. The drafting of the Covenant was accomplished early in 1919, and the signing of the Versailles treaty in June of that year joined together in permanent association the thirty-odd countries—excepting the United States, which failed to ratify it—that had been at war with Germany. Since the League aimed at universal membership, additional states were invited to accede to the Covenant, and forty-two nations were represented at its first meeting in 1920. Later, the defeated states were admitted (Germany in 1926); and by 1935 the League reached a membership of sixty-three, though still without an isolationist-minded United States. But quite as important as the effort to make the League a universal organization was the attempt to create, within a single framework, a piece of machinery sufficient to deal with virtually every aspect of public international affairs. This comprehensiveness of the League's scope and organization established it as the first real experiment with international government.

The League was to carry out three principal purposes: first, to promote international cooperation generally, through such functions as the registration of treaties, encouragement of economic and social advancement, protection of national minorities and nonself-governing peoples, and coordination of the work of international bureaus and technical commissions; second, to be responsible for carrying out some of the provisions of the peace treaties, such as the supervision of the Saar and of Danzig; and, third, to achieve international peace and security. Because the greatest motivating force behind the creation of the League was the desire to prevent war, this last objective was considered by all odds the most important; and the League's success would be measured largely by its effectiveness in maintaining peace.

The League was intended to undertake both indirect and direct approaches to the problem of war. Generally, occasions for war were to be minimized by the more extensive promotion of international cooperation, the practice of "open diplomacy," the review and revision of treaties that might endanger the peace, the achievement of a scheme of armaments limitation, and the employment of peaceful means for the settlement of international disputes. Article 10 of the Covenant obligated members of the League "to respect and preserve as against external aggression the territorial integrity and existing political independence of all members of the League." The most novel feature of the Covenant's approach to the problem of war was found in Article 16, which provided for the collective coercion of a Covenant-breaking state. The League's security system did not declare war illegal, but provided that if a state resorted to war in disregard of certain Covenant obligations, members of the League would subject it to economic sanctions. Finally, Article 16 also anticipated the possibility of collective military sanctions, to be recommended by the Council, though it made no specific provision for them and none was ever attempted.

The League Organs. The machinery of the League to carry out its purposes was new, though its antecedents are clearly recognizable in the forms of international organization developed during the nineteenth century. The Assembly, very much like an annual international conference, was constituted as a representative body in which each member had one vote. It was given power to deal with any matter "within the sphere of action of the League or affecting the peace of the world," and specifically, to admit new members, control the

League's budget, and advise upon the reconsideration of treaties. This body was obliged to adopt its decisions by unanimous vote, except for procedural questions, which required only a two-thirds majority. Generally, the Assembly was intended to serve as a sounding board for world opinion, a center for international cooperation, and a forum for the discussion of international problems where smaller states might be heard.

The Council resembled the earlier Concert of Europe, as well as the various inter-Allied councils of World War I. It was a small body in which the major powers enjoyed predominance and possessed permanent seats; during the League's existence it varied in size from eight to fourteen members, with nonpermanent seats rotated among the smaller states elected by the Assembly. The rule of unanimity applied to all Council decisions so that, in effect, each member had a veto. Although the Council was in no sense an international executive, it was the organ within which major power authority was concentrated, and in practice provided the center wherein the principal world statesmen could exert leadership.

The League's third principal organ—and its only truly international one—the Secretariat, was a more elaborate version of the international bureau, and constituted a permanent international civil service. Headed by a Secretary-General, the Secretariat's staff was responsible for providing secretarial services for the Assembly and Council; registering treaties; preparing for conferences; and maintaining the archives, library, public relations, and translation services. The Secretariat was located at League headquarters in Geneva; its six hundred officials and employees were recruited from over forty different countries. It served as a clearinghouse of information on world problems and the center for the coordination of League activities, and—as the one permanently organized institution of the League— became the repository of accumulated experience and continuity in international administration.

The League system was rounded out by several related agencies. These included the Permanent Court of International Justice, with fifteen judges, the first truly international court for formal adjudication of legal disputes between states; the International Labor Organization, which was supposed to improve working conditions and promote social welfare legislation; and a variety of agencies to perform specialized functions, such as the Economic and Financial Organization, Health Organization, Institute of Intellectual Cooperation, and so forth.

The League Evaluated. Any evaluation of the League presents difficulties, if only because conclusions about its effectiveness and accomplishment tend to vary with the expectations of the evaluator. Since the League did not prevent World War II, and is no longer in existence, the conclusion that it was a failure might seem inescapable. As the first experiment with a general international organization, the League was brought into operation without precedent to guide it, without the wholehearted determination of the major powers to support it, and without any general realization that only a new sense of international community-mindedness could maintain it. It was not remotely a world-state, not a supranational authority, not even an alliance; rather, it was a loose association of states, all continuing to possess undiminished sovereign powers and virtually unlimited freedom of action, so far as their obligations to the League were concerned. It is unreasonable, therefore, as well as unrealistic, to expect the League to have worked some kind of revolution in the nature and conduct of international relations, much less to have reversed all of the tendencies of the nation-state system, within the short period of only twenty years.

The League managed to achieve some successes in technical, health, financial, social, and humanitarian fields, though it operated on an annual budget never exceeding $7 million. It also effectively carried out some of the peace treaty terms relating to plebiscites, internationalized, and mandated territories. But it was hampered by a lack of universality; the United States refused to join, and other major powers were members only part of the time. Its authorization to reexamine treaties and effect a measure of peaceful change proved to be entirely a dead letter. Thus, the partial revision of some treaties was obtained outside the League in ways that clearly lessened esteem for it.

In its ability to restrain aggression and prevent war, however, the League was least effective. It never succeeded in organizing a system of collective security that all, or even most, of its members would support. Some states insisted that no security system could be effective unless there were a general reduction of armaments; but other states were equally insistent that they could not discuss disarmament until they felt reasonably secure! No other problem occupied so much

League time and produced such meager results. Though it dealt with over sixty international disputes, and resolved or saw resolved some thirty-five of them peaceably, these successes were mostly with the smaller states. When the major powers were concerned, success was much more problematical. The kinds of difficulties the League was to encounter were displayed as early as 1923, when both Poland and Italy flouted League authority; other instances of great power intransigence were soon to follow. But most disastrous to the whole League system was the widespread mushrooming of dictatorship throughout postwar Europe, and the accompanying deterioration of peaceful relations among European states.

After its depredations in Manchuria, Japan refused to accept League condemnation as an aggressor and withdrew its membership in 1933. The crisis for the League came when Italy invaded Ethiopia in 1935, and defied both attempts to conciliate the dispute and the application of economic sanctions imposed upon it for going to war in disregard of the Covenant. League machinery was not employed to obstruct later Italian and German intervention in the Spanish civil war, nor German aggressions upon Austria, Czechoslovakia, and Poland—the last launching World War II in 1939. The expulsion from the League of the Soviet Union in December of that year for its attack on Finland was only an anticlimactic gesture of disapproval.

These situations recall the words of Hobbes, from several centuries earlier, that "covenants without the sword are but words." The solution to the League's weakness, it was often suggested, was to put "teeth" in the Covenant; then it could compel states to keep the peace, and coerce any that did not. What must be emphasized is that the League of Nations was not a source or center of power itself; its Covenant provided only the machinery through which collective action could be organized—but machinery is not operative in and of itself. Most fundamentally, what was lacking was a general inclination to employ the League as the common means by which all aggression would be resisted. The failure of the League, then, was really the failure of the major powers: of Germany, Italy, and Japan, which chose to achieve their national aims by force and war; of Britain, France, and the United States, which preferred taking individual views of what acts of aggression directly threatened their security and failed to cooperate to defend it soon enough; and of the Soviet Union, which sought to exploit the failures on both sides. Thus it was that in

1939, the world was confronted with its second global war of the century—a war that could scarcely be put down this time to inadvertence, or to lack of an organization available to settle international disputes. Rather, the moral and material concern to prevent war was not equally shared throughout the international community; this atmosphere was fatal to the League.

World War II. World War II was an even greater disaster than World War I. It lasted for nearly six years; it involved virtually all of the important states of the world; in life and property it was the most destructive conflict in history. Some fourteen million combatants were killed; another thirty-one million were wounded; and twenty-seven million were listed as prisoners of war or missing. Over thirty million civilians lost their lives, and seventy-five million were uprooted from their homes to become displaced persons. It will probably never be known what the total material losses were; one estimate has put the costs at well beyond $1,000,000,000,000! The United States totalled its share alone at over $330 billion—or more than the total for all belligerents in World War I while the Soviet Union claimed even greater costs. Alongside such figures as these must be placed incalculable but very real costs in human anguish and despair; vast destruction of mutual confidence, good will, and creativeness; and tensions and maladjustments from which the world has not yet recovered.

III. The United Nations

The outbreak of war in 1939 meant the effective end of the League of Nations, but so great was the popular impact of the League idea that the Allied powers made re-creation of a general international organization one of their principal war aims. The matter was given attention as early as the Atlantic Conference in mid-1941; and the principles of the Atlantic Charter, which spoke of "the establishment of a wider and permanent system of general security," were affirmed by the Declaration of the United Nations, January 1, 1942, signed by twenty-six states resisting the Axis powers. Altogether, forty-seven states had acceded to the Declaration by 1945, when this wartime alliance could turn to the constructive problems of creating a new international association.

The United Nations Charter. The international conference to draft the Charter of the United Nations—convening at San Francisco,

April 25, 1945—met in a different atmosphere from that of Paris in 1919 when the League Covenant was framed. Although an end to the war now seemed in sight, neither Germany nor Japan had yet surrendered; it was widely hoped, therefore, that the United Nations alliance cooperating for a military victory would help to ensure similar cooperation in the creation of a new general international organization, and that the states associated against a common enemy would be much more inclined to recognize the necessity of making such an organization a strong and effective one. It was also possible now to draw on some twenty years' experience with the League, advice of officials who had served with it, and consultations of those who had carefully studied its operations. Certainly, there was no lack of suggestions, official and unofficial, as to what inadequacies of the League ought to be overcome. Against this background, then, representatives of fifty nations were able to complete their work in two months, and the approved Charter was signed on June 26, 1945.

Despite the attitude of many governments that the new organization would have to improve upon, as well as replace, the League of Nations, the United Nations organization as established proved to be modeled closely upon its predecessor. Its announced purposes also followed those of the League: to maintain international peace and security; to develop friendly relations among nations; to cooperate in solving international problems of an economic, cultural, or humanitarian character; and to be a center for harmonizing the actions of nations in attaining these ends. The Charter indicated further that the organization was based on the principle of the "sovereign equality" of its members, and was not to intervene in "matters essentially within the domestic jurisdiction of any state"; that members would settle their international disputes by peaceful means, refraining from the threat or use of force; and that members would fulfill their Charter obligations in good faith, giving "every assistance" in any action taken in accordance with the Charter.

To augment the original United Nations membership, the Charter provides that other "peace-loving" states may be admitted if in the judgment of the organization they are able and willing to carry out membership obligations. New members are admitted by a two-thirds vote of the General Assembly, upon the recommendation of the Security Council—so that membership nominations are subject to major power veto. The Charter does not mention any right to withdraw from the organization, though in the same manner as states are admitted, the Charter provides, they may be suspended or expelled.

The General Assembly. One already familiar with the structure of the League will not find that of the United Nations strikingly different. The General Assembly is composed of all members, with each state possessing one vote. It is authorized broadly to discuss and make "recommendations" on any matters within the scope of the Charter, general principles of cooperation, and the maintenance of international peace and security. It receives reports from and supervises other UN organs, initiates studies, approves the budget, apportions expenses, admits new members, and has duties in connection with constituting the membership of the several councils, as well as miscellaneous functions. The General Assembly decides "important questions" by a two-thirds vote, others by a majority, and meets at least once annually.

The Security Council. In the belief that the League Council had more responsibilities than it was able to perform effectively, the framers of the Charter provided for three councils in the United Nations organization. The most important is, of course, the Security Council —composed of five permanent members (the United States, the United Kingdom, the Soviet Union, France, and China), and ten non-permanent members, elected by the General Assembly for two-year terms. Organized to function continuously, the Security Council is given primary responsibility for the problem of peace and security. Its principal functions are to investigate any situation or dispute likely to endanger peace; intervene to recommend means of settling it; and, in the event of aggression, decide on measures to restore peace and security. In recognition of their special responsibilities and interests, the five major powers not only enjoy permanent seats in the Security Council, but also a privileged vote, or veto. This results from the requirement that Security Council decisions on procedural questions may be made by the affirmative vote of any nine members; an affirmative vote on substantive questions, however, must also include the concurring votes of all five permanent members. This means that any one of the major powers casting a negative vote on a substantive question may prevent action.

The Economic and Social Council. As the organization to be especially concerned with human welfare, the Charter provides for the Economic and Social Council. It is composed of twenty-seven members, elected for three-year overlapping terms by the General Assembly. Each member has one vote, and decisions are taken by a majority. The Council holds two meetings a year, lasting about one month. The Charter gives it responsibility for promoting higher standards of living, full employment, cultural cooperation, and human rights. The Council undertakes its functions by recommendations to the United Nations members, preparing reports, drafting conventions, calling conferences, and through liaison with the specialized agencies.

The Trusteeship Council. Another organ of the United Nations system is the Trusteeship Council, created to replace the League's Mandate Commission for the supervision of the trust territories. The Council does not have a fixed number of members. The Charter stipulates that its membership shall be composed of those members administering trust territories, the powers having permanent seats on the Security Council which are not trustees, and other states elected by the General Assembly to give an equal balance of representation between administering and nonadministering states. The Trusteeship Council meets at least once a year; each member has one vote and there are no vetoes, with decisions taken by a simple majority. Acting under the authority of the General Assembly, the Council collects information, receives reports, examines petitions with respect to the trust territories, and may send visiting missions to them. Originally, eleven areas were put under trusteeship; as most of these have now achieved independent statehood, the Trusteeship Council has largely completed its work.

The Secretariat. The organ, above all others, which gives continuity and cohesion to the United Nations is the Secretariat. As in the League system, provision has been made for an international civil service to perform the secretarial functions for the whole system of international government. The Secretariat is composed of the Secretary-General, appointed by the General Assembly on the nomination of the Security Council, and the staff appointed by him under regulations determined by the General Assembly. The some twenty thousand officials and employees are recruited internationally on as wide a geographic basis as possible. Protection of the international character of the Secretary-General and his staff is provided by the stipulations that they may not seek or receive instructions from any government or any other authority outside the organization, and that member states agree to respect their status.

The Secretary-General is the chief administrative officer of the United Nations, and is responsible for directing the performance of all Secretariat functions, such as providing research, editorial, interpreting, legal, budgeting, and liaison services. Although the Secretary-General assists at meetings of the General Assembly and the three Councils, he is intended to be more than an administrative officer and to provide much more positive leadership than was permitted to this office under the League system. The Charter authorizes him to exercise certain political functions in the operation and coordination of the various organs, including that of bringing to the attention of the Security Council any matter threatening international peace and security. The first Secretary-General, Trygve Lie, of Norway, served during the years 1946–53; Dag Hammarskjöld of Sweden, from 1953 until his death in 1961 while on a UN mission; U Thant of Burma was given two terms of office, the second ended in 1971.

The International Court of Justice. The principal judicial organ of the United Nations is the International Court of Justice. Modeled closely upon the earlier Permanent Court of International Justice, it is composed of fifteen judges, elected for nine-year terms by the General Assembly and the Security Council. The Court may render judgments in legal disputes between states where the parties agree to adjudication, either in advance or in a particular case, and may deliver advisory opinions to organs of the United Nations and the specialized agencies. The Court is located at the Hague, and is permanently in session. It decides cases submitted to it in accordance with the rules of international law and reaches its conclusions by majority vote. The members of the UN accept the principle that the decisions of the court are binding upon the parties.

The Specialized Agencies. A number of independent technical and expert bodies, though they are not United Nations organs, are recognized as related agencies rounding out the whole system. Known as the "specialized agencies," these thirteen bodies have their own treaty statute, staff, budget, and authority, and perform functions in the economic, cultural, educational, and health fields. They are not created by the Charter, but are "brought into relationship" with the UN, and help to effect its objectives. The specialized agencies include the International Labor Organization (ILO), Universal Postal Union (UPU), Educational, Scientific, and Cultural Organization (UNESCO), World Health Organization (WHO), International Bank for Reconstruction and Development (IBRD), Food and Agriculture Organization (FAO), International Civil Aviation Organization (ICAO), and International Development Association (IDA), among others.

The United Nations Security System. Inevitably, one of the most significant aspects of the United Nations Charter is its arrangement for the maintenance of international peace and security. Fundamentally, the framers of the UN sought to create a tighter and more elaborate system of "collective security" than was provided by the League Covenant. The Charter establishes the general obligation, therefore, that all members shall settle their disputes by peaceful means, and that they shall refrain from the threat or use of force against the territorial integrity or political independence of any state.

The Charter also assumes that the world is imperfect, however, and that the foregoing obligations will not always be self-enforced. So the Security Council is given primary responsibility and special powers, as we have seen, for maintaining international peace and security; and the members agree to accept and carry out Security Council decisions. Under the terms of Chapter VI of the Charter, which deals with the pacific settlement of disputes, parties to a dispute are obligated, first of all, to seek a noncoercive solution by means of their own choice. The Security Council is further empowered to investigate any dispute or situation to determine if it is likely to endanger international peace and security. It may then call on the parties to settle their dispute peacefully, and it may recommend methods for its adjustment. If the parties still fail to settle their dispute, they are obligated to refer it to the Security Council, which may again recommend procedures or terms of settlement.

If these procedures fail, the Charter then provides, in Chapter VII, for enforcement actions. Here the Security Council is authorized to determine the existence of any threat to peace, breach of the peace, or act of aggression, and decide what measures shall be taken to maintain or restore peace. These may be measures short of force, such as the "complete or partial interruption of economic relations, and of rail, sea, air, postal, telegraphic, radio, and other means of communication, and the severance of diplomatic relations"; or the Security Council may decide on action by means of air, sea, or land forces. United Nations members, according to the Charter, undertake to make armed forces available to the Security Council by special agreement. The Charter also provides, finally, for the establishment of a

Military Staff Committee to advise and assist the Security Council, and to command the international forces placed at the Council's disposal.

The whole system of the Charter does assume, however, that the major powers will settle their own disputes. It does not give the Security Council any power to enforce a settlement upon disputing states under Chapter VI, though the Council may take enforcement action under Chapter VII in the event of a threat to the peace. But here the power of the Security Council is subject to the veto, which has proved to be a large obstacle to effective action; for each of the major powers may not only avoid taking action itself, but prevent the others from acting. Further, the agreements to make available standing armed forces for the United Nations, which the Charter anticipated, have never been made. War is still not declared unequivocally illegal, for a state is recognized as retaining "the inherent right of individual or collective self-defense" if an armed attack is made upon it. Finally, the UN is forbidden "to intervene in matters which are essentially within the domestic jurisdiction of any state." It should be obvious, therefore, from the barest outline of its arrangements, that the Charter provides no complete solution to the problem of putting teeth into a security system, and ensuring a certain collective defense of all states.

The United Nations Evaluated. A full and fair evaluation of the United Nations would require the detailed consideration of all its operations for a number of years, to an extent not possible here. Further, we cannot close the books on the UN as we have for the League of Nations; the former is still in operation, an evolving and developing concern, and no observer can know what its future will be. Only some tentative conclusions, therefore, can be made.

Certainly, the United Nations organization got under way with some advantages not enjoyed by the League: it began with the membership of all the major powers, including the United States and the Soviet Union; it could take advantage of some twenty years of League experience, precedents, and trained officials, and thus did not have to blaze an entirely new trail in international organization; and it possessed a much greater degree of popular support, arising out of the widespread belief that international cooperation was now vitally necessary if mankind were not to be led to even greater acts of self-destruction than those of World War II.

Once again, only a loose international association of states, based upon the recognition of their "sovereign independence," had been brought into existence. The United Nations could not begin its operations where the League left off, because many serious new problems had to be faced and procedures established; the worldwide dislocations produced by World War II raised appalling difficulties. The tendency, indeed, to thrust upon the UN a much greater variety of functions, and so burden the organization with such extensive responsibilities, brought many warnings against overenthusiasm about its potentialities. As the Australian delegate to the San Francisco Conference, Mr. Herbert Evatt, warned, the UN must beware of acquiring "more harness than horse." Still worse, no major peace settlements, constituting a viable status quo, accompanied the creation of the UN. The situation prevailing when the Charter was adopted was a military one, and was not thereafter regularized diplomatically by agreement of all states concerned. Thus the new peace organization was really provided with no peace to maintain! Perhaps worst of all, the expected mutuality of trust and fundamental agreement between the major powers which was to be the foundation of the new system never materialized. With the end of hostilities in World War II, differences between the United States and the Soviet Union pyramided so rapidly to the open breach between them that no machinery seemed capable of resolving the East-West schism. The UN became itself one of the battlegrounds of the cold war.

Some United Nations Accomplishments. A large part of the work of the United Nations has been in the area of economic, cultural, and social work, in the effort to create the kind of world conditions that many thought would provide a substantial foundation for world stability and peace. The various UN organs and the specialized agencies have, therefore, sought to undertake such activities as relocation of displaced persons, increase of food production, control of disease, reduction of illiteracy, provision of capital and technical knowledge for backward and undeveloped areas, aid to children, international definition of human rights, and so on. This realm of activity has been called "the UN that nobody knows," for these constructive if undramatic programs generally attract little popular attention. Yet the UN Development Program, for example, shows how much can be done with modest resources, and how the UN and its related agencies may further develop a creative and positive thrust. Of course, international programs are not automatically conceived in wisdom, free of duplication of effort, and always certain to maximize each state's own effort and responsibility. But in the main, the UN's work has been devoted to matters of general concern, amenable to solution only by cooperative international action. Clearly, the UN has already done much that, if unspectacular, is worthwhile and even necessary to the mitigation of world tensions and the advancement of human progress.

Beyond the areas of general cooperation and technical assistance, the United Nations has provided a world forum where contact between East and West continues to be possible, and where states unattached to the groups of contending powers can exert some ameliorating influence. Large and small states alike find advantages in the opportunity for simultaneous negotiation with many governments. The UN is, of course, sometimes used for the dissemination of propaganda; but this practice is not confined to one country or one side alone. That membership in the UN is valued is evidenced by the eagerness with which new states seek entrance to it. Even the Soviet Union, so often negative in its attitude to the organization, has not been inclined to withdraw and leave the field to its adversaries. Thus, the UN does provide a center where world diplomacy could be conducted, if states were minded to use it.

Of high importance are the developments surrounding the great crises in which the United Nations has intervened. At a time when it seemed the UN system might be falling into the kind of desuetude that characterized the League after its failure to halt the Italian aggression against Ethiopia, it gained new esteem from its action following the attack of the North Korean Communist forces on the Republic of Korea, in June, 1950. Here the UN took the strongest action in its history, and with a speed that was scarcely anticipated. This dramatic display of how effective an enforcement action could be was undoubtedly the consequence of a number of factors, uniquely interacting, such as the self-chosen absence of the Soviet delegate to the Security Council, the presence of large American armed forces in Japan, and a resolute President Truman determined to respond with military power to this act of aggression. Whether the ultimate stalemate and armistice achieved in Korea, after bitter fighting and prolonged negotiations, was the kind of a solution the UN should have finally accepted is a question that has been much debated. As a test of UN effectiveness, this experience can scarcely be conclusive, but the organization did respond to this serious and overt challenge.

If the United Nations has not been equally resolute or effective in all controversies, it has at least helped to prevent a number of disputes from becoming a serious threat to international peace. For example, the UN won a cease-fire at Suez in 1956 and established the UN Emergency Force (UNEF) to act as a buffer between Israel and Egypt. Still another precedent was set in 1960 when the UN Congo Force (ONUC) separated warring local elements, forestalled possible major power intervention, and salvaged the disintegrating governmental machinery and services in that troubled African state. It was followed in 1964 when the Security Council authorized the stationing of a UN Peace-Keeping Force in Cyprus (UNFICYP).

Finally, the United Nations has shown itself capable of growth and adaptation to changing international conditions. It seems clear that any successful system of political institutions must possess sufficient flexibility to adjust to unforeseen circumstances and meet newly arising needs. Naturally, not all of the changes in the UN system—as it was envisaged by the Charter—have clearly worked to its strengthening and improvement. If the Security Council has recovered somewhat from its near paralysis during the height of the cold war, the veto power still causes a decline in reliance on that organ, in the number of its meetings, and the significance of its agenda. This development has tended to increase the importance of the General Assembly which, as its membership has swelled far beyond a hundred states, is a much more "democratized" body. At the same time, the specialized agencies, dividing responsibilities on a functional basis, have definitely flourished and expanded because they have met real international needs. Other organs have had indifferent success: the International Court of Justice averages only one case a year, largely because states seek other methods of settling disputes. The Economic and Social Council has produced little in the way of quick results, mainly because states have shown such small interest in the near-utopian objectives set for it. The Trusteeship Council is in decline, but obviously because the transfer of most of the territories to independent statehood properly puts it out of business. Finally, the Secretariat has gained in size, but the role of Secretary-General did not gain in stature during the tenure of U Thant. In this admittedly difficult office many believe his leadership, objectivity, and invention did not match those of his predecessors.

Some United Nations Shortcomings. Certainly, the United Nations organization displays some obvious shortcomings and weaknesses, and nothing is gained by refusing to acknowledge them. These arise, mainly, in attempts to achieve its objectives of maintaining international peace and security. We have already mentioned the Charter's assumption of fundamental unity of purpose among the major powers. Not only has such unity not existed, but some insist that this assumption was so unwise and unfounded as to constitute a fatal defect in the system. The Security Council veto has been employed by the Soviet Union to an extent that has frequently paralyzed that organ; despite extensive discussion of the veto problem, it is probable that no change in the voting machinery would be capable of covering the breach between the communist and anti-communist powers. Even in the absence of East-West conflict, the veto will be a problem as long as there are great powers in competition, and great powers tend always to compete. In 1960, the Soviet Union even sought to extend a veto power to the Secretariat by pressing for replacement of the independent Secretary-General by a "troika" or three-man directorate equally representing the western, communist, and neutralist blocs.

For a while it was possible to be optimistic about some arrangements called forth for the most part to tighten security measures and circumvent Soviet intransigence, such as the 1947 creation of the Interim Committee, or "Little Assembly," and the 1950 "Uniting for Peace" resolution, which were expected to permit the General Assembly to deal with peace problems and possible aggression when the Security Council was deadlocked. But the growth in size of the General Assembly has made it more and more difficult to construct effective majorities in that body, which finds itself increasingly seized with the paralysis affecting the Security Council. Recommendations by the General Assembly in an enforcement action, as authorized by the "Uniting for Peace" resolution, are not a really satisfactory substitute for determined actions by the Security Council, which has the power to move quickly and enforce its decisions. The General Assembly simply does not have the authority to oblige states to act; and its recommendations, often reduced to innocuous compromise in order to win broad support, may represent only a preponderance of votes, and not of power.

Further, states continue to evade stated Charter obligations, despite the solemn promises made when accepting their terms. The his-

tory of international events since 1945 makes it evident how widely
the members of the United Nations have failed to meet their undertakings to observe the principles of international conduct laid down
by the Charter—whether generally to settle all their disputes by
peaceful means, refrain from the use of force, and cooperate for social
and economic advancement, or more immediately, to implement the
Charter by agreements for disarmament, place armed forces at the
disposal of the Security Council, or even to meet their financial obligations to the organization, modest as these are. Some states have refused to pay specific assessments to support activities of which they
disapprove; still others, including some original members, are badly
in arrears. National interests as they are nationally interpreted continue to take precedence over international obligations.

It is once again clear that the creation of a general international organization, such as the United Nations, does not change the actual
distribution of power internationally. Despite attempts to improve
upon the League system, the UN has not solved the problem of how
to apply force effectively against a state engaged in aggression. In the
absence of American military power, the Korean enforcement action
could not have succeeded and would not likely even have been undertaken. In other instances of aggression—the Soviet Union in Hungary and Czechoslovakia, India in Goa, Communist China in India,
Indonesia in Dutch New Guinea, and the many-sided war in Indo-
china, for example—no UN action was forthcoming. States are so far
from feeling any real sense of security from the existence of the UN
that they continue to multiply military alliances, a practice which,
though authorized by the Charter, a really successful international organization would make unnecessary. Thus, the real core of power in
the world today is provided not by the UN, but is found in the military alliances of various groups of states.

Finally, it is impossible to avoid the conclusion that once again, as
with the League, the greatest difficulty is that the United Nations is
not used as the principal means by which states seek to solve their international conflicts and problems. The criticism has become common
that the UN may be weakened more from the neglect of its friends
than the opposition of its enemies. In this respect, then, the western
as well as the eastern world has a share of responsibility for its ineffectiveness. The UN has been used as a place to talk, and properly
so; but it must also be a place in which to act, and here states draw

away. Indeed, it sometimes seems as if the UN may end by drowning in its own sea of words. It must be obvious again that the structural features of the organization are only a part of its difficulty; no machinery can be effective if national political leaders lack the will and the skill to use it. On the closest inspection, therefore, the defects of the UN are those already inherent in our entire system of international relations. Small wonder that some have concluded that the kind of world conditions which would make the UN truly successful would also make it unnecessary!

We can only briefly summarize the situation for the present. If the United Nations has not figured importantly in the affairs of the major powers, it has won an even greater role in those of the new and smaller states, who see it as their international town meeting, the most likely forum in which they can exchange views and information, and represent their particular standpoint on world affairs. Whereas, paradoxically, the original premise was that the major powers should intervene in all international disputes, world peace now seems better served if the major powers are kept out of as many controversies as possible. But most disturbingly, in terms of real world needs and expectations, the UN has become increasingly ineffective; and there are no realistic plans to get at the root causes of its decline. The celebration of the UN's twenty-fifth anniversary in 1970 called for little rejoicing. While many still agreed the organization was indispensable, few could envision its reaching in present form the hopes held for it in 1945. Yet without drastic reform and reorganization, the UN seems destined to pursue its present futile course.

IV. The Search for International Order

How can international order be attained and conflict avoided? What kinds of solutions are proposed? Where can we look for fundamental principles of international organization to aid us? At the very least, it may be asked, what sort of policies in this respect should the United States promote as its contribution to this most perplexing question of our times? There is no end of answers, of course. Statesmen and scholars have advocated panaceas in a wide variety: national armaments, alliances, compulsory arbitration, general disarmament, pacifism, the outlawing of war, unilateral disarmament, and so on, at one time or another. But none of these has proved to be fundamentally effective—except in quite limited circumstances—and none attracts much general support today. The ineffectiveness of various popular solutions to war is undoubtedly the product of their superficiality. Historically, war has been one of man's primary activities; such human inclination is not likely to be altered by wishful thinking. Aggression can be regarded as instinctive, closely related to self-assertion and self-preservation; pacifism is an ideal, not an instinct, and assumes a world without evil, enemies, and so on. Those who expect a perfectly peaceful world delude themselves, for talk about a "world without war" is like talk of a "world without crime." Most contemporary discussion of the problem of controlling war, therefore, tends to be addressed to the relative merits of two other devices, collective security and balance of power, both of which have long ceased to be new ideas, but still enjoy advocacy of their basic principles.

Collective Security—The "Idealist's" Solution

"Collective security" is a political, rather than a legal, term and is used broadly to describe a system by which states, through an agency of international organization, jointly agree to use coercive means against any other state breaking the law, committing violence, or levying war upon them. The collective sanctions, or means employed to resist and coerce such an aggressor, may include reprisals, economic pressures, and even war itself. Because the advocates of such a system assume the possibility of a rational and moral international order, it has been labeled by some critics as a praiseworthy "ideal," impossible of practical achievement, and hence an "idealist's" solution.

Assumptions. The idea of collective security rests upon the proposition that the totality of international power is superior to any national power. Since domestic governments enforce the peace and maintain order against violators of their domestic law, it is asserted, why should not states do the same thing through the framework of international government in the international sphere? States cannot assure their own security by unilateral efforts, but acting in concert the members of the international community can create a force so great that no one state could stand against it. The very existence of such an organization, furthermore, would substantially decrease the occasions when it would have to act, it is maintained, because international order would be strengthened by the fact that aggressive states would face the certainty of being met and resisted by overwhelming force. Hence, international violence would tend to disappear, because people and governments everywhere would be brought to realize its hopelessness.

What would be the concomitant principles of such a system? Clearly, an effective scheme of collective security assumes that war is a matter of moral concern and, indeed, of vital interest to the entire international community. There must, then, be a level of disarmament by individual states that will minimize their ability to undertake aggression or resist collective coercion. Also required is a method to define aggression and determine who is the aggressor in the event of conflict. Such a system will depend upon the availability of some sort of international police force, preferably of components already organized and designated, to apply military sanctions when the necessity arises. It will further exclude the right of a state to adopt a position of neutrality toward the belligerents in such a situation, for no state could be permitted to take an impartial stand against aggression. Finally, within the framework of international government, there must be substituted for resort to violence and war adequate means for making adjustments in the status quo when political, social, or economic inequalities and controversies appear. In a word, methods of "peaceful change" and "peaceful settlement of disputes" must be available. Thus, although the effecting of a scheme of collective security does not require a world government, it does necessitate an assured system of international organization.

Experience with Collective Security. We may now recall our discussion of the League and the United Nations, and of their arrangements and efforts to maintain the peace. These associations provide our only experience with collective security, since nothing of this sort was attempted before 1919. Both provide the machinery for the application of collective sanctions. That of the League was only partly developed, however, despite many proposals to extend it; and in the Italo-Ethiopian war the economic sanctions applied against Italy were not effective, as we have noted. The international tensions then prevailing did not favor cooperation of the major powers through the League; the member states were unwilling to embargo oil shipments to Italy in the face of Italian threats that such action would mean war; and the League could not assure their protection if an Italian attack were provoked. Finally, the League simply did not have the authority to use, or oblige its members to use, armed force against an aggressor. As acts of aggression spread, the League states backed away steadily from all proposals to create any such authority.

The United Nations Charter provides a more elaborate scheme to achieve collective security, as we have seen, but this has only been partly implemented, and suggests once again the unwillingness of states to accept in advance irrevocable commitments to act collectively in the employment of force. At the time of the Korean enforcement action, indeed, which was effected only by an unusual combination of circumstances, forty-four of the then sixty UN members declined to send combat troops or failed even to reply to the Secretary-General's request to come to the aid of the Korean Republic. And of the sixteen nations responding, only the United States, Great Britain, and Canada provided more than token forces. Whatever else may be said of this experience, then, it was scarcely *collective* action to the extent that the terms of the Charter anticipated; and it is perhaps even arguable whether it was a true instance of collective security, as it was achieved almost entirely by American military effort. Certainly no state can yet depend solely on the UN for its protection.

Criticisms of Collective Security. Under the circumstances, some students of international affairs insist that advocates of collective security are vainly seeking a system which logic brands unworkable, and experience demonstrates to be impossible. States have not achieved it, they say, because states would not—and still will not—accept its obligations. Essentially, they assert, such a system obliges states to renounce war in behalf of their own national interest, but expects them to fight in wars that do not concern, or are even contrary to, such national interest. Such disinterestedness in international affairs is most unlikely. Drawing on the experience we have mentioned above, they then insist that all states simply will not act in concert in such a crisis because all do not feel equally threatened at the same time.

They argue, further, that states are not persons, and that coercive measures in collective security enforcement do not consist of action by a group against one—in the analogy of domestic society—but of war against a whole nation. The nation in its very nature is bound to resist to the utmost. Thus, the people of the law-enforcing states who must wage the war are punished as much as those of the law-breaking state, at least until they achieve victory. The critics of the idea also maintain that no satisfactory method has been devised to determine in every controversy which is the state aggressed upon, and which is the aggressor, deserving of coercion and punishment; that collective security substitutes universal war for local war, because all states are obliged to participate in every controversy; and that states cannot reasonably be expected to disarm substantially until they can feel greater assurance of their security—hence, even a prerequisite of the system is almost impossible to achieve.

Finally, it is argued that the disparity between the military strength of the large and small states is so considerable that there is no practicable possibility any longer of an association of small states successfully coercing a major power. Obviously, no combination of states was powerful enough to deter Nazi German aggression in 1939, and only after a long and costly world war, drawing on the efforts of Great Britain, France, the Soviet Union, and the United States, among others, was Germany finally defeated. What combination of states, it may be asked, would challenge the United States, the Soviet Union, or other states armed with and disposed to use nuclear weapons? Further, aggression is not always committed by one state alone, so that the problem can become one of coercing a number of states. In view of all these considerations, the critics of the idea believe it cannot be successfully defended or seriously advocated.

Balance of Power—The "Realist's" Solution

The term "balance of power," in the international community, describes an equilibrium of forces sufficient to keep the peace among states by preventing one member from gaining a dangerous domination over the others. It may constitute a simple balance, as when there is an equilibrium between two states or groups of states; or the balance may be complex, with power distributed widely and fairly equally among a number of states. The advocates of balance of power, whether as a device or a policy to maintain international order, have styled it the "realist's" solution on the grounds that it makes proper allowance for the role of power in international affairs and, indeed, draws on the dynamics of power to accomplish its effect.

Assumptions. Advocates of the balance-of-power system begin with the same constructive goal as the supporters of collective security: the protection of national independence and maintenance of international peace. But they claim to avoid expectations of idealized state conduct and unreal disinterestedness. Their solution depends upon neither moral nor legal standards of action, and requires no formalized machinery of organization. It takes the form, rather, of a *modus vivendi* —with only a general understanding as its basis. The individual security of states can best be maintained, supporters assert, by giving full play to the inclination to combine in resistance to any state seeking to overthrow the international equilibrium. Thus, the balance of power can operate automatically, if not artificially restricted, because states that are threatened have a natural tendency to join together against a common enemy or aggressor.

It is further argued that, in the attempt to achieve and maintain the condition of balance of power, states will be led to adopt its goal as a leading principle of their policy in international affairs. If one state should undertake the dangerous aggrandizement of its power, it will be restrained peaceably if possible, but forcibly if necessary, by other states; and the balance will be restored by the defeat of the aggressor. War is therefore discouraged and likely to be prevented because attempts to disturb the status quo or to employ policies of aggression are made difficult and perilous. Further, states are encouraged to undertake a diplomacy of adjustment and maintain peace by consultation, concessions, compensations, and bargaining. Finally, states are left free to be the judges of their own national interest.

Experience with the Balance of Power. Despite its recent fashionableness, the principle of the balance of power is quite old, and its practice even older. It was recognized in Europe as early as the fifteenth century in the relations of the Italian states. It led to the creation of coalitions which fought in the Thirty Years' War, and its principle was incorporated in the Peace of Westphalia which followed in 1648. The seventeenth century saw the idea further established in European politics. It was recognized in the Peace of Utrecht, in 1713, and revived again by the powers arrayed against Napoleon. The basis of the peace settlements ending the Napoleonic Wars, in 1815, was the establishment of a European equilibrium, which was increasingly extended on a worldwide basis in the decades following.

The work of the Congress of Vienna seemed to have vindicated the doctrine for the nineteenth century, yet at no time did the defeat of an aggressor actually discourage the next one. Far from providing a permanent solution to the problem of international order, the balance of power did not prevent a series of wars throughout the so-called century of peace. And World War I came in 1914 as the culmination of attempts by Germany to overthrow the balance and establish a hegemony over the European continent. The Peace of Paris (1919–20) —based upon the principles of national self-determination, disarming the aggressors, and collective security—clearly constituted a discarding of the idea. But the failure of collective security after both World Wars I and II has led to revival of the idea of the balance, and new advocacy of its utility.

What conclusions, in short, may be drawn from historical experience with the balance of power? It does seem to have been effective in demonstrating the merits claimed for it when power is widely and somewhat evenly divided among a number of fairly equal political units, so that a considerable variety of alignments and combinations of states is possible. A true fluidity of the international situation thus seems almost indispensable for its effective operation. The balance-of-power system has also been able notably to maintain international stability for short periods, thus perpetuating the multistate system and preserving the existence of small states which otherwise would be unable to defend themselves. But the existence of the balance has never completely discouraged the ambition of one or more states to overthrow it, or the anxiety of others to maintain it. Both sides are thus led to secure their ends by military alliance systems, rivalry between heavily armed camps, displays of force, successive crises between the coalitions, and—finally—general war in which few important states are able to avoid involvement.

Criticisms of the Balance of Power. After examining the extensive history of the balance of power—only briefly surveyed here—many students of international affairs insist that dependence upon it as a device to preserve world order can only be blindness in the face of facts. The advocates of such a principle, they say, far from having discovered how power can be controlled, are only pseudorealists guilty of an incomplete analysis of international life. They point out that the balance-of-power system affords no fair representation or protection of the interests of all states—that it permits only the great powers to maneuver for their advantage, while the smaller states are used as pawns and buffers.

They assert, further, that the balance of power is at best a crude and tentative arrangement. It is always uncertain whether it has been truly established and how effectively the states comprising it will continue to sustain their existing positions. The dangerous risk is ever present that someone will miscalculate the situation and precipitate conflict. It is argued, as well, that it is even questionable whether states ever really seek the equilibrium so neatly assumed in theory; rather, they are more likely to strive for what inevitably seems more congenial to their national interest—a superiority of power in their own favor. And this step creates the very condition which balance of power is supposed to prevent: tampering with the balance, and a trial of strength producing war.

Finally, it is asserted that developments in the post-World War II era may have rendered the whole balance-of-power concept obsolete. The effects of World War II and the development of nuclear weapons by the United States and the Soviet Union reduced the number of major contenders in the power contest to two. This produced for some years a simple balance of power, but also an extremely danger-ous and unstable international situation, reaching a crisis in the eye-ball to eyeball confrontation over Cuban missile sites in 1962. If this event then demonstrated the superior power of the United States, it showed clearly as well what little else stands between a modicum of world order and chaos. More recently the two great ideological blocs have split apart. The world is thus no longer polarized about the two superpowers, and new centers of power are emerging. But the result is scarcely balance or stability. Communist ambitions for expansion and aggrandizement have not been extinguished, and wars continue whether by means "hot" or "cold," conventional or unconventional. Further, full-scale nuclear war is still entirely within the realm of pos-sibility. Of its probability, we shall have something to say at the end of this chapter.

V. The Problem of World Authority

Looking at the limited development and modest accomplishments of international organization, one recalls the remark of Victor Hugo, who was once asked what he thought of civilization. "Civilization?" he said, "It's a good idea. Someone ought to start it." Certainly it is clear that we have so far achieved only the most limited forms of any-thing that could be called international *government*, and nothing re-sembling a real world authority that might provide for the globe the kind of peace and security that men claim, at all events, to be seeking. Can we start it?

It is a commonplace to observe that the League of Nations has failed, and that the United Nations has not yet succeeded. They have not produced effective systems of collective security, nor demonstrated that such systems are really practicable in the present world. Furthermore, it no longer seems possible to rely on the operation of a balance of power. There has been inevitable speculation, therefore, upon the opportunities of some new departures in world political arrangements that would carry us beyond the present level of international relations and achieve some kind of world political authority. Several of these merit consideration.

World Empire. One of the most obvious means by which a central world authority could be brought into existence is through the establishment by one state of a political hegemony over all others and the creation of a world empire dominated by that state. Such an entity would constitute a kind of superstate—with a single sovereignty, government, law, and citizenship, presumptively—and might achieve the complete merging of the present multistate system into a single whole. History offers some precedent for this possibility. The Roman empire, though not worldwide, extended partial control over the western world of its time—the Mediterranean rim and Europe. The Pax Romana which it made possible was as great a force for universal peace as man had then known. Even the Pax Britannica of the nineteenth century was acknowledged to be a force for law and order to a larger extent than any previously seen in the modern world. Still other efforts at wide imperial hegemony have been made by Alexander the Great, Genghis Khan, Napoleon, and Hitler, though all ultimately failed.

Could such an attempt succeed in the world today? It seems beyond argument that a single global state could not be brought into existence voluntarily by the acquiescence of existing states; it would have to be created by conquest and force. Yet it can scarcely be denied that the technological means for the establishment of world empire are within the reach of modern man. Those who advocate a world empire almost always envision its creation and control by their own state. Since virtually all states would forcibly resist domination by another, however—and some could put up a fairly effective resistance—it seems likely that such a world dominion could not be achieved except after long and bitter worldwide war; and what could be won in this way would not only create a most unpromising basis for political organization but, for its cost, might not even be worth having. If this, then, is the only avenue to world empire, we may conclude that it is a most unlikely solution to the problem of world order.

World Federation. A second approach proposes the creation of world authority through the union of existing states by federation. Federalism is a form of government wherein, essentially, a constitution divides political power between the central government and the governments of component units of the federation; the sphere of authority of each level of government is defined and may not be altered by either alone; and both levels may exercise authority directly upon individuals. It permits the central government to deal with matters of general interest to the federation which require common action and permits the governments of the component units to manage local matters. The federal arrangement is well known, of course, exemplified in the political systems of Switzerland, the United States, Canada, Australia, Germany, and, in form at least, in the Soviet Union. How would the principle apply in the establishment of world government?

Most proposals for world federation tend to follow many features of the American Constitution. They assume a central world government would be representative and democratic, composed of the usual three branches. Thus, there would be an executive agency to enforce world law and maintain order, a legislature to frame law and policy, and a world court with compulsory jurisdiction for the settlement of disputes. Advocates of world federalism all agree, as a minimum, on the necessity for sufficient coercive authority and monopoly of armaments to maintain peace; others, however, would go further, to provide such features as a common world citizenship, currency, free trade, a bill of rights, and so on, thus tilting the balance of political power in favor of the central government.

The cause of federalism, however, scarcely seems realizable in the political atmosphere pervading the world at present. No government has sought to promote it. Communists oppose it as a "capitalist plot." Nationalists and superpatriots have as readily denounced it for its infringements on national independence and sovereignty, labeling it a dream of "rootless cosmopolitans." Democratic states do not relish the idea of joining a world government when most of the world's people have had no experience of democracy. Those with relatively high standards of living are concerned that they would be reduced to the level of those much lower. It is even argued that the states of the world are by now far too disparate in power to make their federation practicable. The formal abolition of national sovereignty, for instance, would not necessarily abolish the power centers that exist in the world today. The superiority of manpower, natural resources, and industrial potential of the two great superpowers would still remain, in fact, and constitute realities to be reckoned with, even if the United States and the Soviet Union voluntarily relinquished their legal expression in theory. Under all circumstances, then, the belief in the desirability or necessity of world federation is not widely enough shared to provide soon a basis for world political organization.

World Functional and Regional Integration. Despite the unpromising prospects for developing world authority by the creation of a world empire—which would be actively resisted—or by the creation of a world federation—which is simply being ignored—there is a possible third path, which already has advocates. It involves neither a predetermined scheme of action by one state, nor a blueprint of organization agreed upon by all. It is, indeed, little more than a method: the achievement of higher authority through the integration of lesser authorities, by gradual growth and development along lines already discernible. The supporters of this approach to world order reject extreme and sweeping solutions. They point out that stable and truly effective political structures are more like trees than houses; they are grown, rather than built. Thus, the sense of community among people fosters the creation of common institutions, and these in turn help to solidify and maintain the community.

The central weakness of all proposals for the immediate creation of world government, in consequence, is simply that there is no world community upon which it could be constructed. There is, instead, an international community composed of many independent nation-states; and it is to the nation-state that most men still give their highest loyalties. But these considerations, it is asserted, while they may explain the virtual impossibility of creating world government by an immediate and positive act, do not exclude the possibility for its development by the gradual integration of states along functional and regional lines. The process, in fact, is already underway; it may well be continued in greater intensity.

World integration in practice has continued at an accelerated rate in the twentieth century, accompanying the development of the League of Nations and United Nations systems, so that the number of separate international agencies with particular responsibilities—known as *specialized* or *functional* international organizations—has grown greatly. The International Labor Organization, Food and Agriculture Organization, International Civil Aviation Organization, and Universal Postal Union are only a few of the better known agencies of this sort devoted to dealing with a variety of technical international problems. Still others, known as *regional* international organizations, whether of general purpose or specialized in their approach to international affairs, are constituted on a geographic basis. Examples of these include the Organization of American States, Nordic Council, European Economic Community, Organization of African Unity, and North Atlantic Treaty Organization.

In effect, then, a vast network of bonds of association is steadily being drawn around various groups of states. And as these new unions develop in importance and effectiveness, their members find themselves increasingly led to employ them to resolve political as well as technical problems. Thus do they create new bases for the existence of larger communities than those of the nation-states. To be sure, the functional and regional association of states does not invariably feed into a general trend toward world integration; in some cases, for a time at least, it may well obstruct a higher level of world association. But the advocates of functional integration believe that from the continuation and gradual extension of communication, accommodation, and cooperation among the nation-states—in many ways and for many purposes—a wider peace, a larger community, and a higher level of political authority may be brought into existence. Although we may not yet discern its ultimate form, we may imagine its results.

Conclusions. Obviously, we cannot foresee how or if the problem of creating an adequate world authority is to be resolved. Whether it can be done by one of the alternatives we have briefly discussed, or by still some other method, it is probably idle to guess. In the late twentieth century, many men have come to believe that the division of world society into nation-states creates most international trouble and have intensified the search for newer political configurations to meet traditional political needs in more effective ways.

It does seem quite possible that the individual nation-states, in the long run, will be obliged to abandon their conventional claim to sovereignty. So urgent is this necessity, indeed, that the state as we have known it may even be on the road to extinction. What sort of political associations are likely to emerge? We are inclined to expect they will be federal structures of various types, so that the future political life of man may have something in common with the middle ages, and develop a great variety of relatively independent, functional, and territorial groupings.

The achievement of a more effective political integration of the world will certainly take much time—and it is not at all clear that the basic conflicts between the major powers, which can conceivably escalate into full-scale nuclear war, assures us a sufficient margin for it. Yet it is also possible that the equal ability of both the United States and the Soviet Union to destroy all significant military targets in the world has created an atomic weapons stalemate, neutralizing their use by either. Each side may thus be deterred from the suicide pact which employment of the ultimate weapon would involve, if only because each must stop and draw back before a step that could destroy civilization itself. Man has, after all, come a long way from barbarism; perhaps he can outdistance it entirely.

We prefer to think, finally, that mankind will not destroy itself, though in this frequently disordered world, we can scarcely be sure. If future generations are able to look back on our race between education and catastrophe, they may well be inclined to apply to it the Duke of Wellington's blunt summing up of the Battle of Waterloo— "It was a close-run thing, the damned closest-run thing you ever saw in your life!"

14

Epilogue

POLITICS and the political order are no longer identical with "the good life," as the ancient Greeks thought, but neither are they alien to it, as men have often held in the centuries since. In the kind of life many of us in the twentieth century have come to take for granted, and toward which other millions aspire, the order and activity we call "political" is so essential that we cannot avoid being the most political people in history since the days of Plato and Aristotle. If our political regime is faulty, few aspects of our lives will not suffer the consequences. But while any thoughtful person can recognize this if he directs his attention from narrow and immediate interests to their context and implications, no agreement with others on standards to judge the adequacy of political regimes necessarily follows. Not even political science has been able to create or discover universally acceptable criteria. When students of politics observe the world about them, they find not only differences but even contradictions; when along with other citizens they endeavor to make reasonable choices, they encounter dilemmas. Understanding seems at best partial, and what to one man is dispensable is essential to another. However, we must recognize that human freedom, when present at all, is particularly manifested in political life, and that our inability to comprehend politics completely springs from the fact that freedom breeds diversity and conflict, and obliges us to make choices that are not usually easy.

Most political scientists have seen democracy as the form of government most closely related to the condition of freedom, a perspective generally maintained throughout our discussion. In ideal, this is undeniably true. In practice, however, the conclusion is less certain, for if democracy does not work it cannot serve freedom or any other end. The theoretical analysis of democracy presented in our early chapters was supplemented by considerable discussion of how both democracies and dictatorships operate and of the domestic and international issues they confront today. Our conclusion will therefore be most useful if it helps to evaluate the various forms of institution, process, and policy in the light of the urgent political needs of today and tomorrow. Only thus can we understand requirements and possibilities in contemporary politics and discern the place of democracy.

Early in American history, Fisher Ames gave a grudging tribute to the democracy he was not particularly fond of. "Monarchy is like a great ship. It sails majestically on, then strikes a rock, and sinks forever. Democracy is like a raft," he said. "It never sinks, but damn it, your feet are always in the water!" Both criticism and defense of democracy have been couched in these terms, as friends of democracy claimed for it not only unsinkability but also the majesty of truth and justice. In our earlier chapters we sought to show such claims to be of dubious merit. The virtues of democracy, though far from unconsequential, are more modest.

The distinction Ames made appears basically sound. Men imbued with a strong sense of righteousness find it difficult, if not impossible, to accept a regime which promises only to keep us afloat. But the problem of democracy today is somewhat different, and it bothers realists no less than idealists. Ames took it for granted that while democracy did not embody the highest virtues, it was at least durable. It did not occur to him, apparently, that even an unsinkable raft might still break apart—that the qualities of democracy could be inadequate not only in ethical standards but in survival ability. Today, however, there are few things central to our concerns for which effective governmental support is not essential, even if the support is indirect and unnoticed. We are committed at home to broad humanitarian purposes requiring intense and skillful cooperation for their realization. Abroad, we are engaged in remarkably hazardous enterprises in a world full of dangerous conflicts. Miscalculation and ineffective action are likely to be more than merely disappointing; they may be fatal. To be sure, our rather haphazard and pragmatic methods, usually involving much trial and error, probably would produce acceptable results ultimately if sufficient time were at our disposal. But time is of the essence and it may be running short.

We may wonder, though, whether this criticism of democracy is really any more significant than those of old. Indeed, it is much the same, except that survival rather than virtue is set forth as the end democracy allegedly cannot attain. Both the idealists of old and the realists of today insist that men are not equal—or always and equally rational—and that the bulk of mankind is not capable of imaginative genius and creativity. This is quite likely true; most men commonly desire nothing more than the preservation of the status quo once its benefits are generalized. But that argument does not in itself invalidate democratic government. Those who reject democracy must do more than deny the omnicompetence of the average man. If they pretend to a rational demonstration, they must show that those whose rule they would prefer actually possess all the qualities required in modern government—not only knowledge and virtue, but also the capacity to exercise them in effective statecraft. This they have never been able to do. As Plato discovered ages ago, the search for perfect governors is doomed to failure. The complexities of political action and values are too great; politics is inevitably cut of rather coarse cloth. While it is not hard to find this and that wrong with democracy, there is—unfortunately or not—no alternative form of political regime which will effectively remedy all of democracy's failings, or even a substantial number of them.

The possible alternative to democracy is not another form of government, whether better or worse, but a succession of various types of governments, each temporarily serving particular purposes and meeting particular problems, and each in turn being overthrown, as conditions change, with all the confusion accompanying revolutions. Revolutionary zeal is most pronounced precisely among those who do not understand the nature of democracy or its benefits—or are active where democracy does not exist and may be impossible. For democracy in practice is unique; inherently experimental, it is the only form of government in history which specifically tends to promote a reasonably automatic adaptation to changing conditions and objectives. Where democracy has been established—unfortunately in relatively few places—its performance has earned description as institutionalized peaceful revolution. Of course, there is no proof one way or another as to democracy's capacity to continue in this vein, for its experience has been short and our data modest.

Modern political thought and practice traditionally have fluctuated between two poles: one of responsibility and one of leadership. The two contending political theories of the contemporary world differ largely because democracy is rooted in the ideal and processes of responsibility in government, while dictatorship rests its case entirely on the necessity of uncontrolled leadership. Until recently, democrats have paid a quite inadequate attention to leadership and its provision. Responsibility was seen as the key to good government—to be achieved by subordinating officials to the rule of law and to an electoral accountability. So the founding fathers in America aimed to bind down the executive in the chains of the Constitution; power was distributed throughout government as a barrier to tyranny; political factions within society would operate to cancel out each other's threat to the political system. Since it was assumed that leadership would arise spontaneously, no special provision for it was necessary, except to limit and regulate it.

This concern of constitutionalists and democrats to preserve responsibility in political life is worthy of respect; tyranny is the consequence of rejecting it. Yet we have discovered that in some circumstances an exclusive preoccupation with responsible government is no longer meaningful. The need for leadership is particularly overwhelming in times, such as the present, when values and standards relevant to political judgment have been upset by rapid change. The rise of totalitarian dictatorships in this century reflects this fact; they were not the product only of the ruthlessness and demagogic skill of a few men. We do now see that leadership is an essential need of human life, and most obviously and powerfully in periods of great change and confusion, of which the twentieth century is a prime example. Dictatorship can be prevented, therefore, only if some other effective forms of leadership can be provided. Furthermore, while leadership inevitably must come in good part from government—from the political realm—it must also come significantly from the social realm as well: from the leaders of other important institutions of society—the corporations, labor unions, universities, churches, and so on. Only with far better channels of communications between such leaders and those in government are we likely to obtain concentration on the great issues that transcend us.

The problems facing our society today are truly staggering. Where once they emerged slowly, we responded slowly to them; but today great problems appear with frightening speed. A few decades ago we could concentrate on achieving national wealth and international power. Yet the winning of these has brought in their train a host of new problems: of war and nuclear weapons, of population and pollution, of overtaxed resources and underfinanced local governments, of dehumanized urban living and social injustices, of burdensome taxes and fiscal deficits, of irresponsible mass behavior and sheer bad taste. We see that ruin can come from the fulfillment as well as the denial of human hopes. For the first time in man's history, his survival depends not so much on his ability to conquer nature as on his ability to protect nature so that it may sustain him.

It is further the case that we can no longer simply identify evils and assume that the application of good intentions will then remedy them. We have now to face the possibility—and some experience suggests the probability—that men are not capable of solving or even controlling the great social, economic, and political problems before them. In the past, we could quote Abraham Lincoln that the proper function of government is to do those things for the people that they cannot do for themselves. And for long, the performance of private enterprise alone was seen everywhere as leaving much to be desired. But the dismal record of much recent governmental effort to solve various contemporary difficulties suggests that many of these are amenable neither to billions of dollars in expenditures, enlarged bureaucracies, pyramided agencies, renamed and reorganized programs, nor any other of the best efforts of alternating partisan administrations. Governments that grow too large become ungovernable. Governments appear to perform best, as they were so originally designed, as protective institutions. As all good things must end, so must expectations of perfect and omnicompetent governments.

In the decades to come, democracy's severest tests seem to lie before it. We face the question whether through representative democracy a people can meet successfully the unprecedented problems of the 1970's. The answer in part seems to turn upon the possibility of creating a renewed sense of community—of a civic mindedness and personal self-discipline essential to its operation. History makes clear that these are essential ingredients to the enjoyment of freedom without anarchy. The answer in part also turns upon the likelihood of stemming the growing lapse into irrationality, which has become so attractive to some. There have always been certain people, of course, who would act unreasonably, but there has scarcely been a time when so many have chosen to behave irrationally. And it is within the social institutions and intellectual traditions which have long sustained discipline, authority, and rationality that there are gathered large numbers who would attack and undermine them. If, indeed, only a declining number of the privileged members of contemporary society are willing to support, defend, and advance the values of western civilization, the prognosis for democracy is negative.

We can only agree, then, with Sir Winston Churchill that democracy is possibly the worst form of government—except for any other. It may be that responsible democratic government has ceased to be feasible in the face of today's problems, however well it may have served some peoples in the past. But that where democracy exists it may be preserved, and where democracy does not exist it may be promoted, depends much on leaders guiding their actions by democratic standards in an atmosphere of public self-restraint. All communities require leadership, but that alone which democracies can tolerate must arise in a pluralistic social life, with many centers of informed initiative accountable through mutual checks and balances. Wise leaders will promote these conditions.

Would democracies then be able to meet the threats and challenges to life in the world today? There is no guarantee. We seem to be once more in that human crisis, recurrent since the times of ancient Greece, as described by Professor Gilbert Murray in his 1912 Columbia lectures: "Mankind has not yet decided which of two opposite methods leads to the fuller and deeper knowledge of the world: the patient and sympathetic study of the good citizen who lives in it, or the ecstatic vision of the saint who rejects it." We believe the continuing development of an effective political science will help, and the spread of its insights and information among the people, if they will undertake the discipline of politics to make democracy work. Yet politics is more than a science or a philosophy; it is also an art. Thus, the future of democracy cannot be taken for granted. In the end, people cannot be protected from their own stupidity, perversity, and failure of vision; there is no way of ensuring their survival and happiness. Thucydides long ago discerned the only answer: "The secret of happiness is freedom, and the secret of freedom, courage."

A Study Guide to
Modern Government

Reference Materials

Guides to Bibliographic Information

Clifton Brock, *The Literature of Political Science* (Bowker, 1969) is a most useful and thorough guide to information, bibliographies, and reference sources.

Bert F. Hoselitz (ed.), *A Reader's Guide to the Social Sciences*, rev. ed. (Free Press, 1970) contains a section on political science by Heinz Eulau in the form of a critical essay which discusses many of the classics of political science, recent writings on methodology, and important works on politics, public administration, and international relations.

Peter R. Lewis, *The Literature of the Social Sciences: An Introductory Survey and Guide* (The Library Association, London, 1960). While covering the general area of the social sciences, the larger portion of this volume is devoted to political science, public administration, law, and international affairs. Emphasis is on British publications, but others are not excluded.

Carl M. White (ed.), *Sources of Information in the Social Sciences: A Guide to the Literature* (Bedminster Press, 1964) ranges over the various social sciences listing books and other resources by various categories, and is partly annotated.

Robert B. Harmon, *Political Science: A Bibliographical Guide to the Literature* (Scarecrow, 1965) offers an extensive selection, arranged by fields, not completely annotated.

Lubomyr R. Wynar, *Guide to Reference Materials in Political Science*, 2 vols. (Libraries Unlimited, 1968) emphasizes reference sources, partly annotated.

John Brown Mason, *Research Resources: Annotated Guide to the Social Sciences*, 2 vols. (ABC-Clio Press, 1968) is a valuable interdisciplinary guide.

R. L. Merritt and G. J. Pyszka, *The Student Political Scientist's Handbook* (Harper, 1970) is a general guide to source and bibliographic materials for the preparation of investigative papers.

Robert B. Downs, *How to Do Library Research* (U. of Illinois Press, 1966) provides an excellent explanation of how to use libraries and their reference sources.

A. S. Beardsley and O. C. Orman, *Legal Bibliography and the Use of Law Books,* 2nd ed. (Foundation Press, 1947) undertakes full treatment of the subject for the Anglo-American legal system and covers the law report series.

Frederick C. Hicks, *Materials and Methods of Legal Research,* 3rd ed. (Lawyers Cooperative Publishing Co., 1942) is also a full treatment of legal research, law books, legal periodicals, and law reports.

L. F. Schmeckebier and Roy B. Eastin, *Government Publications and Their Use,* rev. ed. (Brookings, 1961) is a substantial and comprehensive guide to government documents in the United States.

Monthly Catalog of United States Government Publications is a useful listing of current publications. *Monthly Checklist of State Publications* records those state documents received by the Library of Congress.

Dictionaries

Harry Back *et al., Polec: Dictionary of Politics and Economics* (Gruyter, Berlin, 1967) is a compilation of English, French, and German terms.

Joseph Dunner (ed.), *Dictionary of Political Science* (Philosophical Library, 1964) defines or briefly identifies several thousand terms and names.

Edwin V. Mitchell, *An Encyclopedia of American Politics* (Doubleday, 1946) constitutes a useful guide to the principal terms and personalities which have figured in American politics.

Jack C. Plano and M. Greenberg, *The American Political Dictionary,* 2nd ed. (Holt, 1967) is organized into broad subject areas.

Edward C. Smith and Arnold J. Zurcher, *New Dictionary of American Politics*, 2nd ed. (Barnes & Noble, 1968) treats both political and legal terms in a wide array of entries.

Hans Sperber and Travis Trittschuh, *American Political Terms: An Historical Dictionary* (Wayne State University Press, 1962) is a substantial work revealing something of the flavor of American politics, with historical emphasis.

F. Elliott and M. Summerskill, *A Dictionary of Politics*, 4th ed. (Penguin, 1964) is an English guide whose entries deal with leading statesmen, political institutions, political parties, and related matters.

Jack C. Plano and Roy Olton, *The International Relations Dictionary* (Holt, 1969) covers the broad area of international relations and associated fields.

Günther Haensch, *Dictionary of International Relations and Politics* (Elsevier, 1965) renders the basic vocabulary of politics—some six thousand terms—in English, French, German, and Spanish.

William Safire, *The New Language of Politics* (Random House, 1968) is an anecdotal dictionary of slogans and catchwords.

Henry C. Black, *Black's Law Dictionary: Definitions of the Terms and Phrases of American and English Jurisprudence, Ancient and Modern*, rev. 4th ed. (West, 1968) also covers the field of legal terminology in concise entries.

Encyclopedias

Encyclopedia of the Social Sciences, 15 vols. (Macmillan), is an extensive compendium. Published originally between 1930 and 1935—and thus out of date at many points—it is still a valuable reference work, international in scope. Articles were contributed by outstanding scholars and authorities and are signed, with accompanying bibliographies. The encyclopedia was reprinted in 1948 in 8 volumes.

International Encyclopedia of the Social Sciences, 17 vols. (Macmillan, 1968) contains nearly two thousand signed articles and biographies by outstanding scholars. It brings up to date and complements information in the above *ESS*.

Worldmark Encyclopedia of the Nations, 3rd ed., 5 vols. (Harper, 1965) devotes Volume I to the United Nations and related agencies; the remaining four contain geographic, historical, political and other data on various regions of the world. There is also much of value for the student in the major general encyclopedias: *Encyclopedia Ameri-*

cana, 30 vols. and supplementary *Annual; Encyclopedia Britannica,* 24 vols. and supplementary *Book of the Year; Collier's Encyclopedia,* 20 vols., providing briefer accounts; and *Columbia Encyclopedia,* a single volume useful for ready reference.

Yearbooks and Handbooks

New York Times Encyclopedic Almanac. Annual. The largest and best collection of factual information and political data among the almanacs.

Whitaker's Almanack. Annual. A British publication, emphasizing data respecting the United Kingdom and the Commonwealth.

Annual Register of World Events. A historical and factual summary of world affairs, with British emphasis.

Survey of International Affairs. Irregularly produced but aimed at systematic coverage of the years, emphasizing recent political developments, national and international. A publication of the Royal Institute of International Affairs.

United States in World Affairs. Annual. An important and objective treatment of American foreign relations and international events of concern to the United States. Published by the Council on Foreign Relations.

Documents on American Foreign Relations. Annual. Contains a substantial selection of representative documents on the subject, also published by the Council on Foreign Relations.

Statesman's Year-Book. Annual. Treats each country, briefly describes its governmental system and other features. Statistical, historical, and diplomatic information for ready reference.

Political Handbook and Atlas of the World. Annual. Contains data on the parliamentary bodies, political parties, the press, and the principal government officials of most national governments.

Europa Yearbook, 2 vols. A directory of international organizations, international agreements, and general political and statistical information about the European countries.

Everyman's United Nations. This compact and comprehensive reference guide, published at intervals by the United Nations, gives details of the organization, functions, and achievements of the UN and its specialized agencies.

Yearbook of the United Nations. Annual. Also published by the UN, it provides a review of its activities and functions.

Official Congressional Directory. Issued frequently, it contains official biographies of the members of Congress, as well as considerable other information about the United States government and its principal officials.

United States Government Organization Manual. Annual. A major and official compilation of information about United States government organization—its departments, agencies, offices, and their statutes, and publications.

Book of the States. Biennial. Issued by the Council of State Governments, it provides extensive and authoritative information about American state governments and their activities.

Municipal Yearbook. Annual. Articles and data on American city government, particularly to meet the needs of municipal officials.

Miscellaneous Reference Aids

Facts on File. Weekly, looseleaf. This American-produced digest of world news includes such categories as world affairs, national affairs, and foreign affairs. Cumulative indexes from fortnightly to annually.

Keesing's Contemporary Archives. Weekly, looseleaf. A British diary of world events containing selections and summarizations of news, reports, statistics, and data drawn from an array of sources. Cumulative indexes.

A. J. Peaslee, *Constitutions of Nations,* 3rd ed., 4 vols. (Nijhoff, 1965–70) provides an English-language version of the constitutions of most states of the world.

A. J. Peaslee, *International Governmental Organizations: Constitutional Documents,* 2nd ed., 2 vols. (Nijhoff, 1961) is a compilation devoted to international organizations created by states and having governmental functions.

Encyclopedia Britannica World Atlas. Unabridged. In addition to its collection of maps, this atlas contains much useful political data and a comprehensive statistical treatment of more than 200 states and political units of the world.

Advanced Atlas of Modern Geography and *Columbus Atlas* (both McGraw-Hill) and *Cosmopolitan Atlas* and *Goode's School Atlas* (both Rand McNally) are also useful reference aids.

Periodicals

Useful in bringing political science subjects up to date is the great variety of periodical literature. Among the scholarly journals available for this purpose, in what must be a highly selective list, are:

American Political Science Review (quarterly); *American Behavioral Scientist* (bimonthly); *Annals of the American Academy of Political and Social Science* (bimonthly); *Canadian Journal of Political Science* (quarterly); *Comparative Politics* (quarterly); *Foreign Affairs* (quarterly); *Journal of Politics* (quarterly); *Midwest Journal of Political Science* (quarterly); *Parliamentary Affairs* (quarterly); *Political Studies* (three times a year); *Polity* (quarterly); *Review of Politics* (quarterly); *Western Political Quarterly* (quarterly); and *World Politics* (quarterly). Most are indexed in *Public Affairs Information Service Bulletin, Social Sciences and Humanities Index,* and similar references.

Supplementary Readings

Chapter 1. The Study of Modern Government

Albert Somit and Joseph Tanenhaus, *The Development of American Political Science* (Allyn, 1967) presents an excellent history of the discipline.

Stephen L. Wasby, *Political Science—The Discipline and Its Dimensions* (Scribner's, 1970) is the most useful general introduction to the discipline.

James C. Charlesworth (ed.), *Contemporary Political Analysis* (Free Press, 1967) treats and evaluates the approaches and methods of political research.

Michael Haas and Henry S. Kariel (eds.), *Approaches to the Study of Political Science* (Chandler, 1970) considers a variety of perspectives and calls for a new synthesis.

G. David Garson, *Handbook of Political Science Methods* (Holbrook, 1971) is aimed at students, treating both traditional and behavioral approaches.

Eugene J. Meehan, *Value Judgment and Social Science* (Dorsey, 1969) considers the relationships between empirical analysis and moral judgments.

Dante Germino, *Beyond Ideology: The Revival of Political Theory* (Harper, 1967) insists that political theory and political science are inseparable.

Seymour E. Lipset (ed.), *Politics and the Social Sciences* (Oxford U. Press, 1969) presents ten essays on the subject.

Chapter 2. Society and the State

Ernest Barker, *Principles of Social and Political Theory* (Oxford U. Press, 1951) is a scholarly analysis of the history and character of political community in the western tradition.

Robert M. MacIver, *The Web of Government*, rev. ed. (Macmillan, 1965) is a penetrating study of the rise and nature of political communities.

Lee Cameron McDonald, *Western Political Theory* (Harcourt, 1968) covers the subject from ancient times to the present.

George H. Sabine, *A History of Political Theory*, 3rd ed. (Holt, 1961) has been the standard history of western thought for many years.

Alfred Zimmern, *The Greek Commonwealth*, 2nd ed. (Oxford U. Press, 1915) remains the standard study of the classical Greek community.

Leon Homo, *Roman Political Institutions*, 2nd ed. (Barnes & Noble, 1962) is a classic study with an extensive bibliography.

Marc Bloch, *Feudal Society* (Routledge, 1961) is an outstanding analysis of the feudal order.

Alexander P. d'Entrèves, *The Notion of State: An Introduction to Political Theory* (Oxford U. Press, 1967) considers the state as a system of force and the rightful holder of power.

Chapter 3. Modern Democracy and Its Challenges

Leslie Lipson, *The Democratic Civilization* (Oxford U. Press, 1964) is a wide-ranging historical and analytical treatment.

C. W. Cassinelli, *The Politics of Freedom: An Analysis of the Modern Democratic State* (U. of Washington Press, 1961) is a cogent study of the relation between procedures and values.

Henry B. Mayo, *An Introduction to Democratic Theory* (Oxford U. Press, 1960) is an excellent study of democratic practices and accomplishments.

Robert Y. Fluno, *The Democratic Community: Governmental Practices and Purposes* (Dodd, Mead, 1971) presents a clear-eyed treatment of this complex subject.

Theodore J. Lowi, *The End of Liberalism: Ideology, Policy, and the Crisis of Public Authority* (Norton, 1969) is an important critique of pluralism and interest-group liberalism.

Shlomo Avineri, *The Social and Political Thought of Karl Marx* (Cambridge U. Press, 1968) is probably the best study of his philosophy.

R. N. C. Hunt, *The Theory and Practice of Communism*, 5th ed. (Macmillan, 1960) is a valuable survey from 1848.

James Chieh Hsiung, *Ideology and Practice: The Evolution of Chinese Communism* (Praeger, 1970) discusses ideology and politics in this new communist state.

Karl D. Bracher, *The German Dictatorship: The Origins, Structure, and Effects of National Socialism* (Praeger, 1971) presents an analysis of the multiple causes of Nazism by a German political scientist.

S. J. Woolf (ed.), *The Nature of Fascism* (Random House, 1969) shows the contemporary relevance of the subject.

A. James Gregor, *The Ideology of Fascism: The Rationale of Totalitarianism* (Free Press, 1969) demonstrates the similarities in communism and fascism.

Carl J. Friedrich and Z. K. Brzezinski, *Totalitarian Dictatorship and Autocracy*, rev. ed. (Harvard U. Press, 1965) provides a comparative analysis.

Paul E. Sigmund (ed.), *The Ideologies of the Developing Nations*, rev. ed. (Praeger, 1967) is a useful collection of speeches and writings from the third-world leaders.

Maurice Cranston (ed.), *The New Left* (Bodley Head, 1970) is a scholarly approach to this movement.

William P. Gerberding and D. E. Smith (eds.), *The Radical Left: The Abuse of Discontent* (Houghton Mifflin, 1970) shows how the means used by the radical left threaten democracy.

Chapter 4. Constitutions: Order and Freedom

C. H. McIlwain, *Constitutionalism, Ancient and Modern*, rev. ed. (Cornell U. Press, 1947) surveys the development of constitutionalism in terms of the restraints of law.

Francis D. Wormuth, *The Origins of Modern Constitutionalism* (Harper, 1949) emphasizes the English contribution to the basic ideas concerning modern constitutionalism.

Walter Bagehot, *The English Constitution* (Oxford U. Press, 1936) is a classic study of the mid-Victorian constitution.

E. S. Corwin and J. W. Peltason, *Understanding the Constitution,*

3rd ed. (Holt, 1964) is an historical and analytical interpretation of the American Constitution.

Arnold J. Zurcher (ed.), *Constitutions and Constitutional Trends Since World War II*, 2nd ed. (New York U. Press, 1955) is a collection of essays on constitution-making in postwar Europe.

Leslie Wolf-Phillips (ed.), *Constitutions of Modern States: Selected Texts and Commentary* (Praeger, 1968) considers a dozen representative constitutions from communist and noncommunist states.

Ivo D. Duchacek, *Comparative Federalism* (Holt, 1970) examines all political systems with federal features.

Milton R. Konvitz, *Expanding Liberties: Freedom's Gains in Postwar America* (Viking, 1966) shows how civil liberties have been substantially enlarged in recent decades.

Abraham Brumberg (ed.), *In Quest of Justice: Protest and Dissent in the Soviet Union Today* (Praeger, 1970) demonstrates how civil rights in the U.S.S.R. are repressed.

Rocco J. Tresolini, *These Liberties: Case Studies in Civil Rights* (Lippincott, 1968) emphasizes contemporary problems.

Harry M. Clor, *Obscenity and Public Morality: Censorship in a Liberal Society* (U. of Chicago Press, 1969) argues the case for censorship to maintain public moral standards.

The Report of the Commission on Obscenity and Pornography (various editions, 1970) concludes by a majority of the commission that public opinion does not support such censorship.

Chapter 5. Interests and Opinion

David B. Truman, *The Governmental Process*, rev. ed. (Knopf, 1971) offers a theoretical basis for the consideration of interest groups.

Henry W. Ehrmann (ed.), *Interest Groups on Four Continents* (Pittsburgh U. Press, 1958) compares and contrasts groups in some nine states.

Harmon Zeigler, *Interest Groups in American Society* (Prentice-Hall, 1964) treats the functions of interest groups in the American setting.

Grant McConnell, *Private Power and American Democracy* (Knopf, 1966) considers group effectiveness in dealing with public agencies.

Geoffrey K. Roberts, *Political Parties and Pressure-Groups in Britain* (Weidenfeld, 1970) is a useful recent treatment.

H. Gordon Skilling and F. Griffiths (eds.), *Interest Groups in Soviet Politics* (Princeton U. Press, 1971) is the best study made of this subject.

Bernard R. Berelson and Morris Janowitz (eds.), *Reader in Public Opinion and Communications*, 2nd ed. (Free Press, 1966) is a collection of articles from a variety of sources.

Leonard W. Doob, *Public Opinion and Propaganda*, 2nd ed. (Holt, 1966) is a survey with special attention to propaganda.

Bernard Hennessy, *Public Opinion*, 2nd ed. (Wadsworth, 1970) provides a useful recent survey.

John Whale, *The Half-Shut Eye: Television and Politics in Britain and America* (St. Martin's Press, 1969) is a balanced view of the subject.

Wilbur Schramm, *Mass Media and National Development: The Role of Information in the Developing Countries* (Stanford U. Press, 1964) discusses the role of communications in the new states.

Chapter 6. Parties and Voters

James C. Davies, *Human Nature in Politics* (Wiley, 1963) is a broad psychological interpretation of politics.

Leon D. Epstein, *Political Parties in Western Democracies* (Praeger, 1967) is the best comparative study of political parties.

Maurice Duverger, *Political Parties: Their Organization and Activity in the Modern State* (Wiley, 1954) is an early effort at comparative study.

Kenneth M. Dolbeare and Murray J. Edelman, *American Politics: Policies, Power, and Change* (Heath, 1971) offers a general discussion of politics and political power in the United States.

V. O. Key, Jr., *Politics, Parties, and Pressure Groups*, 5th ed. (Crowell, 1964) is an authoritative study.

Hugh A. Bone, *American Politics and the Party System*, 4th ed. (McGraw-Hill, 1970) covers all aspects of the subject, theoretical and practical.

R. T. McKenzie, *British Political Parties*, 2nd ed. (St. Martin's Press, 1963) is an important study emphasizing internal structure and operations.

Samuel P. Huntington and Clement H. Moore, *Authoritarian Poli-*

tics in Modern Society: Dynamics of Established One-Party Systems (Basic Books, 1970) ranges over the variety of one-party systems.

Peter Worsley, *The Third World,* 2nd ed. (U. of Chicago Press, 1970) examines the frequent one-party rule in the new states.

Gerald M. Pomper, *Elections in America: Control and Influence in Democratic Politics* (Dodd, Mead, 1968) shows the importance of elections in the political process.

A. J. Milnor, *Elections and Political Stability* (Little, Brown, 1969) discusses plurality, majority, and proportional representation systems.

John S. Reshetar, Jr., *The Soviet Polity: Government and Politics in the U.S.S.R.* (Dodd, Mead, 1971) provides a full treatment of the Communist party and its relation to the power structure.

Chapter 7. The Executive

Gwendolen M. Carter and John H. Herz, *Major Foreign Powers,* 5th ed. (Harcourt, 1967) a durable text, it treats the four major executives of Europe.

Roy C. Macridis and Robert E. Ward, *Modern Political Systems: Europe,* 2nd ed. (Prentice-Hall, 1968), relates the executive to the context of national culture.

W. Ivor Jennings, *Cabinet Government,* 3rd ed. (Cambridge U. Press, 1959) is the classic work on the British executive.

John P. Mackintosh, *The British Cabinet,* 2nd ed. (Stevens, 1968) is a substantial study by a British scholar.

Clinton Rossiter, *The American Presidency,* rev. ed. (Harcourt, 1960) is a readable account with attention to the expanding powers of the presidency.

Joseph E. Kallenbach, *The American Chief Executive: The Presidency and the Governorship* (Harper, 1966) presents a comparative treatment of the offices.

Martin C. Needler (ed.), *Political Systems of Latin America,* 2nd ed. (Van Nostrand, 1969) gives attention to the executive role.

Merle Fainsod, *How Russia Is Ruled,* rev. ed. (Harvard U. Press, 1963) is a standard study of the subject.

Alan Bullock, *Hitler: A Study in Tyranny,* rev. ed. (Harper, 1962) is an excellent study of the dictatorship.

Maurice Latey, *Tyranny: A Study in the Abuse of Power* (Macmillan, 1969) furnishes an informative comparative analysis.

Chapter 8. The Legislature

Peter H. Merkl, *Modern Comparative Politics* (Holt, 1970) draws many useful conclusions about policy-making structures and processes.

K. C. Wheare, *Legislatures,* 2nd ed. (Oxford U. Press, 1968) is a short, thoughtful, and comparative study of the institution.

W. Ivor Jennings, *Parliament,* 2nd ed. (Cambridge U. Press, 1957) is the standard work on the British institution.

Ronald Butt, *The Power of Parliament,* 2nd ed. (Constable, 1970) evaluates criticisms of the British institution and declares them exaggerated.

Lewis A. Froman, *The Congressional Process: Strategies, Rules and Procedures* (Little, Brown, 1967) is a thorough treatment of the formal and informal lawmaking processes.

Roger H. Davidson *et al., Congress in Crisis: Politics and Congressional Reform* (Wadsworth, 1966) examines various theories concerning legislative reform.

Philip M. Williams, *The French Parliament: Politics in the Fifth Republic* (Praeger, 1968) is a short but excellent treatment of Parliament in the current regime.

Gerhard Loewenberg, *Parliament in the German Political System* (Cornell U. Press, 1966) examines the German parliamentary tradition and the contemporary Bundestag.

Allan Kornberg, *Canadian Legislative Behavior* (Holt, 1967) offers a useful analysis of the Canadian Parliament and its parliamentarians.

Sidney I. Ploss, *Conflict and Decision-Making in Soviet Russia* (Princeton U. Press, 1965) seeks to interrelate power influences and policy making.

Franz L. Neumann, *Behemoth: The Structure and Practice of National Socialism, 1933–1944* (Harper, 1966) is instructive on the policy-making process in the Nazi dictatorship.

Chapter 9. The Judiciary

William Seagle, *The Quest for Law* (Knopf, 1941) is a readable discussion of the development of western legal systems.

C. Gordon Post, *An Introduction to the Law* (Prentice-Hall, 1963) is a useful examination of the American system.

Carleton K. Allen, *Law in the Making*, 7th ed. (Clarendon, 1964) is a massive treatise on legal development and jurisprudence.

Rudolf B. Schlesinger, *Comparative Law: Cases and Materials*, 2nd ed. (Foundation Press, 1960) contains materials comparing the common and civil law systems.

John H. Merryman, *The Civil Law Tradition* (Stanford U. Press, 1969) discusses the legal systems of western Europe and Latin America.

John N. Hazard, *Communists and Their Law* (Chicago U. Press, 1969) treats the nature of legal systems in the Marxist states.

J. N. D. Anderson, *Islamic Law in the Modern World* (New York U. Press, 1959) is a short authoritative account.

Robert G. Neumann, *European Government*, 4th ed. (McGraw-Hill, 1968) is a useful comparison of law and justice in several major states.

R. M. Jackson, *The Machinery of Justice in England*, 5th ed. (Cambridge U. Press, 1967) discusses the organization of the judicial system.

Robert McCloskey, *The American Supreme Court* (U. of Chicago Press, 1960) is an historical survey of the court as a policy-making body.

Howard E. Dean, *Judicial Review and Democracy* (Random House, 1966) is also devoted to the lawmaking function of the court.

Theodore L. Becker (ed.), *Political Trials* (Bobbs-Merrill, 1971) ranges over a variety of political trials in different states.

Chapter 10. The Administration

Ferrel Heady, *Public Administration: A Comparative Perspective* (Prentice-Hall, 1966) is a short treatment with attention to the new states.

Stanley Rothman, *European Society and Politics* (Bobbs-Merrill, 1970) usefully compares public policy and its implementation in four European states.

Ralph Braibanti (ed.), *Political and Administrative Development* (Duke U. Commonwealth Studies Center, 1969) represents views on administration in the new states.

John M. Pfiffner and R. V. Presthus, *Public Administration*, 5th ed. (Ronald, 1967) combines several approaches to the subject.

Harold Seidman, *Politics, Position, and Power* (Oxford U. Press, 1970) discusses American administrative organization and "culture."

Donald C. Rowat (ed.), *The Ombudsman: Citizen's Defender* (U. of Toronto Press, 1965) discusses the office which has won much contemporary attention.

Robert T. Golembiewski and M. Cohen (eds.), *People in Public Service: A Reader in Public Personnel Administration* (Peacock, 1970) covers the major areas of the subject.

O. Glenn Stahl, *Public Personnel Administration*, 6th ed. (Harper, 1971) includes attention to the international dimension.

Eugene P. Dvorin and A. J. Misner, *Government Within the States* (Addison-Wesley, 1971) examines organization and process within American state and local government.

Samuel Humes and Eileen Martin, *The Structure of Local Government: A Comparative Study of 81 Countries* (International Union of Local Authorities, The Hague, 1969) amasses a large body of information.

Peter Hall, *The World Cities* (McGraw-Hill, 1966) is a study of seven major metropolitan world centers.

William O. Winter, *The Urban Polity* (Dodd, Mead, 1969) presents a useful comparative treatment of urban problems.

John H. Baker, *Urban Politics in America* (Scribner's, 1971) is an interdisciplinary and intergovernmental approach.

Chapter 11. The Modern State in International Law

J. L. Brierly, *The Law of Nations*, 6th ed. (Oxford U. Press, 1963) is the best brief introduction.

Arthur Nussbaum, *A Concise History of the Law of Nations*, 2nd ed. (Macmillan, 1954) is a readable survey from ancient times.

Gerhard von Glahn, *Law Among Nations: An Introduction to Public International Law*, 2nd ed. (Macmillan, 1970) treats the subject in its broad dimensions.

Richard N. Swift, *International Law: Current and Classic* (Wiley, 1969) is a recent general treatment.

William D. Coplin, *The Functions of International Law* (Rand McNally, 1966) applies recent social science concepts.

Kazimierz Grzybowski, *Soviet Public International Law, Doctrines and Diplomatic Practice* (Rule of Law Press, 1970) discusses the current Soviet interpretation of international law.

Edward Collins (ed.), *International Law in a Changing World*

(Random House, 1970) is a combination text-casebook approach.

Shabtai Rosenne, *The World Court: What It Is and How It Works* (Oceana, 1962) describes the International Court of Justice.

J. D. B. Miller, *The Commonwealth in the World*, 3rd ed. (Harvard U. Press, 1965) evaluates the Commonwealth association.

Eugene Davidson, *The Trial of the Germans* (Macmillan, 1967) covers all facets of the Nürnberg trials.

Chapter 12. The Elements of International Politics

Hans J. Morgenthau, *Politics Among Nations*, 4th ed. (Knopf, 1967) makes an important contribution to "realistic" theory.

A. F. K. Organski, *World Politics*, 2nd ed. (Knopf, 1968) offers an excellent critique of "realistic" theories.

Ivo D. Duchacek, *Nations and Men: An Introduction to International Politics*, 2nd ed. (Holt, 1971) is a concise text analyzing the interaction of nations.

Raymond Aron, *Peace and War: A Theory of International Relations* (Doubleday, 1966) offers an important study by a French scholar.

J. E. Dougherty and R. L. Pfaltzgraff, *Contending Theories of International Relations* (Lippincott, 1971) is a most informative overview.

Carleton J. H. Hayes, *Nationalism: A Religion* (Macmillan, 1960) contains the conclusions of a leading historian.

Roy Macridis (ed.), *Foreign Policy in World Politics*, 3rd ed. (Prentice-Hall, 1967) provides readings on the major powers.

John Spanier, *American Foreign Policy since World War II*, 4th rev. ed. (Praeger, 1971) is an excellent treatment of the period.

Richard F. Rosser, *An Introduction to Soviet Foreign Policy* (Prentice-Hall, 1969) is a short and balanced treatment.

Harold C. Hinton, *China's Turbulent Quest* (Macmillan, 1970) undertakes a survey of Communist China's foreign policy.

David Vital, *The Inequality of States* (Oxford U. Press, 1967) considers the small states in international relations.

John R. Wood and Jean Serres, *Diplomatic Ceremonial and Protocol* (Columbia U. Press, 1970) is a survey of history and practice.

George Lichtheim, *Imperialism* (Praeger, 1971) traces the history of imperialism and challenges its identification with capitalism.

Klaus Knorr, *Military Power and Potential* (Heath, 1970) reflects the change in the factor of military power in the past several decades.

Robert Leckie, *Warfare* (Harper, 1970) is an excellent short treatment of all aspects of warfare.

Chapter 13. International Organization and the Problem of Peace

Inis L. Claude, Jr., *Swords Into Plowshares: The Problems and Progress of International Organization*, 4th ed. (Random House, 1971) is a penetrating analysis of the subject.

David Brook (ed.), *Search for Peace: A Reader in International Relations* (Dodd, Mead, 1970) deals broadly with the problems of world order.

Francis P. Walters, *A History of the League of Nations* (Oxford U. Press, 1952) is a standard history of the League experiment.

Stephen S. Goodspeed, *The Nature and Function of International Organization*, 2nd ed. (Oxford U. Press, 1967) focuses on the United Nations.

David C. Coyle, *The United Nations and How It Works*, rev. ed. (Columbia U. Press, 1969) is an authoritative reference.

Kathleen Teltsch, *Cross-Currents at Turtle Bay: A Quarter-Century of the United Nations* (Quadrangle, 1970) is an interesting journalist's account.

Alan James, *The Politics of Peace-Keeping* (Praeger, 1969) examines the role of the United Nations in the peace-keeping realm.

John G. Stoessinger, *The United Nations and the Superpowers*, 2nd ed. (Random House, 1969) examines the interactions of the United States and the Soviet Union.

M. S. and L. S. Finkelstein (eds.), *Collective Security* (Chandler, 1966) weighs up the pros and cons.

Paul Seabury (ed.), *Balance of Power* (Chandler, 1965) is a collection of varied readings.

David Mitrany, *A Working Peace System* (Quadrangle, 1966) treats the functional approach to world peace.

Ernst B. Haas, *Beyond the Nation-State: Functionalism and International Organization* (Stanford U. Press, 1964) stresses the functional needs of the world community.

Chapter 14. Epilogue

John Lukacs, *The Passing of the Modern Age* (Harper, 1970) argues that the modern age of the past four centuries is ending and discusses what may follow.

Karl W. Deutsch, *Nationalism and Its Alternatives* (Knopf, 1969) asserts that there is little likelihood of early integration of existing states.

Richard A. Falk, *Legal Order in a Violent World* (Princeton U. Press, 1968) examines the regulation of conflict in the contemporary world.

Leonard Freedman (ed.), *Issues of the Seventies* (Wadsworth, 1970) considers the problems Americans face in this decade.

Peter Drucker, *The Age of Discontinuity* (Harper, 1969) speculates about the nature of postindustrial society.

Victor C. Ferkiss, *Technological Man: The Myth and the Reality* (Braziller, 1969) is another interesting speculation about the future.

William I. Thompson, *At the Edge of History: Speculations on the Transformation of Culture* (Harper, 1971) also scans the future.

Index